Rethinking

Edited by
Mechthild Leutner

Berliner China-Hefte

Chinese History and Society

Edited by
Mechthild Leutner

Editorial Management
Jens Damm, Nathalie van Looy
and Alexander Thies

Ostasiatisches Seminar
der Freien Universität Berlin

Volume 31

LIT

Rethinking China in the 1950s

Edited by

Mechthild Leutner

LIT

Bibliographic information published by the Deutsche Nationalbibliothek
The Deutsche Nationalbibliothek lists this publication in the Deutsche
Nationalbibliografie; detailed bibliographic data are available in the Internet at
http://dnb.d-nb.de.

ISBN 978-3-8258-0291-2

A catalogue record for this book is available from the British Library

© LIT VERLAG Dr. W. Hopf Berlin 2007
Ziegelstr. 30
D-10117 Berlin

Auslieferung:
LIT Verlag Fresnostr. 2, D-48159 Münster
Tel. +49 (0) 2 51/620 32 - 22, Fax +49 (0) 2 51/922 60 99, e-Mail: lit@lit-verlag.de

Distributed in the UK by: Global Book Marketing, 99B Wallis Rd, London, E9 5LN
Phone: +44 (0) 20 8533 5800 – Fax: +44 (0) 1600 775 663
http://www.centralbooks.co.uk/acatalog/search.html

Distributed in North America by:

Transaction Publishers
New Brunswick (U.S.A.) and London (U.K.)

Transaction Publishers
Rutgers University
35 Berrue Circle
Piscataway, NJ 08854

Phone: +1 (732) 445 - 2280
Fax: + 1 (732) 445 - 3138
for orders (U. S. only):
toll free (888) 999 - 6778
e-mail:
orders@transactionspub.com

Contents

Rethinking China in the 1950s

Conference Reports

Reviews

Calligraphy: Chen Ning
Orders: Lit-Verlag Münster-Hamburg-London, Grevener Str. 179, D-48159 Münster, Germany,
lit@lit-verlag.de.
Single issue: 20.90 € plus postage, one year subscription (two issues) 25 € plus postage.
Submission of Manuscripts (Articles, Reports, and Reviews):
Chinese History and Society/Berliner China-Hefte, Freie Universität Berlin, Ostasiatisches Seminar,
Ehrenbergstr. 26-28, 14195 Berlin, eChina@zedat.fu-berlin.de.
Manuscripts should conform to the style of Chinese History and Society/Berliner China-Hefte:
http://www.geschkult.fu-berlin.de/e/oas/sinologie/chinesehistoryandsociety

Susanne Weigelin-Schwiedrzik

Back to the Past: Chinese Intellectuals in Search of Historical Legitimacy (1957-1965)*

In the year 1957, prominent historians in the People's Republic of China (PRC) began to voice criticism of the state of the art in the field of history writing. Fan Wenlan (1893-1969), one of the most important among them, was especially outspoken. Others joined in the debate, stressing their discontent with the dogmatism prevailing in educational publications on Chinese history. All those who participated in this debate by backing Fan Wenlan, among them many well-known historians such as Wu Han (1909-1969), Jian Bozan (1898-1968) and Li Shu (1912-1988), were to be severely criticized during the Cultural Revolution (1966-1976).

Wu Han, who was at the time deputy mayor of Beijing and had been a leading historian since the 1930s, summarized his anti-dogmatist stance with his slogan "Let interpretations emerge from facts" (论从史出). He was among the first to be criticized during the Cultural Revolution and he died in prison in 1969. Jian Bozan, Dean of the History Department at Beijing University and close to the Chinese Communist Party (CCP) since the 1930s, although less radical than Wu Han, was also criticized and committed suicide together with his wife in 1968. Fan Wenlan profited from Mao's special protection which the director of the Institute of Modern History (近代史研究所) at the Chinese Academy of Science (中国科学院) had earned as a consequence of his collaboration with Mao in Yan'an. He died in 1969 shortly after he had been elected member of the 9th Central Committee of the Communist Party of China. One of the many prominent spokesmen for the anti-dogmatist line in the 1950s and 1960s who survived the Cultural Revolution and Mao Zedong was Li Shu, the editor of the leading journal, *Historical Research* (历史研究). He is among the few participants of the debate of whom we know more than the sometimes cryptic writings of the 1960s revealed.

As victims of the Cultural Revolution, the group of intellectuals we are dealing with in this paper is often regarded as liberal in its political stance. As they all come from a non-Marxist, bourgeois, pre-1949 background, it seems logical to look upon them as representatives of democracy in China and their often indirect criticism of Maoism as a sign of growing opposition to Communist rule in China.

This paper tries to analyze the debate among historians that started to evolve during the latter half of the 1950s and continued until the beginning of the Cultural Revolution in the context of two different constellations. On the one hand, the paper reads the debate as a reaction to the disaster of the Great Leap Forward and the Great Famine; on the other hand, it looks at the debate in terms of a reaction to the on-going modernization process and the contradictions this inevitably implies. At this point, the paper introduces some of Jürgen Habermas' writings on historical revisionism and neo-conservatism, hinting at similarities in the historical debate that are at the same time astonishing and illuminating.

---

* Earlier versions of this paper were presented at the Harvard Leiden Workshop on Conservative and Revisionist Historiography, March 2005, at the AAS Annual Conference in Chicago, April 2005, at the Brandeis-Vienna Workshop on the Great Leap Forward, April 2005, and at the Leiden Workshop on Historical Revisionism, November 2005. Special thanks go to Peter Bole, Frederic E. Wakeman, jr.†, and Arif Dirlik for their comments on this paper.

As a result, we will try to show that rather than being seen as forming a growing opposition to Maoist rule, this group of intellectuals should be viewed as being eager to redefine the legitimacy of Communist rule over mainland China. Having taken sides with Mao Zedong, they acted as censors in the traditional sense of the word by reminding Mao of his own principles and by looking for roots reaching beyond the victory of the revolution. This is what their form of historical revisionism was aimed at. However, their search for roots in Chinese history and culture meant that they were confronted with the on-going modernization process and with what they perceived as a possible loss of particularity and identity. In this sense, they showed a tendency towards neo-conservatism and elitism and no interest in supporting democracy and mass participation.

The Beginning of the Debate: in Search of Particularity for Chinese History

Fan Wenlan's first and very prominent intervention concerning dogmatism in Chinese Marxist historiography was somewhat meekly entitled "On some questions concerning the writing of history" (Fan Wenlan 1957). He criticized historians for copying Marxist phrases as if they were omnipotent recipes or abstract formulae that could be used no matter what the times, the location or the conditions were like. Fan Wenlan called this kind of historiography "dogmatic" and criticized it as "false Marxism." For him, Marxism was but a tool to be applied to the analysis of Chinese history. "To study Marxism-Leninism means to grasp the spirit of Marxism-Leninism. What we should definitely avoid is to copy it in all detail" (Fan Wenlan 1957: 1).

When Fan voiced his criticism, he must have included his own works. Although he is said to have been the first historian ever to have presented a full account of Chinese history from a Marxist point of view (Guoxue 2000), he states, in his article, that no one had ever succeeded so far in writing Chinese history according to the standpoint (立场), the viewpoint (观点) and the method (方法) of Marxism-Leninism. We know from recent accounts of his life, that he, was, indeed, very critical of the two books he had written during his time at Yan'an, and that he regarded his own early attempt at writing a narrative of Chinese history as "not historicist enough (历史主义), not analytical enough and not well structured" (ibid.). But it also seems plausible that Fan Wenlan criticized Guo Moruo's version of Chinese history (Guo Moruo 1976) which sticks closely to the five stages of social development as canonized by Stalin in his book *On the Problems of Leninism* (Stalin 1947). Fan writes a whole paragraph about those people who study China's early history by copying Engels and linking his sayings to quotations from the Chinese classics (Fan Wenlan 1957: 4).

When Fan published this article, he was the Director of the Institute of Modern History, also known as the "Third Institute" (第三所), and Guo Moruo (1892-1978) was the head of the Institute of Ancient History or "First Institute" (第一所) (Wang 2001, slightly different in *Jindaishi yanjiusuo*) which merged to become the Institute of Historical Research (历史研究所) in 1958. Guo Moruo was responsible for research on early history and a little higher up in the hierarchy than Fan Wenlan as he was also the President of the Institute of History; this was, in a way, the umbrella organization for the First, Second and Third Institutes, although all were given the name of "institute" (所) which made them equal in ranking. Whether Fan intended to criticize Guo Moruo or not, it was quite clear from his article that he was not satisfied with the work that was being done at Guo's institute.

However, Fan Wenlan's article had yet another target which is neither mentioned in more recent articles nor in publications of the time but which has to be considered against the backdrop of what was going on in Chinese historiography at the time. Liu Danian (1915-1999) reported that Fan Wenlan started to think critically about Soviet historiography after he had encountered difficulties with having his book on modern Chinese history translated into Russian and published in the Soviet Union. Russian historians had objected to his negative assessment of Czarist policies towards China and rejected the publication of the book on these grounds. They had even gone so far as to criticize the book as being "pro-American." Although the book was eventually published in Russia after the passages on Czarist politics were omitted, Fan started doubting the truthfulness of Soviet publications from this point on (Liu Danian 1979: 24). This again has to be seen in the context of Soviet dominance over Chinese history writing originating from the People's University (人民大学) and its publications "Teaching and Research" (教学与研究) and "History Teaching" (历史教学). Dogmatism, in this context, meant adhering to an interpretation of world history as well as Chinese history that had its origins in Russia rather than in China. Guo Moruo and the historians in his institute also played a major role in this context. It was Guo Moruo who had proven in the 1930s during the "Debate on the character of Chinese Society" that the Stalinist model of society developing in five stages was applicable to Chinese history (Dirlik 1978, Leutner 1982). This "proof" turned out to be of major importance both in the 1930s and in the 1950s. In both cases, it was instrumental in positioning the Chinese revolution in the context of the world revolution underlining the CCP's claim on power in Marxist terms and on an equal footing with the other members of the Communist International. However, while gaining legitimacy for the Chinese revolution in an international context, historians in China were confronted with difficulties when trying to show how the necessity of revolution emerged from Chinese history. From the early 1950s onwards, they started to debate the question as to whether or not China had gone through a phase of being a slave society and, if so, when this phase had ended and China had changed into a feudal society. If a feudal society had ever existed, when did it end and why did it not naturally change into a capitalist society (Wang 2001)? In these debates, the group of historians around Guo Moruo would usually stress the compatibility of Chinese history with the Marxist view of world history, while the group around Fan Wenlan would become more and more outspoken in demanding "particularity" for Chinese history.

However, the dominance of Soviet scholarship was never uncontested in the field of Chinese historiography and the different schools of thought were not as directly juxtaposed in their attitudes towards the Soviet influence as they were in other questions (Wang 2001). During the 1950s, Guo Moruo as well as Fan Wenlan both accepted the idea that China would follow the five stages development model just as every other country in the world, but they arrived at different answers when it came to defining the end of the slave society and the beginning of feudalism in China. And while disputing among themselves they both came to conclusions that differed from the Russian version with only Shang Yue (1902-1982, Yanhuang Chunqiu 2005), who would soon become a target of open criticism, accepting the Soviet interpretation that China had become feudal in the 3rd century A.C. Q. Edward Wang rightly comments on the intrinsic problem of adapting Marxism-Leninism to Chinese history by saying: "Given the perceived distance between Marxist theory and Chinese history...they [i.e. Chinese historians] can have only two options: find sources that fit with the theory, and the other is, to modify the theory to mesh with the facts" (Wang 2001: 110).

What Wang did not see as a possibility would eventually come up in the next round of discussions after the Great Leap Forward and the Sino-Soviet split: it is the possibility Fan had hinted at in his 1957 article and developed in the 1960s together with colleagues such as Jian Bozan, Wu Han and Li Shu. Marxism was a method (方法) and thus to be seen on a more abstract level than either theory or interpretation. It was a way of looking at things that could help Chinese historians to discover the particularity of Chinese history (Fan Wenlan 1961). Both Li Shu and Fan Wenlan played a major role in publishing this idea. Li Shu legitimized the search for particularity in Chinese history by referring to the Yan'an experience of the CCP: "If a communist cannot properly explain the particularity of a nation, if his work lacks the appropriate national form, he cannot relate to practice and is unable to answer questions which the reality of life puts to him" (Li Shu 1961: 7). Mao-Zedong-Thought was the form of Marxism-Leninism that represented the particularity of China. Historiography should in the same manner relate to its task and to its object of inquiry, i.e. the particularity of Chinese history.

With this argument, Li Shu backed Fan Wenlan and his 1957 article in which he wrote: "China and Western Europe are two different places, both of them dispose of quite a number of particularities. But if we declare the particularity of Western European history to be universal, we lose whatever particularity there is in Chinese history" (Fan Wenlan 1957: 6). By the beginning of the 1960s, Mao's criticism of the Soviet textbook on socialist economy (Mao Zedong, Martin 1977-1982, IV) was in circulation and the distance between China and the Soviet Union was growing wider. The claim for particularity in Chinese history as a way of repudiating Soviet dominance could be integrated into the overall attempt at gaining independence from the Soviets. Just as Mao-Zedong-Thought had been defined by the 7th Party Congress to be the combination of the general truth of Marxism-Leninism with the concrete practice of the Chinese revolution, Chinese history could be both related to the universal aspects of world history and show its particularity when compared with it.

Opening up to the Facts: in Search of Continuity in History
In 1961, Fan Wenlan published another article, this time with the provocative title of "Do not shoot with empty bullets" (Fan Wenlan 1961). At first sight, this article does not show any sign of dissent. On the contrary, it reads like a boring propaganda piece on China's fight against imperialism and revisionism and seems to have been written for the 10th anniversary of the Korean War. However, there is a second part to this article in which Fan takes up his favorite theme of dogmatism in historiography in writing about historians who are eagerly studying Marxism-Leninism, "but when they start writing history, they neglect historical facts to an unimaginable degree" (Fan Wenlan 1961: 3). That is why dogmatism has to be criticized, said Fan Wenlan, explaining that for him, the detailed research on the historical event should be the basis and starting point for any historian's work. Only after the chronology of events had been established could Marxism-Leninism enter the scene as an analytical tool for helping to find the reasons for and consequences of the events (因果) and to assess their role in the process of development. Marxist-Leninists reconstruct the chronology of events in exactly the same way as histori-

ans who do not apply Marxism-Leninism to historical research. It is only in their analysis and assessment of the event that Marxist historians differ from non-Marxist historians.

Li Shu was the editor of the journal *Historical Research* at the time Fan had this article published. As a matter of fact, he reportedly would have liked the article to be more straight-forward. Ding Shouhe remembers his saying that the article was itself more like an empty bullet as it did not dare to argue against specific persons in the field. But even though Fan had obviously tried to avoid criticism, the propaganda department of the CCP Central Committee was notified about the publication and internal criticism launched against it (Ding Shouhe 1998: 103). Again, others joined in the debate and backed Fan Wenlan's arguments. As Ding Shouhe explains today, their interest in debating the relationship between theory and facts was nurtured by the failure of the Great Leap Forward. They were hesitant about theories that were not well grounded in facts and reality. The unrealistic attitude prevalent during the Great Leap Forward translated, in their view, into a form of historiography in which theoretical considerations were more important than historical facts (Ding Shouhe 1998: 99-103). The basis of historical interpretation was not a reconstruction of events as they had happened in the past. It was a theory the plausibility of which was derived from a vision of the future. The dogmatism Fan Wenlan had criticized during the late fifties was therefore different from the dogmatism of the Great Leap Forward period. Back in 1957, he had criticized a form of history writing that neglected facts and was only interested in quotations from Marx and Engels to back the argument. In 1961, the empty bullets were empty because the arguments were not developed on the basis of reconstructing the past, but as a consequence of anticipating the future.

The discussion on "historicism and class viewpoint" is closely linked to this question (see Dirlik 1977). It started in early 1960 as a reaction to the call for "a revolution in historiography" (史学革命) which had been articulated during the Great Leap Forward and was aimed at defining the balance between historical evidence and class analysis based on Marxist-Leninist concepts. When the party journal *New Construction* (新建设) decided to give momentum to the debate in 1963, Li Shu is reported (Ding Shouhe 1998: 110) to have talked Ning Ke into writing his famous article "On historicism and class viewpoint" (Ning Ke 1964, 1984). At this point, the tension between different groups of historians was already comparatively high, and Guan Feng, later to become one of the most prominent critics of anti-dogmatism, jumped into the ring criticizing Ning Ke for his lack of interest in class analysis. According to Ding, Ning was much more balanced in his view than others and had tried to avoid stressing one side of the problem to the disadvantage of the other. But with Guan Feng reacting so vigorously, Ning Ke had to go for another round writing his article "On Marxist historicism." This article would later turn out to be the main piece of evidence against him, but as we are told today, the incriminating sentence in the piece was not his but Ding Shouhe's who had altered Ning's sentence "Class viewpoint is the most important aspect of a materialist view on history" (阶级观点是唯物史观的主要内容) into "Class viewpoint is one of the most important aspects of a materialist view on history" (阶级观点是唯物史观的主要内容之一 Ding Shouhe 1998: 110). Quite obviously both sides were mobilizing all their troops in this round of the discussion, and they would not even hesitate to send their colleagues on suicide squads. Fortunately, Ning Ke survived the mission.

One of the reasons why they might have seen no problem in doing what they did is that they still thought they were backed by Mao Zedong. In Mao's notes on the soviet textbook they could read astonishing remarks on the relationship between facts and theories. Mao criticized the textbook for being unrelated to reality and arguing from one theoretical assumption to the next. Instead he preferred theory to be based on facts, stressing that laws and regularities had to derive their plausibility from facts. He even went so far as to state: "Marxism demands the unity of logic and history. Thought is a reflection of objective reality. Logic evolves from history" (Mao Zedong, Martin 1979-1982, IV: 526). Jian Bozan translated this into his slogan "Facts and theories have to be combined" (史论结合) and must have thought that he was in total agreement with Mao's views (Jian Bozan 1962: 4, also Edmunds 1987, Leutner 1982).

Merle Goldman (1969) describes this period as years characterized by unprecedented open debate. The fact that with the end of the Great Leap Forward the idea of stressing facts rather than theories had gained a certain momentum certainly opened a window of opportunity for revising many of the verdicts that so far had dominated Chinese Marxist historiography. In 1962, Zhou Yang (1908-1989), who was then deputy head of the propaganda department of the CCP's Central Committee, had organized a conference aimed at reassessing the role of Confucianism in Chinese history. Liu Jie gave a speech propagating the idea that Chinese history was different from world history because Confucianism had prevented class struggle from developing fully. Therefore class struggle could not be the main factor behind the development of Chinese society, and Chinese society was not characterized by revolutions propelling it from one stage of development to the next (Goldman 1969, 1972). Instead, Jian Bozan and Wu Han explained that the policy of making concessions (让步政策) had been responsible for progress in Chinese history. The ruling class was not toppled by the ruled because it knew how to make concessions; thus peasants would be able to live more decent lives without having to revert to overthrowing the system. For Feng Youlan and Wu Han, Confucianism had helped bring about a form of ethics that was placed above the interests of the ruling class and was therefore still valid in the present (Chung Wah-min 1968). The discussion that evolved around the issue of taking over ethical standpoints from the past (道德继承论) is closely linked to Wu Han's articles written for the "Three Family Village" (三家村) column of *Forefront* (前线) run by the municipality of Beijing. He was criticized for his argument immediately after he had published the first of several articles on the issue in 1962, without realizing, of course, that this was going to be yet another of the major accusations brought up against him during the Cultural Revolution (Li Yun 2002: 555-556).

However, while Mao criticized the Soviet textbook on socialist economy, he also came to the conclusion that class struggle was the only means to prevent revisionism from taking over as had happened in the Soviet Union after Stalin's death. That was why he developed his theory on the necessity of continuous class struggle. The criticism of dogmatism which was aimed at the re-evaluation of the Chinese past by relativizing the influence of the class struggle and stressing continuity rather than break with the past must have caught his attention. The more he intensified his calls for continuing the class struggle, the more tension increased between the different groups of historians, with younger intellectuals having a more realistic assessment of what was going to be the result of this debate. Guan Feng criticized the prestigious philosopher, Feng Youlan, for his views on Confucianism, stressing that progress was impossible without a class struggle. Feng countered this argument by drawing on Marx's early piece on German classical philosophy in which he had explained the fact that no ruling class could preserve its dominance without developing an ideology which not only reflected its own interests but also the interests of society as a whole. Therefore, historical documents as well as philosophical essays from the past reflected more than the class standpoint of the author and still had some validity in the present (Chinese Studies in History and Philosophy 1968).

In 1964, Qi Benyu, who was almost unknown at that time, published an article together with Lin Jue and Yan Changgui in which he openly criticized Jian Bozan for speaking against dogmatism (Qi Benyu et al 1964). He reproached Jian for attacking Marxism-Leninism and preparing the ground for eventually re-introducing traditional Chinese historiography in the form of evidential text criticism (考证). This argument, which added a new topic to the debate, would later be reiterated time and again. Stressing facts rather than theory is related to the Qing dynasty style of evidential text criticism and thus related to a method of re-assessing the past in which the ruling class was placed in a more favorable light. Reconstructing the past on the basis of facts implied establishing continuity between past and present and thus inevitably relativizing the role of the revolution and putting the CCP on a par with ruling classes in the past. Stressing continuity in history was, therefore, even more dangerous in the eyes of the young critics than establishing the particularity of Chinese history especially if combined with the traditional style of history writing. If the ruling CCP could learn from ruling classes in the past, this would mean that its rule was in essence no different from that of the past. As rulers in the past had been subject to decline, continuity with the past also implied the possibility of decline and loss of power on the side of the CCP.

There is no sign in the publications of Fan Wenlan and others that they intended their criticism of dogmatism to go so far as to imply a possible loss of power on the side of the CCP. But it is quite clear that they were looking for a historical legitimation that would go farther than the victory in the Chinese revolution. One reason for this search for continuity might, as Q. Edward Wang suggests, be growing nationalism (Wang 2001). Nationalism, if rooted in history, very often goes along with a feeling of pride based on a positive assessment of the past. If the contribution of the revolution in overcoming the shortcomings of the past is stressed, the logic of the argument demands a negative assessment of the past in favor of a positive present and a bright future perspective. However, if the present is jeopardized by negative developments such as the economic problems in the wake of the Great Leap Forward, the argument loses its plausibility. That is where the search for continuity begins. Negative experiences in the present need to be relativized by a positive record of historical figures and events in the past. Searching for continuity in history can be regarded as a form of relativizing the contribution of the revolution, but it might also serve to diminish the pressure on the CCP's efficiency in ruling the country. Measured against a long Chinese history with many ups and downs, problems in the economy of the country are only of a temporary character and might soon be overcome. In this sense, Fan Wenlan's search for continuity might well have been part and parcel of an attempt to re-legitimize the CCP's regime after the disastrous failure of the Great Leap Forward.

In the Face of Crisis: Defining a New Identity through History
Most of the prominent authors who voiced their anti-dogmatist opinions in the late 1950s and early 1960s published several articles concerning the teaching of history at schools in the PRC (Wu Han 1980a, Wu Han 1980b, Wu Han 1980c, Jian Bozan 1980a, Jian Bozan 1980c). It is in these articles that they link the criticism of dogmatist historiography to the question of the relationship between historical data and theory, and it is also in these articles that they link their demand for a fact-oriented form of history writing to the question of identity in history. They complain that the image of the Chinese past as presented in textbooks was too negative, saying: "There are certain comrades who speak about China's ancient history as if it were all dark, a pile of garbage and full of crimes." Those comrades had a "nihilist" attitude towards Chinese history and would not look at what people actually did in the past. Instead, they used the method of class analysis to criticize them as "members of the reactionary class." Against this, Jian argued: "In the history of our country, there were outstanding historical figures in each and every époque and in each and every dynasty ... Among them are emperors, kings, generals and ministers. We should be proud of the fact that there are these outstanding historical figures." The discussion about "historical figures" (历史人物) that developed during the early 1960s was aimed at making it possible for young people to identify with them in a positive way.

Fan Wenlan, Jian Bozan and Wu Han had received their training in the field of history before they had allied themselves with the Communists. Fan Wenlan was the off-spring of a prominent family of scholars from Zhejiang known for their contributions to the debate between the New-Text and the Old-Text Schools. He was trained in the tradition of evidential text criticism, but later made a sharp turn towards a very dogmatist form of Marxist historiography, in the light of which many researchers in the West still see him today (Leutner 1982, Liu Danian 1979). Wu Han is linked to Hu Shi (Beijingshi lishi xuehui 1984), and even though he was not negatively affected by the campaign against Hu Shi's pragmatism (Grieder 1980, Chan Lien 1968) launched in the early 1950s, we know today that his affiliation with Hu Shi was one of the grounds on which he was criticized during the Cultural Revolution (Ding Shouhe 1998: 125). Through his closeness to Hu Shi he was certainly open to questions of methodology in the writing of history and more inclined towards a fact-oriented form of historiography. Jian Bozan was an economist before he became a historian, and the earliest pieces on methodology which he produced date from the 1930s. Already at that time, he stressed the necessity to focus on facts rather than theories. His first statements can be read as a reaction to the discussion "On the Character of Chinese Society" in which the imposition of the Stalinist model was the main achievement of CCP related historians (Leutner 1978, 1982; Edmunds 1987, Beijing Daxue Lishixi 1980, Li Honglin 1978).

At the time, his courage in voicing dissent was most probably nurtured by a discussion that was going on in the Soviet Union. When the Soviet Union was threatened by Germany, the Stalinist regime realized that overstressing theory in the teaching of history had made young people unable to relate emotionally to Russian history in a positive way. With patriotism becoming a decisive factor in the struggle against Germany, a kind of historiography was asked for in official documents that could make young people proud of their country's history. The debate instigated by these demands criticized the "sociologization of history" and asked for the emphasis to be placed on facts rather than theory.

It was a common understanding in Russia at the time, that the theory orientation of historiography had created a form of abstract historical thought which was obstructive to the creation of solidarity and a common identity among the peoples of the Soviet Union (Anweiler und Meyer 1961: 204-205; Kernig 1966, II: 940-945; Mazour 1971).

As in the 1930s, Jian Bozan did not speak directly about the question of identity in his articles on the teaching of history written in the 1960s. However, he came up with a similar chain of arguments stressing the necessity to make the facts of Chinese history known to students. Wu Han voiced the same kind of opinion. He wanted the facts to be presented so as to fit the notion of particularity as well as continuity in Chinese history. The basis for a positive relationship of youngsters, described as "being proud of the past" in the debate, was that they should know about the contributions of "outstanding historical figures" to the progress of history (Wu Han 1980d). This progress did not start with the revolution under the leadership of the CCP, but existed all through Chinese history. That is why, according to Jian and Wu, continuity in history existed not only for the "reactionaries," but also for the revolutionaries.

Even though nationalism is a topic which might have been expected to come up in the context of this debate, it was not talked about openly. However, the problem of identity is indirectly hinted at insofar as it was made clear that the dogmatist way of writing a Marxist version of Chinese history was obstructive to fulfilling the task historians like Fan Wenlan, Jian Bozan and Wu Han had defined. This was the task of defining the identity of the Chinese nation. Only if there was particularity and continuity in Chinese history, would the Chinese people be able to recognize themselves in history and develop solidarity on the basis of a common identity. The task of defining this identity was central to historiography, and a common understanding of history was central to the identity of the Chinese nation (Weigelin-Schwiedrzik 2004). Dogmatism in the form of an import from the Soviet Union, as well as in the form of a "sociologization of history" was detrimental to fulfilling this task.

The reason why the discussion became so tense is that it was a reaction to a crisis of legitimacy that had evolved as part of the Great Leap Forward and in the context of the international Communist movement (MacFarquhar 1999, Ding Shu 2003). Communist regimes all over Europe, including the regime in the Soviet Union, had been under stress since the early 1950s. The CCP was well aware of the danger hidden in this development and tried to avoid a loss of legitimacy by launching the Great Leap Forward (Zheng Qian 1999). However, the disaster that evolved from this struck an even heavier blow at the legitimacy of CCP rule. This blow did not only affect the workers' and peasants' loyalty towards the Communist regime; it made intellectuals feel uneasy, too. If intellectuals such as Fan Wenlan, Jian Bozan and Wu Han voiced criticism of dogmatism, they did this in an effort to re-legitimize the regime by defining an identity for the Chinese nation that was not exclusively linked to the victory of the revolution.

Continuing the Revolution in the Field of Historiography

As early as the winter of 1965, Mao Zedong knew in which direction the repudiation of the authorities in the field of historiography would go. He said: "Who are the authorities now? They are Yao Wenyuan, Qi Benyu, Yin Da. ... Determined people of younger age, less expertise, but with a firm standpoint and political experience should become the successors" (Quote from Ding Shu 2003). According to recent memoirs published in the

PRC, the years of open debate had already ended in 1962, when the Great Famine had come to an end and the economy of the country had returned to normal. On the occasion of the 10th Plenum of the 8th Central Committee in September 1962, Mao again stressed the necessity of class struggle and asked the Party to concentrate on the fight against Revisionism. It was under these auspices that the younger generation which Mao was desperately seeking saw the chance to join in the debate and qualify as "successors of the revolution" (Li Yun 2002: 556). By 1965, they had replaced the older generation of historians.

Qi Benyu's first step in this direction was an article on Li Xiucheng which he launched as part of the debate on peasant uprisings and historical figures. In this article, he reproached Li Xiucheng, who was one of the leaders of the Taiping Movement, for betraying the revolt by writing a résumé in which he had added flattering words about the Qing Dynasty (Ding Shouhe 1998: 118, Su Shuangbi 1997: 33. Qi Benyu 1964). So far, Li had been looked upon with respect by Chinese historiography, and Luo Ergang, the most prominent specialist on the Taiping Revolt, regarded the résumé as part of a time-winning strategy on the part of Li Xiucheng (Uhalley 1966). Although not many historians would go as far as Luo, the majority of them regarded Li Xiucheng as an upright peasant leader; Jian Bozan reacted vigorously to Qi's reassessment, saying: "This [the résumé] was hurriedly written in eight days. You cannot say that a whole revolutionary life was all false on these grounds" (Quote from Ding Shu 2003). And he added that Qi Benyu by writing this article "had made his ancestors look bad... If we say that Li Xiucheng was a traitor, we have to rewrite Chinese history completely" (Quote from Ding Shu 2003).

Jian was not the only one to criticize Qi. As a matter of fact, negative reactions to his article seemed overwhelming. However, Mao Zedong was notified of this new young scholar, reportedly by Chen Boda (Ding Shouhe 1998: 133) and after reading the article found that it fitted in with his strategy. That is how Qi who had been an office worker at the Office of the Central Committee (中央办公厅) started a career that would soon make him a member of the editorial board of the Party's leading theoretical journal *Red Flag* (红旗) and later of the Cultural Revolution Small Group (Ding Shouhe 1998: 133, Su Shuangbi 1997). Quite clearly, it was Qi's intention to use the example of Li Xiucheng in order to hint at the possibility that traitors of the revolution could sabotage the revolution from the very heart of its leadership. If we can trust the memoirs published on this issue, most of the leading intellectuals involved in the debate did not know at the time where the debate was heading to. They all underline the fact that none of them knew what Mao's intentions had been and that none of them had expected anything like the Cultural Revolution ever to happen (Su Shuangbi 1997: 37, Li Yun 2002). But somehow Qi Benyu must have had an idea of what Mao was planning even before he made contact with those at the very top of the Party leadership. In his article on Li Xiucheng, at a time when the majority of prominent intellectuals thought they were merely participating in an academic discussion on the issues of "historical figures" and continuity in history, he hinted at what would later become the main topic of the Cultural Revolution It is hardly surprising that Mao decided to help him and forward his career.

Qi Benyu's next important article was co-authored by his colleagues, Lin Jue and Yan Changgui. It appeared in issue No. 4 of *Red Flag* in 1964 and carried the name of Jian Bozan in its title: "Comrade Jian Bozan's view on history has to be condemned" (Qi Benyu et. al. 1964). Although the title of "comrade" was still put in front of Jian's name, it was clear to everyone familiar with the conventions of political debate that by directly using the name of a person who was to be criticized, the debate was in the process of changing its character. Under usual conditions, no name would be mentioned as long as the contradiction between the criticized person and the Party belonged to the category of "contradiction among the people." In the article, Qi and his colleagues described Jian Bozan and Wu Han as representatives of bourgeois historiography who were developing a counter-revolutionary program based on the Croce and Popper version of historicism. Their fight against dogmatism was a fight against Marxism-Leninism (Qi Benyu, Lin Jue and Yan Changgui 1964). In other words, Qi here once more sets the tone for the debate. He had already argued that Jian Bozan and Wu Han were enemies of the Party long before Yao Wenyuan's well known article on "Hai Rui is dismissed from office" would appear in the press (Wagner 1990; Fisher 1986; Su Shuangbi 1997; Zi Ling and Zi Zhen 1986, Ma Zimei [i.e. Mary Mazur] 1996).

In early 1966, the next among those "young scholars" mentioned by Mao Zedong appeared on the scene. Yin Da, vice-director of the Institute for Ancient History, published an article entitled, "We need to bring the revolution of historiography to an end" (Yin Da 1966). Once more, the main target of this article was Jian Bozan, who was seen as the major obstacle to a successful revolution in the field of history writing (史学革命) since the late 1950s. Theory had to take the lead over historical data (以论带史), and only by applying this methodology could a younger generation of historians in China rewrite a comprehensive version of Chinese history according to the needs of the revolution. This time, Yin Da was supported by many authors publishing in all major newspapers and history related journals. They asked for everything that Fan Wenlan, Jian Bozan and Wu Han had rejected a few years earlier: more class analysis, more theory, more repudiation of the past (for example: Gao, Min, Chen, Zhen 1966; Cao Lanting and Liu Shaoyi 1966; Su Wen 1966, Guangming ribao 1966a, Guangming ribao 1966b). Even though the renowned journal "Historical Studies" had been under the leadership of Li Shu and was therefore a stronghold of publications against dogmatism, the journal published one article after another criticizing the anti-dogmatists (Ding Shouhe 1998: 119). The same holds true for the theoretical journal of the Beijing municipality *Forefront* (前线). Authors such as Deng Tuo who had been the closest friends of Jian Bozan and Wu Han published articles critical of them in *Forefront* (Li Yun 2002: 556-558), and Li Shu opened the archives containing the correspondence between Wu Han and Hu Shi (Ding Shouhe 1998: 120) thus helping to prepare for the next round of criticism. Today, those who survived the turmoil try to explain their change of sides by referring to the fact that the situation was totally unclear and that, indeed, Jian Bozan and Wu Han had gone too far in some of their articles (Li Yun 2003). However, the change of sides did not help them. All their articles were criticized during the latter half of 1966 for "false criticism and real protection."

Historical Revisionism in Comparative Perspective

When Jürgen Habermas addressed the Danish public in a discussion about the Germans' attitude towards their own past, he made his point of view very clear: it was the Germans' belief in the *Sonderweg*, a supposedly special path the Germans had taken up until the end of WW 2 as a result of its particular position in Europe, that had set Germany apart from the rest of the Western world and this was at the very root of the Germans' willingness to follow Hitler. A historical consciousness after Auschwitz had to get rid of Germany's hopes of a special position in Europe, and Germany had to live with a radical discontinuity in its history. According to this assessment, the identity of the German nation is to be based on a self-chosen orientation towards the West, on an explicit break with the past and on an attitude towards history that is informed by the ambiguity of tradition (Habermas 1989c).

The debate in the 1980s, forty years after the end of World War II, in which Habermas played a prominent role, was very intense, with far reaching accusations on both sides. Keywords such as the crisis of legitimacy, a new search for identity and ungovernability were passed back and forth just as revisionism, dogmatism and conservatism were used to label the respective opponents in the debate. Two chains of arguments dominated the scene: on the one hand, the demand for historical continuity and particularity, on the other the demand for a historical break, a new beginning and an ambiguous attitude towards the question of collective identity in history (Peter 1995). Although the historical, cultural, political and economic circumstances of the debates in China and Germany were different, there are striking similarities to be observed. How can we explain this?

First and foremost, the questions of particularity, continuity and identity are questions that are inherent to human existence in the context of modernity. As Habermas underlined in his analysis of the German debate, modernity is marked by a particular understanding of time. "The present is understood at each point as a transition to something new...the present perpetuates the break with the past in the form of a continual renewal" (Habermas 1989a: 48) It is this kind of *Zeitgeist* that compels modernity to define its standards without being able to refer to positive models of the past: "Modernity sees itself as dependent exclusively upon itself – it has to draw on itself for its normativity" (Habermas 1989a: 49). But how do we know that the new is better than the old? How can we assess the risks we are undergoing in striving for change? The only possibility for modern man to know the future is by knowing the past. It is only by analyzing the causes and effects of what we did in the past that we can foresee the consequences of our actions in the present for the future. That is why although modernity is based on the assumption of breaking with the past it cannot but relate to the past. In order for these two orientations not to contradict each other, the complementarity of past and future has to be established to enable man to cope with the present (ibid.).

The German as well as the Chinese debates show that the complementarity of past and future is achieved as a result of public debate in which different participants voice their preference for either of the two options. In the Chinese case, the critics of dogmatism clearly distanced themselves from a utopian attitude towards the future. They called this kind of utopianism "empty talk" (空谈) and by using this term, made explicit reference to philosophical debates during the late Ming and early Qing dynasties. Instead of anticipating the future, without being able to assess the implied risk, they believed that knowing the past makes future developments foreseeable. As the Engels version of Marxism, especially Engels' "Dialektik der Natur," explains, history develops according to certain rules, the objectivity of which equals the laws of nature. If man were able to understand these rules, he would be able to apply them not only to understanding the past, but also to creating the future. It is by gaining this kind of knowledge that man is enabled to leave the realm of necessity and act in liberty. This liberty is constrained by rules and laws of social development, but by knowing them, man can make himself an agent of these laws and willfully act on behalf of them (Kolakowski 1977-79, I: 299-306). It is this kind of scientific determinism that Fan Wenlan, Jian Bozan and Wu Han reiterated when explaining that by researching on the history of China, one would be able to find the laws and rules governing the development of Chinese society. They view these laws as inherent in history and propagate the slogan "interpretations emerge from data" (Wu Han 1980c). You have to know that they are there to be able to find them, but you cannot know what they are like before you have found them!

This kind of scientific determinism coincides with what Kolakowski regarded as Engels' contribution to Marxism. It contrasts with the anthropocentric utopianism which can be found in some of Marx's writings. Both interpretations have their continuations in the later development of Marxism-Leninism with the different viewpoints complementing each other to a certain degree (Kolakowski 1977-79). In the Chinese context, it is quite obvious that the so called young historians were oriented towards criticizing the past and underlining the break between past and present which therefore made an assessment of the future based on past experiences undesirable. The Great Leap Forward was a social movement that was closely linked to this line of thought, which was launched without any concern about the outcome (Schoenhals 1987). The same is true for the Cultural Revolution. A line of reasoning based on past experience did not conform to the *Zeitgeist* of the time. Instead, the argument was that the Chinese people had to do something no-one had ever done before. The quality of the action was assessed on this basis and not on the predictability of the outcome. However, the terrible disaster which was brought about by the Great Leap Forward forced those intellectuals into action who believed that future developments should be guided by the knowledge of the past. The result of utopianism made it impossible for them to believe in the necessity or possibility of coexisting with the utopianists. That is when they started to argue openly against dogmatism.

The critics of dogmatism turned to tradition because they wanted the Chinese people to feel at ease with China's history. They started searching for positive aspects of the past which people living in the present could relate to. They defined a set of historical figures, events and thoughts that had already for a long time been included in the repertoire of historical knowledge in the context of Chinese culture. In their attempt to overcome the break between past and present, they quite naturally became traditionalists in the sense of selecting those aspects of the past that were helpful in making people feel at ease with their history, if not proud of it. The key issue here is the assessment of Confucianism which in Feng Youlan's and Wu Han's view could bridge the gap between past and present.

Confucianism was also their main asset in arguing in favor of the particularity of Chinese history. Because of Confucianism, Chinese history developed according to its own laws: without class struggle, without revolutions, without the development of capitalism. In the case of Germany, it is that country's geographical position right at the heart of Europe which explains Germany's historical particularity in the European context. In the case of China, it is the effect of Confucianism which in the past not only exerted an impact on China proper, but also challenged China's neighbors to either adopt or reject it.

In analyzing the German debate, Jürgen Habermas characterizes the modern nation state as resting on two basic assumptions: the universalistic orientation towards democracy, and the particularistic orientation towards nationalism. A universalistic orientation is needed to define a nation's position in the world; particularity is needed to define the reason for its very existence as separate and different from the rest of the world (Habermas 1989c: 254). Again, Habermas sees both tendencies as coexisting with each other.

If we try to transpose this to the Chinese situation, we find the orientation towards Marxism-Leninism as the universalistic side of the nation state, and Chinese history and culture, which supposedly have always made China different from the rest of the world, as the basis of its particularistic orientation. Mao Zedong Thought was defined as the reconciliation of the two orientations with one another. It was defined as the combination of the "general truth of Marxism-Leninism with the concrete practice of the Chinese revolution" (马克思列宁主义的一般原理跟中国革命的具体实践相结合) and regarded as the basis of the CCP's success in claiming power in China. By the time the Great Leap Forward had developed into the Great Famine, Mao Zedong Thought had lost its persuasiveness, and with it the complementarity of the universalistic and the nationalist orientations. For the anti-dogmatist historians, this meant that the time had come to argue in favor of the particularity of Chinese history against the dominance of the Soviet Union. For them, the universalism was Marxism-Leninism in its purified, non-Russian form, and the writing of history as a combination of facts and theories was the result of perceiving particularism and universalism as complementary. What they tried to do was simply to redefine the terms for the combination of both orientations. This is how they understood the "spirit of Yan'an" (延安精神), and that is why they thought they would have the support of Mao Zedong.

On the Relationship between Historical Revisionism and Conservatism

In his analysis of historical revisionism, Jürgen Habermas links the search for historical continuity and historical particularity to the idea of conservatism. He defines conservatism as a form of disillusioned reaction to modernity: "The affirmative stance toward social modernity and the devaluation of cultural modernity are typical for the evaluative scheme implicit in all neoconservative diagnoses of the contemporary situation" (Habermas 1989b: 28). Neo-conservatives, like their predecessors in earlier periods of the twentieth century, claim the existence of an inherent contradiction in contemporary society. Modern society is economically dependent on man becoming more and more conscious of his or her self-interest as individuals. As a consequence of this inward orientation, man becomes unable to cope with the social aspects of life, and thus becomes increasingly more unable to act as a politically conscious member of society. If modernity takes the form of a market economy combined with democracy, the economic side stands for growing self-awareness and self-interest; the political side for the necessity of sociability. Both sides are supposed to complement each other, but will eventually be unable to do so as economic necessity pushes the development of a highly individualized, if not anti-social form of life-style so far that no space is left for the social orientation of man. This is where the search for historical roots begins. In order to safeguard the ability to form and live in groups, man has to relate to history: "Social modernity requires for its stabilization … a renewal of its own historical substance; in other words, the desperate – because paradoxical – effort of a traditionalism enlightened by historicism" (Habermas 1989b: 33). The development of modern society naturally produces a split between society and culture which, according to neoconservative thought, is the cause of the crisis of legitimacy which confronts all modern societies sooner or later. The solution offered by the neo-conservatives is to strengthen "the willingness to assent and obey … based on tradition and a consensus of values, immune to variations in state services" (Habermas 1989b: 26).

Looking at the Chinese debate during the late 1950s and early 1960s, the anti-dogmatists unexpectedly display a number of striking characteristics. Although it is difficult to find direct traces of disillusionment in the works of Fan Wenlan, Jian Bozan and Wu Han, their publications give the reader a strong sense of imminent crisis. These intellectuals were converts. They had known a life without devotion to Marxism-Leninism and to Mao Zedong before investing their hopes of rescuing China in cooperating with the CCP. They had risked their privileged position in society with this conversion and felt, of course, assured that they had made the right decision when the Communist Party took over. However, it is exactly this background that made intellectuals like Fan Wenlan, Jian Bozan and Wu Han extremely sensitive to any sign of a crisis of legitimacy on the side of the Communist regime. Psychologically, the failure of the Great Leap Forward might well have induced disillusion; politically, it forced these intellectuals into a new search for legitimacy. Some of them found it in the cultural heritage of China, others in the realm of politics.

Ding Shouhe tells us a little more about this disillusionment in one of his articles about Li Shu. Li Shu was disappointed with the Party's attitude towards the peasants. He took the Party's propaganda for granted, believing the peasants to be the main social force supporting the CCP's victory. According to Ding, Li Shu realized even during the collectivization campaign that the Party was deceiving the peasants by collectivizing, i.e. taking away the land it had just distributed to them. He also believed that the commune was an organizational form that deprived the peasants of the fruits of their labor and left them with no freedom whatsoever. The people who had helped the Communists to come to power turned out to be the most under-privileged class in the new society (Ding Shouhe 1998: 109).

This argument falls, to a great extent, into the pattern of political disillusionment arising from the pragmatism of politics being juxtaposed to the ideology of politics. Neoconservatives, most prominently among them the US sociologist Daniel Bell (1996), stress that this split between society and culture does not only cause disillusionment but also crisis in society. Bell argues that while the protestant ethic was the motivational force which made capitalism possible, capitalism with its tendency toward secularization destroyed the very motivational force that formed the basis of its existence (see also Habermas 1989b: 27). If we translate this into the Chinese situation, the interpretation would be: the peasants who had invested their hopes in a prosperous peasant society had been the driving force behind the CCP's ascent to power. The necessity for modernization in the form of industrialization, however, allowed the CCP to turn towards a policy of privileging the urban over the rural population and industry over agriculture. Thus the CCP robbed itself of the very motivational force it had successfully relied upon. The consequence of this inherent contradiction was the Great Leap Forward, and the consequence of the Great Leap Forward was not only the Great Famine, but also the kind of disillusionment found in the publications related to the intellectual debate of the late 1950s and early 1960s.

If disillusionment was the trigger that induced this debate, does that mean that we should view Fan Wenlan, Jian Bozan and Wu Han's interventions in the light of conservative or neo-conservative thought? As we saw when dealing directly with their statements, there is a striking similarity between their concerns for historical continuity and particularity and what so-called revisionist historians articulate in their publications. We also argued that Habermas' analysis concerning the inherent contradictions of modernity is applicable to understanding the Chinese debate, although the overall circumstances as well as the specific contents of the debate are quite different in the European context. However, one could raise doubts and argue that the similarity is so much a structural one that it cannot be used on the level of contents analysis. The missing link might be found by looking at current debates on conservatism in China and also at earlier debates such as the one led by scholars publishing in the *Xue Heng* journal. Here we not only find a structural similarity, but also a similarity of topics, which were being discussed in the 1920s and 1930s, in the 1950s and 60s, and today. In all three cases, the assessment of Confucianism plays a major role. In all three cases, Confucianism is linked to the topics of historical continuity. And in all three cases, the interventions aiming at a positive assessment of the role Confucianism played in Chinese history were linked to the idea of a Confucian revival in the respective present. If these statements back in the 1920s and 1930s and their resurgence in the 1990s are viewed as being rightly labeled conservative, why should those from the 1950s and 1960s not be seen in the same light?

On the Particularity of Historical Revisionism in Post-49 China
When comparing neo-conservatism in Germany and the US, Jürgen Habermas sees three basics similarities and one major difference. The similarities consist in neoconservatives in both countries having a strong anti-communist and anti-populist orientation. Their common "enemy" is the class of intellectuals. They regard communism as a form of totalitarianism and prefer the democratic rule of elites to mass democracy. However in their understanding, the ruling elites are not identical with those intellectuals which propel modernization in their respective countries. On the contrary, those intellectuals are regarded as proponents of an "adversary culture" and should be "tamed, under threat of being purged from responsible milieus" (Habermas 1989b: 27). In the US, neoconservatives speak of a "new class of intellectuals" while in Germany they are most commonly called a "new class of priests."

However, neoconservatives in the US have sociology as their professional background while conservative thought in Germany is deeply rooted in the *Geisteswissenschaften,* especially in the fields of philosophy and history. The sociological approach dominating the US scene is characterized by a positive attitude towards modernity as a form of social organization. Their colleagues in Germany are said to have lost their belief in modernity after being confronted with the modernization drive of the 1960s. That is why Habermas qualifies their thought as basically romantic while looking at US neoconservatives with much more respect (Habermas 1989b).

If we compare Fan Wenlan, Jian Bozan, Wu Han and the whole network of intellectuals around them with the situation in Europe and the US, it is quite obvious that the Chinese anti-dogmatists were not anti-communists. However, they were highly critical of the Soviet Union, and some among them, most prominently Li Shu, harshly condemned Stalinism. While they were strongly influenced by the idea of adoring the masses, they were critical of mass movements like the Great Leap Forward. Although they looked for orientation in the Chinese past, they did not oppose modernization in general. They felt motivated to voice their opinions not only as critics of the Great Leap Forward but also as supporters for the readjustment policies applied by the CCP in order to overcome the problems caused by the Great Leap Forward. As we saw earlier, they held to a version of Marxism that had its roots in scientific determinism and thereby can be regarded as believing in modernization as a form of rationalized organization of state, society and economy. In this sense, they are closer to what Habermas describes as US neo-conservatism than to the proponents of historical revisionism in Germany.

However, the criticism of dogmatism which was voiced by Fan Wenlan, Jian Bozan and Wu Han was never directed against intellectuals. Instead, they were quite outspoken in articulating the wishes of the intellectuals to play a central role in the process of modernization. While they perceived themselves as intellectuals, they denied their opponents this label. Especially when it came to debating with the so-called younger generation, they regarded their opponents as badly educated young people who did not deserve to be called intellectuals.

As we stated before, the group of anti-dogmatists were not traditionalist in their historical methodology as some critics tried to suggest. They were traditionalist in their understanding of the role of intellectuals in society. They regarded themselves as having the duty to serve the state while at the same time being obliged to voice their criticism as censors of the political elite, whenever necessary. Only if they referred to themselves as intellectuals in a positive sense, could they claim the right to voice their criticism.

The list of differences would not be complete without referring to the role that Mao played in the debate. As already explained, Mao first refrained from direct interference and only showed his inclinations when the debate changed into a battle. However, he was also always concerned about being present in the debate. When the compromise between different groups and networks of intellectuals broke down in the face of an urgent crisis of legitimacy, the main aim of their discussion was to win Mao for their respective sides. Without Mao's support, neither side of the debate would be able to gain a dominant position. The structure of the political system in the PRC compelled them to think and act in these terms. This means that their criticism was not only meant as a sign of loyalty towards the state and the nation; it also had to be expressed in a form that would testify to their loyalty to Mao Zedong. Exactly because of this complex constellation, the network of anti-dogmatist intellectuals dispersed as soon as Mao decided not to support it. Those who experienced the situation at the beginning of the Cultural Revolution and are still alive, stress that the anti-dogmatists had numerically a much stronger cohort of support, but they knew that they had no chance without Mao (Su Shuangbi 1997: 33).

In the public process of transmitting a culture we decide which of our traditions we want to continue and which we do not. The debate on this rages all the more intensely the less we can rely on a triumphal national history on the unbroken normality of what has come to prevail, and the more clearly we become conscious of the ambivalence of tradition (Habermas 1989c: 263).

This comparatively conservative statement made by Jürgen Habermas helps us to understand why both in Germany and in China, history is such an enormously important field of public debate. In Germany, it is, of course, the 1933 to 1945 period that makes reliance on a triumphal national history impossible. In China, the victory of the revolution has raised enormous expectations as to the future development of the nation. However, as soon as the revolution started to eat its own children, the nation had to face its own history which was just as tainted by defeat and humiliation as it was marked by victory and pride. The fight over the ambiguity of tradition turned out not to be a dinner party as we unfortunately all know.

References

Anweiler, Oskar and Klaus Meyer (1961) *Die sowjetische Bildungspolitik seit 1917. Dokumente und Texte*, Heidelberg: Quelle & Meyer.

Beijing daxue lishixi Zhongguo gudaishi jiaoyanshi 北京大学历史系中国古代史教研室 [Teaching and research center for China's ancient history, Department of History, Peking University] (1980) (ed.) *Jian Bozan tongzhi geming de yisheng* 翦伯赞同志革命的一生 [The revolutionary life of comrade Jian Bozan], in Jian Bozan 1980, pp.490-508.

Beijing shi lishi xuehui 北京市历史学会 [The Beijing historical society] (1984) *Wu Han jinian wenji* 吴晗纪念文集 [Collected Works in memory of Wu Han], Beijing: Beijing.

Bell, Daniel (1996) *The Cultural Contradictions of Capitalism. Twentieth Anniversary Edition*, New York: Basic Books.

Cao Lanting 曹兰亭 and Liu Shaoyi 刘少义 (1966) "Bo 'shiliao ji shixue' de miulun 驳「史料即史学」的谬论 [Refuting the theory that "historical material is historical science"], in *Tianjin ribao,* May 3, 1966, p. 3.

Chan Lien (1968) "Communism versus Pragmatism: the Criticism of Hu Shi's Philosophy," in *Journal of Asian Studies* 27/1968, pp. 551-570.

Ding Shouhe 丁守和 (1998) "Kexue shi wei zhenli er douzheng de shiye: Yi Li Shu de xueshu shengya" 科学是为真理而斗争的事业: 忆黎澍的学术生涯 [Science is a matter of struggling for the truth: in memory of the academic life of Li Shu], in *Li Shu shinian ji* 黎澍十年祭 [Tenth anniversary of death of Li Shu], Bejing: Zhongguo shehui kexue, pp. 99-156.

Ding Shu 丁抒 (2003) "Cong 'shixue geming' dao "wa zufen" 从 "史学革命" 到 "挖祖坟" [From the "revolution of historiography" to "digging family graves"], http://www.boxun.com/hero/dings/47_1.shtml, accessed December 4, 2006.

Dirlik, Arif (1977) "The Problems of Class Viewpoint versus Historicism in Chinese Historiography," in *Modern China* 3/1977, pp. 465-488.

Dirlik, Arif (1978) *Revolution and History: The Origins of Marxist Historiography in China, 1919-1937*, Berkeley, Los Angeles, London: University of California Press.

Edmunds, Clifford (1987) "The Politics of Historiography: Jian Bozan's Historicism," in Goldman, Merle (ed.) *China's Intellectuals and the State: in Search of a New Relationship*, Cambridge, Mass: Harvard UP, pp. 65-106.

Fan Wenlan 范文澜 (1961) "Fandui fangkongpao" 反对放空炮 [Against empty talk], in *Lishi yanjiu* 3/1961, pp. 1-4.

Fan Wenlan 范文澜 (1957) "Lishi yanjiu zhong de jige wenti" 历史研究中的几个问题 [Several problems regarding historical research], in *Beijing Daxue xuebao* 6/1957, pp. 1-10.

Feng Yu-lan (1968) "Criticism and Self-criticism in the Discussion on Confucianism," in *Zhexue Yanjiu / Philosophy Research* 6/1963, reprinted in *Chinese Studies in History and Philosophy*, New York: International Arts and Science Press, I, 4/1968, pp. 70-104.

Fisher, Tom (1986) "The 'Upright Intellectual' as a Model in the Humanities," in Hamrin, Carol Lee and Timothy Cheek (eds) *China's Establishment Intellectuals*, White Plains: Sharpe.

Gao 高, Min 敏, Chen 陈, Zhen 振 (1966) "Zhe shi shenme lichang, guandian he fangfa?" 这是什么立场，观点和方法? [What kind of standpoint, viewpoint and method are these?], in *Shixue yuekan* 2/1966, pp. 27-32.

Goldman, Merle (1969) "The 'Unique Blooming and Contending' of 1961-1962, in *The China Quarterly* 37/1969, pp. 54-83.

Goldman, Merle (1972), "The Role of History in Party Struggle 1962-4," in *The China Quarterly* 51/1972, pp. 500-519.

Goldman, Merle; Cheek, Timothy and Hamrin, Carol Lee (eds) (1999) *China's Intellectuals and the State. In Search of a New Relationship,* Cambridge/Ma.: Harvard UP.

Grieder, Jerome B. (1980) *Hu Shih and the Chinese Renaissance. Liberalism in the Chinese Revolution, 1917-1937.* Taipei: Rainbow Bridge.

Guangming ribao (1966a) "Wu Han tongzhi fan dang fan shehui zhuyi fan Makesi zhuyi de zhengzhi sixiang he xueshu guandian" 吴晗同志反党反社会主义反马克思主义的政治思想和学术观点 [The political and academic viewpoint regarding the anti-party, anti-socialism and anti-Marxism of comrade Jian Bozan], in *Guangming ribao*, April 10, 1966, pp. 2-3.

Guangming ribao (1966b), "Jian Bozan tongzhi de fan Makesi zhuyi lishi guandian" 翦伯赞同志的反马克思主义历史观点 [The historical viewpoint of the anti-Marxism of Jian Bozan], in *Guangming ribao*, April 21, 1966, pp. 2-3.

Guo Moruo 郭沫若 (1976) *Zhongguo shi gao* 中国史稿 [A preliminary history of China], Vol.1-5, Beijing: Renmin chuanshe, 1976-1983.

Guoxue 2000, http://www.guoxue.com/deathfamous/fanwenlan/ fwl00jj.htm, accessed March 14, 2005.

Habermas, Jürgen (1989) *The New Conservatism. Cultural Criticism and the Historians' Debate*, edited and translated by Shierry Weber Nicholson, introduction by Richard Wollin, Cambridge/MA: The MIT Press.

Habermas, Jürgen (1989a) "The New Oscurity: The Crisis of the Welfare State and the Exhaustion of Utopian Energies," in Habermas 1989, pp. 48-70.

Habermas, Jürgen (1989b) "Neoconservative Cultural Criticism in the United States and West Germany," in Habermas 1989, pp. 22-47.

Habermas, Jürgen (1989c) "Historical Consciousness and Post-Traditional Identity: The Federal Republic's Orientation to the West" in Habermas 1989, pp. 249-269.

Jian Bozan (1962) 翦伯赞 "Guanyu 'shi' yu 'lun'jiehe de wenti 关于"史"与"论"结合的问题 [On the problems of how to combine "history" and "theory"], in *Guangming ribao*, Febr. 14, 1962, p. 4.

Jian Bozan (1980) 翦伯赞 *Jian Bozan lishi lunwen xuanji* 翦伯赞历史论文选集 [Selected historical works of Jian Bozan], Beijing: Renmin.

Jian Bozan (1980a) 剪伯赞: 目前历史教学中的几个问题 [Some problems in current historical teaching], in Jian Bozan 1980, pp. 32-47.

Jian Bozan 翦伯赞 (1980c) "Gonggu de queli Malie zhuyi, Mao Zedong sixiang zai jiaoxue yu kexue yanjiu zhong de zhidao diwei" 巩固的确立马列主义，毛泽东思想在教学与科学研究中的指导地位 [Strongly confirm the guiding position of Marxism-Lenism and the ideas of Mao Zedong in teaching and academic research], in Jian Bozan 1980, pp. 133-136.

Jindaishi yanjiusuo 近代史研究所, http://history.1001n.com.cn/ info/infoasp?id=4397, accessed March 15, 2005.

Kernig, Claus D. (ed.) (1966-1972) *Sowjetsystem und demokratische Gesellschaft 1966*, Vol. 1-6, 1. Zusatzband, Freiburg, Basel, Wien: Herder.

Kolakowski, Leszek (1977-79) *Die Hauptströmungen des Marxismus*. Vol.1-3, Zürich: Piper.

Leutner, Mechthild (1978) "Der Fall Chien Po-tsan [Jian Bozan] und die Entwicklung der marxistischen Geschichtswissenschaft in China," in *Geschichtswissenschaft in der Volksrepublik China. Einmalige Beilage zu China Aktuell*, Dec 1978, pp. 18-25.

Leutner, Mechthild (1982) *Geschichtsschreibung zwischen Politik und Wissenschaft. Zur Herausbildung der chinesischen marxistischen Geschichtswissenschaft in den 30er und 40er Jahren*, Wiesbaden: Harrassowitz.

Li Honglin 李洪林 (1978), "Jian Bozan tongzhi shinian ji: Bo Qi Benyu dui Jian Bozan tongzhi de wuxian" 剪伯赞同志十年祭.驳戚本禹对剪伯赞同志的诬陷 [Collected works on the occasion of the tenth anniversary of the death of Jian Bozan. Refute the frame-up of comrade Jian Bozan by Qi Benyu], in *Lishi yanjiu* 9/1978, pp. 27-47.

Li Shu 黎澍 (1961) "Mao Zedong tongzhi de 'gaizao women de xuexi' he Zhongguo lishi kexue" 毛泽东同志的「改造我们的学习」和中国历史科学 ["Reform of our learning" by comrade Mao Zedong, and the science of Chinese history], in *Renmin ribao* July 8, 1961, p. 7.

Li Yun 李筠 (2002) "Wo suo zhidao de 'san jia cun'" 我所知道的「三家村」 [What I know about the "Three Family Village"], in Lu Lin 鲁林, Wei Hua 卫华, Wang Gang 王刚 (eds) *Zhongguo gongchandang lishi koushu shilu* 中国共产党历史口述实录 [Oral reports on the history of the CCP], Jinan: Jinan, pp. 547-565.

Ma Zimei 马紫梅 (i.e. Mary Mazur) (1996) *Shidai zhi zi Wu Han* 时代之子吴晗 [A son of the times: Wu Han], Beijing: Zhongguo shehui kexueyuan.

MacFarquhar, Roderick (1997) *The Origins of the Cultural Revolution: The Coming of the Cataclysm 1961-1966*, Oxford, New York: Oxford UP and Columbia UP.

Mao Zedong (Martin) (1977-1982), "Du Sidalin 'Sulian shehui zhuyi jingji wenti' pizhu" 读斯大林《苏联社会主义经济问题》批注 [After reading Stalin's notes on "Economic problems of socialism in the Soviet-Union"], in Martin, Helmut (ed.) *Mao Zedong Texte*, Vol. I-IV, München: Hanser, Vol. IV, pp. 526-564.

Mazour, Anatole G. (1971) *The Writing of History in the Soviet Union*, Stanford UP.

Ning Ke 宁可 (1964) "Lun lishi zhuyi yu jieji guandian" 论历史主义与阶级观点 [Historicism and the class view], in *Lishi yanjiu* 3/1964, pp. 1-38.

Peter, Jürgen (1995) *Der Historikerstreit und die Suche nach einer nationalen Identität der achtziger Jahre*, Frankfurt/Main: Lang.

Schoenhals, Michael (1987) *Saltationist Socialism: Mao Zedong and the Great Leap Forward 1958*, Stockholm: JINAB.

Stalin, Iosif V. (1947) *Problems of Leninism*, Moscow: Foreign Languages.

Su Shuangbi 苏双碧 (1997) "Guanyu 'Wu Han wenti xingzhi' de gaozeng zhenglun" 关于「吴晗问题」性质的高层争论 [High level discussions on "the nature of the problem of Wu Han"] in *Yan Huang chunqiu* 5/1997, pp. 28-37.

Su Wen 苏文 (1966) "Jian Bozan tongzhi fan Makesi zhuyi de shiyue gangling pipan" 翦伯赞同志反马克思主义的史学纲领批判 [Critique on the historical guiding principle of comrade Jian Bozan's anti-Marxism], in *Guangming ribao*, April 20, 1966, p. 2.

Uhalley, Stephen (1996) "The Controversy over Li Hsiu-ch'eng," in *Journal of Asian Studies*, 25/4, pp. 305-317.

Wagner, Rudolf G. (1990) *The Contemporary Chinese Historical Drama: Four Studies*, Berkeley: University of California Press.

Wang, Q. Edward (2001), "Between Marxism and Nationalism. Chinese Historiography and the Soviet Influence, 1949-1963," in *Journal of Contemporary China*, 9/23, pp. 95-111.

Weigelin-Schwiedrzik, Susanne (1988) "'Shi und lun': Studien zur Methodologie der Historiographie in der VR China," Habilitationsschrift, Fakultät für Ostasienwissenschaften der Ruhr-Universität Bochum (accepted July 1989).

Weigelin-Schwiedrzik, Susanne (1996) "On 'shi' and 'lun'. Towards a Typology of Historiography in the PRC," in Axel Schneider und Susanne Weigelin-Schwiedrzik (eds) *Theme Issue 35, History and Theory*, 35/4, 1996, pp. 74-97.

Weigelin-Schwiedrzik, Susanne (2001) "Die chinesische Historiographie in den 90ger Jahren: Zwischen Erkenntnistheorie und Marktwirtschaft," in Hartmut Kaelble and Dietmar Rothermund (eds) Nichtwestliche Geschichtswissenschaften seit 1945, *Comparativ. Leipziger Beiträge zur Universalgeschichte und vergleichenden Geschichtsforschung*, 11/4 S.53-79.

Weigelin-Schwiedrzik, Susanne (2004) "History and Truth in Marxist Historiography," in Schmidt-Glintzer, Helwig, Achim Mittag and Jörn Rüsen (eds) *Historical Truth, Historical Criticism, and Ideology. Chinese Historiography and Historical Culture from a New Comparative Perspective*, Leiden: Brill, pp. 421-464.

Wu Han 吴晗 (1980a) "Ruhe xuexi lishi" 如何学习历史 [How to learn history?], in Wu Han 1980, pp. 202-210.

Wu Han 吴晗 (1980c) "Guanyu lishi yanjiu zhong de jige wenti" 关于历史研究中的几个问题 [On some problems regarding the study of history], in Wu Han 1980, pp. 211-222.

Wu Han 吴晗 (1980d) "Lishi jiaocai he lishi yanjiu zhong de jige wenti" 历史教材和历史研究中的几个问题 [Some problems regarding historical teaching material and historical research], in Wu Han 1980, pp. 239-245.

Wu Han 吴晗 (1980) *Xuexi ji* 学习集 [Learning: collected works], Beijing: Beijing.

Wu Han 吴晗 (1980b) "Xuexi weida zuguo de lishi" 学习伟大祖国的历史 [Learning from the history of our great country], Wu Han 1980, pp. 198-201.

Yanhuang chunqiu (2005), http://www.sina.com.cn, last accessed March 16, 2005.

Yin Da 尹达 (1966) "Bixu ba shixue geming jinxing daodi" 必须把史学革命进行到底 [On the need to totally revolutionize history] in *Hongqi* 1966/3, pp. 3-10.

Zheng Qian 郑谦 (1999) "Dangdai shehui zhuyi gaige yu Zhongguo de 'wenhua dageming' (jielu)" 当代社会主义改革与中国的"文化大革命"（节录）[The current reform of socialism and China's "Cultural Revolution" (excerpts)], in Zhang Hua 张化, Su Caiqing 素采青 (eds) *Huishou wenge* 回首文革 [Look back at the Cultural Revolution], Beijing: Zhonggong dangshi, pp. 204-217.

Zi Ling 子伶 and Zi Zhen 子真 (1986) "Wu Han he Hai Rui baguan" 吴晗和海瑞罢官 [Wu Han and Hai Rui dismissed from office], in Zhou Ming 周明 (1986) *Lishi zai zheli chensi. 1966-1976 nian jishi* 历史在这里沉思 1966-1976 年记实 [Reflections on history. Events from 1966-1976], vol.1-5, Beijing: Huaxia Vol. 2, pp. 1-15.

Julia Strauss

Rethinking Land Reform and Regime Consolidation in the People's Republic of China: the Case of Jiangnan 1950-1952

Much of the grounding legitimacy of the Chinese Communist Party (CCP) stems from a particular narrative of how it won the support of the people (particularly the poor peasantry on whose backs it marched to power) and vanquished the opposition. Despite the emergence of any number of recent works inside and outside China that have begun to question this linear trajectory of history, the regime's success in carrying out land reform is inseparable from this larger narrative of class struggle, tempering of the CCP's leadership in the rural hinterland, close links to the people, and military victory over the forces of reaction and feudalism in 1949 that ushered in a subsequent "Golden Age" of popularity and successful implementation of key revolutionary policies in the early to mid 1950s (Resolution on Certain Questions in the History of Our Party 1981: 17-27). In this larger narrative of early positive accomplishment, land reform takes on a particular importance. Land reform can be considered *the* linchpin of regime legitimacy in the countryside for the CCP. It was one of the few campaigns aimed at a fundamental and revolutionary transformation of society and economy that was executed on a large scale both before and after the watershed of 1949. As such it is unusual for the way in which it linked pre-1949 progressive pro-peasant policies with very much the same kind of initiative after victory was won in 1949. Indeed land reform stands as the major campaign in which the CCP's post-1949 rhetorical idealization its close links to the poor peasantry was actually put into practice. Between the land reform of the early 1950s until the decollectivization of the early 1980s, the revolutionary PRC simply did what all other revolutionary and developmentalist regimes have done before and since: squeezed the countryside until the pips squeaked by dampening rural consumption, extracting from agriculture mercilessly to fund investment in heavy industry through a system of unified purchase and supply of grain that subsidized urban areas at the expense of the rural, systematically and heavily discriminating against the countryside in favor of urban areas, particularly urban areas in the interior deemed important for strategic reasons of self reliance and defense (Ash 2006, Lardy 1983). Particularly in the light of what came later – collectivization, hyper collectivization with the Great Leap Forward, ideologically driven mass famine in the early 1960s, and the overall stagnation of consumption and living standards in the countryside from the mid 1950s onward, land reform stands out as a case of virtually unquestioned "success" for the CCP. Some have quibbled about the degree to which land reform was an economic success, citing the fragmentation and inefficiency of China's land holdings (Wong 1973, Stavis 1978), but all have concurred that land reform was in aggregate an unquestioned political and social success in clearing the ground of the rural landlord elite that had blocked the modernization of the rural economy. Land, after all, was what most peasants wanted, and this was what the CCP provided, through unique policy instruments of mobilizing class consciousness, investigative work teams, the mass line, and soliciting an extraordinary degree of popular participation, culminating in the dramatic spectacle of public accusation meetings (控诉会) in which landlords were publicly accused by the downtrodden and exploited for their past sufferings.

On the whole, the CCP's own reading of its success in land reform has been buttressed by a sympathetic Western historiography from several quarters: Firstly, contemporary left leaning participant- observers, notably William Hinton (1966) and Isabel and David Crook (1959), all of whom were able to observe particular villages in the Liberated Areas of North China in the late 1940s; secondly, later generations of Communist sympathizers (Myrdal 1965), and thirdly, agricultural economists (Wong 1973, Stavis 1978). While the agricultural economists have disagreed between themselves about how to evaluate the economic successes of land reform, in aggregate all have taken the CCP's claims about land reform at face value: that there was significant demand from below for land reform, that the CCP was unusually pragmatic in solving practical questions and problems associated with the implementation of land reform, that the CCP enjoyed a surge of rural support and mobilized the grassroots as a consequence of land reform, and that on the whole land reform ought to be deemed an unquestioned political and social success, and at least a guarded economic one as well. There are two elements that are implicit in this understanding of land reform: firstly that it was necessary both economically and politically and secondly that the regime's methods of implementing land reform were both comprehensible and reasonable in the light of the actual circumstances in rural China.

Land Reform as Hegemonic Morality Tale: West and East
There are two literatures that converge to produce a fairly uniform story of land reform, more akin to morality play than simple narrative. Most of the Western literature revolves around two sets of contemporaneous "thick descriptions" of land reform by sympathetic, left leaning anthropological observers, who were able to witness the unfolding of land reform as it happened, on the ground, in the particular places of William Hinton's *Long Bow* and David and Isabel Crook's *Ten Mile Village*. Both were predicated on the assumption that the economy was stagnant, fixed, whereby individual families resorted to non productive endeavors such as usury, rents and foreclosure when they could to ensure their own perpetuation as "whoever did not go up went down" (Hinton 1966: 38, Crook and Crook 1979: 8-9). While the honesty of these thick descriptions gives ample evidence of the violence, the individual personalities, the confusion, the initial difficulties in mobilizing the people to speak up and act, and the simple wrong headedness of some of the more aggressively egalitarian policies in economies in which there was only a fixed amount to go around, both implicitly and explicitly see the CCP and its bottom up form of agrarian revolution based on the practice of class struggle to have been the progressive, socially just way out of economic and social backwardness and stagnation. This depiction of land reform dovetails almost perfectly with the CCP's own literature on land reform promulgated in the early 1950s and after. This literature was in the first instance geared to an educated Chinese public perhaps unconvinced of the need for social revolution in the countryside and leery of violence and bloodshed, but was simultaneously part of a larger founding myth of the legitimacy of the CCP. It had two components: heuristic personal testimonial (typically by an ivory tower intellectual, now converted through personal experience to the CCP's understanding of life in the countryside) and "objective" social investigation and exhaustive economic classification of wealth, landholding, occupation, and age throughout the entirety of the countryside. Both buttressed the CCP's educative propaganda of the time, which asserted that the countryside was in crisis, the Guomindang had not only failed but had been part of the problem, and the CCP's smashing of

feudalism by breaking the economic and social power of the landlord class was necessary, proper, and just. Typical, but by no means unique, was the CCP's organization and dispatch of a special delegation of professors and high level academics from Beijing's most elite universities to rural Jiangnan in the spring of 1951 for a month of "investigation and study" (参观与学习), with Pan Guangdan of Qinghua the leading academic in attendance. The subsequent essays and testimonials revolved around such questions as why Jiangnan really ought to be considered feudal and the reasons why land could not be peacefully divided (Shi Wenqi 1951: 88-90), the myriad ways in which "feudalism" and exploitation was perpetuated through landholdings (Pan and Quan 1951: 5-9, Beijing ge daxue jiaoshou huadongqu tudi gaige canguantuan zongjie 1951: 183-193), the change in peasants' consciousness, and reaffirmed the transformative and liberating effect of having participated in the special investigation and study team for the political and social consciousness on the participating individual (Beijing ge daxue jiaoshou huadongqu tudi gaige canguantuan zongjie 1951: 198). These short pieces were initially widely disseminated in *Remin ribao* 人民日报, *Xin guancha* 新观察, and *Guangming ribao* 光明日报 before eventual collection in a volume published by the Su'nan People's Government Public Office Land Reform Commission in late 1951. While it is impossible to know whether the senior academics truly believed what they were writing in their accounts of having participated in investigation and study of land reform in Jiangnan, the content well illustrates the degree to which senior intellectuals were, as early as mid 1951, already acting "as if" they had internalized both the new Marxian categories of class analysis and the moral necessity of the regime in pushing through what would turn out to be a very bloody campaign indeed, with upwards of one million killed in the violent emotions that were whipped up through the mass accusation sessions that immediately preceded the actual division of land.[1]

Although the Chinese official literature on land reform differed in some of its language with its incessant harping on the evils of "feudalism", and made particular use of the heuristic examples of high status ivory tower intellectuals being sent to the countryside to witness appalling conditions and the necessity of land reform, the essential presumptions of both Chinese and foreign variants of this morality tale were identical: a backward and immiserated countryside, the economic and social need for land reform, and the absolute centrality of the CCP, its organizational skill, its application of Marxist categories in pushing through the class based participatory revolution that rid the countryside of the hated exploiters once and for all, clearing the ground for progress, science, development, political awakening and justice.

The depiction of land reform as told by sympathetic observers Hinton and the Crooks – at ground level, with all the immediacy and human drama of revolutionary ferment offers a compelling narrative, one that has been reproduced both implicitly and explicitly in most of our understandings of the campaign. And indeed, the "thick descriptions" of *Fanshen* (Hinton 1966) and *Ten Mile Village* (Crook and Crook 1959) continue to compel, for several reasons. First, both Hinton and the Crooks wrote vividly, and with an unusual combination of sympathy, emotion, and willingness to detail things as the authors perceived them, however unflattering to individuals or even to local cadres in the CCP. Further, these depictions of land reform both manage to capture the micro stories in the inti-

---

[1]   In the different authoritarian context of Syria, see Wedeen 1998.

mate and personal stories recorded, and situate those stories in a context of campaign evolution and violence that is rendered both progressive and enlightened, presented as the only real chance for both the CCP and for China's economic and social breakthrough out of economic stagnation and social exploitation. This sympathy in combination with a baseline ideological view of land reform as fundamentally *necessary* carries one through the uncomfortables of the texts – individuals with muddled motives, violence that got out of hand, cadres could be by turn formulaic and lorded it over everyone else, and the weasly way in which individuals bargained for more preferable class statuses. These are exactly the features that save these works from being mere propaganda, and have contributed to their staying power as an integral part of a wider master narrative of 20th century Chinese history in general and economic history in particular: it posits that rural China was characterized by economic stagnation and exploitation, that underlings resented the economic and social elite, and that the CCP was virtually required to come in and smash the old economic and social order in rural China.

Land Reform Outside of North China

But when we look over the vastness of China and begin to incorporate the kinds of archival and documentary sources that have begun to come available in the past ten years, what do we in fact see was the case on the ground, in the voluminous reports and statistics compiled by those in county, peri-urban, municipal and regional/district offices in charge of overseeing the land reform campaign in its stages of preparation and implementation? We see something more than a little unexpected. This unitary, hegemonic description and understanding of land reform, and the crude "reasons" for it simply does not hold up *at all* when one moves out of the relatively impoverished, historically bandit riven, and physically insecure North China plain of the 1940s to the more commercialized, commodified, and at least relatively physically secure regions of east and south China. Indeed, critical reading of the individual stories and details laid out in such classic works as *Fanshen* and *Ten Mile Inn* suggest that may not hold up all that well even for the North China plain, as both works admit that there was not a huge gap in standard of living between even landlords and poor peasants ("all were pitifully poor" [Crook and Crook 1979: 8], "their [landlords'] lives were luxurious only in contrast to the absolute poverty and near starvation of the great mass of people" [Hinton 1966: 37]). Hinton and the Crooks also go into considerable detail discussing just how difficult it was for individuals to be assigned to particular classificatory statuses, as in practice the seemingly straightforward distinctions between landlords, rich peasants, middle peasants and poor peasants on the basis of relations of exploitation were often extremely difficult to make in practice.

In fact, none of what the Jiangnan archives are now revealing should come to us as that much of a surprise. Ezra Vogel's detailed treatment of land reform in *Canton under Communism: Programs and Politics in a Provincial Capital, 1949-1968* (1969) was published only three years after *Fanshen* and is quite explicit on how differently land reform played out in the commercialized, clan riven, Cantonese speaking Pearl River Delta. Here one sees the enormous difficulty with mobilizing the peasants against the "exploiting classes" given the strong lineages and social welfare functions of clan halls, and an ambivalence so profound on the part of leading Guangdong cadres that it turned to outright obstructionism and resistance, eventually requiring outsiders to come in to the province to implement the kind of violent, class struggle based land reform measures mandated by the

Party center (Vogel 1969: 91-124). But perhaps because of the outlying status of Guang-dong – high level of commercialization, orientation to overseas Chinese communities, different dialect, the anomalous presence of Hong Kong, and the particular social struc-tures characteristic of Cantonese society – the way in which land reform played out in Guangdong could be sidelined as a kind of Cantonese exceptionalism. Indeed, two of the key overview texts in the Western literature perpetuate the baseline assumptions of Hin-ton and the Crooks, as well as the CCP itself, that land reform "consolidated the support of the peasant masses" (Cambridge History of China 1978: 153) and "if the ends of land reform were determined from above, the process itself was carried out from below ... providing peasants ... with the sense that they could be masters of their own destiny" (Meisner 1986: 110). In short, the pre-1949 North China land reform story as filtered through the CCP, the Crooks and Hinton has been uncritically assimilated as a baseline archetype for understandings of land reform ever since, with if anything the suggestion that land reform did not go quite far enough in terms of its egalitarianism, and at any rate was disappointing in its impact on agricultural productivity.

When we turn to the lower Yangzi region, we find that despite the regime's projection of itself as scientific, progressive, and empirically based, the CCP's categories of class based occupation, and the ways in which these were translated to presumptive levels of exploitation, were at least as inapplicable as they were for the Pearl River Delta, even though their imposition does not seem to have sparked the kinds of resistance so endemic in Guangdong. The Jiangnan was, like the Pearl River Delta, highly commercialized and oriented towards external markets; and if there was not the presence of a Hong Kong, there certainly was the anomaly of the urban metropole of internationalized Shanghai that dominated the rural economy in so many direct and indirect ways. But in other respects Jiangnan was lacking in some of the social and economic elements that seemed to go into Guangzhou exceptionalism; clans and lineages were much less important in rural society, fewer villages in Jiangnan exported their people overseas, and Jiangnan had been at the epicenter of rural commercialization and literati culture for many hundreds of years. As least as importantly, the relative physical proximity and good transport links of Shanghai and Jiangnan to the political center in Beijing, in combination with the sheer dominance of Shanghai's industry and the importance of integrating it into the national economy meant that the CCP treated the takeover and integration of Jiangnan in general and Shang-hai in particular with a great deal of sensitivity and care. This was reflected in one of the key differences in the implementation of land reform in the Jiangnan countryside and the Pearl River Delta; Jiangnan did not have the problem of the leadership as well as the rank and file of provincial cadres reflecting local interests who were so obvious in their efforts to deflect central policies to nearly the extent that Guangdong did, nor were outsider troops sent in to finally implement land reform in the more thorough and radical way de-manded by the party center (Vogel 1969: 101-124).

But even without these distinguishing features of "Cantonese exceptionalism," when we turn to Jiangnan, particularly the peri-urban districts around Shanghai and counties in the Su'nan administration(active between mid 1949 and 1953, after which it merged with the Subei district to form the province of Jiangsu) within relatively easy reach of Shanghai, it is clear that in contrast to the relatively straightforward, if emotionally compelling, moral-ity tale of progressive modernization, social justice, and popular participation related by Hinton and the Crooks, land reform was really quite different in Jiangnan. Indeed, there was almost *no* correlation between the standard view of land reform as reasonable, comprehensible, desired by the "masses", and/or socially and economically necessary.

First, the conventional categories for rural social and economic classification of land-lord, rich peasant, middle peasant, poor peasant and poor-and-hired were neither reasonable nor comprehensible when applied to Jiangnan, and cadres in Shanghai entrusted with overseeing the implementation of the campaign at lower levels in the peri-urban *jiaoqu* (郊区) understood this very well. Their own preliminary analyses of local economic stratification repeatedly suggested that in most of the *jiaoqu*, even those that were largely rural, the majority of the rural working population only worked in agriculture part time, almost all rural males aspired to becoming factory workers (and many migrated, at least part time, to where the factories were), and absentee landlords were extremely common. Worse still, the standard division between exploiting and exploited classes that so stirred people to indignation and action in North China simply could not be made for the highly commercialized and commodified Jiangnan, where most small-holders of modest means also rented out their land and could thus be reasonably classified as "exploiting classes" (SMA A71/1/71). As a result, the CCP's fundamental line of demarcation between exploiting vs. exploited classes was virtually impossible to apply.

Second, there was embarrassingly little demand from below for overturning the class order, for two interrelated reasons, both of which had to do with the ways in which the realities of economic and social life in rural Jiangnan blended and fudged the criteria for the clean and clear classifications by economic class made by the CCP. Preliminary investigations of the outlying districts of Shanghai suggested that land ownership patterns and type of "exploitation" were both "very complicated", as definable landlords of any description only owned a fraction of the land, handicrafts and small factories were already ubiquitous, land renting was subcontracted to people outside the local area, and petty rentiers with multiple sources of income actually comprised the largest classificatory group (SMA B14-1-21). Insofar as there was any definable class hatred at all, it tended to be directed against the agents and rent collectors of large absentee landlords, but even here class hatred seemed to be remarkably muted. Indeed, at the outset of the campaign, from early July 1950 until the convening of the Second East China Region Conference on Typical Land Reform Experiments in mid November of the same year, many local cadres in Jiangnan exhibited a remarkable lack of enthusiasm for the parts of the project that involved targeting individuals and stirring up class consciousness and hatreds – at least in part because it was so difficult to match actual local conditions with the kinds of fixed categories being dictated from above. In the first stage of the campaign, cadres in Su'nan typically "focused only on land ... and dangled the prospect of land to get peasants to come to Peasant Association meetings [at all]". It was only after the campaign moved into its second stage more radical stage, with dire warnings from above about the dangers of cadre formalism and lazy thinking that "*my* village does not really have any exploiters" that a set of bureaucratic incentives was established to conform to the targets of higher levels – or else. After the November 1950 conference, however, the campaign lurched in a wild leftward direction that culminated in uncounted instances of "indiscriminate struggle" (乱斗) that in turn alienated and puzzled many. Despite guidelines that absolutely forbade targeting middle peasants, the all important middle peasants were in some places among those struggled against and beaten for having collaborated with the Japanese. Many villagers also looked askance at the common practice of substituting the wives or sons of landlords as struggle objects, as not infrequently landlords were not physically present to be struggled against (JPA 3006-3-271).

More tellingly, the putatively exploited masses themselves tended to not see themselves as exploited and downtrodden by landlords, even after the educative measures of the early part of the campaign. In many places, the masses had a most unfortunate tendency to continue to think that that their landlords were actually good people … "[their] landlords were pretty honest and true, were 'laboring landlords' (劳动地主), [who] ought to [be permitted to] participate in the peasant association as representatives …" In one case in Xibing, such was the local feeling towards one of the local landlords that the masses sent food to him while he was incarcerated pending his struggle session, and in another in Yangjiawan a captured "bandit" was so popular that two hundred of the masses gathered outside the local public security bureau to protest his arrest (JPA 3006-3-271).

Finally, and perhaps most surprisingly of all, the dramatic dénouement of state led retribution through public accusation meetings, when emotionally charged villagers were stirred up at the prospect of wicked and exploitative landlords getting their just deserts did not conform to the scripts of out of hand violence, drama, and free flowing tears laid down in north China. Not only were local landlords not particularly hated a priori, but in many places the clear majority of those who were struggled against at public accusation meetings *were not even landlords,* even by the loose criteria that were by then in use. For example, in Shanghai county, then a largely rural area to the south of municipal Shanghai, of the 779 individuals arrested and struggled against over the course of the campaign, only roughly one quarter (190 of 779) were identified as landlords; 140 were "local bullies" (恶霸), the largest number of all at 236 were "counterrevolutionaries" (反革命), followed by a number almost as large that were completely unclassified in the catch all category of "other" (其他) at 213 (MDA 13/1/37). Local reports bear out these county wide statistics. In rural Dashu xiang, Shanghai county, there were a mere four landlord households of 789, and of these, two were "commercial landlords" (工商业地主), one had fled, and the final one worked his own fields and had no major discernible crimes and evils. Ultimately, the best that the local authorities could do by way of struggle targets in Dashu was to produce two individuals: firstly, a bandit (土匪) by the name of Zhu Jiejun whose past activities had so stirred up the local community that even after he committed suicide in custody, the crowd gathered for the public accusation session against him demanded that his corpse be displayed to receive continued accusations, and secondly, a village bully (乡恶) by the name of Tang Luoxiong who was handed over for a united struggle session at the district center in Beiqiao (MDA 13-1-35). In short, even though the bureaucratic incentives from above to foment class struggle, stir up the masses, and make a proper example of exploitative landlords were intense after the November 1950 conference, there simply were not enough of the right sort of landlords to go around in Jiangnan. The statistics from Shanghai county suggest that where the numbers of clear and obvious landlords were insufficient, local cadres made approximations; typically by targeting those deemed counterrevolutionary, or "local bullies" as those who were either credible dangers to the regime or genuinely hated by the masses. Yet these categories were in practice even more malleable and subjective than was the status of landlord (which in the end had to be based on objective and measurable criteria of landholding and income derived from "exploitation"), and in many cases this crude approximation opened the door to local grudges and/or targeting whichever local elites had previously collaborated with the Japanese. Campaign overlap and campaign approximation (given the bureaucratic incentives to produce landlords, evil gentry and local bullies), the usual suspects could be rounded up and used as statistic fodder.

Yet land reform was accomplished in Jiangnan, and in outline proceeded much as it did in North China, where rural economic and social conditions were so very different. The cadre rank and file was greatly expanded through a process of training – notably in the model and methods derived from North China. Large numbers of basic level cadres were recruited, trained, and dispatched to carry out the campaign. The stages of the campaign were virtually identical: preparation, test sites, preparation and investigation in particular villages, the identification of activists and sympathizers, the public accusation meeting followed by punishment of the accused target, and the division of the land. Work teams duly went in to villages, plans were drawn up, classifications were applied, *kongsu hui* were convened, the land was re-apportioned, peasant associations were created, and mutual aid teams were encouraged. Indeed what stands out about land reform was how in terms of its bureaucratic objectives – the things that could be measured as part of policy implementation – not how flexible and accommodating to local circumstances the CCP was, but rather how inflexibly and didactically they imposed a model and a staged process that had everything to do with ideological filters and the establishment of a uniform hegemony from above, and surprisingly little to do with what was sensible, demanded from below, and provided any kind of "fit" with local conditions.

The Purposes of Land Reform

If land reform in Jiangnan was not about the sorts of things trumpeted by the regime: exploitation, economic stagnation, and demand from below, then what *was* it about? In an exploratory piece of this length, I can only suggest the following in a preliminary manner. The primary *raison d'être* of land reform in the Newly Liberated Areas of China after 1949 had little to do with objective economic and social need for social revolution, but everything to do with a larger process of revolutionary regime consolidation in the countryside. Land reform (along with the concurrent and partially overlapping Campaign to Suppress Counterrevolutionaries) was the primary means by which the regime differentiated itself from its predecessor and illustrated conclusively to Chinese society writ large that after an initial year of moderation and inclusiveness, its agenda was seriously revolutionary after all. The revolutionary regime's method of pushing through land reform was the mobilizational mass campaign, which collapsed five analytically distinct, but temporally overlapping targets into one concentrated push; firstly, moral and ideational differentiation between itself and the outgoing Guomindang, which had ineffectually discussed and promoted gradualist programs of land reform that worked through extant local elites for the previous twenty years, secondly, literal extermination of the main social and economic bulwark against revolutionary programs in the countryside – the landed gentry elite, thirdly, the concurrent expansion of the organizational power of the CCP in the countryside through the simultaneous mobilization of commitments on the part of those who would serve the state and the silencing of those who might otherwise object to it, fourthly, the didactic inculcation of a new set of revolutionary norms, language, and tropes and finally the enlistment of mass participation and mass entertainment in state led dramatic spectacle through *kongsu hui* 控诉会 [public accusation meetings], which in aggregate had the effect of graphically demonstrating the state's new coercive powers and willingness to use them against class enemies, while soliciting the open, public collusion of the majority in state sponsored violence. The methods and organizational matrix inherent to the mass campaign established an environment of urgency and haste, in which it was possible to launch regime consolidation initiatives on all these fronts at once, in a public way that mobilized the emotions and made any kind of active resistance to either the violence or the build up of state power in the countryside well nigh unimaginable. And it does have to be said that in aggregate the land reform campaign was extremely successful. It *did* conclusively break the power of landed rural elites through extermination and expropriation. It *did* expand the ranks of basic level cadres enormously: in the greater Shanghai area alone, over 6000 cadres were initially identified and trained to implement the land reform campaign, many of whom then went on to continue as basic level village cadres (SMA B14/1/80). To judge from the quick acquiescence of those brought in to investigation/study tours of land reform, urban elites were quick to adopt the regime's moral grounding, code words, and new tropes. And what evidence we have from the *kongsu hui* mass accusation sessions suggests that at this early stage, the "masses" usually complied with expectations from above: they jeered, they cheered, and they clapped more or less on cue with a resounding hand at the inevitably bloody dénouement, as the accused were led off to the execution ground (Strauss 2006). But the dynamics of campaigns, as implemented by a coalescing system of bureaucratic domination, led to any number of abuses and dysfunctions, even in this early stage of regime consolidation when popular support for the regime was high. Bureaucratic incentives to perform and meet ill defined targets set from above irrespective of how applicable those targets might be led to dynamics of very rough approximations. When extant reality did not correspond to the targets, policies, and systems of classification imposed from above, cadres on the ground applied policy to proximate groups, leading to the blurring of land reform with the concurrent Campaign to Suppress Counterrevolutionaries in Jiangnan. In the end, the majority of the targets struggled against and executed were not even landlords at all. In this respect, land reform in Jiangnan can be understood as not only the way in which the countryside was brought to heel, rural intermediaries exterminated, basic level organizations of party-state domination established, and elite and mass populations "educated" into the revolutionary regime's new norms and tropes, important as these things all were. Land reform in Jiangnan was, at its broadest, the coalescing state's imposition of a hegemony derived from the categories, values, and world view of impoverished, rural north on the commercialized, urbanized south. It would not be the last campaign for which this would be the case, and would set any number of chilling precedents for the future.

References

Ash, Robert (2006) "Squeezing the Peasants: Agrarian Reform, Agricultural Development and Grain Extraction in Mao's China" in *The China Quarterly* 188 (December 2006), pp. 959-998.

"Beijing ge daxue jiaoshou huadongqu tudi gaige canguantuan zongjie" 北京各大学教授华东区土地改革参观团总结 [General summary of Beijing universities' professorial group visiting tour of the Eastern China region land reform] (1951), in Su'nan renmin xingzhengshu tudi gaige weiyuanhui, pp. 183-198.

Crook, Isabel and David Crook (1959) *Revolution in a Chinese Village: Ten Mile Inn*, London: Routledge (reprinted 1998, 1999, 2000).

Crook, Isabel and David Crook (1979) *Mass Movement in a Chinese Village: Ten Mile Inn*, London: Routledge.

Hinton, William (1966) *Fanshen: A Documentary of Revolution in a Chinese Village*, New York: Vintage.

Lardy, Nicholas (1983) *Agriculture in China's Modern Economic Development*, Cambridge: Cambridge UP.

MacFarquhar, Roderick and John K. Fairbank (eds) (1987) *The Cambridge History of China*, Vol 14, *The People's Republic, Part I: The Emergence of Revolutionary China 1949-1965*, Cambridge and New York: Cambridge UP.

Meisner, Maurice (1986) *Mao's China and After*, New York: Free Press.

Myrdal, Jan (1965) *Report from a Chinese Village*, London: Penguin.

Resolution on Certain Questions in the History of Our Party Since the Founding of the People's Republic of China (1981), Beijing: Foreign Languages Press.

Pan Guangdan 潘光旦 and Quan Weitian 全慰天 (1951) "Su'nan nongcun fengjian shili de jige tedian" 苏南农村封建势力的几个特点 [Some special characteristics of the power of rural feudalism in Su'nan], in *Su'nan renmin xingzhengshu tudi gaige weiyuanhui*, no place, pp. 1-9.

Stavis, Ben (1978) "China and the Comparative Analysis of Land Reform" in *Modern China* 4/1 (January 1978).

Shi Wenqi 施文淇 (1951) "Wo suo jiandaode Su'nan tudi gaige yundong" 我所见到的苏南土地改革运动 [The land reform movement in Su'nan that I saw], in Su'nan renmin xingzhengshu tudi gaige weiyuanhui, pp. 88-89.

Strauss, Julia (2006) "Morality, Coercion and State Building by Campaign in the Early People's Republic of China: Regime Consolidation and After, 1949-1956" in *The China Quarterly* 188 (December 2006), pp. 891-912.

Su'nan renmin xingzhengshu tudi gaige weiyuanhui 苏南人民行政公署土地改革委员会 (ed.) (1951) *Wo suo jiandao de Su'nan tugai gaigeyundong* 我所见到的苏南土地改革运动 [The land reform movement in Su'nan that I saw], no place, 1951.

Vogel, Ezra (1980) Canton under Communism: Programs and Politics in a Provincial Capital, 1949-1968, Cambridge: Harvard UP (1st edition 1969).

Wong, John (1973) *Land Reform in the People's Republic of China: Institutional Transformation in Agriculture*, New York: Praeger.

Wedeen, Lisa (1998) "Acting 'As if' Symbolic Politics and Social Control in Syria," in *Comparative Studies in Society and History* 40/3 (July 1998), pp. 403-423.

Archives

Jiangsu Provincial Archives 江苏省档案馆 (JPA)
Minhang District Archives 闵行区档案馆 (MDA)
Shanghai Municipal Archives 海市档案馆 (SMA)

JPA 3006-3-271. "Guanyu fadong qunzhong douzheng de cailiao zhailü" 关于发动群众斗争的材料摘录 [Notes on materials relating to stirring up the masses' struggle], Su'nan tugai jiancha chu 苏南土改检查处, April 1951.

MDA 13/1/35. "Shanghai xian, di'yi lei xiang dashu xiang zongjie" 上海县，第一类乡大树乡总结 [Shanghai county, No. 1 type village: dashu village summary report], February 1, 1951.

MDA 13/1/37 "Shanghai xian jieshu tugai gongzuo douzheng qingkuang tongji biao (2)" 上海县结束土改工作斗争情况统计表 [Shanghai county final statistics on struggle work], November 18, 1951.

SMA A71/1/71. "Shanghai shi jiaoqu tudi gaige zongjie" 上海市郊区土地改革总结 [A comprehensive summary of land reform in Shanghai's outer districts], November 25, 1952.

SMA B14/1/1. "Shanghai shi jiaoqu tugai gongzuo baogao" 上海市郊区土改工作报告 [Work Report on Land Reform in Shanghai's outer districts], February 21, 1951.

SMA B14/1/80. "Sheng tudi gaige qianhou xiangcun jiceng ganbu bianhua qingkuang tongjibiao" 省土地改革前后乡村基层干部变化情况统计表 [Statistical form on changes in basic level rural cadres before and after land reform], p. 13 of internally numbered file, December 31, 1951.

Klaus Mühlhahn

"Repaying Blood Debt" – State Violence and Mass Crimes during the 1950s in China[1]

When Mao proclaimed the founding of the People's Republic of China on October 1, 1949 at Tianamen Square, his words conveyed the expectation that a new age was being ushered in. The rhetoric of a New China quickly gained popularity in China and among western observers, reflecting the widespread feeling of being part of a truly revolutionary process which was about to turn the old backward Middle Kingdom into a renewed, invigorated and progressive socialist society. And certainly, the 1950s did in fact see a series of policies that changed China profoundly und propelled it in the direction of a socialist system. There can be no doubt that the new government in the 1950s pursued an active reform agenda which affected many areas of daily life, reaching from land reform to a new marriage law. Through these policies, century-old institutions and social relations were displaced, and new social practices slowly began to emerge. On the other hand, although Mao liked to compare China with a clean sheet of paper, on which the most beautiful characters could be written, there was no zero hour and many links can be traced between pre-1949 China and China under socialism. Historians have only recently begun to look into these continuities that bridge the 1949 divide. Up to now, they have mostly studied policy goals (development, modernization), political structures (the one party state) and foreign policy as examples of the continuities which link the 1950s with the 1930s and 1940s. One additional and very important area that still needs to be studied more fully relates to the spasms of violence that connect the 1950s (and 1960s) with the war period in the 1940s. In 1949 as well as in the early 1950s, there was still fighting going on in many parts of China. Various insurgencies continued to threaten the new government far into the 1950s. The new government responded to these challenges with aggressive and violent political and military campaigns. As a matter of fact, the public outbreak of violence was an inseparable part of the experience of living in New China and under socialism in the 1950s. Whether in the villages or the cities, almost every citizen of the new state was likely, at one time or another, to witness violent scenes, which were conducted and organized by the new state against real or perceived enemies.

This paper focuses on the policies of violence – policies characterized by a combination of massacre and expulsion, deliberate acts of terror and looting, social humiliation and mass rape – that the men and women who founded the People's Republic of China (PRC) put in place and allowed to spread throughout China during what official histories now refer to as "the period of basic completion of socialist transformation." The 1950s witnessed mass violence and mass killings on a very large scale, although these are very difficult, if not impossible, to quantify. But this is not the main concern here; rather, I want to understand the historical factors and contexts that allowed such a massive wave of violence to happen, with the victimization of millions of people, and the involvement of large numbers of perpetrators and bystanders. My interest is in the key components of

---

[1] This paper was first presented to the workshop "The History of Human Rights" organized by the Center for the Study of History and Memory and the Department of History, Indiana University, Bloomington, March 8-9, 2006. I want to thank the participants of this workshop and especially my discussants Rosemary Foot (University of Oxford) and Jeffrey Wasserstrom (UC Irvine) for their helpful comments.

those policies, *who* organized the violence and how the policies of violence fitted into what passed for a state apparatus, what they looked like, how they operated, and what some of their key strengths and weaknesses were in the eyes of those who operated them. Mass crimes and mass violence are both characterized by the destruction of large segments of a civilian population, often accompanied by atrocities, which, at first sight, seem to be random or without purpose. Yet, beyond the murderous frenzy of men which we often hold responsible for such crimes, mass violence and mass murder follow a particular "rationality." Mass violence and mass murder do not flow out of the "delirium of the battlefield," a term used by the historian Charles Browning, to describe the atrocities committed by soldiers against each other in the dynamics of war. Rather, they result from a policy deliberately designed to remove and annihilate civilian populations (men, women, and children).

The terms "mass violence" or "mass crime" do not imply a particular technology or specific murder weapons (knives, machine guns, lethal gas, etc.), but rather an act or a series of acts, collectively organized, whose aim is to annihilate entire groups of unarmed individuals. Demanding a high level of organization, mass crimes are often the responsibility of states. It is obvious that private groups, militias, and guerrilla movements could also commit such atrocities in their efforts to gain power. However, this form of violence becomes more effective when its organizers have particularly efficient means at their disposal: only with the help of an army, a police force, administrative capabilities, and various communication networks within the population, can such large-scale acts of murder be carried out.

This paper starts with a description of the discourse behind the leadership's inclination to resort to violence when dealing with real or perceived enemies. Mass crimes and mass violence were carried out in two modes and by two different sets of agencies. The first mode, which is discussed in the second part, was the conducting of mass movements and mass campaigns, organized by local party cells with the support of local state agencies. The other mode of employing violence, through the use of law enforcement agencies, is examined in the third part. The conclusion looks at possible explanations of the role of violence in the 1950s, with the aim of understanding why and how these events occurred.

The State Apparatus as a Weapon

Behind the violence that regularly rippled though China in the 1950s was a particular politico-legal discourse, which shaped and justified the use of force. The leadership of the Chinese Communist Party (CCP) viewed law as a tool of government and power, not as a value in itself. As such, law could never pertain to values or rights existing independently of the state. In the CCP's view, law was also not tied to ideas of justice (or fairness); rather, it was seen as a weapon for dealing with the enemies of socialism. In the words of Mao Zedong: "The state apparatus, including the army, the police and the courts, is the instrument by which one class oppresses another. It is an instrument for the oppression of antagonistic classes" (Mao Tse-tung 1967: 445f.). The party also rejected the idea of equality before the law. On the contrary, since law was seen as the continuation of the class struggle and a tool for dealing with enemies, a clear distinction should always be made between "us" or "the people" and "them," i.e. "enemies of the people". The people were entitled to participate in public affairs, but the so-called "enemies of the people" or "counter-revolutionaries" were subject to the "democratic dictatorship" of the people.

"Democratic dictatorship" meant that counter-revolutionaries had to be dealt with strictly and severely. They should be treated differently and more violently than offenders who came from the ranks of the people. The enemies should be forced to remould themselves through hard labor and become "new persons" (新人). Mao also described this process as "turning rubbish into something useful" (Mao Zedong 1992: 57).

While, in general, the party focused on forced re-education, depending on the circumstances, counter-revolutionaries also needed to be killed because they "were deeply hated by the masses and owed the masses heavy blood-debts" (ibid.). The use of violence was thus justified by popular resentment and "blood-debts". The latter expression frequently occurred in Mao's speeches and writing. The concept of "blood-debts" was used to argue that popular indignation compelled the party to seek retribution and retaliation when dealing with its worst enemies. Mao also made it clear that counter-revolutionaries would still exist in China, so that campaigns would be necessary in the future. The socialist state had to be vigilant and could not afford to renounce the use of violence: "We cannot promulgate [a policy] of no executions at all; we still cannot abolish the death penalty. Suppose there is a counter-revolutionary who has killed people or blown up a factory, what would you say, should that person be executed or not? Certainly such a person must be executed" (ibid.).

Revolutionary justice in Mao's thinking inevitably encompassed "exceeding the limits, in order to right the wrongs of the old order." Justice would come through heavy-handed responses, through open and violent retaliation. The punishments had to be such that they could be understood as a symbolic expression of public indignation over previous heinous crimes. In general, if applied with skill, public spectacles of retribution were a powerful tool. They could be used to suppress and eliminate opponents. At the same time, when staged as a public theatre, the drama of retributive justice could serve as a vehicle to rally popular sentiment behind the party's course and direct indignation towards targeted opponents. Mao made no effort to hide his notion that this should take the form of terror. Terror was not only acceptable as a necessary evil, but in fact indispensable for the revolutionary project.

At the centre of this discourse is a way of thinking that originates, as Michael Dutton has convincingly argued (Dutton 2005: 3ff.), from the binary friend-enemy distinction or, in Mao's words, from the distinction between the people and the enemies of the people. As a result, not only in all legal affairs, but also in political matters and daily life, was a fundamental distinction made between friend and enemy. From the mid-1930s onwards for almost fifty years, the division between friend and enemy framed politics and law in China in a fundamental sense, so that the whole "nation operated almost entirely on the basis of this binary divide" (ibid.: 4). Political and legal matters became over-determined and over-written by the perceived need to police and guard the binary distinction between friend and foe. The State and its agencies were seen as a weapon to fight against the enemies and to protect the people. The question of loyalty or betrayal overrode all other concerns, opening up the way for violent excesses conducted and permitted by the state.

Mass Campaigns, Terror and Regime Consolidation

Some of the most important levers of the new government for wielding state power were so-called People's Tribunals. These existed alongside the People's Courts, but were ad hoc in nature and lasted only through the duration of a campaign (ibid.: 35-39). The introduction of the tribunals first took place in the context of the Land Reform Movement in 1950. On July 20, 1950, the Organic Regulations of People's Tribunals were promulgated. The tribunals were formed by people's governments at provincial level or above and dissolved upon completion of their tasks. The main task was "the employment of judicial procedure for the punishment of local despots, bandits, special agents, counter-revolutionaries, and criminals who violate the laws and orders pertaining to agrarian reform (…)" (ibid.: 36). The tribunals were allowed to make arrests, detain suspects and pass sentences extending from imprisonment to the death penalty.[2] The members serving in the tribunals mostly came from local party organizations. Thereafter, many of them were appointed to the regular courts on the grounds that they had received judicial training through their work in the tribunals.

People's Tribunals used "mass line" devices such as mass trials or accusation meetings in order to dispense justice. Three formats were widely used by the tribunals: "accusation meetings" (控诉会), "big meeting to announce the sentence" (宣判大会), and "mass trial" (公审) (Amnesty International 1978: 56). All forms could involve up to tens of thousands of people. They were organized in ways which would best mobilize the population and educate it through negative examples and the deterrent of public punishment. Bypassing the formal court system, "people's tribunals," in cooperation with public security organs and party organizations, often carried out massive purges implementing the government's policy. Between 1950 and 1953, in the context of nation-wide campaigns and movements, several social groups were singled out and isolated from the rest of society: landlords (the land reform campaign), counter-revolutionaries (the Campaign to Suppress Counter-revolutionaries), corrupt bureaucrats (the Three-Antis Campaign: anti-corruption, anti-waste, anti-bureaucratism), capitalists and private entrepreneurs (the Five Antis Campaign: anti-bribery, anti-tax evasion, anti-fraud, anti-theft of state property, anti-leakage of state economic secrets), and the educational sector and intellectuals more generally (the Thought Reform Campaign).

The following example demonstrates the course of an "accusation meeting" held during the "Campaign for the Suppression of the Counter-revolutionaries" (镇反运动). The Peking Municipal People's Government held a huge public meeting for the accusation of counter-revolutionaries on May 20, 1951. Addressing the aroused crowd, Luo Ruiqing, Minister of Public Security, suggested that some 220 criminals of the 500 or so accused persons be sentenced to death. He was followed by Mayor Peng Zhen, who wrapped up the process by saying:

People's Representatives! Comrades! We have all heard the report given by Minister Luo and the accusations of the aggrieved parties. What shall we do to these vicious and truculent despots, bandits, traitors, and special service agents? What shall we do to this pack of wild animals? ("Shoot them to death!" the people at the meeting shouted.) Right, they should be shot. If they were not to be shot, there would be no justice. (…) We shall exterminate all these despots, bandits, traitors, and special service agents. We shall shoot as many of them as can be found. (Loud applause and loud shouts of slogans: "We support the people's government! We support Mayor Peng"). The other day, the Public Security Bureau transferred the results of its investigation to the Municipal Consultation

---

2 Sentences exceeding a five year term of imprisonment needed a ratification of the provincial government.

Committee for discussion. Today those results were further discussed by all of you. You have expressed your unanimous opinion on that matter. After the meeting, we shall hand over the cases to the Military Court of the Municipal Military Control Committee to be convicted. Tomorrow, conviction; day after tomorrow, execution. (Loud applause and loud shouts).

The present accused only represent a part of the counter-revolutionaries. There is still a group being kept in jail. Moreover, there are not a few who are concealing themselves in Peking. All the people of the municipality should rise and cooperate with the public security organs to liquidate and exterminate them (loud applause) (Wei 1955: 38).[3]

Carefully arranged and organized as they were, mass trials and accusatory meetings were "designed to concentrate free-floating public hatred of counter-revolutionaries while galvanizing support behind the regime in a highly public manner" (Strauss 2002: 97). Through the organization of campaigns, the government tried to deliberately rally popular support behind the regime, extend the coercive formal and informal instruments of the revolutionary state, and vertically integrate and enhance the rule of the bureaucracy. By conducting mass campaigns in the early fifties, the government aimed at ending all potential opposition, pacifying the country and winning compliance and support from the populace. Significant personal and financial resources were set aside for the campaigns that therefore had a high priority for the regime.

In the course of the movements in the early fifties, an estimated 4 million arrests were made by the police, the army or party organs without any real involvement of the regular courts (Dutton 2005: 167). Hundreds of thousands of "class enemies" or "enemies of the people" were sentenced to death and executed. In mass trials, the death penalty was carried out immediately or the next day.[4] As a rule, executions were public. The convicts were forced to kneel and then shot from behind with a single bullet. The public display of excessive violence had a profound impact on society. It showed unequivocally what the "class struggle" ultimately entailed. Millions more were sentenced to imprisonment by irregular ad-hoc courts, the army or the police.[5] Opponents and real or suspected enemies were subjected to a regime of violence and terror. The Chinese Communist Party proved to be ready to employ violence and terror against its own nationals, and, if deemed necessary, to substantially alter or pass over key provisions of the fragile socialist law and regulations at any time of its own choosing.

However, the scope of arrests and executions and the willingness of local cadres to participate in the movement seem to have taken the leadership by surprise. The longer movements like the Land Reform and the Suppression of the Counter-revolution lasted and the more blood was spilled on the execution grounds, the more urgent grew the ap-

---

3   The source is a report in *Renmin zhoubao*, Beijing, June 3, 1951.

4   An example of a mass trial and a mass execution of around 50 landlords during the Land Reform Movement is described by Ruf (1998: 86-87).

5   The total of 800.000 executed counter-revolutionaries is often mentioned. In 1957, Mao Zedong himself explained that during the campaign to eliminate counter-revolutionaries in the years 1950 to 1953, 700.000 people have been killed. In the period from 1954 to 1957, 70.000 people in addition have been executed as counter-revolutionaries. He also admitted that mistakes have been made and innocent peoples were killed (Mao 1989: 142). If on average a third to a quarter of all accused counter-revolutionaries was executed, one can estimate that the total of all accused counter-revolutionaries was between 2.1 and 2.8 million people. This is only the minimum number, the true number is most likely much higher.

peals of the central leadership to local units to exercise restraint.[6] The movements were apparently used by many local actors (cadres, militia) to settle old scores with neighbors and decide long-term local conflicts in their favor.

The masses should not only watch events like the one described above; rather they were meant to participate actively. They should be "stirred up" (发动群众) and were invited to play a vicarious part in the policy imposed by the state, thus collectively reaffirming its popular legitimacy. The close and direct participation of the masses in the criminal process was to be carefully rehearsed. The numerous trials and campaigns drew in people from all sectors of society, mobilizing the rank and file of cadres and rallying them behind the government-sponsored objectives. As Julia Strauss has argued, in respect to the mass campaigns, the most important audiences were the "regional and local layers of the revolutionary state" (Strauss 2002: 85). It was incumbent on the central state to win over the leading local and municipal cadres on whom the Central relied to implement its directives. Campaigns, mass trials and people's tribunals therefore played a very important role for the imposition and enforcement of norms set by the government. By bypassing the formal justice system, they provided the central state with a forceful set of ideological and moral incentives to elicit compliance and responsiveness from low-level cadres and officials as well as from the broad population. While the judicial system continued to serve as the organizational core of the sanctioning process, mass trials and mass campaigns functioned as flexible and informal mechanisms for the effective, direct and rapid transmission of socio-political norms and the mustering of broad popular support for these norms and their enforcement.

The campaign to suppress counter-revolutionaries established not only a more structured form for these mass organizations but, with official encouragement, enabled them to expand their powers. By the time this campaign ended in 1953, China had 170 000 resident or work unit security committees with a mass activist base numbering more than 2 million people (Tao and Luo 1996: 104). These formed a support force for the numerically weak public security units, solving a problem that had plagued that Ministry since the time of liberation. Operating under the leadership of the local public security organs, work units, villages or towns, their combined strength allowed them to stretch across all facets of social life and offer social order protection right down to the street and work unit level.

Labor Reform and Class Struggle

After the military capture of the cities by the People's Liberation Army, a new order was imposed by a military-based administration. The new power holders had first to deal with the civil unrest that had followed the fighting in many, especially urban, areas. Consolidation and the restoration of order in the cities was the first task. The military authorities started searches for alleged war criminals, secret service agents and collaborators in order to mop up existing pockets of resistance and remnant GMD forces. At the same time, the

---

6 In 1950 and 1951 Mao Zedong wrote several comments on the "Movement to Suppress and Liquidate Counterrevolutionaries," see Mao 1986: 189, 112. He expressed increasing uneasiness about the movement to get beyond control. On May 8, 1951 (ibid.: 189) he argued that only perpetrators who have committed the most severe crimes (murder, rape) should be executed immediately, all others should receive a two year delay. A few weeks later, on June 15, 1951 (ibid.: 202) he argued that his earlier policy should not be mistaken to be too lenient. In any case, Mao's frequent comments all demonstrate how difficult the control over the movement was.

PLA took action against criminals, prostitutes, street gangs and vagrants. The combined attack upon military opponents and social troublemakers enabled the new authorities to enlist the popular support that was seen as essential for upholding the new order. Campaigns, work and residential committees, as well as Public Security, were very successful in carrying out their duties in the 1950s and 1960s. Millions of Chinese were rounded up by the various agencies or in campaigns. Some faced immediate execution, but most were to be deported to remote regions for forced labor. While the new authorities made many arrests, they still lacked sufficient facilities to house the arrested. A few months after the promulgation of the PRC, prisons were already severely overcrowded. Soon after 1949, the regime was confronted with the question of how to handle the enormous number of people labeled as bad elements and suspected of being hostile to the Socialist cause. The answer was to build up an extensive labor camp system.

It was in May 1951 that the foundations of the labor camp system were laid down. The "Third National Conference on Public Security" was held at that time and it intended for the first time to systematically discuss the treatment of sentenced offenders and to find solutions concerning the whereabouts of those arrested (Yang 1989: 25). Many important members of the leadership attended the meeting – a fact that illustrates the importance attributed to its discussions. Among others, Liu Shaoqi gave a keynote speech, Peng Zhen made comments and Mao Zedong personally revised the final resolution of the Conference (Yang and Zhang 1998: 30). This is not to say that the "reform through labor system" (劳改) has no precursive forms; these existed in both the Jiangxi and Yan'an periods.

In his address, Liu Shaoqi pointed out the significance of the problem. He told the conference that a solution for accommodating the high numbers of prisoners was urgently needed. Ways had to be found for the prisoners to be guarded, organized, reformed and, if necessary, punished (Cai 1988: 9).[7] He proposed that the Public Security apparatus should be in charge of the prison sector. Liu, furthermore, suggested organizing the camps in such a way that the prisoners were given incentives to comply with the rules and to engage earnestly in labor. Those who work should be rewarded: "If one works well, give him a little reward or give him a little pay. Give him small things like cigarettes, meat, or soap in order to heighten his activity." Another point he made was related to the benefits of prison labor for the national economy: "If we handle this matter well, it has many benefits. This is a workforce numbering XXX people (deleted in the text, KM) as much as the whole workforce of a Bulgaria, [this workforce] does not need insurance or wages; it can do a lot of work, can build great things. In the Soviet Union, prisoners were used to build several canals. If we do this well, it has economic and political benefits. Because we did not kill them, we can let them work and possibly they will at some time in the future turn into good people (好人)."[8]

---

[7] Part of this speech is reprinted in Wang 1992. In this speech Liu Shaoqi mentioned the total number of prisoners, but in the reprint this information has been omitted.

[8] See Liu Shaoqi, Address to the Third National Conference on Public Security. May 11, 1951, in Wang 1992: 163-164. According to UN statistics, Bulgaria had a population of 7.2 Million people in 1951. At that time its total workforce was around 5.4 Million people. See http://www.un.org/esa/population/publications/worldageing19502050/pdf/054bulga.pdf; accessed May 15, 2003. This would point to at least some 5 Million prisoners in 1951 before the establishment of a labor camp system.

The resolution that was adopted on May 15, 1951 was a crucial document that determined the basic organization of the Laogai.[9] One of the important issues addressed was that of the supervision of the prison sector. The conference approved the ruling that the Ministry of Public Security should from now on oversee the whole prison sector. The resolution also contained detailed regulations that mapped out the internal structure of the Laogai (Sun 1994: 22). Convicts sentenced to five years and more should be organized in detachments (大队) that were administered by Laogai organs at provincial level. Major production and construction projects, which were drafted in accordance with the need for national reconstruction, were all to be assigned to Laogai detachments. The Laogai detachments (劳改大队) were, in organizational terms, tantamount to large labor camps; they formed, so to speak, the backbone of the Laogai system (Domenach 1995: 89). Convicts sentenced to more than one year, but less than five years were to be sent to smaller Laogai units administered by special districts or the counties. They would therefore remain in the vicinity of their homes and under the control of local authorities. Convicts sentenced to a prison term of under one year should work under surveillance (管治) and remain in their units and homes. Apart from labor and production, it was stressed that the camps should organize educational measures in order to re-educate the criminals. Education in the Laogai included political, ideological and cultural education as well as hygienic education. Good performance in regard to thought reform and labor should be rewarded with privileges up to parole, while insurgent behavior was to be punished, the most severe available punishment being the extension of one's prison term.

Finally, the resolution called for the creation of an administrative apparatus responsible for the Laogai. The Public Security organs at all levels were called upon to open special bureaus for the administration of the Laogai facilities. The provinces and large cities should assign 20 to 30 officials to the Laogai bureaus, the districts, 5 to 10 and the counties, 2 to 3. The regulations concerning the administrative structure are quite remarkable, in particular when compared with the Soviet Union. The Chinese leadership obviously did not want the creation of separate, central administration for the Laogai, which was the system in the Soviet Union. Instead, the existing Public Security apparatus was used. All large Laogai divisions or Laogai camps were thus governed by the provincial Public Security organs and not by any central agency in Beijing. While the central agency for the corrective labor camps in Moscow (Gulag) was in charge of all camps (Applebaum 2002), the Public Security Ministry in Beijing did not directly have command of the majority of Laogai institutions. Apart from a few inter-provincial infrastructure projects, the "eleventh department" (十一局) of the Ministry confined itself to loosely overseeing the provincial Public Security Bureaus which in turn supervised the day to day operations of the camps.[10]

From May 1951 onwards, the establishment of Laogai started on a large scale. In order to coordinate the Laogai policy, the central government organized joint administrative committees staffed from different departments such as public security, finances, water works, public construction, heavy industry and railways at various branches and levels of the administration. The committees should implement concrete steps for setting up Laogai institutions. A very important issue that was discussed at the meetings was related to the

---

9 See "Resolution of the Third National Conference of Public Security, May 15, 1951", in Wang 1992: 162.

10 The role of the provinces is also emphasized by Domenach 1995: 127-128.

contributions of the Laogai to the national economy. The directives of the central government demanded that the Laogai institutions take over important economic tasks within the national reconstruction. The central government viewed the deployment of Laogai in water control works (Yellow River, Huai River), canal construction and railway construction as particularly appropriate. The party central also urged local authorities to find ways to quickly transfer large numbers of prisoners to the newly founded Laogai institutions so that the Laogai could go into operation without further delay. A few months later, in September 1951, the Fourth National Congress on Public Security was held. Again the question of imprisonment was discussed in detail (Yang 1989: 24). Minister Luo Ruiqing stressed, in his report, the task of reforming counter-revolutionaries. Labor and politics, punishment and education had to be combined in the processes of the Laogai. Despite Luo's emphasis on re-education, the final resolution primarily focused on the organization of labor in the camps. As can be seen from this, right from the very outset, there was tension over whether to prioritize labor or re-education within the Laogai system. Despite a lip-service commitment to re-education, prison labor and prison production in the early fifties appear to have been of most importance to the leadership.

The initiatives from the central government soon produced tangible results. By June 1952, 62% of all inmates were engaged in labor. Prison labor grew to become an essential economic factor. At large construction sites, the deployment of prison labor made it possible for the government to slash the civilian workforce by about 80,000 workers. Apart from the use of Laogai in the infrastructure projects that were coordinated and managed by Beijing, many provincial Laogai facilities were agricultural farms. By 1952, there were a total of 640 Laogai farms; 56 of these were larger camps holding more than one thousand prisoners. On a slightly smaller scale, there were also mining operations and kilns. 217 Laogai units were involved in the industrial sector in 1952; 160 of those were operations that had more than one hundred prisoners; 29 used more than 500 prisoners.[11] By 1952, the government was operating at least 857 Laogai facilities, not including the mobile camps used for the construction of railways and canals.

The implementation of the first Five-Year plan, which formally covered the years 1953 to 1957, provided an opportunity to fully utilize prison labor for the task of national construction on a countrywide scale. The goal was to make maximum economic use of the Laogai system. By 1954, the number of Laogai places had grown exponentially; the central government could count altogether 4.671 Laogai units. Many of these were relatively small units, run by county governments or local cadres. More than 83% of all prisoners were now engaged in forced labor. 40% of the Laogai inmates were working on agricultural farms, 34% in industrial operations such as mining and heavy industry, and 20% in construction sites of canals and railways.

The establishment phase of the Laogai was consummated by the promulgation of the "Statute on Laogai in the Chinese People's Republic" on August 26, 1954. The text of the statute was drafted with the help of Soviet advisors. The language of the statute also suggests that the drafters were primarily preoccupied with technical issues and organizational questions.[12] Only the first two articles of the statute deal with questions of a more princi-

---

[11] Unless otherwise noted the numbers are all from Sun 1994: 23. Harry Wu 1992: 60 gives the similar numbers for the camps. His numbers for inmates are much higher, though.

[12] This point is also made by Domenach 1995: 96.

pal nature. Article 1 articulates the purpose of the Laogai: it is to "punish counter-revolutionaries and other criminal offenders and re-educate them into new persons through labor".[13] As Article 2 makes clear, all Laogai institutions were regarded as "one of the instruments of the people's democratic dictatorship". This explanation of Laogai as an instrument of the people's democratic dictatorship is crucial, it represents far more than a mere general phrase. It should be kept in mind that in his 1949 speech, Mao explained democratic dictatorship as the rule of the people (that is the alliance of workers and peasants) over the counter-revolutionary classes (Mao 1967.IV: 420). To exercise dictatorship over internal enemies is, as he continued to say at that time, a prerequisite for securing the victory of the revolution. It follows that the Laogai was regarded as the state's main instrument for dealing with Socialist China's assumed or real enemies. The democratic dictatorship of the people was a weapon which would deal with the enemy to ensure that the people's government could not be overthrown. At stake was not justice or fairness, but the victory of the revolution. This emphasis on dictatorship and class struggle as established in Article 2 carries an open connotation of being at war and thus vindicates the use of bare violence. As Minister Luo Ruiqing explained, this strategy was an "effective way to eradicate counter-revolutionary activities and all criminal offences" (Luo 1994: 233).

The most controversial paragraph in the statute was, perhaps, Article 62.[14] This Article ruled that after completing their prison sentences, those prisoners wishing to remain in the camps, who had no home nor any prospect of finding work, or who were living in sparsely populated areas where their settlement was possible, should continue to be employed by the labor camps. In short, the paragraph said that prisoners, under certain conditions, had to remain in the camp even after serving their sentences. The crucial question was: which of the prisoners still had a home or work and were not living in sparsely populated areas? Most prisoners lost their residential registration, once they were sentenced, so most inmates no longer actually had a home or work. Although the article was vague, it provided the basis for the so-called job placement system (就业) for prisoners who had completed their terms. Released convicts were placed in jobs and residential units in or near the labor camps where they had spent their prison terms.[15] Their official designation was "job placement personnel" (就业人员), but colloquially they were called "free convicts" (自由犯). In fact, most prisoners, who were officially released after the expiration of their terms, were still retained in the camp as free convicts for an indefinite period of time.[16] This was one of the main features of the Laogai before 1978: only very few inmates were ever able to come back from the Laogai; return to their homes and resume their civilian lives. The number of "free convicts" grew continuously and, in some institutions, the job placement personnel even formed the majority. The job placement

---

[13] An English translation is available in Blaustein 1962.

[14] It seems that the article 62 was controversial within the leadership, too. Luo Ruiqing spent much time discussing this article in his general introduction of the statute (Luo 1994: 23).

[15] The article was elaborated by the "Temporary Statute on the Release of Criminals Completing their Term and the Implementation of Job Placement, Sept. 7, 1954, see Wu 1992: 1, 13-14, 108-110; Domenach 1995: 99-100.

[16] Released were only the following groups: convicts who had served terms under two years, old and infirm prisoners, CCP cadres and their children, those whose families are living in the countryside. See Wu 1992: 111.

system therefore existed alongside the Laogai system; it has to be seen as an extension of the Laogai. It is evident that political, economic and security considerations led the authorities to adopt the general policy of "keeping more, releasing less" (多留少放) (Wu 1992: 111). This policy was tantamount to deporting groups of the civilian population that were considered to be enemies. It also prioritized the general economic demands of the system over specific demands for reform and re-education. The Laogai now had a con- stantly growing workforce at its disposal; at the same time, it was made sure that the counter-revolutionaries and other enemies would never again represent a threat to Social- ist China. This points, however, to another remarkable inconsistency within the official Laogai theory. The whole Laogai was officially praised for being able to reform and re- educate offenders, yet only a very few of those offenders were ever accepted as having been fully reformed.

The rapid and often uncoordinated establishment of Laogai institutions in the early 1950s created a scattered and unprofitable system (Domenach 1995: 89). After 1955, therefore, the central government encouraged provincial authorities to merge and concentrate exist- ing smaller Laogai camps and units. Nearly all the institutions which were created after 1955 were large scale operations with the capacity to hold tens of thousands of prisoners. In 1955, the Laogai units which had originally numbered 4600 were reduced to 2700, and two years later, in 1957, this number was again reduced to 2000 Laogai units. Of these Laogai units, 1323 were industrial enterprises, 619 were agricultural farms and 71 were engaged in infrastructure projects (Sun 1994: 25). As can be seen from these numbers, within a few years, the center of gravity was clearly shifted away from agriculture to industry.

During the years 1955-1958, the Laogai came to be viewed by the leadership as an impor- tant economic asset. This was justified by assumptions that all offenders under socialism had an obligation to contribute to national construction. It was quite bluntly stated that prisoners had the duty to produce "material riches" in exchange for the forgiveness of the collective (Yang and Zhang 1998: 31). Prison labor was theoretically regarded as a means of re-education, but, in fact, labor was accounted an economic resource that the state could not afford to waste. Moreover, the emphasis on labor and production claimed to have many benefits: by gradually turning prisons into self-sufficient farms and factories, the central government could reduce its expenditure on the prison sector. At the same time, Laogai labor became almost indispensable for the sustained implementation and consummation of large scale ambitious construction projects that were regarded as sym- bolic hallmarks to show what a socialist society could achieve. Prison labor took over important functions for huge infrastructure projects; it was systematically used as a replacement for work that civilian workers considered to be too dangerous or too hard. The cultivation of wastelands, the basic construction work for railways and canals, the digging of shafts and galleries for mines was regularly assigned to the Laogai workforce. Only when the strenuous and hazardous preparatory work was completed, were the van- guards of Chinese communism, the workers, brought in by the state to complete the work. The total number of prisoners had increased from 5 million in 1951 to probably some- thing around 40 to 50 million by the eve of the Cultural Revolution.[17] Death rates were

---

[17] Several Chinese internal documents all indicate that there were about 2.000 camps in early 1960s. An average of 20.000 prisoners would result in a total of 40 million prisoners. From several witness reports

high: Jean-Luc Domenach estimated that the death rates in the camp rose by up to 10 % annually during the years from 1959 to 1962. The total number of deaths in these four years was probably around 4 million people (Domenach 1995: 58, 215, 248). Also according to Domenach, approximately 2 million people died in the period from 1949 to 1952. At least six million victims must have died in the 1950s, in the PRC camps and prisons, as a result of execution, starvation, abuse or disease. This number does not include the millions who were executed or killed outside the camps, for instance, during campaigns. These figures may be inaccurate, but, in any event, we cannot ignore the fact that these estimates clearly point to mass deportations, mass violence and mass dying occurring in China in the 1950s.

Conclusion

In this paper, I have tried to explore and address an aspect of the interaction between politics and society – and between the individual and the new socialist state – in the first years of the PRC that has not yet been widely researched. It is clear that socialist China was fundamentally marked by the pervasive spread of violence. As historians have recently argued, war experiences deeply influence political, cultural and social relationships in a country (Sheehan 2003). Legally, morally, and practically, the young socialist state emerged from war and revolution to find itself basically dependent on the right and ability to use violence. Before as well as after 1949, the very real presence of continuous hostilities and civil strife determined the relationships of various forces with one another and of each of those forces with its citizens. What Carl Schmitt once called the state's "monstrous capacity" to exercise the power of life and death over human beings began to fundamentally shape Chinese political culture in the 1950s. The emerging binary divide between friend and enemy led to growing polarization and politicization, which severely affected and, in fact, radicalized life in the 1950s.

The labor camps, in many ways, became the epitome of these intractable developments. The labor camp regime in China imposed forced labor and programs for re-education and seemed to be pursuing a goal. In each and every case, however, release from the camp was uncertain and depended upon the will of the local staff. Since they were rarely even given a specific sentence, none of the prisoners could know the length of his term of imprisonment. And the camps in socialist China became sites of violence, deprivation and a horrendous mass dying. For Giorgio Agamben, the lawlessness of the camps symbolized a "state of emergency" or "state of exception". "In the camp", Agamben writes, "the state of exception, which was essentially a temporary suspension of the rule of law on the basis of a factual state of danger, is now given a permanent spatial arrangement, which as such nevertheless remains outside the normal order" (Agamben 1998: 169). In this space outside society, all human rights, civilized standards, norms and morals were suspended. Those interned were stripped of all their attributes and were, according to Agamben, reduced to their "bare lives". With this operation, then, the state power established a space where it was no longer faced with any limits or restrictions. In the camps, the state proclaimed itself to be on a war footing against its internal enemies and could relentlessly wage an assault against those presumed to be hostile or dangerous. While the establishment of a regular state apparatus and system of government was accompanied by the

---

we know, however, that there were some camps holding more than 40.000 prisoners.

promulgation of legal rules and procedures, the Socialist regime also, clandestinely or openly, set up mechanisms which allowed them to bypass criminal justice operations. This state of exception made possible the mass deportations of civilians and the mass crimes which occurred in the 1950s and 1960s in the PRC.

Rule by socialist law and by fear and terror were the two faces of the new Socialist order in Maoist China. Together these measures and technologies pushed the power of control and norm enforcement in directions not seen in the periods before the revolution. In its continuing assault upon the structure of feudal-capitalist authority, the revolutionary leadership was thus able to score an enormous success. The pre-revolutionary class structure dwindled and most opponents and dissidents to the Party's policy initiatives were eliminated within the first few years. A peculiar structure of authority and social control was established in the PRC. It did not resemble Stalinist totalitarianism because the dynamics, although initiated by directives from above, were fuelled by enthusiastic mobilization and mass participation from below. Chinese "mass line" socialism produced a highly decentralized method of coercion, and a pervasive voluntarism of the victims as well as the victimizers. Such a mechanism drew in everybody and nobody was allowed to remain outside.

References

Agamben, Giorgio (1998) *Homo Sacer: Sovereign Power and Bare Life,* Stanford, Calif.: Stanford UP.

Amnesty International (1978) *Political Imprisonment in the People's Republic of China*, London: Amnesty International Publications.

Applebaum, Anne (2003) *Gulag: A History*, 1st ed., New York: Doubleday.

Blaustein, Albert P. (ed.) (1962) *Fundamental Legal Documents of Communist China*, New Jersey: Rothman.

Cai Yanshu 蔡延澍 (1988) *Laodong gaizao gongzuo gailun* 劳动改造工作概论 [Concise history of the *laogai* work], Guangdong: Gaodeng jiaoyu.

Domenach, Jean-Luc (1995) *Der vergessene Archipel. Gefängnisse und Lager in der Volksrepublik China*, Hamburg: Hamburger Edition 1995.

Dutton, Michael (2005) *Policing Chinese Politics. A History,* Durham: Duke UP.

Luo Ruiqing 罗瑞卿 (1994) *Lun Renmin Gong'an gongzuo* 论人民公安工作 [On public security work], Beijing: Qunzhong.

Mao Tse-tung [Mao Zedong] (1967) *Selected Works*, vol. 4, Beijing: Foreign Languages Press.

Mao Tse-tung [Mao Zedong] (1989) *The Secret Speeches of Chairman Mao: From The Hundred Flowers to the Great Leap Forward*, ed. by R. MacFarquhar et al., Cambridge, Mass., Council on East Asian Studies/Harvard University.

Mao, Zedong (1992) *The Writings of Mao Zedong, 1949-1976*, ed. by Michael Y. M. Kau et al., vol.2. Armonk, N.Y.: M.E. Sharpe.

Ruf, Gregory (1998) *Cadres and Kin. Making a Socialist Village in West China, 1921-1991,* Stanford, Calif.: Stanford UP.

Sheehan, James (2003) "What it Means to be a State: States and Violence in Twentieth-Century Europe" in *Journal of Modern European History* I/1 (2003), pp. 11-23.

Strauss, Julia C. (2002) "Paternalist Terror: The Campaign to Suppress Counterrevolutionaries and Regime Consolidation in the People's Republic of China, 1950-1953" in *Comparative Studies in Society and History* 44 (2002), pp. 80-105.

Sun Xiaoli 孙晓霁 (1994) *Zhongguo laodong gaizao zhidu de lilun yu shijian: lishi yu xianshi* 中国劳动改造制度的理论与实践 / 历史与现实 [*Laogai* – the Chinese prison system's theory and practices: history and reality] Beijing: Zhengfa Daxue.

Tao Siju 陶驷驹 (1996) *Luo Ruiqing: Xin Zhongguo di yi ren gong'an buzhang* 罗瑞卿: 新中国第一任公安部长 [Luo Ruiqing: New China's first minister of public security], Beijing: Qunzhong.

Wang Gengxin 王耿心 (1992) *Mao Zedong laodong gaizao sixiang yanjiu* 毛泽东劳动改造思想研究 [Mao Zedong's thoughts on labor reform], Xi'an: Shehui kexue.

Wei, Henry (1955) *Courts and Police in Communist China To 1952*, Lackland Air Force Base, Texas (Human Resources Research Institute Research Memorandum No. 44).

Wu, Harry Hongda (1992) *Laogai – The Chinese Gulag*, Boulder, Colorado: Westview.

Yang Xianguang 扬显光 (ed.) (1989) *Laogai faxue cidian* 劳改法学词典 [Juristic dictionary on labor reform], Chengdu: Sichuan cishu.

Yang Diansheng 杨殿升 and Zhang Jinsang 张金桑 (eds) (1998), *Zhongguo tese jianyu zhidu yanjiu* 中国特色监狱制度研究 [Studies on the prison system with Chinese characteristics], Beijing: Falü.

Song Shaopeng

The State Discourse on Housewives and Housework in the 1950s in China

During the 1950s, three categories of women were mentioned in the state discourse in China: firstly, rural women, secondly, female workers and staff members and thirdly, housewives who were described as dependants of workers and staff members – that is, *jiashu* 家属. Different discourses were applied by the state to these three categories of women. This article will analyze the discourses on housewives, *jiashu* and housework as found in the *People's Daily* (人民日报), the official newspaper of the Chinese Communist Party (CCP) and the highest authoritative media representing both the CCP and the Government. The article focuses on the development of the state discourses on housewives and housework during the 1950s and places the evolution of the state discourses within the broad historical context of changes in social order and gender order.

Jiashu emerged as a formal identity during the China Soviet Republic in the 1930s. In 1931, the *Outline Constitution of the Chinese Soviet Republic* (中华苏维埃共和国宪法大纲) stipulated that "all workers, peasants, red army soldiers, all laborers and their dependants (*jiashu*) are equal under the laws of the Soviet and are the citizens of the Soviet Republic regardless of their gender, race and religion" (Xiamen daxue 1984: 7). Under the regime of the Chinese Soviet, the qualification for citizenship was related to class identity, and the class identity was determined by a citizen's occupation and related economic position. If the social identity of a citizen had been defined in terms of his/her social labor work and this had also been taken as standard, then housewives would have lost their independent social identities and also their political status in the state. The electoral law of the Soviet defined the "laborer" as "those who make a living by means of production work or serving public welfare," and *jiashu* as "those who manage their housework" (ibid. 103). Although the *Constitution and Electoral Law* did not specifically mention the gender of the *jiashu*, in the discourse context at that time, the reference to "the *jiashu* who manage the domestic work" actually applied to females. With the identity of "the *jiashu*" and "domestic work manager," housewives, on the one hand, gained an independent social identity, political status and political rights equal to their male counterparts. On the other hand, the term *jiashu* indicated the subordinate relationship of the *jiashu* to the bread-winner of the family, *shu* 属 "belongs to," also made the subordinate status clear. The term *jiashu* with the above-mentioned connotation was used until the foundation of the People's Republic of China in 1949.

From Parasites to Socialist Laborers: 1949-1956

There are no accurate statistics available on the numbers of housewives in China during the 1950s. According to *Statistics on Women in China: 1949-1989* (Zhonghua quanguo funü lianhehui funü yanjiuhui 1991: 239), it can be inferred that probably ninety percent of urban women were housewives. At the end of 1953, the number of female workers in state-owned enterprises was 2,132,000 and accounted for 6.6 percent of all urban women. Although some women might have taken part in production activities outside their households in other working units besides the state-owned enterprises, we can still say that most urban women during the early 1950s were housewives.

To understand the political status of the housewife and the social position of housework in the 1950s, the multiple meanings of the term "labor" in socialist China have to be explored. First of all, the laborer was a political identity. The PRC was regarded as a social-ist country of the People's Democratic Dictatorship based on a worker-peasant alliance with the working class as the leader. Thus, the state was seen as belonging to the workers. Therefore, labor and workers were seen in relation to the nature of the state and the legiti-macy of the regime; for the citizen, the identity of "a worker" was not only economic but also political. Labor became the standard for defining the class identity and it was one of the qualifications for citizenship. Secondly, labor was regarded as a kind of morality. Karl Marx believed labor produces value; his labor theory of value (劳动价值论) is not only an economic theory but also a moral theory. In a socialist country, labor does not only re-fer to economic behavior, it is also a moral requirement. In the early days of the People's Republic of China (PRC), therefore, domestic work was not viewed positively, and housewives were despised as "parasites" (寄生虫). On Labor Day, 1 May 1950, Liu Shaoqi 刘少奇 (1950) gave the following address:

We must give the workers, especially those laboring heroes and inventors who have cre-ated great inventions and innovations in the work they have undertaken, all the honor they deserve and give those social parasites the contempt they deserve for idling about and eating without working.

Praising model workers means not only praising their economic contributions but also giving them political and moral recognition. Lastly, and at the lowest level, labor is re-garded as economic behavior and a means of making a living. The political position of workers in the state was decided by two elements: what type of work could be included in the category of labor, and what functions can labor fulfill in the historical evolution proc-ess. The question of whether domestic work could be recognized by the state determined whether the housewife could gain the identity of worker and thus a political position in the state. During this period, the state ideology maintained that only productive work cre-ated history; all women participating in social production outside their households, women in both urban and rural areas, were then granted the same indisputable worker identity as their male counterparts, and were therefore granted political status within the state. However, housework and the social position of housewives was not of any particu-lar value according to that interpretation of labor theory. This did not only amount to the political denial of housewives but also exerted moral pressure on them.

The section "readers' letters" published in the *People's Daily* in 1949 and 1952 called for women to break away from their "parasitical lifestyle" (He Ping 1952, Xue Zehui 1952), and the state played the role of rescuer (Jing 1952). That women walked out of their households and participated in work was regarded as the symbol of women's liberation under the new regime. In the *Resolution on the Issues of Working and Employment* (关于劳动就业问题的决定）released by the State Council on 4 August 1952 (Zhongyang ren-min zhengfu zhengwuyuan 1952) housewives in cities, especially well-educated intellec-tual women were regarded as the extra labor whose employment situation should be re-solved. The editorial in the *People's Daily* on the same day demanded that "universal em-ployment should be realized step by step in a planned way," and also regarded the house-wives as objects of universal employment. Soon after this, a letter from a housewife named Zhong Bilin 锺碧林 (1952) was published in the *People's Daily* expressing the housewives' appreciation and welcoming this resolution.

As a result of collectivization in rural areas in the 1950s, most rural women of working age had to participate in production activities outside their households just like the female workers and staff members in cities; each of these groups of women shared a similar burden of the work inside and outside their households. Their external work was rated highly by the state, and a great number of so-called "female model workers" were found in these two categories. They were expected to resolve problems connected with their domestic work, housework and bringing up children, themselves; these were "their own special difficulties" (特殊困难) (Zhonghua quanguo minzhu funü lianhehui 1954, Zhang Yun 1953). In order to mobilize more women, both in rural and urban areas, to participate in production activities, the state ordered the working units to set up the facilities, such as daycare centers and cafeterias, to socialize domestic work (家务劳动社会化) universally. But many of these day-care centers and cafeterias in rural China were only short-lived.

The state was eager to change the urban population from products' consumers into producers, and the large numbers of women, especially those with some education were looked upon as a potential labor force. From 1949 to 1952 the views of the government expressed in the *People's Daily* obviously inclined to the opinion that housewives were "parasites," and tried to push housewives out of their households and into production. However, the government failed to fulfill the ideal of full employment for all housewives and had to face the heavy cost of providing the public facilities, daycare centers and kindergartens required for the full employment of women, which was economically unfeasible for the new state.

During the period of economic readjustment, the first group mobilized to go home was exactly those housewives who were newly employed. In 1956, the government started to reduce the working staff in the government agencies, and the female cadres with more children were mobilized to go home to their housework or return to the rural areas for agricultural work, which caused discontent among some of female staff (Qian Miaoying 1958). On the other hand, this policy was inconsistent with the theory propagated by the CCP and the government that "work liberates women" so that the value of housework and the position of housewife within the state had to be reassessed. The *People's Daily* held a national discussion through readers' letters on "whether women should leave their jobs and go home to do domestic work". The *People's Daily* selectively published two readers' letters in the names of "a husband" (Yi Fei 1958) and "a housewife with a college level education" (Lin Changkun 1958). "One husband" claimed that he would not despise the wife who did housework full-time, because "how could husbands focus on their own professional work and finish their various tasks if wives did not do the housework?" "A housewife with a college level education" represented the intellectual women and proved that such women had the ability to deal well with their public work outside the household. However, the conclusion was still that "women should do the housework," because "taking into consideration family economic conditions, the education of the children, the reduction of government spending, their contribution to society or their own future, it is always better for female workers with more children to resign and return home to do housework than stay at their working positions ... because housewives have changed from being parasites into those who have made contributions to socialist construction since liberation." The *People's Daily* finally drew an official conclusion from this "discussion" (People's Daily 8 March 1958):

Families have become the cornerstone of socialism and housework plays an important role in its development. A housewife can make a huge contribution to society if she is able to educate her children to become people with lofty communist ideals, if she can manage the family well according to the principle, "work hard and manage the family economically" to help her husband to do his work smoothly. How can we say it is dishonorable if she is engaged in such significant work? ... In our country, the economic basis of the family is not private ownership but the socialist public ownership of the productive materials; relationships among the family members are shaped by equality, mutual aid and harmony, cooperation, and not by 'men are superior, women are inferior" (男尊女卑) or the complete dependence of women upon men. Therefore, the labor fulfillment of family members also includes the achievement of housework". As a result, even if a housewife cannot become independent economically, she will not become a "parasite".

In fact, even when the Women's Federation implemented the "Resolution on Employment Issues" by the State Council and actively mobilized housewives to go out to work, the contradiction between ideal principles and practice became obvious. They, therefore, proposed cautiously, "when we propagate the resolution, we must try to prevent the undervaluing of housework, and we have to explain the significance of housework quite clearly so that those housewives who are not able to be employed or are temporarily not needed for outside work can be content with domestic work (Zhonghua quanguo minzhu funü lianhehui 1952). On the *First Conference on Urban Women's Work* (第一次城市妇女工作会议) held by the *All-China Women's Federation* (ACWF) in April 1955, the housewives were asked to be fully prepared for both eventualities: they could go out to work and also be satisfied with housework. So housework was raised to the position of "one type of public work" as an "indirect contribution to socialism" (Zhang Yun 1955).

It did not take long for the state to realize that the efficiency of male workers in the forefront of production could not be maintained if they were worried about household issues because their wives were not looking after their households. The All-China Federation of Trade Unions (中华全国总工会) (ACFTU) realized the importance, to production, of strengthening the logistical work of the *jiashu*.[1] In this period, the administrative management of the *jiashu*, whose places of residence were the industrial districts, was carried out by the Labor Union; the administrative management of those whose places of residence were scattered in various locations, however, was carried out by the local Women's Federation.

"The Five Goods:" *Jiashu* be Recognized and Honored by the State: 1956-1958

In order to accomplish the goal of the First National Five Year Economic Plan in advance and exceed it, the ACFTU called for the mobilization of a national movement to select the most advanced workers in production competition (先进生产者运动). To coordinate the production competition, the ACFTU made different demands on working women and the

---

1 In most large-scale units, such as industries and mines, railway departments, the workers, staff members and their dependants usually lived in the residences concentrated in the areas around their working places. *The Organization Regulation on Residents' Committees in Cities* (城市居民委员会组织条例), passed in 1954, stipulated that independent residents' committees should be set up. The *jiashu* committees organized by the Labor Union held a position on the residents' committees. ACFTU held a national conference on national workers, staff members and *jiashu* work on October 10, 1951. Li Lisan, the deputy president of ACFTU, emphasized: "The Labor Union must stress that the *jiashu* work is an important component of labor Union work; therefore, all labor unions at every level, but especially those at basic level, must study the methods and steps for the practice of *jiashu* work according to local conditions."

jiashu: the special difficulties of working women would be resolved. Daycare centers would be set up and put under good management to care for children in order to reduce the heavy burden of housework for working women. Meanwhile, the ideological and political education among the *jiashu* would be strengthened, and the *jiashu* would be organized to maintain hygienic sanitation, to eliminate bugs, mosquitoes, flies, and fleas to prevent disease and to ensure that workers could get enough rest (People's Daily 29 February 1956a). For the same purpose, before the March 8th Women's Festival (三八"妇女节) in 1956, the ACWF called on "all national female workers, and those in various production and working positions," "rural working women," "all female youth," "all female intellectuals" to participate in the production competition. It also called on all: "the *jiashu* of the workers and staff members, the *jiashu* of artisans, the *jiashu* of industrialists and merchants and other housewives" to do "five goods" (五好): "Maintain good harmony in the family and neighborhood and give mutual assistance, organize a good domestic life, give children a good education, encourage their dear ones to do good work and study well, and push themselves to obtain good results in their studies" (家庭邻里团结互助好、家庭生活安排好、教育子女好、鼓励亲人生产工作学习好、自己学习好).[2]

At the NMLHC in 1956, Cai Chang 蔡畅 (1956) made a similar call for "all the *jiashu* to work vigorously for the 'five goods', to assist their husbands in better ways and attempt to accomplish the national plan." The ACWF launched the widespread "five-goods" selection movement and a large number of *jiashu* models across the country were chosen as "five goods" families or "'five goods' active individuals." For instance, 80,000 "five goods" workers' families emerged in Wuhan in 1956 (*People' Daily* 18 November 1956c), and over 9,100 active individuals were chosen across Shanghai (*People's Daily* 5 December 1956d). The ACWF pushed the "five goods movement" for all housewives in 1957.

The First National Representative Conference of the *jiashu* was held from 4 June to 12 June 1957,[3] and around 1,300 representatives of the *jiashu* participated. During the conference, the CCP and the government leaders, such as Mao Zedong, Liu Shaoqi, Zhu De and Zhou Enlai gave interviews to the representatives at the conference. The political

---

2   In 1957 the "double-hardworking guideline" was amended at the National Representative Conference of *jiashu* workers: "Good at working hard and thriftily to maintain the family, good at being united and giving mutual assistance, good at educating the children, good at maintaining hygienic sanitation, and good at pushing themselves to study well. There was no essential change, the only difference was the inclusion of "arranging family life well" and "encouraging dear ones to work and study well" within the principle of "working hard and thriftily to maintain the family" and the addition of "maintaining hygienic sanitation". The purpose was to ensure the health of the male workers and staff members. Some local Women's Federations started to extend the "five goods" movement to the countryside. In the rural area, the "five goods" changed into "being hardworking, loving communes, loving the country, giving mutual assistance, working hard and thriftily to maintain the family, studying knowledge and technology well, respecting the mother-in law, loving the daughter- in- law, educating the children well, and maintaining hygienic sanitation" (Zhang Yun 1957).

3   Lao Ruoyu 赖若愚, the president of the ACFTU, was the chairperson of the Preparatory Committee for the National Representatives' Conference of the *jiashu* workers. Zhang Yun 章蕴, the deputy president of the All-China Democratic Women's Federation, and Yang Zhihua 杨之华, the Head of the Female Workers Department of the ACFTU were deputy chairs. This reflected the leadership of the ACFTU with regard to the *jiashu* work and the cooperative position of the Women's Federation (*People's Daily* 23 January 1957a).

treatment they received was the same as that given to model laborers for the NMLHC. This was indicative, first of all, of the great interest shown by the government in the work of the *jiashu*; it confirmed their political status and gave them political recognition for their work. In 1957, the Chinese government propagated the slogan: "Be hardworking and thrifty to construct the country, be hardworking and thrifty to maintain the family" (勤俭建国，勤俭持家) – commonly known also as "the double-hardworking guideline." On the other hand, the government was affirming the gendered division of labor for housework. For instance, *China's All-Women Federation* selected "five goods *jiashu*" ("五好"家属) models and these *jiashu* model workers participated in the First National People's Congress (NPC). Specific "national conferences of *jiashu*" were held and *jiashu* were granted audiences by the party and state leaders (*People's Daily* 13 June 1957c).

There were some *jiashu* among the 147 female representatives at the First NPC in 1954. Gao Fengqin 高凤琴, a *jiashu* in Shenyang, was chosen as a people's representative with the identity of a *jiashu* (Xin Zhongguo funüshe 1954). *Jiashu* model workers attended the NMLHC in large numbers both in 1956 and 1959. As for those who were praised at local level, *jiashu* model workers could also be found among the model workers at city level in Beijing in 1952 and 1959. The fact that some *jiashu* were elected as NPC representatives showed the visible social identity and political status of the *jiashu* in China in the 1950s. The NMLHC in 1956, one of the model *jiashu* representatives whose name could be found in the *People's Daily* was Sun Ruizhi (孙瑞芝), the Dean of the *jiashu*' Committee of Beifengwo 北蜂窝 of the Beijing Railway Management Bureau (*People's Daily* 9 May 1956b). The government published a list of all the representatives of NMLHC in 1959, among them there were 49 *jiashu* model workers (*People's Daily* 7 November 1959b).

Rural women were in a similar – or even more difficult – situation as other female workers during the collectivization period, when they were confronted with the double burden of domestic and external work. As a matter of fact, rural women were at a disadvantage compared with urban women – they did not have the socialized domestic work facilities provided by the working units. Rural women therefore took on the double roles of female workers and *jiashu*. In order to resolve the conflict between production work and domestic work in rural areas during the collectivization period, the government advocated the gendered division of labor (*People's Daily* 26 March 1957b). First came gendered labor division in production: women were organized to participate in agriculture and sideline production. Next came gendered labor division in production work and domestic work. The state required agricultural producers' cooperatives to take the necessary free time into account when they assigned women to production work. Women should "rush to finish making the clothes, socks and shoes for the whole family during the slack season in farming, so that they could concentrate on production during the busy season; or the division of labor should be applied within the household: some women should mainly participate in production work in the fields and others should spend more time taking care of housework" (ibid.). The government also called on the cooperatives to set up some mutual assistance daycare organizations to reduce the housework burden of rural women. Among those women praised by the state, however, not one single rural woman appeared except the *jiashu* in cities. When the government mobilized female cadres working within the government departments to resign and return to housework in 1957, the *People's Daily* published an article from the *Liaoning Daily* to explain the reasons why women must return to housework:

According to the division of labor which forms naturally in human society, women have been always been mainly responsible for housework, and housework will continue to be an indispensable component of the whole area of social work even in a communist society. As a result, there is still a large number of women who will be engaged in housework even in a communist society. We cannot imagine what society would be like, if all women in society were engaged in other social work and not dealing with housework any longer" (*People's Daily* 17 December 1957d).

To summarize, domestic work was not recognized by the state as part of socialist work until the middle of the 1950s, when the *jiashu* were seen as taking care of male workers, which was regarded as beneficial for their production work. The *jiashu* then obtained visible social status and political identity, and the *jiashu* models were also included in the model workers praised by the party and state. Although the state officially recognized the value of domestic work in the 1950s, it also defined the principal and the subordinate relationships between production work and domestic work, and the service status of domestic work. As a result, when the state judged and measured women with double burdens, the standards were taken from work in the public sphere, and work in the private sphere was disregarded (Hershatter 2003).

Honored Work: From Domestic Work to External Production Work: 1958-1960

The labor content for which the *jiashu* were praised at the NMLHC in 1956 was different from that in 1959. In 1956, the selection standards for model *jiashu* and "five goods" had focused on domestic workers, especially on those who took such good care of (male) workers and staff members that production improved; the latter were praised by the government.

In 1959, China entered the Great Leap Forward era; now domestic work was no longer regarded as honorable; in the *People's Daily* the liberation of women through the socialization of domestic work was mentioned once again; women were mobilized to walk out of their households to participate in production activities outside – the function of domestic work, however, was not taken into consideration.

The "five goods" selection process which was once seen as a way of praising the domestic work of women was also stopped. For the *jiashu* living in industrial and mining regions, the Great Leap Forward Movement also meant that they had to "assist with production and participate in production" (Cai Chang 1959) in addition to doing their domestic work and community work to ensure the efficiency of male production workers. At the "National Heroes of Work Conference" (群英会) in 1959, Wang Xiulan 王秀兰, one of the *jiashu* from the steel factory of Anshan, related that 160 *jiashu* in the Anshan Steel Cooperation had taken part in the production processes in one factory and learnt techniques such as mixing ingredients for making bricks, and baking bricks. They also set up 15 factories for the production and direct supply of wooden articles, hardware and hemp rope, which contributed greatly to the "leaping forward" of production by the Anshan Steel Cooperation. Huai Xiuying 怀秀英, the representative of the "*jiashu* Committee of the Jinan Railway Station Bureau," said that, on one occasion, three *jiashu* under her leadership had worked continuously for 17 days to help the railway station clear a great quantity of overstocked materials. Despite the cold weather, in order to improve the living standard of workers, the *jiashu* from the Tulinhe Forestry Bureau (图里河林业局) in the Inner Mongolia Autonomous Region were said to have tried every possible way to grow

vegetables and produce foodstuffs (*People's Daily* 6 November *1959a*). At this conference, Kang Keqing 康克清, the Deputy President of the ACWF at that time, gave a
speech, praising the outstanding contributions that all the *jiashu* had made towards the
socialist construction work (ibid.).

The *jiashu* were also asked to continue to participate actively in production, to utilize
every possible means of setting up a collective welfare life and serving the workers and
staff members. They should also adhere to the policy of being hardworking and thrifty in
constructing the country and managing the household manage their housework well and
serve the industrial production and construction processes in every way possible to make
their own contributions towards guaranteeing the continuing Leap Forward in 1960 and
speeding up the pace of the socialist construction.

After the Great Leap Forward, the national economy entered a readjustment period, the
cafeterias were closed and many women workers returned to their families. Some industries and mines held a competition entitled "do housework well to guarantee the attendance rate [of the workers]" (*People's Daily* 5 April 1961), and city street committees
once again selected "five goods" (*People's Daily* 19 January 1962), but this time emphasized a link between good thoughts and politics (政治挂帅思想好).

The editorial of the *People's Daily* on 8 March 1963, entitled "Women, struggle for new
achievement," still called on urban housewives and the *jiashu* to further develop the spirit
of serving production and the masses and doing the housework well to ensure that workers could throw themselves with full vigor into the struggle to construct socialism.

After 1964, however, housewives and the importance of domestic work gradually disappeared from the state discourses and the People's Daily has not mentioned these topics
since then.

Conclusion: Historical Continuity and Changes in Terms of Gendered Labor Division and Gendered Norms within the Household

The model *jiashu* and the selection of "five goods" activists showed that the state con-
structed a gender order in the public sphere outside the family, that is, women entered the
public sphere and joined men in production work, while the state at the same time
intentionally propagated the traditional gender role and duties of women within the family. If the changes in women's work and the sex roles of women within the family are
placed in a broader work context and gender order, it is quite clear that demands for
changes in the gender order have never been oriented towards men; male gender roles
both within the family and outside have never been questioned. The demands for the reform of the gender order were aimed at women. In order to receive the same citizenship
identity as their male counterparts, women were required to take up social roles and
responsibilities in the public sphere like men. However, their traditional gender roles and
responsibilities within the family were never challenged; they were in fact confirmed by
the party and state. The working standards for women in the public sphere were the same
as the men's, which could also be seen in the neutral selection standards for national
model workers;[4] however, a gendered model type was hidden behind the neutralized stan-

---

4 Among the standards for model workers at past conferences, there were no specifically assigned quotas on
   the participation of women and minorities. There was also no other regulation related to gender. In interviews with government agencies responsible for selecting model workers, the explanation given was that
   gender-neutral selection standards for model workers reflected the gender equality in general employment.

dards. Model *jiashu* praised by the state were one of the special categories which applied exclusively to women.

Some women were able to get out of the household into the public sphere; this was thanks to the internal labor division among women. When some women went out to work and took up the same roles as men, other women became public child-care workers and carried out their assumed gender roles for them. Nevertheless, all these women were still required to conquer their own "special difficulties" as females, connected with the bringing up of children and domestic work (Zheng Tian 1961).

No matter whether it was in the socialization of housework during collectivism, or during the commercialization of housework in the market economy; no matter whether it was the "special difficulties" of urban workers and rural women in the 1950s, or the "traditional virtues" of women today, the continuity of women's roles as care-takers and servants within the family extends beyond time and political or economic institutional changes. When more and more Chinese women gained a decent education and entered the public sphere as workers, they did not only face the very real burdens of work inside and outside the home; they also came under a great deal of pressure from the double morality of "traditional virtues" and "career standards."

The Marxist theory of women's liberation propagated by the state could not provide any relief from the weight of this double burden. According to the Marxist theory, the gendered division of labor is "natural" due to the different reproductive function of the two sexes (MacKinnon 1989: 13-36). The early members of the CCP, such as Mao Zedong (1919) believed that the basic differences between men and women were found in their physical attributes and reproduction functions and that the essential source of the exploitation of women was the fact that women had to rely on men to support them during their reproductive period (Mao Zedong 1919):

Therefore, Mao Zedong's idea for freeing women from men's exploitation included giving women economic independence and having "children raised by society" (ibid.). Because of his belief in women as a "great force of revolution" (Mao Zedong 1939) and a "great human force resource" (Mao Zedong 1955), Mao thought that the main function and contribution of women should come from outside the family. However, along with other male leaders, Mao never questioned the "natural labor division" within the family, which was based on reproduction, and promised only the "socialization of housework". When it emerged that the state was not fully able to take on the public function of "raising the children", Mao proposed in 1957 that women should '(be) hard-working and thrifty in managing family" (Mao Zedong 1977: 456-465) and the responsibilities of managing the household continued to rest on women's shoulders.

In some ways, the gendered role of women in the household has shown no changes during the last fifty years, but in other ways, political changes have transformed the roles of wife and husband. In the 1950s, the requirements of the "five goods" included the traditional duties of wives to assist their husbands, such as organizing family life and encouraging husbands to work and study hard, and the duties of mothers, such as educating their children well. During this period, the state recognized the domestic identity of housewives and maintained the traditional duties of women within the family. At the same time, however, women went outside the house to work and became "the housewives of the state;" they thus owned the double identities of wives and citizens. Housework therefore became public work; as the "housewives of the state," women had not only domestic duties but also external responsibilities. These included to "create harmony in the community and to provide mutual assistance," which referred to the mutual assistance among the *jiashu* that was necessary to ensure that all workers would work well and not only their own husbands; this would eventually benefit the general production process and the collective. Mutual assistance and altruism were moral requirements during the collectivization movements. "Push themselves to study well" meant that the *jiashu* had to concern themselves with politics and pay attention to the serious political issues of the state."[5] Loyalty to the state was rated higher than loyalty to husbands when the demands on the housewives as "wives" conflicted with the demands on them "as citizens." The government praised the work of the *jiashu*, not for their contributions to the family and loyalty to their husbands, but for their contributions to the state. The government mobilized and encouraged the *jiashu* to denounce any corrupt behavior on the part of their husbands or other relatives' in the "Movement against the Three Evils" (三反运动) and the "Movement against the Five Evils" (五反运动) in 1952 (Huang Lianghuai 1951, Beijingshi minzhu fulian tongxunzu 1952, Zhang Duannian 1952, Huan Zhong 1952, Beijingshi disan qu renmin zhengfu tongxunzu 1952).[6]

Important changes also occurred after the upheavals of the 1950s. During the Cultural Revolution, the policy was to give priority to the public interest over private interest (崇公抑私) so "the double-hardworking guideline" came under severe attack.[7] The *jiashu* has gradually disappeared since the 1980s, not only from the state discourses but also from all the various state institutions; the *jiashu* no longer have a political identity. The *jiashu* workers, of course, were the first group to feel the impact of the market reform of enterprise institutions. Many of them had to buy out their working years under unfavorable conditions when they had to leave their positions (退岗), forfeiting any rights to claim retirement pensions (Xinjiang Petroleum Management Bureau 2003). Since then, they have been working as temporary workers without any formal employment relationship with the enterprises. The domestic work of the female has once again been praised by the government as "the traditional virtue" (传统美德). Thus, the historical function and contribution of the *jiashu* gradually vanished from historical discourses. Instead, the traditional gender norms for women within the family once again became part of the general discourse.[8] The *jiashu* of the 1950s thus lost their social identities which were once recognized by the state and were entirely forgotten as a group.   (revised by Jens Damm)

---

5   The *jiashu* and housewives were brought into the state system through the *jiashu* committees and residents' committees. Participation in the political studies organized by these committees was the main means of introducing the *jiashu* and housewives to politics (Wang Zheng 2003: 165-198).

6   In other words, the requirements of the "five goods" included not only maintaining the traditional gender duties of assisting husbands and educating children, but also betraying the traditional Confucian moral norms of " relatives should help each other and hide each other's misbehavior" (亲亲相隐).

7   In the Hua Guofeng era directly after the Cultural Revolution, the industrial model of Daqing 大庆 also involved and praised "model jiashu workers." However, what was cited was their production work outside the households, that is, the subsidiary function of their agricultural work for Daqing industrial work.

8   For example, in the middle of the 1990s, Han Suyun 韩素云 became a national model worker. The selection processes to find the "five goods civilized families" and "ten outstanding mothers" are still operating in present-day China. Han Suyun's domestic virtues were defined as "patriotism," her contributions to her family were seen as indirect contributions to the state and represented the harmony

References

Beijingshi di san qu renmin zhengfu tongxunzu 北京市第三区人民政府通讯组 [The news group from Beijng No. 3 District People's Government] (1952) "Beijingshi disan qu junshu yangjihua jianyu le ta zhangfu de tanwu xingwei 北京市第三区军属代表杨际华检举了她丈夫的贪污行为" [The Representative of Soldier's *jiashu* from Beijing No. 3 district, Yang Jihua, reported a crime of corruption committed by her husband], in *People's Daily*, 10 August 1952.

Beijingshi minzhu fulian tongxunzu 北京市民主妇联通讯组 [The Beijing Democratic Women's Federation] (1952) "Beijingshi minzhu fulian zhaoji gejie funü daibiao kaihui, dongyuan guangda funü canjia fan tanwu fan langfei yundong, Zhangxiaomei tongzhi guli gejie funü jiechu gulü jiji canjia jianyu 北京市民主妇联召集各界妇女代表开会动员广大妇女参加反贪污浪费运动 张晓梅同志鼓励各界妇女解除顾虑积极参加检举[Beijing Democratic Women's Federation called for a meeting of female representatives from different fields, mobilized women to take part in anti-corruption anti-waste movements, and comrade Zhang Xiaomei encouraged women from every field to free their minds of apprehension and participate actively in exposing any corruption and wasteful behavior], in *People's Daily*, 6 January 1952.

Cai Chang 蔡畅 (1956) "Zhigong jiemei yao jiji canjia xianjin shengchanzhe yundong" 职工姐妹要积极参加先进生产者运动 [Workers and staff sisters must take an active part in the advanced production movement – the address of Cai Chang at the National Advanced Production Representatives Conference], in *People's Daily*, 9 May 1956.

Cai Chang 蔡畅 (1959) "Zai quanguo qunyinghui zhigong jiashu daibiao xianjin jingyan jiaoliuhui shang de jianghua" 在全国群英会职工家属代表先进经验交流会的讲话 [The address to the meeting of the representatives of worker's *jiashu* in the national worker heroes on the exchange of experiences related to progress], in *People's Daily*, 3 November 1959.

Han Zhong 韩中 (1952) "Chazhong dianyejü zhigong jiashu shiguangxiang dongyuan zhangfu tanbai tanwu zuixing" 察中电业局职工家属史光香 动员丈夫坦白贪污罪行 [A *jiashu* from the Chazhong electrical business bureau encourages her husband to confess his crime of corruption], in *People's Daily*, 30 January 1952.

He Ping 何萍 (1949) "Zuzhi jiating zhishifunü canjia gezhong shengchanlaodong: dui Huangpiao wenti he bian xiaofei chengshi wei shengchan chengshi de yijian" 组织家庭知识妇女参加各种生产劳动: 对黄飘问题和变消费城市为生产城市的意见》 [Organize intellectual housewives to participate in productive work – the suggestion relating to Huangpiao issues to turn consuming cities into productive cities], in *People's Daily*, 10 April 10 1949.

Hershatter, Gail (2003) "Making the Visible Invisible: The Fate of 'The Private' in Revolutionary China," in Lü Fangshang (ed.) (2003) *Wusheng zhi sheng: jindai Zhongguo de funü yu guojia* 无声之声□: 近代中国的妇女与国家 1600-1950 [The silent voice: modern Chinese women and the state; 1600-1950], Taipei: Institute of Modern History, Academia Sinica.

Huang Lianghuai 黄亮怀 (1951) "Funü yinggai canjia fan tanwu douzheng" 妇女应该参加反贪污斗争 [Women should join the anti-corruption struggle], in *People's Daily*, 28 December 1951.

Jiang Zemin 江泽民 (2002) "Quanmian jianshe Xiaokang shehui, kaichuang Zhongguo tese shehuizhuyi xin jumian: zai Zhongguo gongchandang di shiliu ci quanguo daibiao dahui shang de baogao" 全面建设小康社会，开创中国特色社会主义新局面: 在中国

between the identity of "wife" and the identity of "citizen" (*People's Daily* 5 January 1995).

共产党第十六次全国代表大会上的讲话 [Build a well-off society in an all-round way and create a new situation in building socialism with Chinese characteristics: report at the Sixteenth National Congress of the CCP] http://www.cass.net.cn/yaowen/16da/3.htm（accessed 5 September 2006).

Jing 静 (1952) "Renmin zhengfu wei women jiatifunü xiang de zhen zhoudao" 人民政府为我们家庭妇女想得真周到 [The People's government thoughtfully considered our housewives] in *People's Daily* 15 August 1952, Special Column: Readers' letters.

Lin Chuangkun 林昌坤 (1958) "Wenhua chengtu gao yie yinggai congshi jiawu laodong" 文化程度高也应该从事家务劳动 [(Women) should engage in housework regardless of high education], in *People's Daily*, 24 February 1958.

Liu Shaoqi 刘少奇 (1950) "Zai Beijing wuyi laodongjie ganbu dahui shang de yanshui" 在北京五一劳动节干部大会上的演说 [A speech at the cadre conference on May 1, Labor Day in Beijing], in *People's Daily*, 1 May 1950.

MacKinnon, Catharine A. (1989) *Toward a Feminist Theory of the State*, Cambridge, Mass: Harvard University Press.

Mao Zedong 毛泽东 (1919) "Nüzi zili wenti" 女子自立问题 [The issue of women's independence], in Zhongyang wenxian yanjiushi 中央文献研究室编 [The literature research department of the Central Committee of the CCP] (ed.) (1990) *Maozedong zhaoqi wengao* 毛泽东早期文稿 [Early articles and drafts of Mao Zedong], Changsha: Hunan Publishing House (First published in *Nüjiezhong* 女界钟, *Special Version* November 21, 1919).

Mao Zedong (1939) "Zai Zhongguo nüzi daxue kaixue dianli shang de jianghua" 在中国女子大学开学典礼上的讲话 [A Speech at the opening ceremony of the women university of China] in Zhonghua renmin gongheguo quanguo funü lianhehui 中华人民共和国全国妇女联合会 [All-China Women's Federation] (ed.) *Mao Zedong zuxi lun funü* 毛泽东主席论妇女 [Chairman Mao Zedong's speeches on women], Beijing: Renmin, 1978, p. 11.

Mao Zedong (1955) "'Fadong funü touru shengchan, jiejue le laodongli buzu de kunnan' yi wen anyu 发动妇女投入生产，解决了劳动力不足的困难"一文按语 [Comment on "mobilizing women into production resolved the difficult of deficient labor force"] in Zhonghua renmin gongheguo quanguo funü lianhehui 中华人民共和国全国妇女联合会 [All-China Women's Federation] (ed.) *Mao Zedong zuxi lun funü* 毛泽东主席论妇女 [Chairman Mao Zedong's speeches on women], Beijing: Renmin, 1978, p. 21.

Mao Zedong (1977) [1957] "1957 nian xiaji de xingshi" 一九五七年夏季的形势 [State of affairs in Summer of 1957], in Mao Zedong: *Maozedong wenxuan* 毛泽东文选 [Selections of Mao Zedong], Vol. 5, Beijing: Renmin.

People's Daily (14 November 1951) "Zhonghua quanguo zong gonghui zhaokai quanguo zhigong jiashu gongzuo huiyi; jueding jiaqiang zhigong jiashu gongzuo" 中华全国总工会召开全国职工家属工作会议，决定加强职工家属工作 [The all-China federation of trade unions held a national conference on jiashu workers to decide how to improve their work].

People's Daily (29 February 1956a) "Guanyu dongyuan quanguo zhigong yingjie Zhongguo gongchandang di ba ci quanguo daibiao dahui, kaizhan shehuizhuyi jingsai, tiqian wancheng ti yi ge wunian jihua de jueyi" 关于动员全国职工迎接中国共产党第八次全国代表大会，开展社会主义竞赛，提前完成第一个五年计划的决议 [The resolution on the mobilization of all workers and staff to welcome the 8th National Congress of the CCP, to carry out the socialist competition and fulfill in advance the first national plan].

People's Daily (9 May 1956b) "Xianjin shenchanzhe zhong de xuduo jiashu renyuan biaoshi nuli zhangwo xianjin jishu wei zhuguo fuwu" 先进生产者中的许多家属人员表示努力掌握先进技术为祖国服务 [Lots of technical staff of advanced producers declare that they will gain mastery of the advance technology to serve the state].

People's Daily (18 November 1956c) "Fulian zuzhi shenru zhigong jiashu kaizhan wuhao yundong, Wuhan chuxian jin bawan ge xinjiating" 妇联组织深入职工家属开展五好运动，武汉出现近八万个新家庭 [Women's Federation carried out "five goods" movement around *jiashu* workers, 80,000 new families in Wuhan].

People's Daily (5 December 1956d) "Shehui xinfengshang, Jiati xinqixiang, wuhao jijifengzi dapi chuxian 社会新风尚，家庭新气象"五好"积极分子大批出现 [New social customs, new family phenomena. "Five goods" activists emerged in large numbers].

People's Daily (23 January 1957a) "Quanguo zhigong jiashu daibiao huiyi jiang zai jinnian liuyue zhaokai"全国职工家属代表会议将在今年六月召开 [National representation conference on jiashu workers to be held in June].

People's Daily (26 March 1957b) "Heli de anpai he shiyong nongcun laodong funü laodongli" 合理地安排和使用农村妇女劳动力 [Rational arrangement and utilization of the Rural Women's Labor force].

People's Daily (13 June 1957c) "Guojia lingdaoren Jiejian zhigong jiashu daibiao" 国家领导人接见职工家属代表 [The state's leaders see the Jia-shu representatives]

People's Daily (17 December 1957d) "Weishenme dongyuan yibufen nüganbu qu caochi jiawu?" 为什么动员一部分女干部去操家务 [Why mobilize some female cadres to do housework?]. Special Column: the digest of newspaper and magazines. First published in *Liaoning daily* 辽宁日报, December 4, 1957. "Nü ganbu tuizhi cao jiawu shifou jiu shi zuo jishengchong" 女干部退职操家务是否就是做寄生虫呢 [Whether female cadres will become parasites if they resign and do housework].

People's Daily (8 March 1958) "Tuizhi he jinbu: 'gai bu gai tuizhi huijia congshi jiawu laodong de' de jiesuyu" 退职和进步：'该不该退职回家从事家务劳动'的结束语 [Resignation and progress – the conclusion on "whether to resign and go back home to the housework"].

People's Daily (6 November 1959a) "Baozheng zhigong shenghuohao shengchanhao qunyinghui zhigong jiashu daibiao jiaoliu xianjin jingyan" 保证职工生活好生产好 群英会职工家属代表交流先进经验 [Ensure workers and staff live happily and work well, the *jiashu* representatives exchanged their experiences on progress at the all-national heroes meeting].

People's Daily (7 November 1959b) "Chuxi quanguo gongye, jiaotong yunshu, jiben jianshe, caimao fangmian shehui zhuyi jianshe xianjin jiti he xianjin shengchanzhe daibiao mingdan" 出席全国工业、交通运输、基本建设、财贸方面社会主义建设先进集体和先进生产者代表名单 [The representatives' roll at the national conference on advanced collective activities and the building of socialism in the industrial, transportation, infrastructure, financial and commercial sectors].

People's Daily (5 April 1961) "Chongqi zhonglianshan meikuang pei zhuanzhi ganbu zuo jiashu gongzuo" 重庆中梁山煤矿 配专职干部做家属工作 [Zhongliangshan mine of Chongqing assigned special cadres for the *jiashu* work].

People's Daily (19 January 1962) "Wuhan jiedao funü shenru kaizhan wuhao huotong, qinjian jianguo qinjian chijia" 武汉街道妇女深入开展"五好"活动 勤俭建国 勤俭持家 [Women in the streets of Wuhan carried out an intensive "five goods" movement, working hard and thriftily to construct the country, working hard and thriftily to maintain their households].

People's Daily (5 January 1995) "Xiang hao junsao Han Suyun xuexi" 向好军嫂韩素云学习 [Learn from the good soldier's wife Han Suyun].

Qian Miaoying 钱妙英 (9 February 1958) "Gai bu gai tuizhi huijia congshi jiawu laodong?" 该不该退职回家从事家务劳动 [Whether to resign and return home to their housework?].

Quanguo fulian deng shisan ge danwei 全国妇联等十三个单位 [All-China Women's Federation and thirteen working units] (1956) "Guanyu jinian sanba funüjie de lianhe tongzhi" [The joint notice on the celebration of the 'march 8 women's festival'], in *People's Daily*, 10 February 1956.

Quanguo fulian wuchanjieji gemingpai 全国妇联无产阶级革命派 [The proletarian revolutionary group of the all-China women's federation] (1968) "Laotong funü jianjue zou Mao zhuxi zhiyin de geming daolu: chedi pipan Zhongguo heluxiaofu fangeming xiuzheng luxian" 劳动妇女坚决走毛主席指引的革命道路—彻底批判中国赫鲁晓夫反革命修正主义妇女运动路线 [Working women are determined to follow the revolutionary road pointed out by chairman Mao – criticizing thoroughly the Chinese Khrushchew's anti-revolutionary revisionist women's liberation route], in *People's Daily*, 7 March 1968.

Wang Zheng 王政 (2003) "Juweihui de gushi: shehuixingbie yu 1950 niandai shanghai chengshi shehui de congxin zuzhi" 居委会的故事: 社会性别与 1950 年代上海城市社会的重新组织 [The stories of the residents' committee: gender and the reorganization of urban society in Shanghai], in Lü Fangshang (ed.) (2003) *Wusheng zhi sheng: jindai Zhongguo de funü yu guojia 1600-1950* [The silent voice: modern Chinese women and the state. 1600-1950], Taipei: Institute of Modern History, Academia Sinica.

Xiamen daxue falü xi 厦门大学法律系 [The department of Law of Xiamen university] and Fujiangsheng danganguan 福建省档案馆 [The archives of Fujian province] (1984) *Zhonghua suweiai gongheguo falü wenjian xuanbian* 中华苏维埃共和国法律文件选编 [Selections of laws and documents of the Chinese Soviet republic], Nanchang: Jiangxi People Publication, p. 7-103.

Xin Zhongguo funü she 新中国妇女社 [The women's news agency of new China] (1954): "Yi bai si shi qi wei nü daibiao" 一百四十七位女代表 [One hundred forty seven female delegates], in *People's Daily*, 21 September 1954.

Xinjiang Petroleum Management Bureau 新疆石油管理局 (3 September 2003) "2003164 hao jianyi ji dafu" 对 2003164 号建议的答复 [Reply on no. 2003164 proposal], http://www.klmyq.gov.cn/klmyzf/kqrd/Article_Show.asp?ArticleID=81 (accessed 6 September 2006).

Xue Zehui 薛泽晖 (1952) "Juexin zuo yige renmin qinwuyuan" 决心做一个人民勤务员 [Determined to become a servant of the people], in *People's Daily*, 17 August 1952, Special column: readers' letters.

Yang Zhihua 杨之华 (1957) "Qinjianjianguo, qinjianchijia: wei shehui zhuyi jianshe gongxian Gengda de liliang" 勤俭建国，勤俭持家: 为社会主义建设贡献更大的力量 [Work hard and thriftily to construct the country, work hard and thriftily to maintain the family: contribute more to socialism construction], in *People's Daily,* 5 June 1957.

Yi Fei 义非 (1958) "Tongyiang shi guangrong de laodong" 同样是光荣的劳动 [The same honorable work], in *People's Daily*, 16 February 1958.

Zhang Duannian 章端年 (1952) "Ying zuzhi ganbu jiashu canjia fan tanwu fan langfei fan guanliangzhuyi yuntong" 应组织干部家属参加反贪污反浪费反官僚主义运动 [The *jiashu* cadres should be organized to participate in the movement against corruption, wastefulness, bureaucratism], in *People's Daily;* 19 January 1962, column: readers' letters.

Zhang Yun 章蕴（1953）"Guanyu dangqian funü gongzuo wenti de baogao" 关于当前妇女工作问题的报告 [The report on the issues of current women work], in *People's Daily*, 12 January 1953.

Zhang Yun 章蕴 (1955) "Guojia guodu shiqi chengshi funü gongzuo he dangqian de jixiang juti gongzuo" 国家过渡时期城市妇女工作的任务和当前的几项具体工作 [Women's work in cities during the transition period of the state and some specific work at present], in *People's Daily*, 7 September 1955.

Zhang Yun 章蕴 (1957) "Genghao de fahui guangda funü zai jianshe shehui zhuyi zhong de zuoyong" 更好的发挥广大妇女在建设社会主义中的作用 [Improve women's important role in the building of socialism], in *People's Daily*, 15 July 1957.

Zheng Tian 征天 (1961) "Wuhao jia-shu fanyuhua" 五好家属范玉花 [Five goods *jiashu* Fan Yuhua], in *People's Daily*, 18 May 1961, special column: Shanxi news.

Zhong Bilin 锺碧林 (1952) "Jiating funü zhong bilin laodong jiuye le" 家庭妇女锺碧林劳动就业了 [Housewife Zhong Bilin is employed], in *People's Daily*, 4 September 1952, special column: readers' letters.

Zhonghua quanguo funü lianhehui funü yanjiuhui 中华全国妇女联合会妇女研究室 [Research institution of all-China women's federation] and Shanxisheng funü lianhehui yanjiuhui 陕西省妇女联合会研究会 [The research office of Shaanxi provincial women's federation] (eds) (1991) *Zhongguo funü tongji ciliao 1949-1989* [Statistic materials on Chinese women: 1949-1989], Beijing: Chinese Statistics Publishing House.

Zhonghua quanguo minzhu funü lianhehui 中华全国民主妇女联合会 [All-China democratic women's federation] (1952) "Wei xiezhu zhixing zhongyang renmin zhengfu zhengwuyuan guanyu laodong jiuye wenti de jueding gei geji fulian de tongzhi" 为协助执行中央人民政府政务院关于劳动就业问题的决定给各级妇联的通知 [The circular to women's federations at all levels to assist in carrying out the resolution on employment issued by the Central People's Government Council], in *People's Daily*, 10 August 1952.

Zhonghua quanguo minzhu funü lianhehui 中华全国民主妇女联合会 （1954） [All-China democratic women's federation] "Guanyu dangqian nongcun funü gongzuo de jueding" 关于当前农村妇女工作的指示 [Direction on current rural women' work] in *People's Daily*, 31 July 1954.

Zhongyang renmin zhengfu zhengwuyua 中央人民政府政务院 （1952） [Central People's Governmen Council] "Guanyu Laodong jiuye wenti de jueding" 关于劳动就业问题的决定" [Resolution on the Issues of Working and Employment] in *People's Daily*, 4 August 1952.

Mechthild Leutner

Parteigeschichte pluralistisch? Neukonstruktionen der 1950er Jahre in Historiographie und Literatur der VR China[1]

Die Geschichte ist Gegenstand einer Konstruktion, deren Ort nicht die homogene und leere Zeit sondern die von Jetztzeit erfüllte bildet (Walter Benjamin, Über den Begriff der Geschichte, 1939).

Scholars and ordinary Chinese alike are apt to point to the 1950s as a kind of golden age – a period of unusual harmony and goodwill, marked by a special closeness between the Chinese people, particularly the working class, and their new socialist government (Perry 1997: 234f).

Fast ein Jahrzehnt nach Elizabeth Perrys Feststellung zur Perzeption der 1950er Jahre in der VR China hat eine Revision ihrer Stilisierung zum „goldenen Zeitalter" stattgefunden. In wissenschaftlichen und literarischen Werken werden aus sehr unterschiedlichen Motiven und Perspektiven heraus Ereignisse und Entwicklungen der 1950er Jahre thematisiert, analysiert und kritisch kommentiert. Die „erlebte Gegenwart", die Zeit nach 1949, wird zu einem „Teil der Geschichte" (Fitzgerald 1994: 24) transformiert, zugleich eine „mit Jetztzeit geladene Vergangenheit" (Benjamin). Ich benutze den Begriff der „Konstruktion" im Benjaminschen Sinne[2], um den aktiven Part von Akteuren in der Ideologie- und Wissensproduktion zu betonen, wobei der Gebrauch des Plurals auf die Divergenz und Gegenläufigkeit dieser „Konstruktionen" verweist. Dabei konzentriere ich mich auf die Neukonstruktionen der Geschichte aus politikgeschichtlicher Perspektive, die Partei- und Nationalgeschichte zugleich ist.[3]

Meine These ist, dass sich im Unterschied zu früheren Perioden bislang keine neue normative und monoperspektivische Geschichtssicht[4] oder eine neue historische Meistererzählung hat etablieren können, sondern dass sich in den Neukonstruktionen der 50er Jahre eine Pluralität von Bewertungen und eine Multiperspektivität in der Einschätzung

---

1 Für hilfreiche Anregungen zu diesem Beitrag bedanke ich mich bei den Kolleginnen Zang Jian (Peking-Universität) und Nicola Spakowski (International University Bremen) sowie den Kollegen Cai Lesu (Qinghua-Universität) und Manfred Gailus (TU Berlin).

2 Auf die breite Diskussion zum „Konstruktions"begriff in den Wissenschaften kann ich hier nicht eingehen.

3 Die im Folgenden ebenfalls analysierten Geschichten der VR China von Jin Chunming 2004 und Xiao Donglian u.a. 1999 unterscheiden sich in ihren inhaltlichen Schwerpunkten und Deutungslinien nicht von denen der expliziten Parteigeschichten. In jüngsten Aufrufen politischer Führer und Wissenschaftler zur Entwicklung einer Nationalgeschichte kommt allerdings das Bestreben der Trennung beider Perspektiven zum Ausdruck. Die Aufrufe, die u.a. in der Zeitschrift *Dangdai Zhongguo shi yanjiu* 4 (2002) und 5 (2002) publiziert wurden, fordern eine Nationalgeschichte (国史), die den Erfordernissen der von Jiang Zemin entwickelten „Theorie der Drei Repräsentationen" gerecht werden soll. Die präzisere Bestimmung des Verhältnisses von Partei- und Nationalgeschichte bedarf einer eigenen Untersuchung. Einzelne sozialhistorische Studien (z.B. Li Lizhi 2002) werden hier nicht berücksichtigt, zumal trotz der relativ guten Quellensituation – zu nennen wären hier beispielsweise die bereits in den 1980er Jahren veranlassten Erstellungen von Lokalchroniken zu den 1950er Jahren -, die sozialhistorische Aufarbeitung dieser Periode noch in ihren Anfängen steht.

4 Vgl. dazu die Ausführungen von Spakowski 1999: 56.

zeigen. „Historische Meistererzählung" verstehe ich hier als dominantes, Identität stiftendes und gesellschaftliche Orientierung vermittelndes Deutungsmuster der Vergangenheit, welches zugleich verknüpft ist mit politischen Hegemonieverhältnissen (Middell et al. 2000: 24ff). Dies wirft letztlich die Frage auf, welche Schlussfolgerungen aus der Pluralität und Multiperspektivität der historischen Interpretationen hinsichtlich der gegenwärtigen politischen Verfasstheit der VR China zu ziehen sind.

Auch wenn die politische Führung nach wie vor eine „Durchherrschung der Gesellschaft" (Kocka)[5] und ein Deutungsmonopol anstreben mag, so findet de facto ein Wettstreit um die Neukonstruktionen der 50er Jahre statt, an dem ein breites Spektrum von Akteuren aus Partei- und Staatsinstitutionen beteiligt ist. Dominante Akteure in diesem Wettstreit sind zwar weiterhin die professionellen Historiker der staats- und parteinahen Institutionen, die versuchen, neue „Festsetzungen" (评论) zur Einschätzung der Geschichte zu treffen. In diesem Wettstreit zeigen sich parallel zu den innerhalb der Kommunistischen Partei (KPCh) stattfindenden Pluralisierungsprozessen stark divergierende Positionen, die einen allgemeinen Grundkonsens zu haben scheinen: die Nichtinfragestellung der Herrschaftsposition der KPCh. Eine eindeutige Zuordnung dieser divergierenden Positionen zu bestimmten Schulen oder politischen Strömungen ist dabei kaum möglich.

Zum anderen, und dies ist von größerer Bedeutung, sind im Unterschied zu früheren Perioden historiographischer Neubewertung in der VRCh in zunehmendem Maße Nicht-Historiker an diesem Prozess beteiligt. Es sind einmal die unmittelbar oder mittelbar von den historischen Ereignissen betroffenen Zeitzeugen, die Opfer der politischen Bewegungen. Es sind zum anderen Autoren, die keine professionellen Historiker sind und zum Teil auch außerhalb partei- und staatsnaher akademischer Institutionen stehen. Sie stützen sich vielfach auf *oral history* und präsentieren, auch den Bedürfnissen des Marktes und der Öffentlichkeit folgend, die Geschichte vorwiegend in Form von Biographien oder historischen Reportagen[6], und bringen damit verstärkt die (auto)biographische und damit auch eine mikrohistorische Perspektive in die Konstruktionsprozesse ein. Sie fordern implizit und explizit, an der Aufarbeitung der Geschichte mitzuwirken, ihr Schicksal bzw. das Schicksal der Opfer als integralen Bestandteil dieser Geschichte zu akzeptieren und – als logische Folge – die jeweils Verantwortlichen, die Täter, zu benennen und die Opfer zu rehabilitieren. Dabei geht es über die Rehabilitierung hinaus um die Implikationen dieser Bewegungen für heute. Diese Narrationen rivalisieren mit denen der professionellen Historiker der Staats- und Parteiinstitutionen und stehen diesen teilweise oppositionell gegenüber. Damit repräsentieren sie eine erweiterte Öffentlichkeit, die nicht nur Deutungspluralität fordert, sondern die Deutungshoheit der KPCh tendenziell in Frage stellt. Durchaus im Bewusstsein der assoziativen Kraft und Mehrdeutigkeit der Begrifflichkeit bezeichne ich daher diese Autoren als zivilgesellschaftliche Akteure.

Die Narrationen der professionellen, staatsnahen Historiker und die der zivilgesellschaftlichen Akteure lassen sich freilich nicht streng voneinander trennen. Es gibt vielmehr Überschneidungen, die Diskurse sind durchlässig und beeinflussen sich wechselseitig, das heißt: auch professionelle Historiker staatsnaher Institutionen können partiell Positionen zivilgesellschaftlicher Akteure vertreten. So dienen die Selbstzeugnisse und

---

5 Zitiert nach Middell et al. 2000: 16.

6 Weigelin-Schwiedrzik spricht auch von „unabhängigen Historikern" und unterscheidet sie von der „akademischen Historiographie" (Weigelin-Schwiedrzik 2001: 63ff).

biographischen Studien in zunehmendem Maße als Quellenmaterial auch für eine Reihe von Historikern: einmal zwecks Erweiterung der (Partei-)Perspektive auf die gesellschaftliche Ebene und auf die Opfer, zum anderen, um die Unterschiede zwischen politischer Propaganda und Rhetorik und der tatsächlichen Situation dieser Jahre zu verdeutlichen.[7] Dies wird beispielsweise beim Rückgriff auf das Tagebuch des zum „Rechten" degradierten Wissenschaftlers Gu Zhun in der zweibändigen Geschichte Xiao Donglians praktiziert (1999, II: 597). Umgekehrt erscheinen die Publikationen zivilgesellschaftlicher Akteure in Verlagen der Volksrepublik, deren Publikationsprogramme einer staatlichen Meldepflicht unterliegen und somit entsprechend auch hier – in Aushandlungsprozessen zwischen Autoren und Verlagen – als Hintergrundfolie das Spektrum von Deutungen professioneller und staatsnaher Akteure präsent ist.[8]

Die Neukonstruktionen der Geschichte, denen notwendigerweise Dekonstruktionsprozesse parallel laufen, sind zugleich politisch höchst brisant. Erstens weil sie auch den Charakter einer Art „historiographischen Wiedergutmachung" haben, nämlich durch die schrittweise Durchbrechung von Tabus und die Aufarbeitung der Vergangenheit als einer Geschichte verfehlter Politik und einer Geschichte von Tätern und Opfern. In der Regel geht es dabei um politische Rehabilitation, eine juristische Aufarbeitung von Täterschaft steht nicht zur Diskussion. Zweitens beinhalten die Neukonstruktionen in zunehmendem Maße kritische Reflexionen der „Jetztzeit", wollen politische Orientierungshilfe für aktuelle gesellschaftliche Probleme sein.

Meine These werde ich zunächst aus der Akteursperspektive beleuchten, bevor ich exemplarisch auf zwei große Themenbereiche eingehe: zum einen auf den Großen Sprung ab 1958, die Volkskommunen und die Kollektivierung als zentrale Komponenten der sozialistischen Transformation auf dem Land, zum anderen auf die Bewegung gegen die Rechten 1957 als größte politische Bewegung gegen die städtische Intelligenz.

Akteure und Perspektiven

Als höchste politische Ebene agierte im Juni 1981 das Zentralkomitee (ZK) der KPCh, als es in Abkehr von der Kulturrevolution und der maoistischen Geschichtsinterpretation mit der „Resolution über einige Fragen in unserer Parteigeschichte seit Gründung der VR China" („Resolution") erste allgemeine Vorgaben zur möglichen Etablierung einer neuen historischen Meistererzählung auch für die 1950er Jahre vorlegte.

Gegenwärtig sind weitere fünf Institutionen (drei direkt dem ZK zugeordnet) führend bezüglich der Neukonstruktionen dieser Periode: 1. das Institut des ZK der KPCh für Schrifttum, 2. das Institut des ZK der KPCh für Parteigeschichte, 3. die Parteihochschule des ZK

---

7 Die Ausführungen Wemheuers (2005: 26, 38f), die von Vorstellungen von einer Einheitlichkeit der Parteigeschichtsschreibung geprägt sind, sind ebenso wie seine tendenzielle Parallelisierung von Parteigeschichtsschreibung und (mündlichen) Erinnerungen, inzwischen – seine Daten hat er 2002 erhoben – nicht mehr aktuell.

8 Den Einfluss der außerhalb der VR China stattfindenden Diskurse zu den 50er Jahren auf die Historiographie aufzuzeigen, ist im Rahmen dieses Beitrages nicht möglich; in den hier untersuchten Studien finden – mit einer Ausnahme, nämlich Xu Jing (2004), – Werke, die außerhalb der VR Ch erschienen sind, keine Erwähnung. Zur Problematik des Verhältnisses VR-Historiographie und westliche Historiographie vgl. Leutner 2003.

der KPCh, 4. das Institut für Zeitgeschichte an der Akademie für Sozialwissenschaften und 5. das Institut für die Geschichte der KPCh an der Volksuniversität in Peking.[9]

Die von diesen Institutionen herausgegebenen Publikationen, wie die Quelleneditionen, Studien und (Auto-)Biographien von Parteiführern, denen der Status von „Autoritäten" (Wang Shunsheng und Li Jun 2006: 10) zugesprochen wird, sind von dem Versuch geprägt, unter Berücksichtigung der Vorgaben der „Resolution" neue Geschichtskonstruktionen zu etablieren. Es geht um die Einschätzung der jeweiligen politischen Linien und deren Umsetzung, um deren gänzliche oder partielle Affirmation (肯定) oder Verwerfung (否定). Als Parteigeschichte im klassischen Sinne konzentriert sich diese Historiographie auf die Parteiführer und die politischen Entscheidungsebenen, mit einer Relativierung der Rolle und Person Mao Zedongs zu Gunsten anderer Parteiführer[10]. Dass sich der Entwicklungsprozess einer neuen historischen Meistererzählung seit der „Resolution" von 1981 sehr kontrovers gestaltet, zeigt am eindrucksvollsten die neueste im Verlag des Instituts des ZK der KPCh für Schrifttum publizierte Parteigeschichte. Sie benennt zwar die zu behandelnden Themen einer möglichen neuen historischen Meistererzählung, doch sie nimmt keine eindeutige historische Einordnung oder monokausale Bewertung der historischen Ereignisse vor. Stattdessen werden zu den 499 als parteigeschichtlich wichtig identifizierten Ereignissen und Problemen Fragen gestellt, in deren Beantwortung die divergierenden und teils widersprüchlichen Deutungen der Forschungsliteratur aufgelistet werden – häufig unter Angabe der Quellen und mit dem Zusatz, dass (noch) keine einheitlichen Auffassungen existieren (Liu Shukai und Guo Simin 2006). Parteigeschichte wird hier also nicht mehr als ein linear fortschreitender Entwicklungsprozess von 1921 bis 2002 dargestellt, sondern als fragmentierter, chronologisch geordneter Problemkomplex von unterschiedlich und sogar widersprüchlich bewerteten historischen Einzelereignissen.

Das Geschichtsverständnis dieser Werke ist nahezu durchgängig geprägt von dem in den 1990er Jahren formulierten Postulat eines gesellschaftlichen Nutzens der Geschichte für die Lösung aktueller Probleme, sowohl im aufklärerischen Sinne einer kritischen Aufarbeitung der Vergangenheit und Reflexion gegenwärtiger gesellschaftlicher und politischer Probleme als auch ideologiebildend in der Etablierung eines pluralistischen Deutungswettbewerbs als Ausdruck unterschiedlicher Entwicklungskonzeptionen und Modernisierungsmodelle[11]. Die professionelle Historiographie kann kaum noch als „dienende Herrin" der

---

[9] Diesen Institutionen sind jeweils Verlage angeschlossen, die eine rege Publikationstätigkeit entfalten. Das Institut für Zeitgeschichte gibt seit 1994 die zweimonatlich erscheinenden „Studien zur chinesischen Zeitgeschichte" (当代中国史研究`) heraus, die Volksuniversität die Reihe „Beiträge zur Geschichte der KPCh" (中共党史研究丛书).

[10] Dies drückt sich auch in der Hierarchisierung und Klassifizierung der Quellen aus: Es sind an erster Stelle die „Klassiker", nämlich die Werke Mao Zedongs, Deng Xiaopings, Jiang Zemins, Zhou Enlais und anderer Parteiführer sowie wichtige Parteidokumente, die extensiv zitiert werden. Darüber hinaus werden hauptsächlich (Auto)Biographien weiterer Politiker – Bo Yibo spielt eine wichtige Rolle – benutzt und zitiert, punktuell ergänzt durch Zeitungs-, lokales Quellen- und Archivmaterial sowie vereinzelt durch (auto-)biographische Texte von betroffenen Intellektuellen (z.B. Wang Shunsheng und Li Jun 2006: 189 und ähnlich He Yonghong 2006: 247-251). Dabei wird insgesamt die Bibliotheks- und Materiallage von den Wissenschaftlern als unzulänglich empfunden (Cao Shuji 1998: 205).

[11] Nach einer Phase der Marginalisierung der Geschichtsschreibung, die in Abkehr von ihrer politischen Indienstnahme während der maoistischen Periode sich zeitweise vor allem auf empirische und politikferne Forschungen konzentrierte, war das Postulat vom gesellschaftlichen Nutzen der Geschichte im

chinesischen Politik (Chevrier 1987: 117) bezeichnet werden oder sich als Opfer profitorientierter marktwirtschaftlicher Interessen stilisieren (vgl. Barmé 1993: 260ff).

Zunächst im Bestreben, die 1950er Jahre als eine Vorgeschichte der Kulturrevolution zu begreifen – so programmatisch im Titel von Xiao Donglian u.a. (1999) –, sollte diese Periode zwecks Vermeidung künftiger „Fehler" – aufgearbeitet, sollten „Lehren" für künftige Entwicklungen[12] aus den (negativen) Erfahrungen gezogen[13], „offene Fragen" geklärt, existierende, als „unzureichend" qualifizierte Argumentationen revidiert werden (Wang Shunsheng und Li Jun 2006: 1). Es ist insgesamt eine auf politische Orientierung zielende Erinnerungsarbeit.

Die Explizierungen dieser Erinnerungsarbeit verweisen zugleich auf die Weiterexistenz des in der traditionellen Geschichtsschreibung wie auch in der maoistischen Periode gängigen exemplarischen Geschichtsverständnisses.[14] So formuliert ein Autor in seiner Studie zur Geschichte der Wandzeitungen:

Zwar sind die Wandzeitungen inzwischen vergangen wie vorüberziehende Wolken, doch ein kurzes Zurückdenken an den Prozess ihres Aufstiegs und Niedergangs könnte man als hilfreich für uns bezeichnen, den kurvenreichen Entwicklungsweg seit der Errichtung des neuen China ernsthaft zu reflektieren. Die Geschichte zu reflektieren, um Windungen und Wendungen künftiger Wege zu vermindern, hierin besteht de facto das Ziel dieses Buches. (Luo Pinghan 2003c: 4).

Sollten aus den Lehren der Geschichte zunächst Erkenntnisse im allgemeinen Sinne gezogen werden und dazu dienen, sie vor „realitätsfernen Träumen" (und realitätsferner Politik) zu warnen (Luo Pinghan 2003b: 421), so erfolgt die historische Aufarbeitung in jüngster Zeit – hier spielt der Terminus der „Hilfe" eine zentrale Rolle – explizit im Bestreben, kritische Stellungnahmen zur Politik der Marktwirtschaft, zur Korruption und zu den drängenden sozialen Fragen der Gegenwart abzugeben und den Charakter direkter politischer Handlungsanleitungen anzunehmen.[15]

Darüber hinaus geht es auch den Historikern um die Rehabilitierung von durch die politischen Bewegungen betroffenen einzelnen Personen und Personengruppen, um das Aufzeigen historischer Verdienste inhaftierter und verfolgter Parteimitglieder und Intellektueller – im Sinne einer kontributorischen Geschichtsschreibung. Das „wahre Gesicht der

---

aufklärerischen, erzieherischen und ideologiebildenden Sinne auch für die Sozialgeschichte formuliert worden (Leutner 1996: 60).

[12] Auch Jin Chunming (2004:86) betont bezüglich des Großen Sprungs die gemachten „Erfahrungen".

[13] „Positive" Erfahrungen werden in der Regel mit dem Adjektiv „wertvoll" versehen: s. Wang Shunsheng und Li Jun 2006: 7.

[14] So beziehen sich eine Vielzahl der Fragen in der Parteigeschichte Liu Shukais und Guo Simins auf die zu ziehenden Lehren aus den (falschen) politischen Entscheidungen und der ihnen folgenden (gänzlich falschen oder in Teilen zu kritisierenden) politischen Umsetzung (Liu Shukai und Guo Simin 2006). „Geschichte dient als Spiegel", oder man will „von der Vergangenheit auf die Gegenwart schließen, um der Politik als Lehrmeister zu dienen" (Wang Shunsheng/Li Jun 2006: 7).

[15] He Yonghong (2006: 229-245) nutzt seine Studie zur Fünf-Anti-Bewegung vor allem dazu, die Notwendigkeit politischer, ökonomischer und juristischer Maßnahmen zur Einschränkung des Privatkapitals, zum Festhalten an der Massenlinie (nicht an der Massenbewegung!) als eines Kontrollsystems des Volkes, zur Verbindung des Kampfes gegen innerparteiliche Korruption mit illegalen Aktivitäten in der Gesellschaft allgemein und zur Stärkung des Rechtssystems in der Gegenwart zu begründen.

Geschichte" soll rekonstruiert werden, eine „wissenschaftliche, objektive Analyse" ist beabsichtigt (Xu Jing 2004: 324). Das Objektivitätspostulat im Rankeschen Sinne wird dabei teils einer „erklärenden Interpretation" entgegengesetzt, teils einer solchen als inhärent angesehen. Insbesondere an den Universitäten, wo die Zeitgeschichte inzwischen einen festen Platz im Lehrkanon und als Forschungsthema gefunden hat[16], stehen empirisch fundierte Analysen im Vordergrund. Theoretische Erörterungen, einschließlich der Bezüge zum historischen Materialismus, finden sich allerdings vereinzelt. Wang Shunsheng und Li Jun formulieren etwa einen theoretischen Anspruch, nämlich „eine Einheit dreier Ebenen, nämlich eine organische Einheit der Geschichte der Tatsachen, der Geschichte der Überlegungen und der Geschichte der Philosophie herzustellen"[17] und grenzen sich so von rein empirischen oder rein reflektierenden Studien ab (Wang Shunsheng und Li Jun 2006: 10). Eine Widerspiegelung dieses Postulats in ihrer Schrift ist allerdings nicht auszumachen.

Es ist also die Partei- und Staatsperspektive, die die Werke der Historiker dominiert und den Blick – als Teil der Grundfrage nach der Korrektheit der jeweiligen Linien – zunehmend auf die innere Verfasstheit der Partei selbst lenkt: auf Fragen der innerparteilichen Demokratie in der Beschlussbildung, den Stellenwert der Beschlüsse und Linien im historischen Entwicklungsprozess und die Möglichkeit der korrekten Erkenntnis der historischen Ausgangsbedingungen. Eine zentrale Position nimmt hier nach wie vor die Bewertung der Rolle Mao Zedongs ein.[18]

Im Unterschied dazu ist bei den zivilgesellschaftlichen Akteuren die Opferperspektive dominant. Sie thematisiert, ausgehend von den Fragen der Umsetzung von Beschlüssen, vor allem die Auswirkungen auf die Betroffenen: die Bauern, die (Basis-)Kader, die (angegriffenen) Intellektuellen. Freilich findet diese Opferperspektive zunehmend Berücksichtigung auch in der Historiographie und ergänzt die Partei- und Staatsperspektive.

Bei den zivilgesellschaftlichen Akteuren lassen sich drei Kategorien von „Betroffenen"[19] sowie darüber hinaus die Nicht-Historiker, die sich die Perspektive dieser Betroffenen zu eigen machen, unterscheiden: einmal (zumeist führende) Mitglieder der KPCh, zum anderen bekannte Demokraten und zum dritten Parteilose oder Studenten, Intellektuelle und Basiskader, die nicht zur Prominenz zählten. Während die Werke „betroffener" Parteimitglieder zunehmend in der Historiographie als Quellen herangezogen werden, ist dies bei den Werken der zweiten und dritten Kategorie nur selten der Fall. Diese zivilgesellschaftlichen Akteure können ihre Schriften häufig erst nach Jahren der Suche nach einem Verleger publizieren. Die Erinnerungen Xu Zhuchengs (1907-1991), des Herausgebers der

---

16 Auch ein erstes Nationales Forum zu *oral history* der 50er Jahre fand im Jahre 2004 statt, s. *Dangdai Zhongguo shi yanjiu* 1 (2005), 93ff.

17 Der Bezug zum Marxismus taucht an anderer Stelle auf, wenn die Absicht geäußert wird, „den theoretischen Schatz des Marxismus zu bereichern" (Wang Shunsheng und Li Jun 2006: 7).

18 Die im Verlag des Instituts des ZK der KPCh für Schrifttum erschienene zweibändige Biographie Mao Zedongs (Auflage 20 000) von Pang Xianzhe und Jin Chongji 2003, stets entlang der Schriften Maos argumentierend, zieht zugleich Wertungen und Urteile weiterer Parteiführer zu historischen „Problempunkten" heran. Die Biographen selbst nehmen sich dabei als „Wertende" zurück und lassen andere Partei-Autoritäten sprechen.

19 Eine ganz andere Art von „Betroffenheit" reklamiert Luo Pinghan (2003c: 1f) für sich: Er führt als Motivation für seine Studie zu den Wandzeitungen an, dass er im Jahre 1957 als Grundschüler nichts mit den zentralen Begriffen der Bewegung anzufangen wusste, aber darüber Wandzeitungen schreiben sollte.

Dagongbao und der *Wenhuibao* und prominenten Demokraten, der 1957 als „Rechter" kritisiert worden war und seitdem de facto ein „entrechtetes" Dasein fristete, konnten beispielsweise erst 1998, sieben Jahre nach dessen Tod, von seinem Sohn herausgegeben werden (Xu Zhucheng 1998: 426).[20]

Doch diese Werke finden, sichtbar an Auflagenzahlen und Raubdrucken, einen – für die marktwirtschaftlich arbeitenden Verlage profitablen – großen Leserkreis. Die biographischen Skizzen Zhang Yihuos über ihren Vater Zhang Bojun (1895-1969) und andere führende Demokraten fanden großen Absatz, stießen zugleich allerdings auf Kritik politischer Stellen, so dass der Verlag selbst das Werk nicht nachdruckte. Es erschien umgehend ein Raubdruck, der außerhalb der Buchhandlungen erhältlich war.[21] Diese Konstruktionen von Geschichte erheben – in stärkerem Maße als ihre literarischen Vorläufer[22] – den Anspruch auf Historizität, verbunden mit der impliziten oder expliziten Forderung an Wissenschaft und Politik, (noch) bestehende (falsche) Geschichtsbilder zu revidieren und die individuell erfahrenen Geschichten in die neuen Geschichtskonstruktionen zu integrieren. Der Schriftsteller You Fengwei (geb. 1943) betrachtet diese Aufarbeitung auch als eine „Verantwortung gegenüber der Geschichte", als eine „historische Wahrheitsfindung" und nutzt zu seiner Positionsbestimmung die Metapher vom unverdorbenen Kind: „Ich hoffe, dass ich wie ein reines, unverdorbenes Kind bin, welches beim Sehen, Hören und Denken so offen sein kann, wie es möchte, das heißt auch eine Kindersprache ohne Tabus hat" (You Fengwei 2004: 453).

Während also die professionellen Historiker um neue Deutungen der 1950er Jahre aus divergierenden Staats- und Parteiperspektiven ringen und eine eher abstrakte Zuschreibung von Verantwortlichkeiten für falsche Politik durch die Charakterisierung politischer Linien vornehmen, findet zugleich, dominant bei den zivilgesellschaftlichen Akteuren, die Opferperspektive Berücksichtigung. Das betrifft „die Bauern" und „die Intellektuellen" jeweils als gesellschaftliche Gruppe sowie die individuell von den politischen Bewegungen Betroffenen. Erstmals geraten auch wie bei Zhang Yihuo über die Opfer hinaus – und hier ist

---

[20] Xus erster Versuch einer Veröffentlichung im Jahre 1989 scheiterte, da kein Verlag die Herausgabe gewagt hatte (Xu Zhucheng 1998: 426). Erst 2003 werden Xus ungekürzte Erinnerungen an das Jahr 1957 in einem Sammelband publiziert (Xu 2003). Auch Li Mei arbeitete 15 Jahre an der Biographie ihrer Mutter Liao Mengxiang (1904-1988), bevor sie 2004 publiziert wurde (Li Mei 2004: 384). Liao Mengxiang ist die Tochter He Xiangnings und Liao Zhongkais, und Ehefrau von Li Shaoshi (Sekretär Zhou Enlais), der 1943 von der Guomindang in Chongqing ermordet wurde.

[21] In die Kategorie der Rehabilitationsliteratur fallen beispielsweise die Erinnerungen der Kinder Hu Fengs an ihren Vater (-1985), der 1955 inhaftiert, 1979 freigelassen und erst nach 33 Jahren in einem dreistufigen Prozess vollständig rehabilitiert wurde. Zugleich dokumentieren diese Erinnerungen die gravierenden sozialen und ökonomischen Auswirkungen der Inhaftierung auf ihr eigenes Leben (Xiaofeng, Xiaoshan und Xiaoyu 2001). Hu Fengs Frau, Meizhi, die jahrelang ebenfalls inhaftiert war und später die Verbannung mit ihm teilte, „überwand nahezu unüberwindbare Schwierigkeiten" beim Verfassen einer umfangreichen Biographie ihres Mannes (Mei Zhi 1998). Etwa 100 der 800 Seiten zählenden Biographie sind der Zeit seiner Inhaftierung gewidmet. Hu Fengs Erinnerungen an diese Zeit, ergänzt durch Erinnerungen seiner Freunde und Kollegen, wurden ebenfalls veröffentlicht (Ji Xianlin 2001). Der Fall Hu Feng findet allerdings in der Parteigeschichte von Liu Shukai und Guo Simin 2006 keine Erwähnung.

[22] Vgl. dazu Weigelin-Schwiedrzik 2003, die Belletristik auswertet, welche die Hungersnot 1959-1961 thematisiert.

ein eklatanter Tabubruch im Unterschied zu früheren Biographien und Selbstzeugnissen zu verzeichnen – einzelne Täter oder Tätergruppen in den Blick, seien es Bauern während der Bodenreform oder seien es führende Persönlichkeiten der Demokratischen Liga oder KPCh-Mitglieder, deren individuelle Rolle in der parteihistoriographischen Narration nicht sichtbar ist. Die Täter und ihre Angriffe auf Kollegen und Freunde, die Verantwortung und Schuld derjenigen, die auf allen Ebenen die politischen Beschlüsse und Linien „erfolgreich" umgesetzt haben, werden damit zum integralen Teil der Geschichte gemacht.[23] Damit erreichen Erinnerungsarbeit und historische Aufarbeitung der 1950er Jahre ein Ausmaß, das an das der Kulturrevolution heranreicht.

Der Große Sprung, die Volkskommunen und die Kollektivierung

Autoritativer Ausgangspunkt der Geschichtskonstruktionen sind für die Historiker nach wie vor die in der „Resolution" von 1981 gemachten Festsetzungen. Für die Jahre von 1949 bis 1956 werden hier eine „völlig korrekte" politische Linie und „glänzende Erfolge" bei ihrer Umsetzung konstatiert. Doch die übertrieben schnelle, oberflächliche und der Form nach zu einseitige Kollektivierungspolitik wird als „Fehler" bezeichnet. Für die Jahre von 1956 bis 1966 ist ebenfalls von „enormen Erfolgen", aber auch von „Rückschlägen" und „Erfahrungen", „schwerwiegenden Fehlschlägen" und einem beträchtlichen Auf und Ab" in der Arbeit der KPCh die Rede (Resolution 1981: 30). Es wird von „überhöhten Planzielen, blindem Dirigismus, Übertreibung von Produktionskennziffern und ,kommunistischen Tendenzen'" des Großen Sprungs und von dem „zu Unrecht" geführten Kampf Mao Zedongs gegen seinen Gegenspieler Peng Dehuai gesprochen. Die „Fehler" während des Großen Sprungs und im Kampf gegen die „rechte Abweichung" werden zugleich mit den Naturkatastrophen und der Aufkündigung der Abkommen durch die Sowjetunion für die „ernsten Schwierigkeiten" und den „großen Schaden" für Land und Volk in den Jahren 1959 bis 1961 verantwortlich gemacht (Resolution 1981: 32). Diese Argumente verweisen letztlich auf die Frage nach der Verantwortung und Schuld für die „Tragödie", die große Hungersnot in den Jahren 1959 bis 1961, eine Frage, die bis heute zentral für die Historiographie und die KPCh insgesamt geblieben ist.

Die in der „Resolution" skizzierten Deutungslinien wurden zunehmend ab den 1990er Jahren von den Historikern konkretisiert und neu gewichtet, die gesteckten Grenzen überschritten und Tabus gebrochen, indem eine stetige Verbreiterung und Differenzierung der Themen erfolgte.[24] Zunächst ging es um die Einschätzung der Parteibeschlüsse vor allem in Bezug auf die Feststellung „linker" und „rechter" Abweichungen sowie um die Umsetzung dieser Beschlüsse. Diese Diskussion wurde allmählich ausgeweitet bis hin zu einer Verwerfung der politischen Linie und der Umsetzung des Großen Sprunges insgesamt. Dabei spielte die Unterscheidung zwischen Volkskommunen-Bewegung, nämlich der

---

[23] Ein Beispiel für eine solche Integration von (auto-)biographischem Material in die Geschichte ist Ma Si 2003.

[24] Selbst der 8. Parteitag von 1956, lange lediglich affirmativ behandelt, gerät inzwischen in die Diskussion (Yang Shengqun und Chen Jin 2006: 325), auch wenn innerparteiliche demokratische Abstimmungsprozesse (Yu Guangyuan in: Yang Shengqun und Chen Jin 2006: 36ff, auch Wu Hongxiang in: Yang Shengqun und Chen Jin 2006: 51ff) und die hier praktizierte kollektive Führung auf dem Hintergrund späterer Entwicklungen zu „Diktatur" und „Personenkult" positiv gewertet werden (Zhao Jianmin, in: Yang Shengqun und Chen Jin 2006: 35).

Zeit von 1958 bis 1961, der Volkskommunen-Periode, die erst 1984 mit deren Auflösung endete, sowie dem Volkskommunen-System eine wichtige Rolle. Damit war die Möglichkeit gegeben, die Kritik zunächst auf die Volkskommunen-Bewegung im engeren Sinne zu beschränken und sich erst nach und nach mit dem Volkskommunen-System und der Volkskommunen-Periode insgesamt kritisch zu befassen oder das System als integralen Bestandteil des sozialistischen Weges bis zu Beginn der Reformperiode ganz zu verwerfen. Dieser schrittweise Prozess der Dekonstruktion wird in jüngster Zeit noch ausgeweitet. Nun geht es auch um eine Neureflexion der frühen Kollektivierungs- und selbst der Bodenreformpolitik.

Es waren führende Parteifunktionäre, die den Weg dafür ebneten, den Großen Sprung und die Volkskommunen-Bewegung in ihrer Gesamtheit als eine verfehlte politische Linie zu bezeichnen und diese für die Katastrophe der folgenden Jahre verantwortlich zu machen. Bahnbrechend waren hier die Erinnerungen von Xie Chuntao (1990) und Bo Yibo (1991) sowie die Aufzeichnungen Li Ruis (1999). Eine große Fragestellung, die die Debatte bis heute dominiert, ist die nach den Ursachen des Großen Sprungs.

Allein sechs Ursachen- und Einflussfaktoren für den Großen Sprung werden von den Historikern identifiziert und jeweils unterschiedlich gewertet.[25] Eine erste Deutungslinie stellt sozialhistorische Ursachen in den Vordergrund: der Wille des Volkes, Armut und Rückständigkeit zu überwinden; eine psychologische Grundhaltung in der ganzen Gesellschaft, die Entwicklung zu beschleunigen; feudales Denken von Kleinproduzenten; Gleichheitsdenken; eine Haltung der Massen, Autoritäten blind zu glauben; die Begrenztheit des damaligen Wissens und simple Übertragung von Methoden aus der Periode des revolutionären Kampfes; unzureichende theoretische Vorbereitung; mangelhafte Qualität der Kader; das böse Erbe feudaler Diktatur. Eine zweite Deutungslinie verweist auf internationale Einflüsse: Die äußere Bedrohung des Imperialismus habe den Übergang von einem armen Land notwendig erscheinen lassen, da ein zukünftiger Krieg unvermeidbar schien und man sich mit dem Imperialismus, aber auch mit der Sowjetunion habe messen wollen. Eine dritte Deutungslinie stellt den Zusammenhang zur Bewegung gegen die Rechten 1957 her: Diese habe die Partei zu der Überzeugung gebracht, dass der Enthusiasmus der breiten Massen zum Aufbau des Sozialismus gestiegen sei und die materielle Basis des Sozialismus erweitert werden müsse (Huang Aijun 2002: 86ff). Eine vierte Deutungslinie verweist auf die erfolgreiche und breit akzeptierte Kollektivierung. Die Regierung habe damit eine Administration zur dirigistischen Kontrolle von oben geschaffen. Zudem hätten die Zwangsmaßnahmen zur Umsetzung der Kollektivierung ein falsches Signal an die Basiskader vermittelt, so dass deren „schlechtes" Verhalten hier ihre Grundlage gehabt habe.

Die entscheidende Rolle Mao Zedongs bei der Initiierung des Großen Sprungs wird von keinem Autor in Frage gestellt.[26] Doch sie wird außerordentlich kontrovers gewertet.

---

[25] Ich stützte mich im Folgenden weitgehend auf Huang Aijun 2005, dessen Literaturbericht sich freilich nur auf die Zeit bis 2002 bezieht, d.h. dass etwa drei Jahre von der Fertigstellung des Beitrages bis zu seiner Veröffentlichung vergangen sind. Die Monographien Luo Pinghans ebenso wie die umstrittene Studie von Zhang Letian von 1998 werden nicht referiert.

[26] Unter Rückgriff auf Formulierungen der „Resolution" von 1981 wird in der Biographie Mao Zedongs der Große Sprung und die Volkskommunenbewegung nicht nur Mao, sondern der gesamten Führungsgruppe, dem Politbüro und dem ZK der KPCh, insgesamt angelastet. Beide seien „katastrophal" gewesen und hätten Staat und Volk Schaden zugefügt (Pang Xianzhe und Jin Chongji 2003, I. 844f). Zentral ist dabei auch die Deutung der Lushan-Konferenz. Sie habe zunächst „linke" Tendenzen korrigieren sol-

Eine Linie argumentiert, dass Mao zur Überwindung der Armut, zur Stärkung des Landes, zur Erreichung der Unabhängigkeit von der Sowjetunion – dies habe auch inneren psychischen Druck auf ihn ausgeübt – den Großen Sprung angestrengt habe. Demgegenüber betonen die Anderen die negativen Auswirkungen des Personenkults, der Verletzung der innerparteilichen Demokratie und des Prinzips der kollektiven Führung. Darüber hinaus werden persönliche Charakteristika Maos als Einflussfaktor für die Initiierung des Großen Sprungs genannt, u.a. dessen übersteigertes Selbstvertrauen bei der Umsetzung seiner „falschen" Theorie in die Praxis. Die sechste Deutungslinie stellt systembedingte Gründe in den Mittelpunkt: das Fehlen von politischer Demokratie und eines politischen Kontrollsystems, Bürokratismus, Diktatur, das Beamtensystem, die zentralisierte Führung, das planwirtschaftliche System, die eisernen Regeln und Pflichten der Kader, die nach oben verantwortlich waren und nicht gegenüber dem Volk (Huang Aijun 2002: 90f). Letztere Deutungslinie schließt eine grundsätzliche Kritik am sozialistischen System mit ein. Andere, oben genannte Argumente sind lediglich als partielle Systemkritik zu werten. Sie werden auch bei der Bewertung anderer historischer Ereignisse genannt.

Es handelt sich einmal um das Argument von der Begrenztheit des Wissens. So schreibt ein Autor:

Wenn wir heute das Gefühl haben, dass die Erkenntnis der Menschen in jener Zeit so naiv und lächerlich war, dann sollten wir wissen, dass richtige Erkenntnis stets erst nach Umwegen und Enttäuschungen erlangt werden kann und von daher sollten wir es würdigen, dass der Sozialismus chinesischer Prägung teuer erkauft ist. (Luo Pinghan 2006: 214)

Die Relativität historischer Erkenntnis wird damit zu einem Argument bei der Konstruktion der Geschichte, zugleich dient es quasi als „Entschuldigung" und fordert Verständnis des Lesers ein.[27] Zum anderen ist es das Argument der Verletzung der innerparteilichen Demokratie und des Prinzips der kollektiven Führung und damit der Verurteilung des Personenkults um Mao Zedong. Dieses impliziert in besonderem Maße „Lehren" für die Gegenwart.

Neben diesen kritischen Bewertungen und Verwerfungen gibt es auch heute noch Versuche, Maos Ausgangspunkt zur Initiierung des Großen Sprungs und die Direktiven zur Steigerung der Wirtschaft positiv zu bewerten (Song Haiqing 2000, II: 431,434,439),

---

len. Mao Zedong jedoch habe sich ab der zweiten Hälfte der Konferenz fälschlicherweise – so bereits die „Resolution" – gegen Peng Dehuai gewandt und dementgegen einen Kampf gegen „rechte Abweichungen" eingeleitet. Die Erklärung für diesen Wandel Maos ist, dass gerade der Brief Peng Dehuais – von den Biographen auch als „Zufallsmoment" bezeichnet – die Situation in einer Weise zugespitzt habe, dass Mao, der sein „linkes" Denken im Grunde nicht korrigiert hätte, den Wechsel von der Kritik an „links" in eine Kritikbewegung gegen „rechts" vollzogen und damit – so schlussfolgern die Autoren der Biographie – den Klassenkampf direkt in die Partei getragen habe (Pang Xianzhe und Jin Chongji 2003, II: 1010). Dieses „Zufallsmoment" konstatiert auch Luo Pinghan, doch er sieht in Pengs Haltung ein notwendiges Element des Widerstandes gegen den Personenkult und den diktatorischen Arbeitsstil eines Einzelnen. Die falsche Kritik an Peng Dehuai sei nicht nur eine Tragödie für Peng selbst und für Mao Zedong, sondern ein Unglück für Partei und Nation geworden (Luo Pinghan 2003a: 158)

27 Das Argument von der Begrenztheit des Wissens taucht auch im Zusammenhang mit der Bewertung anderer historischer Ereignisse auf. Wang Shunsheng und Li Jun 2006: 2 sprechen bezüglich der „Drei-Anti"-Bewegung von der „historischen Beschränktheit".

auch wenn gewisse „Fehler"[28] zugestanden werden. Andere Historiker entziehen sich einer Stellungnahme und meinen, dass es angesichts der Breite der „Lehrmeinungen" noch einiger Zeit bedürfe, um zutreffende Schlussfolgerungen zu den „recht komplizierten Ursachen" der Initiierung der Volkskommunen ziehen zu können (Jin Chunming 2004: 87).[29]

Ähnlich kontrovers wie die Ursachen werden auch die Auswirkungen des Großen Sprungs und damit seiner Bewertung insgesamt diskutiert. Der Große Sprung und nahezu gleichgesetzt damit die Volkskommunen werden zunehmend für die Hungerkatastrophe, die von mehr und mehr Autoren auch als solche bezeichnet wird, verantwortlich gemacht. Der Sozialanthropologe Zhang Letian brachte mit seiner Studie zum Volkskommunen-System, programmatisch als „Abschied von der Utopie"[30] betitelt, die Opferperspektive ins Zentrum der Diskussion. Die Studie wurde zum Politikum, zumal sich die Kritik auf das System insgesamt bezog: „Das zentralistische System der Volkskommunen war wesentliche Ursache dafür, dass die landwirtschaftlichen Erträge zurückgingen und die Dorfwirtschaft ruiniert wurde" (Zhang Letian 2005: 78). Gestützt auf eigene Erfahrungen[31] und Quellenmaterial, einschließlich der Tagebücher eines lokalen Kaders sowie von Feldstudien im Norden Zhejiangs bezog Zhang Letian Position gegen die „öffentliche Propaganda der Regierung", die die „Tragödie", die Hungerkatastrophe von 1959 bis 1961, auf Naturkatastrophen zurückführe. Er zeigte auf, wie die Maßnahmen des Großen Sprungs die Erfolge der Kollektivierung praktisch zunichte machten (Zhang Letian 2005: 67ff). Er kritisierte die Unklarheit der Eigentumsverhältnisse, die ständige Neuordnung der Feldgrenzen, die paramilitärischen Organisationsformen, die notdürftige kurzlebige Einrichtung von Behelfsschulen, die bloß Land und Ressourcen der Bauern kosteten, und die materiellen Verluste der Bauern durch die Hochöfen-Bewegung. Er belegte den Rückgang der Getreideproduktion und berechnete die Getreidemenge, die dem Einzelnen in der von ihm untersuchten Produktionsbrigade zum (Über-)Leben zur Verfügung stand (Zhang Letian 2005: 75f).[32]

---

28 Als „Fehler" werden genannt: eine zu einfache Sicht auf den Aufbau des Sozialismus und die Einengung durch traditionelles Denken, man sei nur gegen „rechts", nicht auch gegen "links" vorgegangen, habe mit Massenmobilisierung den ökonomischen Aufbau durchsetzen wollen und habe die Traditionen der Untersuchung, wie sie in der revolutionären Periode existierten, verlassen (Song Haiqing 2000, II: 434).

29 Ähnlich auch in: Liu Shukai und Guo Simin 2006: 923-940. Jin Chunming sieht auch positive Momente des Großen Sprungs, selbst wenn er dessen Leitidee und die Umsetzungsmethoden keinesfalls „bejahen" will (Jin Chunming 2004: 86).

30 Zhang Letian hatte die Studie, die sich eigentlich mit der Errichtung von Regierungen im ländlichen Raum befasste, bereits 1987 begonnen und 1992 fertiggestellt.

31 Zhang Letian hatte als Kind das Gebiet verlassen, war im Zuge der Landverschickung als Jugendlicher aus Shanghai wieder zurückgekommen, bevor er dann in den 1980er Jahren als Wissenschaftler in eben diesem Gebiet seine Untersuchungen durchführte: Ein Rezensent verweist daher darauf, dass er in seiner Studie versucht habe, ein Gleichgewicht zwischen Lebenserfahrungen und rationaler Welt(erklärung)" zu finden (Cao Shuji 1998: 205).

32 Nach Erscheinen der Studie folgten lebhafte Diskussionen und Rezensionen. Zhangs wissenschaftlicher Zugang wurde mit Fei Xiaotongs Dorfstudien der 30er Jahre verglichen. In methodisch-theoretischer Hinsicht wurde das Werk als „neuer Beitrag zur chinaspezifischen Theorie der Modernisierung des Dorfes" bewertet (Cao Shuji 1998: 206).

Die katastrophalen Auswirkungen etwa des kollektiven Versorgungssystems der Volksküchen und den immensen Niedergang des Lebensstandards zeigt auch Luo Ping-han auf[33] und bewertet die zweite Welle des Großen Sprungs nach der Lushan-Konferenz, als die Gemeinschaftsküchen zum Kern des Kommunismus erklärt worden waren, als einen „armen Übergang zum Kommunismus" (Luo Pinghan 2000a: 176ff). Er kontrastiert Berichte der Basis und höchster politischer Stellen mit den realen Auswirkungen der Direktiven vor Ort. Die in der Propaganda hoch gelobte Einrichtung von sog. Versuchsfeldern, in denen Kader höherer Ebenen sich in der Produktion qualifizieren sollten, ebenso wie die Entsendung von Kadern an die Basis zwecks Übernahme von Leitungsaufgaben in den Gemeinschaftsküchen trugen seiner Lesart nach beträchtlich dazu bei, die Anzahl der zusätzlichen Esser in den Küchen (und damit die Not der Bauern) zu vergrößern. Allein in Henan seien 243 608 Kader in die ca. 330 000 Küchen und in Guizhou gar 30 000 in 26 000 Küchen entsandt worden (Luo Pinghan 2000a: 186). Dass diese Maßnahmen de facto der Sicherstellung der Ernährung der Kader auf Kosten der Bauern dienten – diesen Schluss kann der Leser selbst ziehen. Auch die Kampagnen zur Mechanisierung der Küchengeräte und zur Durchführung des Klassenkampfs in den Küchen, die den Ausschluss von Grundbesitzern, reichen Bauern, Konterrevolutionären, schlechten Elementen und „Rechten", also nach Luo Pinghan u.a. den „gebildeteren" Schichten der Landbevölkerung, von Arbeiten in den Küchen nach sich zog, charakterisiert Luo Pinghan als „Verschwendung von Material und Arbeitskraft" (Luo Pinghan 2000a: 190). Freilich wird bei Luo nicht die Idee der Gemeinschaftsküchen als solche verworfen, sondern die Art und Weise und der Zeitpunkt der Umsetzung. Weder der Entwicklungsstand der Produktivkräfte auf dem Land, noch das Bewusstsein der Bauern – so seine Argumentation – seien reif gewesen für den Übergang zum Kommunismus, ganz abgesehen davon, dass man zu dieser Zeit Kommunismus ganz einfach gleichgesetzt habe mit Volkseigentum, mit „Essen ohne Bezahlung". Damit sei nicht nur der Idee des Kommunismus geschadet worden, auch die Interessen der Massen seien geschädigt und deren Produktionsaktivitäten behindert worden (Luo Pinghan 2003b: 416f). Für die Volkskommunen-Periode insgesamt hält Luo jedoch auch an Positivem fest: Steigerung der Produktion, Finanzierung des industriellen Aufbaus durch die Landwirtschaft, Verbesserung des Bildungs- und Gesundheitssystems. Nicht von ungefähr sind Bildung und Gesundheit die beiden Bereiche, die heute teilweise privatisiert sind und großen sozialen Konfliktstoff bergen.

Die unterschiedlichen Deutungen des Großen Sprungs und der Volkskommunen reichen inzwischen von differenzierteren Urteilen zur politischen Linie und deren Umsetzung bis hin zur gänzlichen Verwerfung. Während die Kritiker die großen ökonomischen Disproportionen, die „drei schwierigen Jahre" und die „Tragödie" für die Landbevölkerung anführen, beziehen sich die positiven Argumente vor allem auf die Erfolge des industriellen Aufbaus in der gesamten Periode bis 1984. Bei aller Pluralität einzelner

---

[33] Luo schildert auch, dass die Einrichtung von Gemeinschaftsküchen anfangs von den Bauern auf freiwilliger Basis erfolgt sei, eben als notwendige Folge der Zunahme von Gemeinschaftsarbeiten und auch der Freistellung der Frauen zu Gemeinschaftsarbeiten (Luo Pinghan 2003a: 74-85). Die Abbildungen in seiner Schrift zu den Gemeinschaftsküchen zeigen allesamt die Verteilung von Nahrung. Luo belegt im Einzelnen die ungleichmäßige Umsetzung und Entwicklung der Volksküchen in einzelnen Provinzen und verweist darauf, dass in der zweiten Hälfte des Jahres 1958 mehr als 90% der Bauern in den 3,45 Millionen Gemeinschaftsküchen aßen.

Einschätzungen sind sich die Autoren in ihrer Gesamtdeutung darin einig, dass Großer Sprung und Volkskommunen den wirtschaftlichen Aufbau und den Sozialismus schwerwiegend geschädigt haben und in der Praxis von der Phase des Aufbaus des Sozialismus abgegangen worden sei (Liu Shukai und Guo Simin 2006: 940-965).

Diese Um- und Neudeutungen greifen inzwischen auf die Historiographie zur „Vorgeschichte" des Großen Sprunges aus. Die frühe Kollektivierung der Landwirtschaft wird zwar nach wie vor mehrheitlich für richtig und notwendig erachtet (Liu Shukai und Guo Simin 2006: 776-798), als eine „herausragende Tat" (Luo Pinghan 2003b: 415) und als „wichtiger integraler Bestandteil eines großen Sieges von historischer Bedeutung" gewertet und auch deren Umsetzung im Großen und Ganzen als erfolgreich angesehen. Darüber hinaus wird sie zudem als notwendige Voraussetzung für das Verantwortungssystem der Gegenwart angesehen (Luo Pinghan 2004: 376). Allerdings werden inzwischen auch gravierende Unzulänglichkeiten und Fehler in der Umsetzung hervorgehoben (Liu Shukai und Guo Simin 2006: 776-798). Sie sei zu schnell, von den Forderungen her zu strikt, von der Arbeit her zu grob und der Form nach zu vereinfacht gewesen. Doch – auch hier das Argument der relativen Erkenntnis – solle man sie nicht nur aus heutiger Perspektive messen (Luo Pinghan 2004: 376).[34]

Die Bodenreformpolitik wird ebenfalls nach wie vor wesentlich unter Erfolgsaspekten abgehandelt, Unterschiede zwischen der Politik vor 1949 und nach der Staatsgründung oder auch Unterschiede zur Entwicklung in der Sowjetunion werden aufgezeigt (Liu Shukai und Guo Simin 2006: 640-648). Mit dieser Einschätzung rivalisierende Deutungen kritisieren, dass die Bodenreformbewegung vor 1949 in Teilen den Charakter von (unkontrollierten) Massenbewegungen und „linken" Abweichungen wie in der Kulturrevolution zeige; die Übergabe der Entscheidungsgewalt an die Bauern, uneinheitliche Klassifizierungen und nicht zuletzt die Willkürlichkeit der Beschlüsse von Bauernversammlungen, beispielsweise selbst Kader der Partei zu kritisieren, abzusetzen oder sogar aus der KPCh auszuschließen (Luo Pinghan 2005: 175ff, 187ff). Luo Pinghan belegt dies an Hand von Daten aus dem Jahre 1948[35] über 2024 Todesfälle im Kreis Xingxian in Shandong.[36] Doch aus Parteiperspektive wird die innerparteiliche Demokra-

---

[34] Luo stützt seine Einschätzung auf eine repräsentative Untersuchung aus dem Jahr 1957, nach der sich nur 7 von 1000 Personen für eine Aufhebung der Kollektivierung ausgesprochen hätten (Luo Pinghan 2004: 371). Neben parteioffiziellen Dokumenten hat er wesentlich die Biographie des Landwirtschaftsministers Deng Zihui ausgewertet und baut diesen bezüglich der frühen Landwirtschaftspolitik als Gegenspieler Maos auf. Deng habe sich vielfach gegen die Beschleunigung der Kollektivierung gewandt, zuletzt im Oktober 1955 auf der 6. Tagung des 7. ZK, auf der er von Mao Zedong der „rechten Abweichung" beschuldigt wurde: Erst 1981 wurde er rehabilitiert, seine Auffassungen als korrekt bezeichnet (Luo Pinghan 2006: 56f).

[35] Diese Materialien entstanden als Ergebnis von Untersuchungen der KPCh-Leitungsorgane im Zuge der Korrektur der „linken" Abweichung (Luo Pinghan 2005: 183ff).

[36] Unterschieden wird nach Todesart (Totschlag, Selbstmord, Verhungern) sowie jeweils nach Klassen-Klassifizierung (Grundbesitzer, reiche Bauern, mittlere Bauern, arme Bauern und Pächter) und nach Arbeitskraft bzw. Nicht-Arbeitskraft (Arbeitsunfähige, Kinder, Alte) (Luo Pinghan 2005: 211, 221). Die Zahl der zu Tode gekommenen mittleren Bauern und ihrer Familienangehörigen (657) ist dabei fast so hoch wie die der Grundbesitzer (666); allein 73 Kinder starben und 525 alte Menschen, die Mehrzahl durch Totschlag (492) (Luo Pinghan 2005: 184). Angesichts dieser empirischen Daten sieht Luo die Befreiung und die damit beginnende Vereinheitlichung der Bodenreform als Wiederherstellung der

tie als positiv hervorgehoben, beispielsweise die innerparteiliche Kontroverse um die Einbeziehung des Landes reicher Bauern in die allgemeine Neuverteilung des Landes und den letztendlich erreichten Beschluss, dieses Land nicht zu verteilen (Luo Pinghan 2006: 12).[37]

Auch wenn in den Studien zur Bodenreform die Bauern erstmals auch als Täter in den Blick geraten, so ist es immer noch die Perspektive auf sie als die eigentlichen Opfer der Politik, die mit der Verlagerung der Thematik auf die Hungersnot und deren Ursachen von einigen Autoren in den Fokus des Interesses gerückt wird.[38] Sie wird durch Einzelstudien, etwa zur Lage von Professoren der Qinghua-Universität in der Zeit der Hungersnot[39] aber insbesondere in (auto-)biographischen Schilderungen der Betroffenen argumentativ verstärkt. Auch in der von Li Yuan verfassten Biographie des Parteisekretärs von Yunnan, Yan Hongyan (1909-1967), wird die katastrophale Situation der ländlichen Bevölkerung geschildert: In Yunnan seien im Jahre 1958 3 Millionen Menschen allein an großen Wasserbauprojekten – mehr als in der Landwirtschaft selbst – und 4 Millionen in der Stahlkampagne eingesetzt gewesen und hätten das Eigentum des Volkes beschädigt (Li Yuan 2003: 66). Auch wenn der Begriff der Hungersnot nicht verwendet wird – in Li Yuans Mikroperspektive eines Basiskaders nimmt diese Katastrophe einen breiten Platz ein: Bereits Anfang 1958, also weitaus früher als in den offiziellen Quellen angeführt, spricht er von ersten Berichten aus mehr als 70 Kreisen und Städten über „Wassersucht-Tote", und zwar insbesondere in den Kreisen, in denen „rote Banner", d.h. eine hundertprozentige Umsetzung der Politik des Großen Sprungs erfolgte. Nicht die eigentlichen Ursachen – aus Sicht Li Yuans: die von oben ständig geforderte übermäßige körperliche Arbeit, Getreidemangel und Hunger – seien in den Berichten genannt, sondern die unzureichende Umsetzung des Kampfes gegen die Rechten sei dafür verantwortlich gemacht und die betroffenen Gebiete als „rückständig" klassifiziert worden (Li Yuan 2003: 68f).[40] Li Yuan entfaltet eine Geschichte der Opfer, nicht nur der Bauern, die den unmenschlichen Anstrengungen und dem Hunger nicht entkommen konnten, sondern

---

Ordnung und die KPCh als „Ordnungsfaktor" (Luo Pinghan 2005: 211, 221).

[37] Beispielsweise wird auch die kleinere Kontroverse zwischen Liu Shaoqi und Gao Gang über die Bildung von Gruppen zur gegenseitigen Hilfe Anfang 1950 thematisiert. Luo führt seine These von der zu schnellen Kollektivierung auf dem Land aus (2006: 14-24). Er überträgt Deng Xiaopings Slogan auf diese frühe Zeit, nämlich dass man nach der Landreform korrekterweise erst einige Bauern hätte reich werden lassen sollen bevor der nächste Schritt zur Kollektivierung hätte erfolgen können.

[38] Tatsächlich existiert auch in Bezug auf die Hungersnot ein breites Spektrum von Auffassungen, und die Opferperspektive ist noch nicht dominant. Während einige Autoren diese hauptsächlich als Ergebnis der falschen Politik sehen, machen andere für die schweren wirtschaftlichen Probleme – der Begriff der „Hungersnot" wird hier gemieden – wesentlich „Linienfehler" verantwortlich, neben den Naturkatastrophen und dem Abzug der Sowjets (Jin Chunming 2004: 102). Seit der 1993 in Peking erschienenen Übersetzung von Penny Kanes Studie (1988) *Famine in China, 1959-1961. Demographic and Social Implications* (London: Macmillan Press) hat der Begriff „Große Hungersnot" allmählich Eingang in wissenschaftliche Publikationen gefunden.

[39] Luo Pinghan wertet beispielsweise Selbstzeugnisse und Kochanweisungen der Mensa der Qinghua-Universität aus (Luo Pinghan 2003a: 232-241).

[40] Das Provinzkomitee hatte bereits im Juli 1958 in einem Bericht an das ZK die Probleme aufgezeigt, leichte Korrekturen waren erfolgt, doch erst nachdem der neue Parteisekretär im Februar 1960 selbst mit Wassersucht-Toten konfrontiert wurde, wurden wirksame Gegenmaßnahmen ergriffen (Li Yuan 2003: 75f).

auch der Kader an der Basis, die selbst Familienangehörige verloren und die im Zwiespalt zwischen Realität und unsinnigen Direktiven der oberen Leitungen sich zu positionieren hatten – einige mit Versuchen, gegen die Interessen der Bauern den Leitungen gerecht zu werden, andere mit Versuchen, die Probleme der Basis mit Hilfeersuchen nach oben zu vermitteln.

Auch in der Biographie der langjährigen Vorsitzenden des Frauenverbandes von Jiangxi, Zhu Danhua (geb. 1911),[41] werden die Probleme der Volksküchen (Ma Shexiang 2002: 320f) und – neben Zhus Beobachtungen auf der Lushan-Konferenz – die Not der hungernden und sterbenden Menschen in den Jahren der Hungersnot geschildert: die Fehler der Leitungen, die Verschleierung der Todesursache, der krude Umgang mit den bettelnden Hungerflüchtigen in Nanchang, die festgenommen und aus der Stadt vertrieben wurden, aber auch die Hilfslieferungen aus Jiangsu in die Hungergebiete Shandongs (Ma Shexiang 2002: 348ff).

Nicht zuletzt zeichnen gerade die Selbstzeugnisse der sogenannten Rechten, die im Folgenden thematisiert werden, nicht nur die Intelligenz, sondern auch die Bauern als Opfer.

Die „Bewegung gegen die Rechten" 1957

Außerordentlich kontrovers und polarisiert ist inzwischen die Deutung der „Bewegung gegen die Rechten". War in der „Resolution" von 1981 der Kampf gegen Rechts noch als „korrekt" und „notwendig", lediglich sein Ausmaß als „beträchtlich überzogen" charakterisiert worden (Resolution 1981: 30f), so vertreten immer mehr Historiker die Position, dass diese Bewegung grundsätzlich falsch war und dem Sozialismus großen Schaden zugefügt hat.

Das Jahr 1957 steht für diese Bewegung und damit für die innerparteiliche Säuberung der KPCh und die Ausschaltung kritischer Parteimitglieder und Intellektueller sowie führender Mitglieder der Demokratischen Liga und anderer Einheitsfrontparteien aus dem politischen und wissenschaftlichen Leben. Insgesamt etwa 550 000 Menschen, 10% der Intelligenz, waren betroffen – unter ihnen viele hoch qualifizierte Experten. Sie verloren ihre Bürgerrechte, wurden zu jahrelanger Gefängnishaft und zur Umerziehung verurteilt. 540 000 wurden inzwischen vollständig rehabilitiert, d.h. sind nach heutiger offizieller Auffassung fälschlich angeklagt worden. Sie alle konnten viele Jahre keine produktive Rolle beim wirtschaftlichen Aufbau spielen. Aus Staats- und Parteiperspektive kennzeichnen die Historiker dies heute als eine Verschwendung von Wissensressourcen (Liu Shukai und Guo Simin 2006: 887). Etwa 10 000 Betroffene sind bis heute nicht rehabilitiert worden, d.h. die politische Führung hat die damaligen Entscheidungen nicht vollständig revidiert.

---

[41] Zhu Danhua (1896-1943) war die Frau Mao Zemins, des Bruders Mao Zedongs; nach dem Tod ihres ersten Mannes heiratete sie Fang Zhichun (1905-1993), einen Bruder Fang Zhimins (1899-1935), der ebenfalls führende Parteifunktionen in Jiangxi innehatte. Wie ihr Mann wurde auch Zhu Danhua in der Kulturrevolution angegriffen und von 1968 bis 1972 im Gefängnis inhaftiert, bevor sie 1980 voll rehabilitiert wurde (Ma Shexiang 2002: 464ff).

Über das allgemein bemühte ökonomische Argument[42] hinaus sind sich die Historiker freilich in ihrer Einschätzung des politischen Stellenwerts der Bewegung keineswegs einig. Einige bezeichnen das politische Ziel der Bewegung nach wie vor als „notwendig und richtig" oder (nur) als „notwendig", dessen Umsetzung jedoch als „übertrieben" und zu „ausgeweitet" und nennen dafür als Grund die Sicherung und Stabilisierung der politischen Macht der jungen Volksrepublik und der KPCh. Sie betonen zugleich den schwerwiegenden langfristigen Schaden der Bewegung für den Aufbau des Sozialismus, das sozialistische Rechtssystem und die innerparteiliche Demokratie. Die Historiker der Gegenfraktion verwerfen die Bewegung insgesamt als falsch und charakterisieren sie geradezu als „Hindernis" für die Entwicklung der KPCh und des sozialistischen Aufbaus. Die Leitgedanken der KPCh und die Beschlüsse des 8. Parteitags seien revidiert, das Vertrauen der breiten Volksmassen in die Partei zerstört und „die sozialistische Demokratie und das sozialistische Rechtssystem [seien] mit Füßen getreten worden" (Liu Shukai und Guo Simin 2006: 883-887). Nicht nur zum Desaster des Großen Sprungs, auch zur Kulturrevolution werden enge Verbindungen gesehen. Wie beim Großen Sprung ist auch hier die Frage nach den Ursachen der Bewegung zentral. Angeführt werden die unzureichenden Erfahrungen der KPCh – also wie bezüglich des Großen Sprungs das Argument von der Begrenztheit der Erkenntnis –, eine falsche Einschätzung der Intelligenz und der Situation insgesamt, der Einfluss internationaler Faktoren, Arbeitsstil und Bürokratismus in der Partei, Widersprüche zwischen den Arbeiter- und Bauernkadern der KPCh und den Intellektuellen sowie Subjektivismus und ein diktatorischer Arbeitsstil Mao Zedongs (Liu Shukai und Guo Simin 2006: 889ff).

Unter den Historikern spielt die Bewertung der These Maos, dass der Kampf gegen die Rechten eine „sozialistische Revolution an der politisch-ideologischen Front" gewesen sei, eine zentrale Rolle. Zwar wurde bereits ein Grundkonsens darüber erzielt, dass es ein Fehler der KP-Führung gewesen sei, die Intellektuellen entsprechend den Positionen Mao Zedongs als „Bourgeoise" zu klassifizieren und damit die 1956 von Zhou Enlai getroffene Feststellung, dass die Intellektuellen bereits das Denken der Arbeiterklasse angenommen hätten, wieder revidiert zu haben (Luo Pinghan 2003a: 12-19). Doch einige Historiker betrachten darüber hinaus diese These überhaupt als falschen Ausgangspunkt für die Politik der nachfolgenden 20 Jahre insgesamt, in der es keine korrekte innerparteiliche Demokratie mehr gegeben habe (vgl. Liu Shukai und Guo Simin 2006: 893ff).

Während die Historiker einerseits um die Einschätzung der politischen Linie ringen, gerät andererseits auch bei ihnen aus mikrohistorischer Perspektive mehr und mehr das Schicksal der Opfer dieser Bewegung in den Blick.[43] Luo Pinghan beispielsweise führt die Par-

---

[42] Zugleich hatten die politischen Verfolgungen gravierende ökonomische Konsequenzen nicht nur für die eigentlich Betroffenen, sondern für die Intelligenz insgesamt. So stellt Luo Pinghan die These auf, dass das Denken der Intellektuellen in diesen Jahren wesentlich von der Frage bestimmt war, wie sie ausreichend zu essen bekommen konnten (Luo Pinghan 2003a: 232ff). Die Erinnerungen Wang Defens (gest. 2001) an ihren Ehemann, den Schriftsteller Xiao Jun (1908-1988), der immer wieder in den politischen Bewegungen kritisiert oder dem keine Arbeit zugewiesen wurde, sind in langen Passagen bestimmt von Fragen des Überlebens (Wang Defen 2004).

[43] Ma Si etwa nennt eine Reihe von Namen und verweist auf die unterschiedlichen Schicksale bestimmter Opfergruppen: Während die meisten Professoren in ihren Einheiten verblieben und lediglich degradiert wurden, seien Schriftsteller und Medienvertreter vielfach mit Verbannung und Gefängnis „bestraft" worden (Ma Si 2003: 362ff).

tei- und Staatsperspektive und die Opferperspektive zusammen – nicht nur das Land insgesamt, sondern auch die Intellektuellen individuell seien zu Schaden gekommen (Luo Pinghan 2003a: 45). So legt er kritisch die Anfänge der Bewegung offen: Die Propagierung der Losung Mao Zedongs „Lasst Hundert Blumen blühen" im März 1957, die er als politische Strategie wertet,[44] die ersten Wandzeitungen und die Demokratiemauer an der Peking-Universität im Mai.[45] und in der Folge an anderen Universitäten, nachdem die Shanghaier Zeitung *Guangming Ribao*, das Organ der Demokratischen Liga, darüber berichtet hatte. Luo charakterisiert präzise das Umschlagen der Bewegung: Bis zum 8. Juni seien die Wandzeitungen alle spontan angeschlagen worden, doch nach diesem Datum, mit der Initiierung der Bewegung, seien diese von den Parteieinheiten organisiert worden, um den Kampf gegen die Rechten vorzubereiten. Während also anfangs die Wandzeitung ein „Werkzeug der rechten Elemente gewesen sei, um die Partei anzugreifen", seien sie in der Folge in der Bewegung gegen die „Rechten" umgekehrt zu einer „Angriffswaffe" gegen diese geworden (Luo Pinghan 2003c: 3).[46]
Sind es bei den Historikern eher Themen wie die „Geschichte der Wandzeitungen" oder die „Situation der Intelligenz", unter der sich der Problematik der Bewegung genähert wird, steht das Jahr 1957 explizit im Blickpunkt der zivilgesellschaftlichen Akteure. Es wird als dramatischer Ausgangspunkt der Verfolgung der Intellektuellen gezeichnet und geradezu zum Symbol der Opferliteratur schlechthin. Zunächst erregte der historische Roman des 1943 geborenen Schriftstellers You Fengwei: „China im Jahr 1957", der aus der Ich-Perspektive das tragische Schicksal des „Rechten" Zhou Wenxiang verarbeitet hat, große Aufmerksamkeit.[47] You Fengwei prangerte die Bewegung als „wirklich große Katastrophe für die Intellektuellen und den gesamten demokratischen Prozess der Gesellschaft" an. Sie sei der Beginn der ultralinken Politik gewesen und werde anders als die Kulturrevolution bis heute nicht offiziell negiert (You Fengwei 2004: 453ff).[48] Yous Roman wurde als eine „Anklage der totalitären Gesellschaft", die Parallelen sowohl zur Sowjetunion als auch zum faschistischen Deutschland und Italien aufweise, gelesen (You Fengwei 2004: 477).[49] Mit seiner Schrift setzte You Akzente, wie sie auch in anderen

---

44 Laut Luo hat das ZK einerseits „die normale Tatsache", dass neben „Blumen" auch „Unkraut" „geblüht" hätten, „zu ernst" genommen, andererseits das Strategem des „die Schlange aus der Höhle locken" angewandt. So seien viele Wandzeitungsschreiber zu „rechten Elementen" gemacht worden (Luo Pinghan 2003c: 3).

45 Am 19. Mai 1957 sei die erste Wandzeitung angeschlagen worden, über die dann der Journalist Liu Guanghua am 27. in der *Wenhuibao* berichtet habe. Liu wurde später selbst zu einem „Rechten" erklärt (Luo Pinghan 2003c: 9ff, 39).

46 Der Wechsel des Begriffs markiert bei Luo deutlich den Funktionswandel der Wandzeitungen auch für alle folgenden Bewegungen. Mit Verweis auf die spätere Kulturrevolution vertritt Luo Pinghan die These, dass die propagierte sog. „große Demokratie" der Wandzeitungen in Wirklichkeit nur die „große Reaktion" gegen die Demokratie gewesen sei (Luo Pinghan 2003c: 3).

47 Allein 88 Besprechungen werden im Anhang der dritten Auflage von 2004 gelistet. und noch im Oktober 2006 sind zu diesem Werk 253 chinesische Internetseiten mit Google abrufbar.

48 Ausdrücklich verweist You darauf, dass bis heute einige Personen nicht rehabilitiert worden seien (You Fengwei 2004: 454).

49 Dabei wurde den faschistischen Diktaturen noch zugestanden, dass diese sich – anders als die Bewegung gegen die Rechten und die Kulturrevolution – nicht um „Privates" gekümmert hätten (You Fengwei 2004: 477).

literarischen, literarisch-dokumentarischen und historiographischen Beiträgen beobachtet werden können. Die Autoren dieser Werke lehnen die Bewegung grundsätzlich ab, schätzen sie als „totalitär" und „faschistisch" ein und beschreiben ihre katastrophalen und weit reichenden Folgen für Demokratie und Meinungsfreiheit. Sie erweitern nicht zuletzt die Opfer-Perspektive um die „inneren Faktoren der Menschen", beziehen sich sowohl auf die Opfer wie die Täter, die „mitgemacht" haben und die letztlich die Bewegung zu solch einem „Erfolg" geführt haben. Diese Deutungslinien unterscheiden sich signifikant vom allgemeinen Grundkonsens der Parteihistoriographie und bedeuten eine grundsätzliche Verwerfung der Politik und der sozialistischen Linie der 1950er Jahre. Yous Roman wurde ob dieser Fundamentalkritik zu einem der am meisten diskutierten Werke der letzten Jahre.

Hu Pings historische Reportagen „Internes 1957: Opferaltar des Leidens" war ähnlich Aufsehen erregend.[50] In der Auswertung zahlreicher Interviews mit Betroffenen trat Hu Ping explizit mit dem Anspruch auf Authentizität und Objektivität auf. Er wählte eine emotionsgeladene Sprache und die Form der historischen Reportage – es sollte ausdrücklich weder ein literarisches, noch im strengen Sinne ein wissenschaftliches Werk sein (Hu Ping 2004, I: 10) –, um die „Geschichten des Leidens, der Intrigen und des Verrats" von prominenten Führern der Demokratischen Liga wie Zhang Bojun und Luo Longji, aber auch die Verwicklung führender KPCh-Politiker in die Bewegung nachzuzeichnen. So wurde das Zusammenspiel von Einzelwillkür und politischen Entscheidungsorganen wie etwa des Vorstandes der Demokratischen Liga und des Nationalen Volkskongresses[51] im Prozess des „zum Rechten Machens" besonders deutlich, auch wenn Hu Ping eine strikte Scheidung von Opfern und Tätern zu vermeiden sucht. Die Umdeutung des Jahres 1957 zu einem zentralen Wendepunkt in der Geschichte der VRCh, den Hu in seiner Wirkung mit der der Kulturrevolution gleichsetzt, ist ein wichtiger Baustein für die Etablierung einer neuen (oppositionellen?) Meistererzählung. Im Einklang damit plädiert Hu Ping vehement für die Nutzung des „eigenen Denkens und der eigenen Stimme" und ruft dazu auf, nicht auf offizielle Versionen und Erklärungen zu warten (Hu Ping 2004, I, Vorwort: 8).

Zhang Yihuo (geb. 1942), Tochter des Führers der Demokratischen Liga, Zhang Bojun, der zu den prominentesten Opfern zählte, schreibt ihre Erinnerungen aus der Sicht des Kindes ebenfalls als eine Geschichte von menschlichem Leid, Verrat und Intrige. Zhu Anping (1909-1966), Luo Longji (1896-1965) und Shi Liang (1900-1985) sind neben Zhang Bojun die Hauptpersonen eines Dramas, welches in seiner detaillierten Schilderung des Verlaufsprozesses von Denunziation, Kritik, Selbstkritik und Verbannung der gesamten Familie in den Nordwesten nicht nur einen politischen Tabubruch bedeutete, sondern auch die Frage der Täter vehement in die historiographische Diskussion gebracht hat. Zhang Yihuos Werk ist Anklage und Aufruf zugleich, sich mit den „wirklichen Problemen, denen lange eine Absage erteilt worden sei" (Zhang Yihuo 2004, Vorwort: 1) zu befassen.[52]

---

50 Am 20.10.2006 waren noch 250 chinesische Internetseiten zu diesem Buch abrufbar. Hu Pings Vater gehörte zu den sogenanten „Rechten".

51 So erhoben alle Abgeordneten „wie ein Wald" ihre Hände und stimmten geschlossen für den Ausschluss von 10 Vorstandsmitgliedern der Demokratischen Liga und weiterer 28 Mitglieder aus dem Vorstand bzw. aus dem Kongress (Hu Ping 2004, II: 490).

52 Das Werk verschwand schnell aus den Buchhandlungen und war nach kurzer Zeit nur noch als Raubdruck erhältlich.

Auch in den posthum veröffentlichten Erinnerungen Xu Zhuchengs (1907-1991) ist das Schicksal als „Rechter" die dominante Perspektive (Xu Zhucheng 1998: 426). Xu hatte sich erst nach einem Gespräch Mao Zedongs mit ihm und anderen Journalisten, bei dem er sich bei Mao rückversichert hatte, dass nun offene Meinungsäußerung die politische Linie sei, für die Bewegung „Lasst Hundert Blumen blühen" eingesetzt. Er zeichnet sich als jemand, der sich selbst zwar nicht besonders kritisch geäußert, wohl aber positive Berichte über eine gerade durchgeführte Delegationsreise in die Sowjetunion veröffentlicht hat (Xu Zhucheng 1998: 264). Danach begann sein Weg als Rechter: Absetzung von seinem Posten, Teilnahme an körperlicher Arbeit in der Landwirtschaft in der Nähe Shanghais, später Zuweisung eines untergeordneten Lektorats, die ökonomischen Probleme, die politische Diskriminierung, die soziale Isolation, eine relative Besserstellung ab 1961, bevor in der Kulturrevolution erneut öffentliche Kritikversammlungen, Hausdurchsuchungen und Demütigungen, wie die Degradierung zum Toilettenreiniger stattfanden (Xu Zhucheng 1998: 304ff). Es ist zunächst die distanziert-nüchterne Schilderung eines prominenten Demokraten, der in die politischen „Fangnetze" geriet und die Leser an seinem Erkenntnisprozess der politischen Desillusionierung durch Kontrastierung von Erinnerungen der Jetztzeit mit Tagebuchaufzeichnungen teilnehmen lässt. Weit weniger distanziert lesen sich Xus einige Jahre später separat veröffentlichten ausführlichen Erinnerungen speziell an das Jahr 1957. Sie thematisieren nun auch die Täterschaft von prominenten Intellektuellen, wie etwa Ba Jins, und Mitgliedern der Demokratischen Liga, bevor diese selbst zu Opfern wurden (Xu Zhucheng 2003).

Ein erschütterndes Zeugnis ihres Lebens in Arbeitslagern und Gefängnissen hat He Fengming, eine damals 25jährige Redakteurin der *Gansu Ribao*, mit ihrer Autobiographie vorgelegt. „Es ist ein mit Blut geschriebenes Buch (...) Wir müssen uns mit ihnen – den Toten und Lebenden – gemeinsam, dieser tiefgehenden Geschichte stellen, alles überdenken und dann unsere eigenen Schlüsse ziehen" (*Gansu Ribao* 12/2006) – fordert der Literaturwissenschaftler Qian Liqun im Vorwort zur zweiten Auflage.

He Fengming wurde 1957 zugleich mit ihrem Ehemann Wang Jingchao 王景超 wegen einer Sympathiebekundung für einen kritisierten Kollegen der „Bandenbildung" angeklagt. Beide wurden in Arbeitslager verschickt. Wang verhungerte, He überlebte, wurde 1978 rehabilitiert und begann 1989, ihre Erinnerungen zu schreiben.[53] He zeichnet ihre Geschichte als eine Geschichte von Hunger, Arbeit und Mühsal (He Fengming 2006: 372), schildert detailliert die soziale Isolation der „Rechten", auch untereinander. Häufig ist die Rede von Grausamkeit, Angst und „Leidenden" (He Fengming 2006: 424, 458, 488). Hes Erinnerungen verdeutlichen, warum gerade die „Rechten" Opfer der Hungerkatastrophe wurden, sie zugleich aber auch diejenigen waren, die den Großen Sprung und die jeweilige Politik verbal besonders unterstützten und ihre „Umerziehung" zu loyalen Anhängern Mao Zedongs als „gelungen" zu präsentieren wussten, um so wenigstens ihre Familien, ihre Kinder vor Verfolgung zu schützen (He Fengming 2006: 7).

Qian Liqun, der Wissenschaftler, verweist in seiner Analyse der Autobiographie auf die „Entmenschlichung" der Opfer,[54] die als „Rindergötter und Schlangengeister" bezeichnet

---

[53] 1996 erfolgte die erste Veröffentlichung; danach hat Qian weitere 4 Jahre daran gearbeitet und Materialien ergänzt (He Fengming 2006).

[54] Hes Ehemann Wang suchte sein „Menschsein" durch Tagebuch-Schreiben aufrechtzuerhalten, aber das Schreiben wurde ihm untersagt. Tagebuchschreiben galt als reaktionärer Akt. Man wollte – so Qian –

– hier zieht er auch die Parallele zur Kulturrevolution – und sozial und familiär völlig isoliert wurden (in: He Fengming 2006: 2ff).[55] He Fengming und Qian Liqun suchen das
Ausmaß der Grausamkeit und des Leidens der Einzelnen zu erklären. Während He ihre
aussichtslose Situation anführt, in der sie nur von dem Gedanken an Umerziehung und
vom Kampf um ihr nacktes Leben beherrscht gewesen sei (2006: 6, 156), sucht Qian nach
einer „Logik der Bewegung". Für ihn war es nicht bloß die Grausamkeit Einzelner, sondern das System selbst bzw. die Notwendigkeit, die Ordnung der „revolutionären Hölle"
aufrechtzuerhalten, welches letztlich zu einer völligen „Entfremdung des Menschen" geführt habe (in: He Fengming 2006: 9f). Er macht insbesondere den Personenkult um Mao
Zedong und dessen Idee vom Opfer des Einzelnen für das Kollektiv dafür verantwortlich.
Die „Rechten" hätten sich selbst sehr kritisch und das Volk als ihr Vorbild gesehen,
Arbeiter und Arbeit seien idealisiert worden. Sie hätten daher nicht nur kein Mitleid
untereinander gehabt, sondern sich sogar gegenseitig Schaden zugefügt (in: He Fengming
2006: 10). Dieses Argument der Internalisierung der propagierten politischen Werte
durch die Intelligenz läuft dabei He Fengmings Argument vom Selbstschutz parallel.
Die neue Deutungslinie durch die zivilgesellschaftlichen Akteure wird bei He Fengming
am treffendsten expliziert: Die Geschichte der 1950er Jahre ist eine Geschichte des „großen Sterbens und des großen Hungerns", eine Geschichte, die He mit der Bewegung gegen Hu Feng 1954 beginnen lässt und die bis zur Kulturrevolution andauert (He Fengming 206: 377). Doch unter dieser Perspektive geraten nicht nur bei He die „Vorläufer"
der Bewegung von 1957 in den Blick, sondern letztlich alle politischen Bewegungen, die
auf die Intelligenz oder städtische Bevölkerungsschichten abzielten. Die öffentliche Kritik
an dem Philosophen Zhang Dongsun durch den marxistischen Historiker Jian Bozan in
der „Drei-Anti"-Bewegung 1951/52 wird dabei ebenso angeführt (Zhang Yihuo 2004b:
403ff) wie die „politischen Erziehungsmethoden" und die Kritik- und Selbstkritik der
„demokratischen Persönlichkeit" Liao Mengxiang (1904-1988),[56] die nach der Verhaftung ihres Freundes Pan Hannian (1906-1977)[57] 1955 ständig krank war bzw. sich in ihre
Krankheiten flüchtete (Li Mei 2004: 270ff). Auch die Kritikbewegung an den Forschungen zum *Traum der Roten Kammer*, die 1954 initiiert wurde, ist ebenfalls wie die
nachfolgenden Kritikbewegungen an der Zeitschrift *Wenyibao*, an Hu Shi (1891-1962)
sowie an Hu Feng[58] sowie Ding Ling (1904-1986) und Chen Qixia 陈企霞 (1913-1988)

Menschen total „auslöschen" (Qian in: He Fengming 2006: 4).

[55] Es hieß auch innerhalb der Familie „klare Grenzlinien zu ziehen". He und ihr Partner waren in einer
ähnlichen Situation und daher nach Qian Liqun noch relativ gut gestellt. Andere seien völlig isoliert gewesen. Selbst als He krank war, sprach niemand mit ihr. Qian zieht hier den Vergleich mit faschistischen Konzentrationslagern (in: He Fengming 2006: 5, 342, 246, 255f).

[56] Liao Mengxiang (1904-1988) war die Tochter des 1925 ermordeten Liao Zhongkai (1897-1925) und
He Xiangnings (1878-1972) und Ehefrau Li Shaoshis, der 1943 in Chongqing ermordet wurde. Die
Tochter Liao Mengxiangs, Li Mei, hat gestützt auf viele Briefe und Manuskripte ihrer Mutter die
Biographie verfasst. Liao Mengxiang, He Xiangning und Liao Chengzhi nahmen an der
Eröffnungszeremonie zur Gründung der VR China am 1.10.1949 auf dem Tian'anmen teil (Li Mei
2004: 259).

[57] Pan Hannian, der von 1955 bis zu seinem Tode 1977 inhaftiert oder im Arbeitslager war, wurde 1982
voll rehabilitiert. Kürzlich erschien Zhang Yun 2006.

[58] Im Kontext der Anti-Hu Feng-Bewegung und der Bewegung gegen Konterrevolutionäre wurden auch
weniger Prominente, wie der zur Gruppe um den Dramatiker Wu Zuguang (1915-2003) gehörende Du

Teil der Aufarbeitung des Jahres „1954" geworden. Der Literaturwissenschaftler Sun Yumin sucht hier beispielsweise „die historischen Fakten" ausgehend von den jeweils involvierten Personen abzuhandeln (Sun Yumin 2003).

Auf diese Weise wird nicht nur die Bewegung von 1957, sondern werden auch die frühen, einstmals als korrekt klassifizierten Bewegungen zu willkürlichen politischen Kämpfen und letztlich zu einer Geschichte politischer Unterdrückung transformiert. Als Beginn dieser Geschichte wird die im März 1951 gestartete Bewegung zur Kritik des Filmes „Das Leben des Wu Xun" konstruiert. Sie sei die erste Bewegung gegen die Intelligenz gewesen, die den Weg für die späteren Bewegungen größeren Ausmaßes eröffnet habe.[59]

Die inneren Zusammenhänge der frühen politischen Bewegungen zu der des Jahres 1957 werden zwar auch von den professionellen Historikern hergestellt, doch sie tragen diese Konstruktion der historischen Ereignisse zu einer durchgehenden Geschichte der Unterdrückung nicht mit. Gegenüber den „Vorläufern" von 1957 herrscht eine zumindest teilweise affirmative Haltung und aus der Partei- und Staatsperspektive werden diese Bewegungen, trotz Fehlern in der Umsetzung, letztlich als Sicherung der ideologischen Basis der jungen Volksrepublik bewertet. So gilt als positiv bei der Kritikbewegung des Films „Das Leben des Wu Xun", dass sich mit dieser Kritik am Reformismus auch Ideen des Marxismus-Leninismus verbreitet hätten und eine klare Unterscheidung zwischen Revolution und Reform vorgenommen worden sei. Im Vergleich zur Bewegung von 1957 sei überdies das Ausmaß der Bewegung relativ klein und die Konsequenzen für die Betroffenen verhältnismäßig gering gewesen (Liu Shukai und Guo Simin 2006: 681-685ff). Diese affirmative Haltung ist auch in Bezug auf die „Drei-Anti" – und die „Fünf-Anti"-Bewegung von 1951/52[60] zu beobachten. Sie werden als notwendige, wenn auch „übertriebene" Auseinandersetzungen zwischen Idealismus und Materialismus im Kultur- und Ideologiebereich angesehen, wenngleich eine Vermischung der politischen und der wissenschaftlichen Ebene beklagt wird (Liu Shukai und Guo Simin 2006: 774ff). Einige Historiker integrieren allerdings auch bei der Bewertung der frühen Bewegungen die Opferperspektive. Sie verweisen auf die hohe Selbstmordrate der in der „Drei-Anti"- und der „Fünf-Anti"-Bewegung als „Tiger" Bezeichneten und „Entlarvten" und üben Kritik bezüglich der Verhängung der Todesstrafe, zumal die Anschuldigungen zu einem Großteil nicht den Tatsachen entsprochen hätten (Wang Shunsheng und Li Jun 2006: 85, 129-

---

Gao (geb. 1930) und seine Freunde als „kleiner Familienclan" öffentlich angeprangert und jahrelang inhaftiert. Die auf ihn bezogenen Materialien der Sicherheitsbehörde wurden durch Zufall vom Historiker und Journalisten Li Hui, der sich auch mit Hu Feng befasst hatte, entdeckt und 2004 als erschütterndes Dokument über die Arbeitslager in Peking veröffentlicht. S. auch Du Gao 2004.

[59] So auch Tang Wenquan, der die Bewegung als wesentlich gegen das Ansehen des bereits 1946 verstorbenen Tao Xingzhi gerichtet interpretiert und dessen Auseinandersetzung mit Jiang Qing in den 30er Jahren dafür verantwortlich macht (in: Xu Zhucheng 2003: 43ff).

[60] Positiv hervorgehoben werden die „rechtzeitige und kraftvolle Korrektur und Beschlüsse" der KPCh zur Lösung dieser Fragen (und nicht zuletzt zur Beendung der Bewegung) (Wang Shunsheng und Li Jun 2006: 135). Wie die „Reportageliteratur" von Bai Xi zur Bewegung zur Unterdrückung der Konterrevolutionäre 1950-1953 zu lesen ist, ist nicht so einfach zu bestimmen. Unter dem Motto: „Lass die Geschichte uns die Zukunft voraussagen" will er – so die Rhetorik – die Erinnerung an die Geschichte, an die damalige Unterdrückung wachhalten und deutlich machen, wie wichtig der Kampf gegen die Konterrevolutionäre war, um dem Land Frieden und Sicherheit zu geben (Bai Xi 2006, Vorwort: 1f). Faktisch präsentiert Bai Xi hier eine Geschichte der Opfer.

135, 777).[61] Sie thematisieren die Bewegung gegen die sog. „weißen Experten" im Jahr 1958 und die hier geführten Angriffe auf einzelne Gelehrte u.a. die Philosophen Feng Youlan (1895-1990) und He Lin (1902-1992) sowie den Linguisten Wang Li (1900-1896) von der Peking-Universität, die Historiker Cai Shangsi (geb. 1905) und Zhou Gucheng (1898-1996) von der Fudan-Universität und Chen Yinge (1890-1969) von der Zhong-shan-Universität, und nennen erstmals hohe Zahlen[62] weiterer von dieser Bewegung betroffenen Hochschulangehörigen (Luo Pinghan 2003a: 126-141).

Fazit

Die Neukonstruktionen der Geschichte der 1950er Jahre erfolgen aus zwei gegenläufigen, manchmal sich allerdings überlappenden Perspektiven: einmal der Partei- und Staats-perspektive, zum anderen der Opferperspektive. Die Partei- und Staatsperspektive, vertre-ten von der Mehrzahl der Historiker, ist nach wie vor geprägt vom Abwägen richtiger und falscher Linien und dem Versuch, – trotz aller „Windungen und Wendungen" und Linien-fehler und den daraus resultierenden jeweiligen weitreichenden Rückschlägen für den Aufbau des Sozialismus in China –, eine Erfolgsgeschichte der Volksrepublik zu präsen-tieren und die gravierenden Fehler als Ausgangspunkt für neue Erkenntnisse, als (letzt-endliche) Durchsetzung einer richtigen Politik umzudeuten. Das Argument der be-schränkten Erkenntnismöglichkeit der politischen Führer in dieser Periode dient einerseits dazu, von Fragen nach Schuld und Verantwortung abzulenken, andererseits wird damit vom Anspruch einer erkenntnistheoretischen „Allmacht" der Partei abgegangen. Das An-führen „korrekter" Gegenpositionen und „Gegenspieler" – auch wenn sie sich zu einem bestimmten Zeitpunkt nicht durchsetzen konnten – bietet darüber hinaus die Möglichkeit, kritisches und selbstkritisches Potential innerhalb der KPCh selbst aufzuzeigen. Inner-parteiliche Demokratie und kollektive Führung (als Gegenpol zur Diktatur und zum Personenkult Mao Zedongs) sind zu entscheidenden Deutungskriterien historischer Ereig-nisse geworden: Die Partei – so lautet das Fazit – hat aus den historischen Fehlern gelernt und muss künftig daraus lernen. Das Kriterium der innerparteilichen Demokratie, wie es für die politische Ebene gefordert wird, entspricht auf der ideologischen Ebene dem ein-geforderten und praktizierten Deutungswettbewerb. Die Pluralität der Meinungen zu be-stimmten historischen Ereignissen ist Ausdruck des Bemühens, einen Grundkonsens bei-zubehalten, nämlich die führende Position der KPCh nicht in Frage zu stellen. Doch die-ser Grundkonsens scheint bei einigen Historikern nicht mehr zu bestehen. Ihre Verwer-fungen des Großen Sprungs, der Volkskommunen, der Kollektivierung und der Bewegun-gen gegen die Intelligenz, deren Integration der Opferperspektive in die Narration, stellen die Präsentation der Geschichte der 50er Jahre als einer wirtschaftlichen und politischen Erfolgsgeschichte mehr und mehr in Frage.

---

[61] 292 000 Personen seien im gesamten Land wegen Bestechung und Korruption über mehr als 10 Mio. Yuan einer Untersuchung unterzogen worden, von denen 105 000 Personen fälschlicherweise angeklagt worden seien (Wang Shunsheng und Li Jun 2006: 135, die sich hier auf eine 1992 publizierte Rede An Ziwens stützen).

[62] Allein an der Wuhan-Universität wurden 391 Personen als „weiße Experten" eingeschätzt, darunter 84 Dozenten und 32 Professoren und Assistenzprofessoren. Überdies wurden 305 Studierende, viele mit sog. „bürgerlichem" Hintergrund, zu „weißen Experten" abgestempelt. Die Medizinische Fakultät der Wuhan-Universität kritisierte 79 ihrer Angehörigen als „weiße Experten" und zwang sie zu Selbstkriti-ken, davon waren die Hälfte Professoren und Assistenzprofessoren (Luo Pinghan 2003a: 140).

An diesem Punkt scheinen die zivilgesellschaftlichen Akteure bereits angelangt zu sein. Ihre Neukonstruktionen der 50er Jahre gänzlich aus der Opferperspektive zeichnen die Periode als eine Geschichte des Leidens und des Hungerns für die Bevölkerung sowie der politischen Unterdrückung und damit des politischen und wirtschaftlichen Misserfolgs. Ob und auf welche Weise diese beiden gegenläufigen Perspektiven in eine neue historische Meistererzählung münden werden und welche Konsequenzen dies für die historische Legitimierung der politischen Herrschaft haben wird, bleibt abzuwarten.

Literatur

Barmé, Geremie R. (1993) „History for the Masses", in Jonathan Unger (Hg.) *Using the Past to Serve the Present. Historiography and Politics in Contemporary China*, Armonk: Sharpe, S. 260-286.

Bo Yibo 薄一波 (1991) *Ruogan zhongda juece yu shijian de huiyi* 若干重大决策与事件的回忆 [Erinnerungen an wichtige Beschlüsse und Ereignisse], Beijing: Zhonggong zhongyang dangxiao.

Cao Shuji 曹树基 (1998), "Rezension zu Zhang Letian" in *Zhongguo shehui kexue* 4/1991, S. 206.

Chen Guidi 陈桂棣 und Wu Chuntao 吴春桃 (2004) *Zhongguo nongmin diaocha* 中国农民调查 [Untersuchungen zur Lage chinesischer Bauern], Beijing: Renmin wenxue chunbanshe (Deutsche Ausgabe: Chen Guidi und Wang Chuntao [2006] *Zur Lage der chinesischen Bauern. Eine Reportage*, Frankfurt/M. : Zweitausendeins).

Chen Minzhi 陈敏之 und Gu Nanjiu 顾南九 (Hg.) (2002) *Gu Zhun biji* 顾准笔记 [Aufzeichungen von Gu Zhun], Beijing: Zhongguo qingnian.

Chevrier, Ives (1987) „La servante-maitresse: condition de la réference à l'histoire dans l'espace intellectuel chinois", in *Extrème Orient – extrème occident. Cahiers de recherches comparatives* 9/1987, S. 117-144.

Du Gao 杜高 (2004) *Wo bu zai shi „wo": yi ge youpai fenzi de jingshen siwang dang'an* 我不再是「我」：一個右派分子的精神死亡檔案 [Ich habe kein „Ich" mehr: Archivmaterialien zum geistigen Tod eines „Rechten"], Hongkong: Ming bao .

Fitzgerald, John (1994) „‚Reports of my Death have been greatly exaggerated'. The history of the death of China", in David S.G. Goodman und Gerarld Segal (Hg.) *China Deconstructs. Politics, Trade and Regionalism*, London und New York, pp.21-58.

He Fengming 和凤鸣 (2006) *Jingli wode yi jiu wu qi nian* 经历我的一九五七年 [Meine Erfahrungen im Jahre 1957], Lanzhou: Dunhuang wenyi.

He Yonghong 何永红 (2006) *„Wufan' yundongyanjiu* "五反"运动研究 [Studie zur „Drei-Anti"-Bewegung], Beijing. Zhonggong dangshi.

Hu Ping 禅机 (2004) *1957: Ku'nan de jitan* 苦难的祭坛 [1957: Altar des Leidens], Guangzhou: Guangdong lüyou.

Huang Aijun 黄爱军 (2005) „‚Da yuejin' yundong fasheng yuanyin yanjiu shuping" 「大跃进」运动发生原因研究述评 [Literaturbericht zu den Entstehungsursachen der „Großen Sprung"-Bewegung], in *Dangdai Zhongguo yanjiu* 12/1 (2005), S.86-92.

Ji Xianlin 季羡林 u.a. (Hg.) (2001) *Zhi man cong cong de huiyi* 枝蔓丛丛的回忆 [Komplizierte Erinnerungen], Beijing: Shiyue wenyi.

Jin Chunming 金春明 (2004) *Zhonghua renmin gongheguo jianshi* 中华人民共和国简史 [Kurze Geschichte der VR China, 1949-2004], Beijing: Zhonggong dangshi 2004.

Leutner, Mechthild (1996) „Sozialgeschichte in der VR China: Modernisierungsparadigma oder Marxismus?", in *Berliner China-Hefte* 11 (1996), S. 47-63.

Leutner; Mechthild (2003) „Die ‚sozialgeschichtliche Wende' in China seit den 1980er Jahren. Chinesische und westliche/deutsche Historiographie: ein Dialog?", in *Zeitschrift für Weltgeschichte* 4/2 (2003), S.103-120.

Li Hui 李辉 (2004) *Yizhi cangliang. Du Gao dang'an yuanshi wenben* 一直苍凉. 杜高档案原始文本 [Eine Trostlosigkeit. Originaltexte aus dem Archiv Du Gaos], Beijing: Zhongguo wenlian.

Li Lizhi 李立志 (2002) *Bianqian yu chongjian 1949-1956 nian de Zhongguo shehui* 变迁与重建 1949-1956 年的中国社会 [Wandel und Aufbau. Die chinesische Gesellschaft 1949 bis 1956], Nanchang: Jiangxi renmin.

Li Mei 李湄 (2004) *Muqin Liao Mengxing bai nian ji* 母亲廖猛醒百年祭 [Zum 100. Geburtstag meiner Mutter Liao Mengxing], Beijing: Zhongguo gongren.

Li Rui 李锐 (1994) *Da yuejin qin liji* 大跃进亲历记 [Persönliche Aufzeichnungen des Großen Sprungs], Haikou: Nanfang.

Li Yuan 李原 (2003) *Zhi wei shi. Yan Hongyan shangjiang wangshi zhuizong* 只唯实. 阎红彦上将往事追踪 [Nur die Tatsachen. Spurensuche in der Vergangenheit des Generals Yan Hongyan], Kunming: Yunnan renmin.

Liu Shukai 刘书楷 und Guo Simin 郭思敏 (2006) *Zhonggongdang shi bianyi* 中共党史辨疑 [Erörterung strittiger Fragen zur Geschichte der KPCh], Beijing: Zhonggong wenxian.

Luo Pinghan 罗平汉 (2000a) „*Da guo fan" gonggong shitang shi mo* 「大锅饭」公共食堂始末 [„Die Große Reisschüssel". Die Volksküchen von Anfang bis Ende], Nanning: Guangxi renmin.

Luo Pinghan 罗平汉 (2002) *Nongcun renmin gongsheshi* 农村人民公社史 [Geschichte der Volkskommunen], Fuzhou: Fujian renmin.

Luo Pinghan 罗平汉 (2003a) *Dangdai lishi wenti zhaji* 当代历史问题札记 [Notizen zu Problemen der Zeitgeschichte], Guilin: Guangxi shifandaxue.

Luo Pinghan 罗平汉 (2000b) *Hongse renliu* 红色人流 [Rote Menschenströme], Nanning: Guangxi renmin.

Luo Pinghan 罗平汉 (2003c) *Dazibao de xingshuai* 大字报的兴衰 [Aufstieg und Niedergang der Wandzeitungen], Fuzhou: Fujian Renmin.

Luo Pinghan 罗平汉 (2004) *Nongye hezuo yundongshi* 农业合作运动史 [Geschichte der Kollektivierung der Landwirtschaft], Fuzhou: Fujian renmin.

Luo Pinghan 罗平汉 (2005) *Tudi gaige yundongshi* 土地改革运动史 [Geschichte der Landreformbewegung], Fuzhou: Fuzhou renmin.

Luo Pinghan 罗平汉 (2006) *Dangdai lishi wenti zhaiji erji* 当代历史问题札记二记 [Notizen zu Problemen der Zeitgeschichte] 2, Guilin: Guangxi shifandaxue.

Ma Shexiang 马社香 (2002) *Yige nü gemingzhe de lishi jianzheng* 一个女革命者的历史见证 [Historisches Zeugnis einer Revolutionärin], Beijing: Zhonggong dangshi.

Ma Si 马嘶 (2003) *20 shiji Zhongguo zhishi fenzi shenghuo zhuangkuang* 20 世纪中国知识分子生活状况[Das Wohlergehen der Massen: Die Lebensverhältnisse der Intellektuellen im China des 20. Jahrhunderts], Beijing: Beijing tushuguan.

Middell, Matthias; Monika Gibas und Frank Hadler (2000) „Sinnstiftung und Systemlegitimierung durch historisches Erzählen. Überlegungen zu Funktionsmechanismen von Repräsentationen des Vergangenen", in *COMPARATIV* 10/2 (2000), S. 7-35.

Meizhi 梅志 (1998) *Hu Feng zhuan* 胡风传 [Biographie Hu Fengs], Beijing: Shiyue wenyi.

Pang Xianzhi 逄先知 und Jin Chongji 金冲及 (2003) 毛泽东传 1949-1976 [Biographie Mao Zedongs, 1949-1976] 2 Bde., Beijing: Zhongyang wenxian.

Perry, Elizabeth J. (1997) „Shanghai's Strike Wave of 1957", in Timothy Cheek und Tony J. Saich (Hg.), *New Perspectives on State Socialism in China*, Armonk, New York, London: M.E. Sharpe, S. 234-261.

Resolution über einige Fragen zur Geschichte der KP Chinas seit 1949. angenommen von der 6. Plenartagung des XI. Zentralkomitees der Kommunistischen Partei Chinas am 27. Juni 1981 (1981), Beijing: Verlag für fremdsprachige Literatur.

Song Haiqing 宋海庆 (2000) *Renmin gonshe xingwang lu* 人民公社兴旺录 [Aufzeichnungen zum Aufstieg und Fall der Volkskommunen] Urumuqi: Xinjiang qingshaonian.

Spakowski, Nicola (1999) *Helden, Monumente, Traditionen. Nationale Identität und historisches Bewußtsein in der VR China*, Hamburg: Lit.

Su Zhongxian 宿忠显 (1994) „Dui fan you douzheng de lishi sikao" 对反右斗争的历史思考 [Erörterungen zur Geschichte des Kampfes gegen die Rechten], in *Dangshi yanjiu ziliao* 12.

Wang Shunsheng 王顺生 und Li Jun 礼军 (2006) *„San fan" yundong yanjiu* 「三反」运动研究 [Studie zur „Fünf-Anti"-Bewegung], Beijing: Zhonggong zhongyang dangsi.

Wang Defen 王得芬 (2004) *Wo he Xiao Jun fengyu wu shi nian* 我和萧军风雨五十年 [Meine 50 mühseligen Jahre mit Xiao Jun], Beijing: Zhongguo gongren.

Wang Yugui 王玉贵 (2004) *Lun fan you douzheng dui „da yuejin" yundong de yinxiang* 论反右斗争对「大跃进」运动的印象 [Der Einfluss des Kampfes gegen die Rechten auf die „Große-Sprung"-Bewegung], in *Shixue yuekan* 11.

Weigelin-Schwiedrzik, Susanne (2001) „Chinesische Historiographie in den neunziger Jahren: Zwischen Problemen der Erkenntnistheorie und der Marktwirtschaft", in *COMPARATIV* 11/4 (2001), S.53-79.

Weigelin-Schwiedrzik, Susanne (2003) „Trauma and Memory: The case of the Great Famine in the People's Republic of China (1959-1961)", in *Historiography East & West* 1/1 (2003), S. 39-67.

Wemheuer, Felix (2005) „Der Weg in die Hungersnot: Erinnerungen chinesischer Inellektueller an den ländlichen ‚Großen Sprung nach vorne' (1958-1961)", in *Asien* 94 (2005), S. 25-41.

Xie Chuntao 谢春涛 (1994) *Da yuejin kuanglan* 大跃进狂澜 [Die Wogen des Großen Sprunges], Zhengzhou: Henan renmin.

Xiaofeng 晓风, Xiaoshan 晓山 und Xiaogu 晓谷 (2001) *Wo de fuqin Hu Feng* 我的父亲胡风 [Unser Vater Hu Feng], Shenyang: Chunfeng wenyi.

Xiao Donglian 肖冬连 *Qiusuo Zhongguo – wenge qian shi nian shi* 求索中国—文革前10年史 [China auf der Suche. Geschichte der 10 Jahre vor der Kulturrevolution] 2 Bde. Beijing: Hongqi.

Xu Jing 许静 (2004) *Da yuejin yundong zhong de zhengzhi chuanbo* 大跃进运动中的政治传播 [Politische Propaganda in der Großen-Sprung-Bewegung), Hong Kong: Shehuikexue..

Xu Zhucheng 徐铸成 (1998) *Xu Zhucheng huiyilu* 徐铸成回忆录 [Erinnerungen Xu Zhuchengs], Beijing: Sanlian shudian.

Xu Zhucheng 徐铸成 (2003) *Qinli yi jiu wu qi* 亲历一九五七 (Persönlich Erlebtes im Jahr 1957), Wuhan: Hubei renmin.

Yang Shengqun 杨胜群 und Chen Jin 陈晋 (Hg.) (2006) *Wu shi nian de huiwang. Zhonggong ba da jishi* 五十年的回望中共八大纪实 [Rückblick auf 50 Jahre. Aufzeichnungen zum 8. Parteitag der KPCh]. Beijing: Sanlian shudian.

You Qiwei 尤其为 (2004) *Zhongguo de yi jiu wu qi* 中国的一九五七 [China im Jahr 1957], Shenyang: Chunfeng wenyi.

Zhang Letian 张乐天 (2005) *Gaobie lixiang renmin gongshe zhidu yanjiu* 告别理想人民公社制度研究 [Abschied von der Utopie – Studien zum Volkskommunensystem], Shanghai: Shiji.

Zhang Yihuo 章诒和 (2004) *Wangshi bing bu ru yan* 往事并不如烟 [Die Vergangenheit ist überhaupt nicht wie Rauch, der verfliegt], Beijing: Renmin wenxue.

Zhang Yihuo 章诒和 (2004) *Yi fuqin yu Jian Bozan de jiaowang* 忆父亲与翦伯赞的交往 [Die Beziehungen meines Vaters zu Jian Bozan] in Zhang Lifan 章立凡 (Hg.) 记忆往事未付红尘 [Erinnern: vergangene Dinge werden nicht ins Jammertal übergeben], Xi'an: Shaanxi shifandaxue, S. 391-440.

Zhang Yun 张云 (2006) *Pan Hannian zhuan* 潘汉年传 [Biographie Pan Hannians], Shanghai: Shanghai renmin.

Luvsanvandan Manlajav

Chinesisch als Fremdsprache – Die Peking Universität in den 1950er Jahren und aktuelle Trends[1]

Über Auslandsstudenten, die in den 1950er Jahren in der Volksrepublik Chinesisch studiert haben, ist bislang bis auf wenige Ausnahmen (Schwarcz 1999, Polonyi 1982) kaum geschrieben worden. Der vorliegende Artikel will dem ein wenig abhelfen, ohne dabei zu sehr in Memoiren oder aber allzu wissenschaftliche Analysen didaktischer Methoden von Chinesisch als Fremdsprache (ChaF) zu verfallen. Es geht schlicht um die Darstellung der Anfänge und der aktuellen Situation von ChaF in China auf der Basis persönlicher Erfahrungen als Auslandsstudentin der ersten Generation in der gerade erst gegründeten Volksrepublik China und aus der Perspektive jahrzehntelanger beruflicher Tätigkeit als Linguistin, Chinesischlehrerin und Direktorin der Fremdsprachenfakultät der Universität für Geisteswissenschaften in Ulanbaataar, Mongolei.

Im Jahr 2004 betrug die Zahl der Chinesisch Lernenden weltweit bereits mehr als 25 Millionen, an über 2300 Universitäten in 85 Ländern waren Chinesischkurse eingerichtet.[2] Die Zahl der Auslandsstudenten in China wächst stetig weiter. Das internationale Interesse an Chinesisch als Fremdsprache ist groß. Staatlich zertifizierte und standardisierte Feststellungsprüfungen wie der HSK (汉语水平考试), Chinesisch-Wettbewerbe wie *Chinese Bridge* (汉语桥) und weitere Einstufungsverfahren, die für Chinesisch im In- und Ausland durchgeführt werden, haben wesentlich zur Popularisierung und Verbreitung von Chinesischunterricht an den Hochschulen beigetragen. Fachorganisationen wie das *Hanban* (Akronym für: 国家对外汉语教学领导小组办公室 Nationale Staatliche Leitungsgruppe für Chinesisch als Fremdsprache) auf nationaler Ebene und die Internationale Wissenschaftliche Gesellschaft für Chinesischunterricht (世界汉语教学学会) auf internationaler Ebene veranstalten regelmäßig Forschungstagungen für ChaF, sowohl in China als auch im Ausland. Trotz dieser offenkundigen Expansion des Fachs hätte vor mehr als 50 Jahren niemand vorhergesagt, dass ChaF einmal eine so umfangreiche Unternehmung werden würde. Die Ursachen für dieses Phänomen dürften in der immer bedeutenderen Stellung, welche China in den letzten Jahrzehnten wirtschaftlich und politisch in der Welt eingenommen hat, begründet liegen, auf deren gesellschaftliche Hintergründe an dieser Stelle jedoch nicht weiter eingegangen werden soll.

Entwicklung von Chinesisch als Fremdsprache in China bis Ende der 1950er Jahre
ChaF hat eine lange Geschichte in China. Bereits in der Früheren (Westlichen) Hanzeit (206 v.u.Z.-220 n.u.Z.) gingen junge Aristokraten der westlichen Regionen in die Hauptstadt Chang'an (das heutige Xi'an), um dort die chinesische Sprache und Kultur zu studieren. Als die ersten Lernenden von ChaF müssen jedoch diejenigen Ausländer gelten, die als buddhistische Mönche nach China kamen.

---

[1] Mein Dank gilt Frau Prof. Mechthild Leutner und Nathalie van Looy. Der vorliegende Artikel ist im Rahmen eines von der DFG geförderten Forschungsaufenthaltes an der Freien Universität Berlin (März bis Juni 2006) entstanden.

[2] Vgl. Fachverband Chinesisch 2004, vgl. auch die Eröffnungsrede des siebten Internationalen Symposiums für Chinesisch-Unterricht in Shanghai, 2002.

Im Verlauf der Sui- (589-618) und der Tang-Dynastie (618-907) wurde das chinesische Reich geeint; gesellschaftlich und wirtschaftlich erreichte es einen hohen Entwicklungsgrad. Die Tang-Dynastie war geprägt durch einen mächtigen Staat, kulturelle Blüte, umfangreiche Beziehungen zu den Nachbarländern, und nicht zuletzt eine große Zahl an Ausländern, die zum Studium nach China kamen. Die Hauptstadt Chang'an entwickelte sich zum Zentrum für Chinesischunterricht. Auch westliche Missionare haben bereits in früheren Jahrhunderten zum Teil beachtliche Chinesischkenntnisse erworben.

Die Geschichte von ChaF im Neuen China begann in den 1950er Jahren. Zu dieser Zeit kam eine Gruppe osteuropäischer Studenten, darunter Ostdeutsche, Polen, Tschechoslowaken, Bulgaren, Ungarn, Rumänen, außerdem Koreaner und Vietnamesen sowie einige wenige Mongolen zum Studium nach China. Obwohl Chinesischunterricht für Ausländer zu diesem Zeitpunkt bereits eine lange Geschichte aufwies, bedeuteten die 1950er Jahre einen Neubeginn des Fachs unter vollkommen neuen historischen Voraussetzungen: Die Volksrepublik China war gerade erst gegründet worden und knüpfte erste diplomatische Beziehungen zum Ausland. Das internationale Interesse an China war groß.

Zu diesem Zeitpunkt war das Ziel der meisten ausländischen Studenten in China ein geisteswissenschaftliches Studium. Erst später begannen Ausländer auch Naturwissenschaften und Ingenieurwesen zu studieren. Zu Beginn der 1950er Jahre wurden nicht nur ausländische Studenten zum Studium nach China, sondern auch Chinesischlehrer aus China zum Unterricht ins Ausland entsandt.

Um die chinesische Sprache ausreichend zu beherrschen und ihr jeweiliges Fachstudium antreten zu können, mussten ausländische Studenten zunächst so genannte Vorbereitungskurse (专修班) absolvieren. Ihre Dauer war von den Hochschulen klar vorgegeben: für Geisteswissenschaften (Literatur, Geschichte, Philosophie oder Philologie) zwei Jahre, für Außenwirtschaft, Internationale Beziehungen, Naturwissenschaften, Ingenieurwesen, Medizin und Landwirtschaft ein Jahr. In den geisteswissenschaftlichen Vorbereitungskursen wurden im zweiten Jahr bereits chinesischsprachige Werke gelesen, im Kurs der Autorin selbst zum Beispiel Mao Zedongs „Untersuchungsbericht über die Bauernbewegung in Hunan" von 1927 sowie Romane und Erzählungen von Lu Xun, Lao She, Ba Jin und Guo Moruo. Im zweiten Vorbereitungsjahr gab es außerdem eine Einführung ins klassische Chinesisch, unter anderem wurden die „Gespräche" des Konfuzius behandelt – Vorkenntnisse, die sich für das spätere Studium der chinesischen Sprache und Literatur als außerordentlich nützlich erweisen sollten.

Die Autorin des vorliegenden Artikels gehörte zum Vorbereitungsjahrgang 1954, war also gewissermaßen eine der ersten Abnehmerinnen von ChaF im Neuen China. 1956 nahm sie ihr Studium an der Fakultät für Chinesische Sprache und Literatur der Peking Universität auf, welches zu diesem Zeitpunkt auf fünf Jahre angelegt war. Hier lehrten unter anderem die Professoren Wang Li 王力, Gao Mingkai 高名凯 und Zhou Zumo 周祖模. Zu den interessantesten Kursen gehörten „Geschichte der Chinesischen Sprache", „Modernes Chinesisch" und „Geschichte der Chinesischen Literatur". Gao Mingkai unterrichtete im ersten Jahr „Einführung in die Linguistik", im dritten Jahr „Theorie der Grammatik". Der Kurs „Geschichte der Chinesischen Literatur" dauerte mit 8-9 Semestern am längsten, was angesichts einer der längsten Literaturtraditionen nicht weiter erstaunt. Die Lektüre zahlreicher klassischer Werke trug bei den ausländischen Studenten nicht nur zum Spracherwerb, sondern auch maßgeblich zum Wissenserwerb über die chinesische Kultur bei.

Die Autorin studierte im Vorbereitungskurs als auch an der Fakultät für Chinesische Sprache und Literatur der Peking Universität gemeinsam mit zahlreichen deutschen Kommilitonen: Irmtraud Fessen-Henjes, Ilse Schmidt, Roland Felber, Dieter Gasde, Eberhardt Treppt sowie Eva und Rainer Müller. Sie alle wurden später Chinaspezialisten, gingen wie Eva Müller oder Roland Felber selbst in die sinologische Lehre und betätigten sich als Übersetzer (Irmtraud Fessen-Henjes). Abgesehen von den deutschen Studenten studierten in diesem Jahrgang zwei Ungarn, Eva Podochony und Peter Polonyi, heute hauptberuflicher Übersetzer, sowie die Koreanerin Cui Dongjin.

Aus der Mongolei kamen in diesem Jahrgang an der Fakultät für Chinesische Literatur und Sprache insgesamt vier Studenten; ein weiterer studierte an der Fakultät für Geschichte. Obwohl die Mongolei ein Nachbarland Chinas ist und beide Länder eine lange Geschichte der gegenseitigen Beziehungen verbindet, begann man erst im 19. Jahrhundert mit einer Intensivierung auch des wissenschaftlichen Austauschs. Zu dieser Zeit wurden mehr als 30 klassische chinesische Werke vom Chinesischen (einige vom Mandschurischen) ins Mongolische übersetzt, darunter „Die Drei Reiche" (三国演义), „Der Traum der Roten Kammer" (红楼梦), „Die Räuber vom Liangshanmoor" (水胡撰) und „Die Inoffizielle Geschichte des Gelehrtenwaldes" (儒林外史). Darüber hinaus gab es auch bereits zweisprachige (mongolisch-chinesische) und dreisprachige (mongolisch-chinesisch-mandschurische) Wörterbücher. Die traditionelle mongolische Sinologie beschränkte sich demnach auf Übersetzungen und das Erstellen von Wörterbüchern, die Lexikografie. Erst diejenigen mongolischen Studenten, die in den 1950er Jahren von der Regierung zum Studium nach China entsandt worden waren und später selbst in die Lehre gingen, begründeten eine moderne Sinologie in der Mongolei. Zu ihnen gehören der Historiker Dr. Chulunn Dalay, heute Mitglied der Mongolischen Akademie der Wissenschaften (Ulanbaataar), sowie die Professoren Choijav Lubsanjav[†] und Luvsanvandan Manlajav. Letztere unterrichteten lange Zeit Chinesisch an der Universität und bildeten mongolische Sinologen aus.

Zhang Yajun 张亚军, ehemals Sekretär der Weltgesellschaft für Chinesischunterricht und Spezialist für ChaF-Didaktik, zog folgende Bilanz:

Während der gesamten 1950er Jahre hat sich ChaF fachlich erfolgreich entwickelt, Gruppe für Gruppe durchliefen Auslandsstudenten die entsprechenden Vorbereitungskurse und nahmen dann ihr Fachstudium an chinesischen Hochschulen auf, während wir gleichzeitig Chinesisch-Spezialisten für andere Länder ausbildeten. Heute arbeiten diese ehemaligen Studenten in verschiedenen Ländern im diplomatischen Dienst, im Außenhandel, im Bildungs-, Medien- und Kultursektor und in anderen Bereichen, einige in hohen, verantwortungsvollen Posten, und sie alle sind in den 1950er Jahren Auslandsstudenten gewesen (Zhang Yajun 1990).

Chinesisch als Zweitsprache: Unterrichtsinhalte und -Methoden

Im Vorbereitungskurs für Auslandsstudenten an der Peking Universität herrschte eine internationale Atmosphäre, Disziplin und kollegiale Beziehungen untereinander wie auch zu chinesischen Studenten. Die Betreuung der Studenten durch die Universität war vorbildlich. Charakteristisch für viele ausländische Studenten war auch ein hohes Maß an Akkulturation.

Unterrichtssprache war Hochchinesisch; Hauptanliegen war die Vermittlung eines bestimmten Wortschatzes und systematischer Grammatikkenntnisse. In den Kursen wurden alle vier

Fertigkeiten – Hören, Sprechen, Schreiben und Lesen – gelehrt; besonders gefördert wurden jedoch das Hörverständnis und die mündliche Ausdrucksfähigkeit. Die Unterrichtsmethoden waren dem damaligen Schwerpunkt des Unterrichts, der Erklärung der Grammatik, entsprechend. Heute wird dies „Grammatik-Übersetzungs-Methode"[3] genannt.

Welches Unterrichtsmaterial wurde benutzt? Im Jahr 1958 wurde für die Studenten des Vorbereitungskurses das „Chinesische Sprachlehrbuch der Peking Universität" (北大汉语教科书) zusammengestellt. Dieses Buch setzte sich aus Unterrichtsmaterial zusammen, welches während der vorangegangenen acht Jahre Chinesischunterricht für Ausländer erprobt und für gut befunden worden war.

Unterrichtsschwerpunkt waren grammatische Fragen, aber die Lehrer sprachen während des Unterrichts ausschließlich Chinesisch und verwendeten somit in ihrem Bemühen, bei ihren Studenten alle vier Fertigkeiten zu perfektionieren, zumindest unbewusst Elemente moderner Unterrichtsmethoden, wie die „direkte Methode"[4] (直接法), die „funktionale Methode"[5] (功能法) und die „kommunikative Methode"[6] (交际法).

Aktuelle Trends und Desiderate der ChaF-Didaktik in China

Die Fachdiskussion und Produktion von Fach- und Forschungsliteratur über ChaF-Didaktik, über die Entwicklung der chinesischen Sprachforschung und die moderne chinesische Sprache sind gegenwärtig außerordentlich rege. Es gibt zahlreiche chinesische und ausländische Fachperiodika[7] sowie wissenschaftliche Konferenzen, die von chinesischer oder ausländischer Seite organisiert werden. Meines Erachtens kann der Unterricht der chinesischen Sprache umso effektiver gestaltet werden, je besser die chinesische Sprache erforscht ist. Darüber hinaus sind sprachtypologische und sprachvergleichende Studien für

---

3 Charakteristisch für die „Grammatik-Übersetzungs-Methode" sind: 1. Unterricht in der Muttersprache, geringer Gebrauch der Zielsprache; 2. Erweiterung des Wortschatzes anhand von isolierten Vokabellisten, 3. ausführliche Erläuterungen der Grammatik; 4. Grammatikkenntnisse als Grundlage für eigene Satzbildungen, viele Konjugations-, Deklinationsübungen; 5. frühe Lektüre klassischer Texte; 6. wenig Inhaltsanalysen von Texten, Lektüre als grammatikalische Übungen (Brown 2000: 52f.).

4 Merkmale der „direkten Methode" sind: 1. Prinzip der Einsprachigkeit: Die Zielsprache ist auch Unterrichtssprache; 2. Vermittlung alltagsrelevanter Vokabeln und Sätze ; 3. Stärkung der mündlichen Ausdrucksfähigkeit durch Rollenspiele und spielerische Dialoge; 4. induktive Grammatikerklärungen; 5. Einführung neuer Elemente durch Vorführung und Wiederholung; 6. Veranschaulichung durch Demonstrationen, Objekte, Bilder; 7. Schwerpunkte Sprechen und Hören; 8. Betonung der korrekten Aussprache und Grammatik (Brown 2000: 52f.).

5 Die „funktionale Methode" betont die sprachliche Funktion (semantisch, syntaktisch, pragmatisch; appellativ, expressiv, ästhetisch u.a.) und die kommunikative Funktion (Wirkung) eines grammatischen Elements im *Kontext* (Dorn 2005).

6 Die „kommunikative Methode" begreift die Fremdsprache als Kommunikationsmittel, hebt ab auf die Aktivierung einer eigenständigen Kommunikation des Lerners und eine stärkere Berücksichtigung der Umgebungsvariablen des jeweiligen Lernerumfelds wie Alter, Geschlecht oder Beruf (Dorn 2005).

7 So zum Beispiel die Fachzeitschriften „Sprachdidaktik und –Forschung" (语言教学与研究 *yuyan jiaoxue yu yanjiu*), „Chinesisch als Fremdsprache weltweit" (世界汉语教学 *shiji hanyu jiaoxue*); den alle drei Jahre erscheinenden „Konferenzbericht der Guoji Hanyu Jiaoxue Taolunhui" (国际汉语教学讨论会报告 *guoji hanyu jiaoxue taolunhui baogao*); sowie entsprechende Periodika für den deutschen resp. englischen Sprachraum, „CHUN – Chinesischunterricht" und „Journal of the Chinese Language Teachers Association" u.a.

die Entwicklung von ChaF unverzichtbar, denn erst im Vergleich mit anderen Sprachen können die Besonderheiten der chinesischen Sprache bestimmt werden.

Den wachsenden Ansprüchen an die Ausbildung und die kommunikativen Fähigkeiten von Fremdsprachenspezialisten im Zeitalter der Globalisierung konnten herkömmliche Methoden wie die Grammatik-Übersetzungs-Methode, die audiolinguale Methode und die direkte Methode allein jedoch immer weniger genügen. Daher mussten den neuen Ansprüchen entsprechend neue funktionale Methoden entstehen.

Die theoretische Grundlage der funktionalen Methoden bilden die Soziolinguistik, die Psycholinguistik sowie die „generative Transformationsgrammatik" und die Theorien über Zweitspracherwerb des amerikanischen Linguisten Noam Chomsky (chinesisch: 诺姆•乔姆斯基). Wenn wir uns die Geschichte von ChaF in China ansehen, so sind die alten Methoden nicht vollständig von neuen abgelöst worden, sondern parallel und miteinander verbunden entstanden, sie haben sich gegenseitig beeinflusst und existieren gleichberechtigt nebeneinander. Chomsky hatte dies bereits in seinem Konzept einer „Universalgrammatik" erkannt. Hier zeigt sich erneut, dass Unterrichtsmethoden immer auch von den Zielen und den Rezipienten des Unterrichts abhängen.

Nach dem Tod Mao Zedongs und seit Beginn der Reform- und Öffnungspolitik im Jahr 1979 wird der Entwicklung von ChaF-Didaktik und ChaF als eigener Disziplin große Aufmerksamkeit geschenkt. Angesichts eines weltweiten Mangels an qualifizierten Chinesischlehrern gelten besondere Bemühungen der Ausdehnung der Lehrerausbildung und Verbesserung der Qualität der Lehrer. Eine wichtige Voraussetzung hierfür ist die Entwicklung eines wissenschaftlichen Bewusstseins bei den Lehrern.

Lu Jianming 陆建明, Linguist an der Peking Universität, formulierte das Problem so:

Im Allgemeinen kommen praktizierende ChaF-Lehrer aus den verschiedensten Disziplinen, so zum Beispiel Literatur, Philologie, Geschichte, Philosophie, Fremdsprachen, Psychologie usw. Obwohl sie persönlich den Beruf des Chinesischlehrers ausüben, forschen sie üblicherweise lediglich in ihren Herkunftsdisziplinen weiter und denken kaum darüber nach, wie sie ihre Fachkenntnisse nun in den Chinesischunterricht einbringen oder gar zu einem organischen Bestandteil desselben machen könnten (Lu Jianming 2004: 178).

Lu Jianming fordert eine professionelle Arbeitshaltung von ChaF-Lehrern: Sie sollen selbst eine stärkere (lebenslange) Lernhaltung einnehmen, aktuelle Forschungen verfolgen und eigene Forschungsbeiträge leisten. Lu hat außerdem betont, dass ChaF-Unterricht in der Hauptsache Sprach- und Zeichenunterricht sei. Dies mag selbstverständlich scheinen; man kann die Bedeutung dieser Aussage jedoch nicht genug hervorheben, denn sie hat eine entscheidende Wende herbeigeführt: Seitdem ist in China viel dafür getan worden, die Entwicklung von ChaF als eigene Fachdisziplin voranzutreiben.

Die chinesische Sprach- und Schriftforschung wie auch die Fremdsprachendidaktik hat seither zahlreiche Arbeiten zu den Bereichen Grammatik, Lexikografie, chinesische Schriftzeichen, Phonologie und Phonetik hervorgebracht. In der ChaF-Didaktik gibt es neue Arbeiten zur Ton-, Wortschatz-, Grammatik- und Zeichenlehre, sowie auch Analysen der häufigsten Fehler, die Ausländer beim Erlernen der chinesischen Sprache machen. Ein weiteres großes Thema ist die Verwendung von Multimedia und Netzwerken (Fernstudienmodelle) im Unterricht. Neue interessante Konzepte und Sichtweisen beginnen herkömmliche abzulösen: So gibt es zwar noch Wissenschaftler, welche das zeichenbasierte Konzept verteidigen.[8] Aufgrund der Besonderheiten der chinesischen Sprache wie Form, Tonalität, Bedeutung gehen sie vom einzelnen Schriftzeichen aus und meinen, dass dieses die Grundeinheit der chinesischen Sprache darstelle. Die Mehrheit vertritt jedoch ein grammatikbasiertes Konzept: Hier gilt das Wort, welches sich aus Ton und Bedeutung zusammensetzt, als Grundeinheit der chinesischen Sprache.

Ein weiterer wichtiger Aspekt der Fremdsprachendidaktik ist die Verbindung von Sprache und Kultur. Die chinesische (deutsche, kubanische…) Gesellschaft und Kultur erschließt sich nur *dem* Lernenden, der auch die chinesische (~) Sprache beherrscht – und umgekehrt. Wichtig am Fremdsprachenunterricht ist beides: die Vermittlung von Sprachkenntnissen und von kulturellem Wissen zur Entfaltung eines „Sprachgefühls" (语感). Moderner Sprachunterricht konfrontiert die Lernenden in Form von Rollenspielen u.ä. mit alltagsrelevanten und lebensnahen Situationen, Problemen und Vokabeln. In praktischen Übungen muss die Technik des situativen Dialogs ausgeweitet werden, damit Studenten Sprachsicherheit gewinnen, das Gefühl bekommen die Sprache zu beherrschen. Wenn man dieses Gefühl bei den Studenten weckt und ihnen eine authentische Spracherfahrung verschafft, so ist es leicht, auch ihre innere Motivation zu stimulieren.

Ein Grundkonzept ist aus der Grammatik-Übersetzungs-Methode geblieben, nämlich der humanistische Ansatz der geistigen Bildung des Lernenden, des Heranbildens der eigenen Persönlichkeit. Von diesem Standpunkt betrachtet ist Sprache nicht nur das wichtigste Kommunikationsmittel, sondern auch die wichtigste Funktion im menschlichen Leben. Die sprachlichen Fähigkeiten eines Menschen zu erweitern, bedeutet also, zu seinem persönlichen Wachstum beizutragen.

Der Unterschied zwischen verschiedenen Sprachen liegt nicht nur in Klang und Bedeutung, sondern auch in den dahinter verborgenen nationalen Kulturen und Mentalitäten. Wenn wir das Erlernen von Fremdsprachen mit dem Erwerb der Muttersprache vergleichen, so ist der auffälligste Unterschied der, dass es sich bei Ersterem um eine transkulturelle Aktivität handelt. Im ChaF-Unterricht ist die Entwicklung der Eigeninitiative des Lernenden die Quelle jeglicher Lernmotivation. Studenten verfügen bereits über muttersprachliche Kenntnisse, daher sind sie sensibilisiert für die Parallelen und Unterschiede zwischen den Sprachstrukturen und auch den kulturellen Merkmalen ihrer Muttersprache und der Fremdsprache. Diese Fähigkeit zum Vergleich stellt ein gewaltiges Potenzial zum Erlernen von Fremdsprachen dar. Wenn wir den Unterricht richtig anleiten und vielseitige Lernmodelle verwenden, dann können wir einen Wandel von passiven zu aktiven Lernstrategien[9], von der passiven Anerkennung einer Information zum aktiven Verfügen über eine Information herbeiführen, die Lernenden dazu bringen, eine Forschungshaltung zum Lernen aufzubringen und ihre Selbstlernmotivation vorantreiben. Nicht zuletzt fördern wir auf diese Weise auch ihre interkulturelle Kommunikationskompetenz.

Kennzeichnend für die späten 1970er Jahre war die Suche nach verlässlichen Partnern für Bildungs- und Lernkooperationen und die Gründung von Bildungsinstitutionen im Ausland. Die Zahl der Auslandsstudenten in China ist heute ungleich höher als in den 1950er Jahren. Viele kommen aus Chinas Nachbarländern. Die Gründe hierfür sind: eine verbesserte Infrastruktur, verbesserte Transportwege und relativ niedrige Studiengebühren. Die

---

[8] So zum Beispiel der in Shanghai ansässige Linguist Fan Wenguo 翻文国
[9] Vgl. hierzu auch die Termini „surface learning" vs. „deep-learning" bei Biggs 1996.

wichtigsten Faktoren sind jedoch die positiven Ergebnisse der Hochschul- und Bildungsreform seit 1978 und die erhöhte Qualität des chinesischen Bildungsangebots. Shen Wenzhong 沈文忠, Institut für Internationale Beziehungen der Shanghaier Fudan Unversität, bezifferte die Nachbarländer, aus denen Studenten nach China kommen, auf 19: Nord- und Südkorea, Japan, Philippinen, Brunei, Malaysia, Indonesien, Vietnam, Laos, Myanmar, Indien, Nepal, Pakistan, Afghanistan, Tadschikistan, Kirgisistan, Kasachstan, Mongolei und Russland (Shen Wenzhong 2004: 118). Die meisten dieser Studenten hätten nicht nur die chinesische Sprache erlernt, sondern vielseitige berufliche Aktivitäten aufgenommen, mittels derer wiederum mehr Menschen weltweit die Möglichkeit erhielten, Chinesisch zu lernen. Dies sei auch das Ziel, das China im 21. Jahrhundert erreichen will. Lu Jianming, Peking Universität, prognostizierte:

Die chinesische Sprache ist international immer gefragter und könnte bald weltweit zur zweitwichtigsten Sprache nach Englisch aufsteigen. Der Unterricht von Chinesisch als Zweitsprache wird daher bislang ungekannte Fortschritte machen (Lu Jianming 2004: 227).

Abschließend bleibt zu wünschen, dass weiterhin eine Mischung der besten sprachdidaktischen Traditionen und Erfahrungen verschiedener nationaler und theoretischer Herkunft genutzt wird, um die Fachdisziplin ChaF voranzubringen. Dies wird nicht nur zur Entwicklung aller Sprachen, sondern auch der Weltsprachforschung beitragen.

(übersetzt und bearbeitet von Nathalie van Looy)

Literatur

Biggs, John B. (1996) "Western Misperceptions of the Confucian-heritage Learning Culture" in John Biggs und David A. Watkins (Hg.) *The Chinese Learner: Cultural, Psychological and Contextual Influences*, Hongkong: Hongkong UP, S. 45-68.

Brown, Douglas H. (2000) *Teaching by Principles: An Interactive Approach to Language Pedagogy*, Upper Saddle River, New Jersey: Pearson ESL.

Chomsky, Noam (1957) *Syntactic Structures*, Den Haag: Mouton.

Chomsky, Noam (1975) *The Logical Structure of Linguistic Theory*. New York und London: Plenum Press.

Dorn, Nico (2005) „Methodiken des DaF-Unterrichts", http://www.texttexturen.de/arbeiten/daf_methodiken/, aufgerufen am 1.6.2006.

Lu Jianming 陆建明 (2004) *Hanyu jiaoyuan yingyou de yishi* 汉语教员应有的意识 [Über die Notwendigkeit eines Fachbewusstseins bei Chinesischlehrern], in *Zhongguo* 2004, S. 227-232.

Lu Jianming 陆建明 (2004) *Zengqiang xueke yishi, fazhan duiwai hanyu jiaoxue* 《增强学科意识，发展对外汉语教学》 [Das Fachbewusstsein stärken, ChaF-Unterricht entwickeln], in *Shijie hanyu jiaoxue* 世界汉语教学, 1/2004.

Lü Bisong 吕必松 (Hrsg.) (1999) *Yuyan jiaoyu wenti yanjiu lunwenji* 语言教育问题研究论文集 [Aufsatzsammlung zu Problemen des Fremdsprachenunterrichts], Beijing: Huayu jiaoxue.

Polonyi, Peter (1982) *Diák voltam Pekingben* [Auslandsstudenten an der Peking Universität], Budapest: Gondolat.

Schwarcz, Vera (1999) "Garden and Museum: Shadows of Memory at Peking University", in *East Asian History* 17-18 (June-December 1999), S. 169-192.

Shen Wenzhong 沈文忠 (2004) *Shanghai zhoubian guojia liuxuesheng jiaoyu jiqi jige wenti* 上海周边国家留学生教育及其几个问题 [Fragen bezüglich der Bildung von Auslandsstudenten aus Nachbarländern Chinas in Shanghai], in *Zhongguo* 2004, S. 118-126.

Wang Li 王力 (1981) *Zhongguo yuyanxue shi* 中国语言学史 [Geschichte der chinesischen Linguistik], Shanxi: Renmin.

Zhang Yajun 张亚军 (1990) *Duiwai hanyu jiaofaxue* 对外汉语教法学 [Lehrmethoden für ChaF], Beijing: Xiandai.

Zhongguo yu zhoubian guojia jiaoyu jiaoliu ji hanyu jiaoxue yantao hui 中国与周边的国家教育交流及汉语教育研国会 (Hg.) (2004) *Huiyi lunwence* 会议论文册 [Konferenzbeiträge der Konferenz über Bildungszusammenarbeit und Chinesischunterricht in China und seinen Nachbarländern], Jinan: Shandong Universität.

Zhu Dexi 朱德熙/Lu Jianming 陆建明 (1987) *Xiandai hanyu yanjiu xianzhuang yu fazhan* 现代汉语研究现状与发展 [Zur gegenwärtigen Lage und Entwicklung der modernen chinesischen Sprachforschung], Beijing: Yuwen.

Marianne Bastid-Bruguière

China's Internationalization and Foreign Language Learning*

Internationalization means increased communication between various people across borders. It means the need for a common language or several common languages as tools for that communication. Conversely, the teaching of foreign languages within a country can be regarded as an index of its internationalization. A related but more complex issue is the significance of the spread of a country's national language outside that country's borders. How far does promotion of the national language abroad give evidence of, or help, the internationalization process inside that country or elsewhere?

The Chinese, like other nations, have always closely related their identity to their own language, but in China, the written characters have played a specific role in creating a common identity. I am going to give a brief historical survey of their attitude towards foreign language learning and practice, as a way of gauging the extent of China's internationalization today and the changes this development is bringing inside and outside the Chinese world. My focus will be on who has been learning foreign languages and how.

Multilingualism in Ancient Times

The first point to be made is that foreign language teaching in China did not start with the Opium War or even with the regular contact with Europeans which began in the 16th century; it is much older.

Archaeological findings have shown us that, in ancient times, there was nothing like a single Chinese language. In the Classics, interpreters are mentioned who helped in communications with the Northern tribes but in Zhou times, however, the various kingdoms spoke different languages. How they managed to communicate and learn the various idioms is unknown. The language differences in the Warring States period were still great enough to prompt Li Si's language reform in 221 BC, as soon as Qin had established a unified empire. This reform unified not only the script but also the language use, at least in the written form and, from this time onwards, the use of foreign languages in China can really be scrutinized and compared with a clearly identified Chinese language, albeit in the written form.

At that time, foreign languages were required for communicating with people beyond the borders or with non-Han people within the empire, but neither the Qin Empire nor the Han Empire established any special device to provide for linguistic go-betweens; it was mostly foreigners who acted as translators or interpreters. Learning foreign languages was not at all integrated into the education of the Han ethnic group, except on a very personal basis, one famous example being General Zhang Qian 张骞, who remained a prisoner for ten years in Central Asia, then joined the Yuezhi (月氏) in Bactria and married a Xiongnu woman there. He later came back to Chang'an and persuaded Emperor Wudi to launch an offensive against the western regions using the intelligence he had acquired while living there. It is quite likely that in those times, among the Han educated elite, more women

* Lecture at the International Workshop "The Internationalization of China," 22 June 2006, at Freie Universität Berlin, Institute of East Asian Studies. This workshop took place at the newly established Confucius Institute at Free University Berlin, which aims at promoting Chinese language and culture world-wide.

than men would have learned foreign languages due to the practice of sending Chinese wives to the barbarians in order to pacify the latter. It should be noted that very early textbooks and glossaries exist, which were compiled by Vietnamese, Koreans and, later, Japanese and people from the Ryukyu Islands, in order to help them to learn Chinese. On the Chinese side, it is only in the 12th century that we find the equivalent, in the form of the bilingual Tangut-Chinese glossaries for use in communications with the foreign Xixia dynasty (1038-1227) in the North.

The linguistic situation both inside and outside the empire came to pose a challenge to the ruling elites after the fall of the Eastern Han in 220. For several centuries afterwards, the big families and dynasties competing for domination were interbred with many different ethnic groups or came from completely alien stock. They spoke Altaic or Tibeto-Burmese languages. They did not have a script, so that Chinese remained the learned language, and that learned language gradually gained ground among the elites of nomadic populations. However, the Northern aristocracy west of the Taihang range, who dominated society under the Sui and Tang, continued to speak a Turkic language, while east of the Taihang range, the Han aristocracy fought to keep cultural purity and opposed any concession to nomadic cultures.

The Han Chinese had, in fact, lived in a multilingual society for many centuries, but multilingualism became a real issue for Han elites from the 10th century onwards. From the fall of the Tang in 907 to the fall of the Yuan in 1368, Chinese was no longer the only official language in China. Alien conquerors created their own scripts, and used their own languages as *Guoyu* (国语), that is, the official language. We know that under the Liao (916-1125) and the Jin (1115-1234) written translations were made into Khitan and Jurchen.

Among the Han elite, a sustained interest in foreign languages had already been developing in the wake of the translation of Buddhist scriptures. In the 2nd century, the first translations of Buddhist texts had been made by Indian monks, Sogdians, Parthians, Indo-Scythians (Yuezhi 月氏), who had come to Luoyang and learned Chinese. By the end of the 2nd century, the Chinese would tell foreigners which Buddhist texts were to be translated, which means that they could roughly understand the original texts. At the end of the 4th century and in the early 5th century, the great translations were still being made by foreigners: Kumarajiva (Jiumo Luoshi 力鳥摩羅什), for example, was of Kuchean origin. At this time, the Chinese monk Faxian 法顯, though he had traveled to India, did not have a good knowledge of Sanskrit. In the 7th century, the Chinese monks sent their young students (for instance, Xuanzang 玄奘) to Kashmir and Nepal. They came back with new texts and Indian translators. They then worked with those translators to edit translations using the oral translation method: the texts were read aloud by foreigners, and then rewritten by the Chinese. That same method was widely used in the 19th and early 20th century for translating European works.

The manuscripts unearthed in Dunhuang and Turpan give evidence of the large variety of languages in use in the empire from the 10th to the 13th centuries: Sogdian, Tangut, Turkic, Tibetan, Uighur. The bilingual lexicons show that the Han Chinese were then learning and using those languages. The Song emperors did not feel the need to establish any institution for teaching foreign languages, but in the schools which were created for aliens, the so-called *fanxue* (藩学) and *xinminxue* (新民学), Han teachers were hired who could write and speak foreign languages.

Official Teaching of Foreign Languages under the Yuan and Later Dynasties

The official teaching of foreign languages was an innovation of the Yuan dynasty, and has remained a state institution ever since. Under the Yuan, Mongolian was the official language. The Yuan created a system in which each major ethnic group had its schools and examinations leading to official appointments. At the top, in the Mongolian School for Sons of the State (蒙古国子学) in Peking, sons of the Mongolian nobility and officialdom were paid for studying Mongolian translations of the Classics for two or three years; they then passed examinations and received appointments. Later, the sons of Han high officials were also admitted to that school. A Moslem College (回回国子学) on the same model was created in 1289 where Turkic and Persian were taught. In the schools reserved for the Han, only Chinese was taught, but all across the empire, a hierarchy of other schools where the Han Chinese could be admitted up to provincial level offered teaching in other languages and Mongolian. Moreover, at each level of government administration, there were secretary translators in official positions in charge of writing or translating official documents into Mongolian. From the previous *de facto* multilingualism, the Yuan dynasty had stepped forward to official multilingualism; this was also a time of great cultural creativity.

Multilingualism was suppressed by the Ming dynasty, but the official training of interpreters and translators was maintained at the Bureau of the Four Barbarians (四夷馆), where officials in charge of relations with tributary countries were offered the opportunity to learn many languages (Tartar, Jurchen, Mongolian, Turkish, Tangut, Persian, Burmese or Thai). Some of the teachers were foreigners from those regions. The Bureau was also an intelligence office where books and documents regarding those countries were translated. This was the place where the study of the frontier (边学) was born, which became a special and highly developed branch of geopolitics (方志学), especially in the Qing period; Western studies (西学) were grafted onto this in the first half of the 19th century.

The Qing dynasty reactivated official multilingualism, but the Manchu elite was already much more sinicized than the elite of Mongol conquerors had been. Although the Manchu language became the official language alongside the Chinese language, only a small number of government documents needed a Manchu version (imperial proclamations and edicts, and documents related to the management of Manchu population and border regions) and the Manchus did these themselves. They learned Chinese in a special system of schools and examinations established for the sons of the Manchu, Mongol and Han Bannermen and for a few Moslems. The teaching was in Manchu or Mongolian; Chinese was taught, as well as military skills. The Han Chinese who were not Bannermen were totally excluded from those schools: they had to attend their own schools. The training at the Banner schools gave access to ordinary official employment and to government posts that were ethnically reserved for Bannermen.

In addition to affirmative action in favor of their own ethnic minority and of their Mongol allies, which provided a fair number of bilingual or multilingual talents, the Manchus readily developed special programs open to all ethnic groups for training translators and interpreters, according to government needs. The Bureau of the Four Barbarians was maintained under the Hanlin Academy. Then in 1748, since it was redundant with a Bureau for Mongolian translation under the Grand Secretariat and with several provincial offices of translation, it was merged into a service in charge of the reception of foreign envoys (会同馆) under the Board of Rites. In 1758, the Imperial Household created a school for interpreters working in Persian, and ten years later, in Burmese. Since 1708, the Grand Secretariat had arranged for Bannermen children to learn Russian with the help of Russian merchants and servicemen, but a real school of Russian interpreters was established in 1756 (俄罗斯学). The students were taught by Russian residents in Peking and were sent to Russia for further training. At that time, the Imperial College (国子监) received a regular flow of foreign students who studied Chinese: Japanese, Koreans, Vietnamese, Russians since 1728, and many from the Ryukyus.

It is along this line of experience that the official teaching of English and French was introduced in 1862, after the Second Opium War. For that purpose, Prince Gong established the College of Languages (同文馆) in Peking, under the newly created Bureau of Foreign Affairs (总理各国事务衙门). Russian was soon added to the teaching, and the former Russian School was suppressed. German was introduced in 1871, and Japanese in 1897. Originally, admission was going to be restricted only to students who were the sons of Bannermen, but the college was opened to the ordinary Han Chinese right from the beginning. They received a salary from the government. Some foreigners were among the teaching staff; subjects such as, science, law, history and geography also appeared on the curriculum. The school was conceived as an information centre; books and newspapers were collected and a program of translations was set up. Other government schools of this type were opened in Shanghai and Canton. In all military and technical schools then created by the imperial government, learning a foreign language was mandatory.

The methods and textbooks used for teaching foreign languages were based on an empirical and mechanistic approach. We have in our keeping a textbook for learning Mongol dated 1260, which introduces the letters of the alphabet, then the composition of syllables, then words with their pronunciation in Chinese characters. In Ming and Qing times, many textbooks would arrange the words by themes with a Chinese translation. Some of these glossaries would combine five languages, (Manchu, Tibetan, Mongolian, Uighur and Chinese). Students would first learn the words, and then learn the texts by heart. For European languages, primary school textbooks from the related countries were used. That was also the device used by foreign missionaries in schools where they taught their native languages. Latin was the first foreign language for which a Chinese grammar was produced; the second one was French. In 1863, a Dutch missionary, hired to teach French in the *Tongwenguan*, produced a French vocabulary and a French grammar (法国话料，法国话规) in Chinese. For English, the Shanghai College of Languages (方言馆) used the Webster dictionaries and textbooks. The textbooks in Chinese that had been compiled by Protestant missionaries since the 1880s were used only in missionary schools, not in government schools. In 1890, a censor remarked that most graduates were unable to talk with foreigners and that they should be sent for language practice to the various Chinese legations abroad. This proposal was actually carried out after 1896.

On the whole, prior to the Sino-Japanese war of 1894, European languages were studied only by young Manchus and Mongols, by a few Han Chinese from poor gentry families who badly needed a salary, or by people engaged in trade. These language studies were not included in the ordinary and main scope of learning for scholars, nor were they widespread; the same applied to the study of Asian languages.

In this regard, the Han Chinese elites of the last five centuries were very different from top elites elsewhere and even within China itself during earlier periods. These Han elites were almost totally devoid of foreign connections and intercourse: none of them had any interest in becoming a polyglot. Foreign intercourse was left to ethnic minorities, half-blood people, and people with a low social status.

Establishing Foreign Languages within the Scope of Modern Chinese Learning

The situation changed after the defeat by Japan. The golden boys of the big Han families turned eagerly to the study of foreign learning, but they did not invest that much effort in learning foreign languages. Emperor Guangxu certainly showed much more real commitment than most reformers around him when he started to study English regularly in 1895. Many new schools established between 1895 and 1900, however, offered courses in foreign languages. Such courses became the rule in the Chinese elite curriculum with the School Regulations of 1902. The Regulations established a national school system based on the Japanese model, which was, itself, based on the German system. In 1902, foreign language learning appeared at higher primary school level, as optional, for three or four hours a week. The subject was compulsory at secondary school level, for 8 hours a week, and also in practically every specialization at higher education level.

Thus, it was ultimately through the study of European languages that knowledge of foreign languages was able to make its way to the core of Chinese conventional learning and scholarship, in the second half of the 19th century. Initially, this new trend owed much more to the impulse of the Manchu aristocracy than to the will of the Han elites. It was Prince Gong who wrested the creation of the *Tongwenguan* from the Han Chinese high officialdom.

The inroads of foreign language learning into Chinese general education and scholarship continued and broadened in the 20th century, although at an uneven pace, and also with setbacks.

The strong position of foreign languages adopted in the 1902 School Regulations was maintained, with very little variation, until 1950. Although the implementation of government regulations was very uneven, the efforts of local elites in the 1920s and 1930s were successful in producing at least one secondary school with foreign language teaching in each county. Japanese and English were the favorite languages. A high standard of learning was then seen as inseparable from foreign language knowledge and from knowledge of the foreign world. Such a practice was maintained consistently in Taiwan, but the mainland experienced a turnabout. Foreign language teaching remained only at higher middle school level, mostly for Russian, with hours cut by half and then reduced to three hours a week. English regained some ground in the early 1960s. In that period, from late 1960 to 1965, 14 special secondary language schools were opened, copying the pattern found in Soviet Russia, with intensive language training of 7 to 9 hours a week from the first year of lower middle school, and part of the general subjects taught in a foreign language. Some of these schools also had an attached primary school with early foreign language training. They were highly selective and produced excellent linguists. Nevertheless, since many ordinary middle schools could not provide any foreign language education, that subject was suppressed in University entrance examinations, and remained only as a special field in university curriculum.

The Cultural Revolution suppressed all foreign language teaching in middle schools. It came back in higher middle schools in 1978, with 4 hours a week, then 7 or 8 in 1981, and today 4 or 5 hours a week, 8 or 9 in the fifty secondary language schools. Now, foreign languages are taught also 4 or 5 hours a week in lower middle schools, and they have become a compulsory subject in university entrance examinations and in most higher education curricula. Today, some 90 million pupils are supposed to be learning a foreign language in middle schools, and over 15 million in primary schools, English in over 95 percent cases. However, an official figure released in April 2006, on the occasion of the visit to New York of Chinese Education Minister Zhou Ji, claims that more than 200 million Chinese children are learning English (Xinhua 2006). New pedagogy, modern audiovisual equipment, internet devices, cooperation with or borrowing from foreign specialized institutions like the British Council, and the Goethe Institut have been widespread, so that the quality and efficiency of teaching has greatly improved and compares quite favorably to the achievements in countries with good performances in this field like Holland or Scandinavian countries.

Efforts have also been made to induce the Han Chinese to learn the "inner" foreign languages, that is, the languages of national minorities. Results have been far less successful in this respect, since in 2005 only 5 percent of the population could communicate in those languages; at the same time, only 53 percent of the whole population was able to communicate with others in Standard Chinese 普通话) (China Daily 2005). However, among a large number of the generation now between 15 and 30, a foreign language is part of their life, and they tend to use it for their own individual purposes, whether business, professional or intellectual promotion, or simply pleasure. This situation and the paramount importance given to foreign languages in the training and evaluation of students have recently caused widespread protests.

The protests have been voiced at the meetings of the People's Congress and in the media (Cai Shihong 2004, Foshanshi diyi xiaoxue 2006, Gu Haibin 2003).[1] The argument against the stress on foreign languages is not a blunt plea for national culture, as was the case in the 1920s and 1930s; it uses the much more obnoxious grievance that the stress on foreign languages discriminates against children from poor families and from rural areas, and increases social inequality. This argument seems quite misplaced, because today, knowledge of foreign languages is no longer the privilege of a top elite, it has become freely accessible to the young middle class to whom it offers access to new thoughts, new experience, new exchanges, and new types of artistic expression through the internet and other media.

A Linguistic Turn in Foreign Policy: Promoting the Chinese Language Abroad

At the same time, and only partly as a response to the attacks against the growing role of foreign languages in Chinese learning and culture, the Chinese government has recently engaged in an active policy of promoting the Chinese language abroad. This linguistic turn in foreign policy is a very significant phenomenon. Imperial China had always been careful to help her neighbors, or at least some of their elites, to learn some Chinese. When Chinese emigration was growing steadily in the 19th and early 20th century, attention and material means were given to help the overseas Chinese to keep their native language and culture. This policy was maintained consistently by the Communist regime.

However, very little interest had ever been shown in promoting the Chinese language and culture to the non-ethnic Chinese in more distant regions; rather the reverse was true. The

---

[1] See also the reports from the 2003 session of the People's Congress; http://www.people.com.cn/GB/shizheng/252/10307/10352/20030313/943154.html, accessed 3 August 2004.

Americans had to claim the right to buy Chinese books and to hire Chinese teachers in the Wangxia treaty of 1844,, because such actions were so far forbidden to foreigners by imperial regulations. For many years, Macao still remained the only place for Westerners to learn Chinese. After the Second Opium War, the Qing government donated Chinese books to foreign sinological libraries on several occasions, but these were return gifts for books presented by foreign governments. Eventually, in the summer of 1919, after the Versailles Peace Treaty, the Republican President Xu Shichang adopted a program for a bold foreign cultural policy suggested to him by a young returned student from Belgium who had been a fellow of the Carnegie Foundation in Japan.

In a bid to win over European public opinion to the Chinese side and to foster more understanding, the idea was to organize and subsidize the teaching of the Chinese language and civilization for a wide audience. This initiative resulted, in 1920, in the founding of the Institute for Chinese Studies in the Sorbonne building in Paris, at Chinese expense, with some support from the French Ministry of Education. It met with fierce opposition from Paul Pelliot who refused to accept that French sinology should be placed under the political control of China. Marcel Granet, whom Pelliot hated and had so far kept out of any university position, was put in charge. Scholarships were granted to students from other European countries to come to study at the Paris Institute and other institutes were planned for the near future, in Berlin and Vienna.

As a matter of fact, the Chinese side was unable to provide any more funding after 1922. The Institute managed to survive on a low profile through some French funding, and was really rescued after 1926 by a regular allowance from the Boxer Indemnity Fund, but kept under tight management control by the French sinology establishment, including Pelliot. The Guomindang government nevertheless went on giving support to institutions that promoted the Chinese language and culture abroad and even enlarged its commitments in this field, particularly through participation in the Organization of Intellectual Cooperation under the League of Nations. That policy was continued after 1949 from Taiwan, but it was completely dropped by Peking, except towards close Communist allies.

Recently, the first step taken by Chinese authorities to internationalize the Chinese language has been the establishment of the HSK (汉语水平考试) test in 1990. The progression rate of the number of applicants in the first ten years has been as high as for the TOEFL (Test of English as a Foreign Language) during its first ten years. Today, there are more than 30 million people learning Chinese as a foreign language in over 85 countries. The National Office for Teaching Chinese as a Foreign Language, Hanban (汉办), was established in 1987, headed by 11 State Departments (Foreign Affaires, Finance, Trade, Culture, Education, Publications, Radio, TV and Film). In late 1996, research centers were established in Shanghai and later Peking to monitor foreign sinology. The number of scholarships for foreign students was increased, a fellowship program for sinologists was started in 2002, and special foreign sinologists' conferences have been convened since 2004. The major Chinese embassies have lately been endowed with an enlarged cultural center and generous funding for organizing exhibitions, lectures, and film shows and for publishing lavishly illustrated journals. A major offensive in the last two years has been the opening of Confucius Institutes.

It is interesting to note that in his third memorial to the Guangxu Emperor, in June 1895, Kang Youwei suggested that China should adopt an active cultural policy abroad. He proposed sending literati well trained in Confucianism to teach barbarians abroad in the various centers of scholarship. They would, at the same time, gather intelligence from the local elites and propagate the Chinese standpoint. The first Confucius Institute opened in South Korea in November 2004. Up to June 2006, agreements had been signed in 25 countries for the establishment of 40 such institutes and the plan is to set up one hundred. A specificity of this program is that it bypasses national governments and relies directly on the foreign local society.

Transnationalization?

We thus find a very unusual situation. For a very large proportion of the Chinese top elite over the age of 50, foreign languages are not part of their culture. This type of learning belongs more to a middle class group outside government control or intervention. They use it for their own purposes and it makes them change their "Chineseness" through the new tastes, aspirations and ideas which the foreign language tool conveys to them. It also changes their Chineseness in the eyes of others. On the other hand, learning Chinese is spreading spontaneously all over the world; there is obviously a drive everywhere to learn more about China. The political agenda that clearly underlies the Chinese government's new cultural foreign policy is not perceived by the general public abroad. Chinese government initiatives are well received; universities are competing to attract a Confucius Institute. Also, the Chinese teachers who, at grass-roots level, are promoting the cultural expansion belong to that middle class group of internationalizing Chinese. Some similarities can be identified here with the spread of Greek in the Roman Empire or the spread of Arabic in the Middle Ages, despite the background to China's economic rise. In fact, the role of the Chinese state in these linguistic developments is not so important since they belong more to the realm of transnational phenomena, or what is called *minjian* 民间, "the people's space," in Chinese. It is a case perhaps of transnationalization, ahead of internationalization.

References

Bastid, Marianne (1971) *Aspects de la réforme de l'enseignement en Chine au début du 20e siècle*, Paris/La Haye, Mouton.

Bastid-Bruguière, Marianne (2004) "Republican China's early attempt at foreign cultural policy," in *Kitai v dialoge tsivilizatsii. K 70-letiyu academika M. L. Titarenko* [China in the dialogue of civilizations. For the 70th jubilee of academician Mikhail L. Titarenko], Moscow: Pamyatniki istoricheskoi mysli, pp. 741-749.

Cai Shigong 采石工 (2004) "Waiyujiaoyu ying yi zhenshi shichang xuqiu wei daoxiang" 外语教育应以真实市场需求为导向 [Foreign language teaching should be oriented towards the real needs of the market], 4 June 2004, website of Foshanshi diyi xiaoxue 佛 山 市 第 一 小 学 [First Primary School of Foshan City], http://xy.ccjy.cn/jyxx.asp?id=89, accessed 2 August 2006.

China Daily (2005) "Mandarin's Influence Reaches Deep in China: Survey, 3 January 2005, http://www.chinadaily.com.cn/english/doc/2005-01/03/content_405494.htm, accessed 3 August 2006.

China National Office for Teaching Chinese as a Foreign Language website: http://english.hanban.edu.cn.

DeFrancis, John (1984) *The Chinese Language: Fact and Fantasy*, Honolulu: University of Hawaii Press.

Eberhard, Wolfram (1952) *Conquerors and Rulers: Social Forces in Medieval China*, Leiden: Brill.

Gu Haibin 顾海兵 (2003) "Zhongguo gonggong waiyujiaoyu fansi" 中国公共外语教育反思 [Reflection about public foreign language education in China], originally published in *Nanfang zhoumo* 南方周末 [Southern Weekly], http://www.asust.cn/xcb/srwjb/info_Print.asp?ArticleID=1051, accessed 3 August 2006. See also reports from the 2003 session of the People's Congress, http://www.people.com.cn/GB/shizheng/252/10307/10352/20030313/943154.html, accessed 3 August 2004.

Jiaoyu da cidian 教育大辞典 (1991-1992) [The great dictionary of education], Shanghai: Shanghai jiaoyu, 3 vols.

Norman, Jerry (1988) *Chinese*, Cambridge: Cambridge UP.

Ross, Heidi (1993) *China Learns English: Language Teaching and Social Change in the People's Republic of China*, New Haven: Yale UP.

Su Jing 蘇精 (1985) *Qingji Tongwenguan ji qi shisheng* 清季同文館及其師生 [The late Qing College of Languages, its teachers and students], Taipei: Shanghai yinshua 1985.

Xinhua News Agency (2006) "China, US Announce New Chinese Language, Cultural Initiative," 20 April 2006, http://www.chinaview.cn, accessed 3 August 2006.

Zhongguo jiaoyu nianjian 1949-1981 中国教育年鉴 1949-1981 (Chinese Education Yearbook 1949-1981) (1984), Peking: Zhongguo da baike quanshu / Chinese Encyclopædia Press.

"Zhongguo xianxing waiyujiaoyu zhidu de falü sikao" 中国现行外语教育制度的法律思考 [A legal examination of the current system of foreign language education in China], 7 July 2006, http://www.6318.cn/peixun/yy/200607/46081.html, accessed 3 August 2006.

Zhu Youhuan 朱有瓛 (1983-1993) *Zhongguo jindai xuezhi shiliao* 中国近代学制史料 [Materials on Chinese Scholars of Modern Times], Shanghai: Huadong shifan daxue.

Joachim Krüger

Die KPD und China (1921-1927)*

Die Entwicklung in China, vor allem der Einfluss der Guomindang unter Führung Sun
Yat-sens, bestärkten die Komintern (KI) in ihren Bemühungen um die maximale
Unterstützung der nationalen und sozialen Bewegung in diesem Lande. So entschloss
man sich, eine größere Zahl politischer und militärischer Berater für die Guomindang zu
entsenden. Der bekannteste Repräsentant war Michail Borodin.

Das Auslaufen der revolutionären Nachkriegskrise in Europa, besonders in Deutschland,
rückten die Geschehnisse in China noch stärker ins Zentrum der Aufmerksamkeit der KI.
Neue Hoffnungen auf den weiteren Aufschwung eines revolutionären Weltprozesses,
diesmal im Fernen Osten, wurden genährt. So schrieb der sowjetische Außenkommissar
Čičerin am 4. November 1924 an den sowjetischen Vertreter in China, Karachan: „.... dass
der Osten ebenso wichtig und sogar noch wichtiger als der Westen sei. Die breiten Massen interessieren sich für ihn".[1] Gemäß dieser Einschätzung organisierten das Exekutivkomitee der KI (EKKI) und unter seiner Leitung einzelne kommunistische Parteien vielfältige Aktionen und machten große Teile der Bevölkerung ihrer Länder mit den Ereignissen in China bekannt. Die KPD nahm dabei einen herausgehobenen Platz ein. Aus zunächst nur geringen und kaum diversifizierten Beziehungen erwuchs in wenigen Jahren
eine breite internationale Solidaritätsbewegung für das chinesische Volk und seine Revolution. Sie umfasste nicht nur bedeutende Teile der Arbeiterbewegung, sondern auch
eine erhebliche Zahl von Intellektuellen, unter ihnen bekannte Schriftsteller, Hochschul-
lehrer, Forscher und Journalisten. Es war kein Zufall, dass die zunächst in der UdSSR ge-
gründete Internationale Rote Hilfe (MOPR) als Internationale Arbeiterhilfe (IAH) in Berlin ihren Sitz nahm. Deutsche Kommunisten standen an der Spitze dieser Organisation
und erwarben sich das Verdienst, die internationale Unterstützung für die chinesische Revolution 1925 bis 1927 wesentlich mit vorangebracht zu haben.

In Deutschland trug die Solidaritätsbewegung neben ihren Leistungen für China vor allem
dazu bei, dass das bis dahin entstandene und teilweise verblasste, stark kolonialistisch ge-
prägte Chinabild durch ein genaueres, die sozialen Bedingungen besser widerspiegelndes
ersetzt wurde. Viele Klischees kolonialen Ursprungs wurden überwunden oder doch zu-
rückgedrängt. Die Leiden, aber auch die Kampfbereitschaft und der Stolz des chinesischen Volkes fanden Eingang in das Alltagsbewusstsein großer Teile der deutschen Bevölkerung.

Nicht übersehen kann man dabei, dass die Reaktion und Berichterstattung durch die KPD
vor allem ihrem ideologischen und politischen Kampf in Deutschland diente. So kam der
kommunistische Reichstagsabgeordnete Robert Neddermayer in seinem Bericht an das
Organisationsbüro der KPD-Zentrale über das Auftreten zweier Guomindang-Vertreter
aus Göttingen bzw. Berlin auf dem Bezirksparteitag der KPD Hessen-Waldeck hinsichtlich der Übersetzung ihrer Ansprachen zu dem Eingeständnis, es sei „praktisch ja ziem-

---

* Beitrag auf der Konferenz des Fernost-Instituts der Russischen Akademie der Wissenschaften „China,
  die chinesische Zivilisation und die Welt. Vergangenheit, Gegenwart und Zukunft", Moskau 27.-28.
  Oktober 2006.
[1] AVP RF, F.0100, op.8, d.2, p.110, l.234.

lich gleichgültig, was dieser Mensch gesagt hat, da kein Casseler Arbeiter seine Ausführungen verstand".[2]

In der ersten Entwicklungsphase der KPD spielten Elemente der organisatorischen Festigung, die Erfordernisse der revolutionären Krise in Deutschland, bewaffnete Kämpfe und Aufstände wie auch utopische Vorstellungen vom Herannahen eines weltweiten Triumphes der Revolution die vorherrschende Rolle. Abgesehen von dem Blick auf Sowjetrussland hatte man den internationalen Faktor noch kaum im Visier.

Die Bildung der KP Chinas erfolgte nach der Gründung der KPD. Gegenseitige Beziehungen waren vor allem wegen geringer Kraft und Möglichkeiten auf chinesischer Seite zunächst nicht zu realisieren. In der deutschen kommunistischen Presse erschienen erste Meldungen über China eher sporadisch und zufällig, nicht kontinuierlich. Die Zentrale der KPD bezog ihre Informationen durch die Mitarbeit in Kominternorganen und über die Führung der KI. So hatte sie, wie die Führungen anderer kommunistischer Parteien, vom Leiter der Agitprop-Abteilung des EKKI, Bela Kun, den Auftrag erhalten, „unverzüglich" die Presse und die Arbeitermassen über die Ereignisse in China zu informieren. Kun hatte in seinem Schreiben vom 10. September 1924 allerdings nur die „außergewöhnliche Bedeutung für die Entlarvung der demokratisch-pazifistischen Form des englischen, amerikanischen und französischen Imperialismus" hervorgehoben. [3] Zusammen mit diesem Auftrag war Informationsmaterial übersandt worden.[4] Es behandelte detailliert den „Kampf der Imperialisten gegen die nationale Bewegung in Südchina" und dessen „Folgen in Mittel- und Nordchina". Der Bürgerkrieg, hieß es, sei „nicht bloß durch Einmischung der Imperialisten, sondern auch durch innere wirtschaftliche Prozesse bedingt". Die Kämpfe könnten sich zu „einem allgemeinen nationalen Bürgerkrieg entwickeln". Sun Yat-sens Kampf entziehe die „schaffenden Schichten der Bevölkerung" dem Einfluss der Militaristen, und die revolutionäre Studentenschaft und die Arbeiterorganisationen bildeten „den Mittelpunkt der antiimperialistischen Bewegung". Eine Orientierung auf Solidaritätsaktionen und Großkundgebungen wurde noch nicht gegeben.

Auch wenn sich in jenen Jahren chinesische KP-Mitglieder in GMD-Organisationen in Deutschland aufhielten, kam es zunächst nicht zum Kontakt zwischen ihnen und der KPD-Zentrale. Zhou Enlai und Zhu De waren in der KPD nicht bekannt, obwohl es in der KPD bereits einen festen Apparat für Ausländer gab und später eine „chinesische Sprachgruppe" geschaffen wurde. Veranstaltungen über China wurden zumeist noch von Chinesen selbst bestritten. So fand am 1. Februar 1924 in Berlin, organisiert von der Zeitung „Neuer Tag", ein erster Vortragsabend mit Lichtbildern über China statt. Chinesen informierten über die allgemeine politische Lage, die neue chinesische Erziehung, die Jugend- und die Frauenbewegung sowie über die moderne Industrie in China. Umrahmt wurde das Programm von musikalischen Darbietungen. Das Mitglied der KP Chinas, Liao Huanxing, sprach zum Thema „Sun Yat-sen und Deutschland", über die Sun-Yat-sen-Bewegung und das industrielle China.

Gut ein Jahr danach wurde auf Initiative der KPD und weitgehend von ihren Mitgliedern getragen eine außerordentliche Solidaritätskampagne für das chinesische Volk ins Leben

---

2   Barch, SAPMO, RY 1/I 2/3/211, Bl. 68.
3   SAPMO, R 1507/1084b, Bl. 102-106.
4   Ebd., Bl. 103-106.

gerufen. Sie entfaltete sich nun zu einem Kennzeichen der KPD-Politik überhaupt und war verbunden mit einer breiten Informationstätigkeit über die Politik der Guomindang und den beginnenden Nordfeldzug. Als wichtiges Instrument diente dabei die IAH, die mit ihren Aktivitäten ihre vierte internationale Kampagne durchführte.

Nur wenige Tage nach dem Massaker in Shanghai begann in Deutschland eine Serie von Versammlungen und Kundgebungen. In einem Brief an das EKKI vom 26. Juni 1925 konnte Heinz Neumann berichten: „Unsere Chinakampagne geht gut vorwärts. Die Versammlungen sind überall gut besucht."[5]

Solche Veranstaltungen besuchten auch im Namen der Guomindang in Deutschland studierende Chinesen, bei denen es sich zum erheblichen Teil um Kommunisten handelte. Sie trugen dazu bei, dass die Zusammenkünfte zu Demonstrationen der festen Verbundenheit beider Völker genutzt wurden. In einem Schreiben der deutschen Gesandtschaft in Peking vom 6. Mai 1925 an den chinesischen Gesandten in Berlin hatte man bereits auf „eine kleine aber laut und anmaßend auftretende Schar unter den chinesischen Studenten ... die kommunistische Propaganda betreibt und in Versammlungen durch hetzerische Reden das Volk aufreizt" aufmerksam gemacht und gewarnt: „Dieses Treiben ... kann die deutsche Regierung im Interesse der Ruhe und Ordnung in ihrem Lande auf die Dauer nicht dulden ... sie sind eine Gefahr und eine Plage für beide Länder."[6]

In Berlin hatten die kommunistischen Mitglieder des chinesischen Studentenklubs im August dessen Führung übernommen, um ihn gegen die deutsche Verwaltung und die chinesische Gesandtschaft zu verteidigen.[7] Auf vielen Zusammenkünften der KPD in Deutschland und allen großen Solidaritätskundgebungen nahmen vor allem Mitglieder aus diesem Verein teil und trugen mit Ansprachen zu eindrucksvollen gemeinsamen deutsch-chinesischen Manifestationen bei.

Als einzige deutsche Partei kondolierte die KPD am 12. März 1925 dem Zentralen Exekutivkomitee (ZEK) der Guomindang zum Tode Sun Yat-sens. In ihrem Schreiben hob sie Gemeinsamkeiten der werktätigen Massen beider Länder im Kampf gegen das europäische und das amerikanische Großkapital hervor. „Die Befreiung der Welt von der Zwangsherrschaft des Großkapitals ist nur möglich durch den solidarischen Kampf der Werktätigen des Ostens und des Westens, Asiens und Europas. Es wird für alle Zeiten das Verdienst Dr. Sun Yat-sens bleiben, dass er die Notwendigkeit dieser internationalen Solidarität erkannte." (Tiedke 1989:23). Was die Zentrale der KPD versicherte: „Die deutsche Arbeiterschaft wird auch weiter alles tun, um den Befreiungskampf der chinesischen Werktätigen zu fördern" (ebd.) wurde schon auf einer Trauerkundgebung in einer großen Versammlungsstätte am Potsdamer Platz in Berlin sichtbar. Liao Huanxing hatte als Sekretär der „Chinesischen kommunistischen Gruppe in Deutschland" Vertreter der KPD-Zentrale eingeladen, und Arthur Rosenberg hielt eine Rede, in der die oben genannten Schwerpunkte wiederholt wurden.

Nachdem die ersten Nachrichten über die Massaker vom 30. Mai 1925, den Beginn des Generalstreiks der Arbeiter, Kaufleute und Studenten in Shanghai und des Generalstreiks in Hongkong Deutschland erreicht hatten, stellte die KPD die erprobten Schwerpunkte in den Mittelpunkt ihrer Initiativen und Aktivitäten. Am 22. Juni wurde in den Berliner Pha-

---

5 SAPMO, RY 5/I/6/3/145, Bl. 25.
6 PAAA, Berlin, Peking 472, unpag.
7 Ebd.

rus-Sälen eine öffentliche Kundgebung abgehalten, auf der ein Mitglied der Guomindang sowie Ruth Fischer für die KPD und Willi Münzenberg für die IAH sprachen. Weitere Kundgebungen organisierte die KPD in jenen Tagen in Hamburg, Saarbrücken, Mannheim, Frankfurt am Main, Bremen, Leipzig, Düsseldorf, Jena, Essen, Magdeburg, Chemnitz, Dresden, Halle und Breslau. Beim Deutschen Komitee für Chinahilfe gingen vom 22. Juni bis zum 8. Juli 1925 Spenden in Höhe von 4 805,25 Mark ein Tiedke 1989:23). Die erste Sammlung der IAH für die Streikenden in China erbrachte 20 802 Mark (*Not und Brot* 43:5). Bis zum 2. Juli gingen bei ihr weitere 27 145,05 Mark ein (Tiedke 1989:34).

Ende Juli/Anfang August 1925 fanden in Deutschland rund 500 China-Kundgebungen statt, darunter mehr als 45 in Sachsen. In Oberschlesien waren es sechs, mit über 13 000 Teilnehmern (*Not und Brot* 45:6). Im August verfassten deutsche Intellektuelle einen Aufruf zur Unterstützung der Hilfsaktionen und wandten sich an chinesische Professoren und Studenten. Es waren unter anderen die Maler Käthe Kollwitz, Otto Nagel, Heinrich Vogeler, Heinrich Zille, die Schriftsteller Alfons Paquet, Erich Mühsam, Ernst Toller, die Pazifisten Gubel, Otto Lehmann-Rußbüldt sowie Erwin Piscator, Wieland Herzfelde und Theodor Lessing. Zu einem Höhepunkt wurde der IAH-Kongress vom 16. August in Berlin unter der Losung „Hände weg von China", auf dem 800 Delegierte aus vielen Ländern und mehrere Tausend Gäste ihre Solidarität mit dem chinesischen Volk bekräftigten.

Die IAH-Zentrale in Berlin hatte ab dem 22. Juli weitere Sympathieerklärungen von Gewerkschaftsgruppen in ganz Deutschland initiiert. Seit dem 19. Juni gab sie außerdem mit insgesamt acht Nummern ein Bulletin der Hilfsaktion „Für China" heraus. Darin wurde über die Kundgebungen im Lande und die Spendenaufkommen wie auch über die Vorgänge in China informiert. Für die Veranstaltungen erschien ein Referentenmaterial mit dem Titel „Der revolutionäre Freiheitskampf in China und das internationale Proletariat". Andere IAH-Materialien waren, in jeweils 10 000 Exemplaren, die Broschüren „Der kapitalistische Kindermord in China" und „Die kapitalistische Hölle in China", in denen über die soziale und politische Lage Chinas berichtet wurde. Mit Unterstützung der IAH erschien am 10. Oktober zum 14. Jahrestag der chinesischen Revolution in 10 000 Exemplaren die Broschüre „Das kämpfende China" des „Hauptverbandes chinesischer Studenten in Deutschland". Sie informierte umfassend über China und gab vor allem einen detaillierten Überblick zu den Kämpfen zwischen dem 31. Mai und dem 12. September 1925. Im Vorwort schrieben die chinesischen Studenten: „Wir danken unseren deutschen Freunden und Brüdern aufrichtig für die von Herzen kommende Sympathie und Solidaritätsbezeugungen und für die praktische Hilfe, die sie zu Beginn des Freiheitskampfes unseren revolutionären Kämpfern erwiesen haben." (Tiedke 1989:39).

Die Hauptkennzeichen aller dieser Veröffentlichungen bestanden in Folgendem: Als politische Kraft in China wurde lediglich die Guomindang, nicht aber die KP Chinas angeführt. Schwerpunkte der Darstellungen waren die Grausamkeit der chinesischen Reaktion und der ausländischen Mächte sowie deren Einmischung und der nationale Aspekt des Kampfes in China. Der aus der Zeitschrift der Roten Gewerkschaftsinternationale Nr.9/1925 im selben Jahr als Buch im Führer-Verlag erschienene Sonderabdruck „Arbeiterbewegung und Revolution in China" zeichnete mit seinen Beiträgen von Karl Radek, Leo Heller, M. Galkowitsch, T. Mandaljan, S. Mstislawski, Sen Katayama und anderen ein umfassendes Bild von der chinesischen Revolution und der Arbeiterbewegung insgesamt. Radek schrieb: „Wenn die Entwicklung der chinesischen Revolution zu einem offenen Zusammenstoß zwischen diesen Massen (Chinas) und dem Imperialismus führt, so werden dadurch der europäischen Revolution die Hände frei." Er plädierte für eine „kolossale Erweiterung des Horizonts der europäischen Arbeiterbewegung, die jetzt erst tatsächlich in ihre internationale Phase tritt" (*Arbeiterbewegung ...* 1925:39). Die unter Führung der IAH in Deutschland ausgelöste kämpferische Solidaritätsbewegung wirkte in genau diese Richtung.

Am 7. Juli hatten die Zentrale der KPD und der „Chinesische kommunistische Studentenklub in Deutschland" (Berlin) eine Vereinbarung über ihre künftige Zusammenarbeit getroffen (Tiedke 1989:36). Die Initiative dazu war von chinesischer Seite ausgegangen. Sie hatten am selben Tag unter Bezugnahme auf die Position der Komintern vorgeschlagen, dass von nun an die Verbindung mit der KPD nicht mehr durch beliebige Vertreter, sondern bevollmächtigte Mitglieder der Exekutive des Studentenklubs erfolgen sollte und dafür Zhang Bojun (Harnisch 1999:248ff) und Hsing Chi Cheng (Hsing Dschi Tscheng) benannt. Verbunden damit war der Hinweis, man sei in der Zentrale der KPD über die Verhältnisse in der Guomindang nicht genau im Bilde, was ihren rechten und linken Flügel anbelangte. Bei den letzten Aktionen der KPD hätten teils Mitglieder der Guomindang und teils Mitglieder des kommunistischen Studentenklubs in einzelnen Städten gesprochen, und so ergaben sich „verschiedene Auffassungen in der Behandlung der aufgeworfenen politischen Fragen". Es wurde empfohlen, den KPD-Unterbezirken künftig mitzuteilen, ob der Redner der Guomindang oder der KPCh angehöre, und die KPD-Organisationen sollten alles tun, um die Guomindang-Vertreter für den Kommunismus zu gewinnen.[8]

Der dann aus dem „Klub chinesischer Studenten" im Sommer 1925 abgespaltene „Hauptverband chinesischer Studenten" in Berlin wurde zu einem wesentlichen Partner von KPD und IAH. Auf dem IAH-Kongress am 16. August in Berlin unter der Losung „Hände weg von China" hielt einer der Führer des Verbandes, Zhang Bojun, als erster Redner ein Referat in deutscher Sprache zum Thema „Die gegenwärtige Phase im chinesischen Befreiungskampf". Zhang trat zu dieser Zeit auch für die Sektion der Guomindang in Deutschland auf.

Das Jahr 1925 kann als ein Höhepunkt der Solidaritätsbewegung für China in Deutschland angesehen werden. Doch auch in den Jahren 1926 und 1927 blieben die Ereignisse in China Anlass für viele Aktivitäten der deutschen Kommunisten. Regelmäßig und eindrucksvoll informierte die Wochenzeitschrift „Arbeiter-Illustrierte Zeitung" (AIZ).

Am 5. Februar 1926 übermittelte das ZK der KPD der KP Chinas und der chinesischen Nationalregierung Glückwünsche zum Sieg über die englischen Imperialisten in Shanghai (*Die Rote Fahne* 5.2.1926). Protestkundgebungen und Sammelaktionen blieben in den folgenden Monaten wichtige Maßnahmen einer tätigen Solidarität.

Der von der Reichsregierung am 17. Dezember 1925 angekündigte Beitritt zum Washingtoner Abkommen hatte eine lange öffentliche Debatte in Deutschland ausgelöst. In einer Interpellation vom 7.12.1926 (Drucksache 2788) stellte die KPD-Reichstagsfraktion die die Anfrage: „Ist die Reichsregierung endlich bereit, sich vor dem Reichstag (wegen der Ratifizierung des Washingtoner Mächteabkommens) zu rechtfertigen?" (*Verhandlungen* 1926). Die Ratifizierung im Reichstag wurde immer wieder aufgeschoben und schließlich nicht vorgenommen.

---

8 SAPMO, RY 1/I 2/3/211, Bl. 28f.

Das ZK der KPD hatte der Guomindang, der chinesischen Gewerkschaftszentrale, dem chinesischen Bauernverband und dem revolutionären Hauptquartier der National-revolutionären Armee anlässlich der Übersiedelung der Regierung nach Wuchang am 8. Dezember 1926 in einem Telegramm u. a. versprochen, „durch die Arbeitermassen von der deutschen Regierung die Anerkennung Eurer Kuomin[Guomindang]-Regierung als Zentralregierung Chinas zu erlangen" (*Inprekorr* 1926). Am 31. März 1927 beantragte die KPD-Fraktion im Reichstag von der Reichsregierung zu fordern, „die national-revolutionäre südliche Regierung sofort als Regierung des chinesischen Volkes anzuerkennen" (Antrag Nr. 3256) sowie „die sofortige Zurückziehung aller imperialisti-schen Truppen und die sofortige Aufhebung aller dem chinesischen Volk aufgezwunge-nen räuberischen Verträge" (Antrag Nr. 3255) (*Verhandlungen* 1927). Beide Anträge fan-den im Reichstag am 5. April keine Mehrheit.

Gleichzeitig fanden im ganzen Land Kundgebungen zur Unterstützung der revolutionären Kämpfe in China statt. Eine Massenkundgebung mit 20 000 Teilnehmern im Berliner Sportpalast am 5. April 1927 verabschiedete eine Resolution, die in dem Aufruf endete: "Nieder mit dem Krieg der Imperialisten in China! Nieder mit den Henkern der chinesi-schen Revolution! Sofortige Abberufung der Truppen und Kriegsschiffe in China! Aktive Unterstützung der chinesischen Revolution! Brüderliche Solidarität mit den um ihre Frei-heit kämpfenden chinesischen Massen!" (Tiedke 1989:70).

Das Jahr 1927 schloss mit vielen Kundgebungen und Manifestationen gegen den Terror und die Massaker an den Kantoner Kommunarden ab.

In diesen Jahren des Beginns und der Entfaltung eines ersten Abschnitts in der China-Politik der KPD und des Zusammenwirkens von fortschrittlichen Repräsentanten beider Länder traten einige deutsche Kommunisten besonders hervor.

Einer von ihnen war der Arzt Dr. Richard Schmincke (1875-1939), ein Internist und Schüler von Robert Koch, dessen Tätigkeit für die deutsch-chinesischen Beziehungen von Bedeutung gewesen ist und der bisher weder in den Darstellungen der China-Politik der KPD noch in chinesischen Abhandlungen Erwähnung gefunden hat. Schmincke wirkte 1923 als Arzt der proletarischen Hundertschaften im sächsischen Vogtland und war Abgeordneter im sächsischen Landtag. Im Oktober 1924 reiste er über die UdSSR mit der Transsibirischen Eisenbahn nach China, wo er sich einige Monate aufhalten wollte. Aus Harbin schrieb er am 23. Oktober 1924 einen längeren Bericht, den die kommunistische Zeitung „Der Kämpfer" am 18. Februar 1925 veröffentlichte. Darin versprach er, nach seiner Rückkehr im Vogtland darüber zu referieren, „was der ferne Osten für die proleta-rische Revolution bedeutet". In Peking angekommen, stellte Richard Schmincke enge Kontakte zur sowjetischen Botschaft her und trat auch mit der Guomindang in Verbin-dung, die ihn als ihren „politischen Freund" bezeichnete. Am 2. Januar 1925 nahm er als konsultierender Arzt und Mitglied eines Ärztekonziliums an einer Untersuchung des kranken Sun Yat-sen teil. Beides bestätigte der deutsche Gesandte Boyé in einem Bericht nach Berlin vom 4. April 1925. Boyé schrieb von einer „engen Fühlung", die Richard Schmincke zum „radikalen Flügel der Guomindang" hatte.[9]

Richard Schminckes aufmerksamen Blick auf die Ereignisse in China und sein politisches Verantwortungsbewusstsein bezeugt ein Brief, den er am 16. Januar 1925 an die Zentrale der KPD in Berlin sandte. Er informierte darin über in China bekannt gewordene deutsche

---

[9] SAPMO, R 1507/1085, Bl. 271.

Waffenlieferungen. „Diese Waffenlieferungen ... schädigen aufs schwerste den Befreiungskampf des chinesischen Volkes aus den Fesseln des Weltimperialismus". Deutlich unterstrich er die zwei Seiten, die in der China-Politik der KPD zum Ausdruck kamen. Er hielt „eine scharfe Campagne gegen die Waffenlieferungen, welche eine versteckte Intervention darstellen, von Seiten unserer Partei für unbedingt und dringend notwendig im Interesse Chinas. Dann ist eine solche Campagne auch geeignet, die deutsche Bourgeoisie vor den Augen des deutschen Proletariats zu kompromittieren".[10]

Richard Schmincke begab sich bereits mehrere Wochen vor dem Tode von Sun Yat-sen nach Japan. Er reiste mit dem deutschen Dampfer „Frieden" nach Yokahama, wo er am 18. Februar 1925 eintraf, kam jedoch wenige Tage später noch einmal kurz nach Shanghai zurück.

Richard Schmincke bewahrte sein tiefes Mitgefühl mit dem Kampf des chinesischen Volkes. Seine Stimme vereinigte sich mit der anderer deutscher Intellektueller, als Anfang der 1930er Jahre die japanische Aggression begann und sich gleichzeitig die antikommunistischen Verfolgungen in China verstärkten.

Noch vor ihrer großen China-Kampagne entsandte 1925 die Internationale Rote Hilfe von Berlin aus den hochrangigen KPD-Funktionär Karl Schulz (1884-1933) unter dem Namen Friedrich Lienhardt nach China. Am 30. Juli verlas er auf der Massenkundgebung in Peking vor 100 000 Teilnehmern einen Aufruf der IAH. Im direkten Zusammenhang mit dem Massaker der britischen Polizei am selben Tage wurde die chinesische Sektion der Internationalen Roten Hilfe gegründet. Chen Duxiu gab ihr den Namen „Vereinigung zur Hilfe von Menschen in Not". Sie war eine Hilfs-, zunächst aber vor allem eine Propagandaorganisation.

Karl Schulz blieb noch mehrere Monate in China und beriet die antiimperialistischen und nationalen Aktivitäten. In Berlin übernahm er 1927 die Funktion des Sekretärs des Reichsausschusses „Hände weg von China".

Am 20. Mai 1925 traf in Shanghai Adam Lindner (1902-1958) aus Wladiwostok kommend ein, wo er als Funktionär des Internationalen Propagandakomitees der Transportarbeiter (IPKT) im Hafenbüro tätig gewesen war. Unter dem Namen Xia Dalin nahm er als Instrukteur der IPKT Verbindung mit Funktionären des chinesischen Gewerkschaftsverbandes auf und wurde Mitglied der Guomindang. Außerdem hielt er Verbindung mit dem Shanghaier Studentenbund. Von Shanghai aus suchte er auch japanische und koreanische Hafenstädte auf. Zu den Aufgaben Adam Lindners gehörte es, chinesische Kader für ein Studium an der Sun-Yatsen-Universität in Moskau vorzuschlagen (Schwarz 1970).

Vom Dezember 1926 bis zum Mai 1927 arbeitete Mojzes Grzyb (1896-1941) für das ZEK der Guomindang im Hauptquartier der National-revolutionären Armee in Wuhan. Dort war er Redakteur des Organs des Pressebüros der Politischen Abteilung des Hauptquartiers der National-revolutionären Armee Chinas, der zweimal monatlich erscheinenden „China Correspondence". Er stand in engem Kontakt zum Leiter der Abteilung, Deng Yanda. In seiner Arbeit wurde er von Karl Schulz (Friedrich Lienhard) unterstützt. Von M. Grzyb stammen zahlreiche Artikel, die er im Auftrag des Chefs der Propaganda-Abteilung des ZEK bzw. einzelner Ministerien der Guomindang-Regierung verfasste. Er trug so wesentlich dazu bei, die offizielle Meinung der Guomindang-Führung der chinesi-

---

[10] SAPMO, RY 1/I 2/3/211, Bl. 21 f.

schen und ausländischen Öffentlichkeit zu vermitteln. Zugleich machten seine Veröffentlichungen deutlich, dass er mit scharfem politischen Verstand die Vorgänge in China zu analysieren vermochte. Als Redakteur formulierte er klar die daraus abzuleitenden Schlussfolgerungen für den Kampf der progressiven Kräfte Chinas und die entsprechende Profilierung der Guomindang. In der zweiten Hälfte des Nordfeldzuges waren seine Artikel nicht zuletzt von Bedeutung für den Klärungsprozess in der Guomindang-Führung und die Profilierung der linken Guomindang. Er zog u. a. ein wirtschaftliches Fazit des Boykott Kantons gegen Hongkong, entwickelte Argumentationen für die Herstellung der chinesischen Zollautonomie, entlarvte das Vorgehen insbesondere Großbritanniens in China. Im Frühjahr 1927 schrieb er auch für die halbamtliche „People's Tribune" der Wuhaner Nationalregierung. M. Grzyb hat eine große Anzahl seiner damaligen Artikel und Dokumente aus dem chinesischen Bürgerkrieg 1928 in seinem Buch „Von Kanton bis Shanghai 1926-1927" unter dem Pseudonym Asiaticus veröffentlicht. Dieses Pseudonym hat er später noch öfter verwendet, als er unter den Namen Möller, Schippe u.a. in China agierte.

In der KPD hatte sich mittlerweile eine kleine Zahl von China-Kennern herausgebildet. Zum zweifellos wichtigsten wurde Karl August Wittfogel (1896-1988). Angeregt durch die Shanghaier Ereignisse vom 30. Mai 1925 veröffentlichte er im Jahr darauf die Broschüre „Das erwachende China. Ein Abriß der Geschichte und der gegenwärtigen Probleme Chinas" aus marxistischer Sicht. Wittfogel machte für Deutschland erstmalig 1927 Sun Yat-sen als Begründer der Guomindang und des Sunyatsenismus bekannt. Seinen Darlegungen fügte er die bearbeitete Übersetzung eines 1926 in Moskau veröffentlichten Buches „Sun Yat Sen: Aufzeichnungen eines chinesischen Revolutionärs" an.

In diesem Zusammenhang sei auch auf das damals populäre und weit verbreitete Buch des Guomindang-Propagandisten Tang Leang-Li „China im Aufruhr" aus dem Jahr 1927 verwiesen. Es vermittelte dem deutschen Leser aus nationaler Sicht ein Bild von der Entwicklung Chinas seit der Mitte des 19. Jahrhunderts bis zum Jahr 1926 mit deutlicher Distanz zur kommunistischen Bewegung in China.

Umfangreiches Material über die genauen Vorgänge in China und die Politik der KPCh stand den Mitgliedern und Sympathisanten der KPD zur Verfügung. An erster Stelle ist hier ein Material der KPCh in deutscher Übersetzung vom 1. Mai 1926 zu nennen: „Die politische Linie in den 5 Jahren des Bestehens der Kommunistischen Partei Chinas" (137 MS). Es enthält den Wortlaut von 30 Dokumenten, darunter der Deklarationen des 2. bis 4. Parteitages sowie vieler Einschätzungen und Appelle des ZK der KPCh.[11] Unter dem Titel „Zur Lage in China" informierten 16 Thesen für Referenten, ebenfalls aus dem Jahr 1926, über die jüngste chinesische Geschichte und gaben eine Einschätzung der aktuellen Entwicklung. „Die chinesischen Arbeiter führen gegenwärtig ihren Kampf gegen die feudalen Militärcliquen und die ausländischen Imperialisten, ohne auf die Bourgeoisie zu hoffen und auf sie zu rechnen, sondern unter der eigenen Klassenfahne, indem sie provisorische Kampfbündnisse mit jenen sozialen Schichten und politischen Parteien schließen, die heute die gleichen Ziele wie das Proletariat verfolgen."[12] Der hier formulierte Kurs wurde vom Exekutivkomitee der Komintern im Frühjahr 1927 bekräftigt. Sein Präsidium beschloss im Februar Maßnahmen zur Verstärkung der China-Kampagnen der

---

[11] SAPMO, RY 1/I/2/8/84, Bl. 8ff.
[12] SAPMO, RY 1/I 2/707/28, Bl. 98.

kommunistischen Parteien. Der stellvertretende Leiter der Abteilung Agitprop des EKKI, Alfred Kurella, übermittelte am 18. Februar der Abteilung Agitprop des ZK der KPD die Weisung, dafür Sorge zu tragen, „dass von den Gewerkschaften und anderen Arbeiterorganisationen weiterhin Sympathietelegramme an die Kuo-Min-Tang [Guomindang] und die chinesischen Gewerkschaften geschickt werden, um die Aufmerksamkeit der Arbeiter für die chinesischen Ereignisse zu verstärken und außerdem das Ansehen der proletarischen Kräfte in der Revolution zu verstärken".[13]

Trotz erheblicher Anstrengungen der KPD erschien deren Pressearbeit dem Leiter der Abteilung Agitprop des EKKI, A. Bennet, nicht ausreichend. In einem Brief vom 1. April 1927 an die Abteilung Agitprop des ZK der KPD kritisierte er fehlendes Reagieren auf bürgerliche Tendenzmeldungen. Bestimmte Ereignisse in China würden „schwächer als die bürgerliche Presse" sie beleuchtete behandelt.[14]

Nach dem Bruch Tschiang Kaisheks [Jiang Jieshi] mit den chinesischen Kommunisten verstärkte die KPD ihre Solidaritätsaktionen für die chinesische Revolution. Sie folgte dabei der Einschätzung, die Robert (Gerhard Eissler) in einem Brief vom 13. April 1927 dem Politbüro des ZK der KPD übermittelt hatte, wonach sich „die proletarischen Elemente der Kuo-Min-Tang [Guomindang] ... unter dem Druck des Verrates Chian-Kai-Sheks [Jiang Jieshi] immer mehr zusammenschließen werden, der rechte Flügel immer mehr isoliert wird und immer breitere Massen in den Kampf gezogen werden".[15]

Teils angeregt durch den direkten Verlauf der chinesischen Revolution, teils in Reaktion und Antwort auf die vielfältigen Aktionen der deutschen Arbeiterbewegung erschienen Mitte der 1920er Jahre zunehmend Beiträge, die zur Herausbildung eines neuen China-Bildes in Deutschland beitrugen. So ergab sich ein breites Spektrum, das von den solidarischen und begeisterten Darstellungen der revolutionären chinesischen Arbeiterbewegung und ihrer Repräsentanten bis hin zur Eröffnung eines China-Instituts im November 1925 in Frankfurt am Main als Zentrum für den kulturellen und wissenschaftlichen Austausch mit seiner Zeitschrift Sinica reichte (Leutner und Steen 2006:500ff). Letztere war zwar wesentlich auf das alte China ausgerichtet, trug aber zu einem größeren Verständnis und realeren Bild des fernen Landes in Deutschland bei. Der erste Direktor des Instituts, der Sinologe Richard Wilhelm, legte seine Erfahrungen und Kenntnisse nach 25-jährigem Aufenthalt in China in dem Werk „Die Seele Chinas" dar. Das Ehepaar Hans und Margarete Driesch beschrieben ihre Erlebnisse während der Vortragstragsreisen des Philosophen in den Jahren 1921 bis 1923 („Fern-Ost. Als Gäste Jungchinas"). Der linksorientierte Intellektuelle Arthur Holitscher berichtete direkt von den Ereignissen in China 1925 („Das unruhige Asien", Berlin 1926). Der Journalist Erich von Salzmann, den es seit der Jahrhundertwende immer wieder nach China gezogen hatte, veröffentlichte Romane („Yü Föng der Nephrit Phönix", 1926 und „Zeitgenosse Fo", 1927), die dem Leser Vorgänge der chinesischen Revolution anschaulich nahe brachten. Gleiches geschah mit dem Roman von Norbert Jaques „Der Kaufherr von Shanghai", 1925.

Insgesamt hatte sich so in Deutschland, maßgeblich vorangebracht durch die entschlossene und aktive Propaganda- und Solidaritätsaktionen der KPD wie ihr nahe stehende Organisationen und Persönlichkeiten, Mitte der 1920er Jahre ein auch von breiten Kreisen

---

[13] SAPMO, RY 05/I 6/3/360, Bl. 16.
[14] SAPMO, ebd., Bl. 19.
[15] SAPMO, RY 05/I 6/3/159, Bl. 34.

linker und anderer demokratischer Kräfte getragenes und vermitteltes Bild von den wahren Vorgängen in China und der Befreiungsbewegung in diesem Lande herausgebildet. Es war an die Stelle vieler Klischees und kolonialistischer Sichten getreten, ohne auch selbst neue Vereinfachungen und Entstellungen zu vermeiden. Eine tatsächliche Kommunikation zwischen Deutschen und Chinesen kam damals allerdings noch kaum zustande.

Literatur

Arbeiterbewegung und Revolution in China (1925), Berlin: Führer.

Harnisch, Thomas (1999) *Chinesische Studenten in Deutschland. Geschichte und Wirkung ihrer Studienaufenthalte in den Jahren von 1860 bis 1945*, Hamburg: Institut für Asienkunde (Mitteilungen des Instituts für Asienkunde 300).

Inprekorr 10/XII/151 (1926).

Leutner, Mechthild (Hrsg.), Andreas Steen (Verf.) (2006) Deutsch-chinesische Beziehungen 1911-1927. Vom Kolonialismus zur „Gleich¬berech¬ti¬gung. Eine Quellensammlung, Berlin: Akademie.

Not und Brot 44, Berlin o. J., S. 12.

Not und Brot 43, Berlin o. J., S. 5.

Not und Brot 45, Berlin o. J., S. 6.

Die Rote Fahne, Berlin, 5.2.1926.

Schwarz, Rainer (1970) „Adam Lindner – ein Pionier des proletarischen Internationalismus", in *Mitteilungen des Instituts für Orientforschung* XVI/4 (1970), S. 587-595.

Tiedke, Kurt et al. (Hrsg.) (1989) *Aus dem Kampf der deutschen Arbeiterklasse zur Verteidigung und Unterstützung der Revolution in China. Dokumente und Fotos aus den Jahren 1918/19 bis 1988*, Berlin: Dietz.

Verhandlungen des Reichstages. III. Wahlperiode 1924, Band 411, Anlagen zu den Stenographischen Berichten, Berlin 1926.

Verhandlungen des Reichstags. III. Wahlperiode 1924, Band 414, Anlagen zu den Stenographischen Berichten, Berlin 1927.

Archive

Archiv Vnejšnej Politiki Rossijskoj Federacii (AVP RF)
Bundesarchiv Berlin (Barch)
Politisches Archiv Auswärtiges Amt (PAAA), Berlin
Stiftung Archiv der Parteien- und Massenorganisationen der DDR (SAPMO)

Izabella Goikhman

The Internationalization of Chinese Research on Jews in China since the 1980s*

"If you do not understand Jews, you do not understand the world" (不了解犹太人就不了解世界) states the back cover of the "Compendium of Chinese research on jewish studies in the 1990s" (Zhu and Jin 1992). "Understanding the Jews" has become an important issue in the Chinese[1] academic community since the beginning of the "open-door-policy" at the end of the 1970s.

Several Chinese scholars noticed the rapid growth of Chinese academic research on Jews in general and on Jews in China[2] in particular and published papers on this development (Xu Xin 1999, Xu 2000a, Yang 2000, Huang 2000). Although these accounts are quite detailed and informative and even mention some important political events such as the establishment of diplomatic relations between China and Israel which had an impact on studies on Jews in China, they neither analyze the lines of arguments of the discourse nor put them into larger national or international context. In fact, all of the authors construe a Chinese tradition of academic research on Jews in China starting as early as during the Yuan dynasty (1280-1368) (Huang 2000: 653) or at the latest in 1897 (Yang 2000: 205, Xu Xin 1999: 16, Xu 2000a: 3) and, though interrupted between 1949 and 1980, lasting till nowadays. Only some short notes suggest that there have been some connections between Chinese scholars and their colleagues abroad: the results of Chinese research were introduced to foreign specialists (Yang 2000: 211) and "direct contacts with foreign scholars and the availability of their works stimulated many Chinese scholars" (Xu 2000a: 6).

In the last few years there is a growing academic interest in processes of internationalization and its impacts on knowledge transfer between different cultural contexts. Some of them even concentrate on the People's Republic of China. Yet, most of these studies deal with knowledge management in international organizations and businesses.[3] There is almost no research on internationalization of science in China[4] or abroad.[5]

---

*   This paper is partly based on chapters of the authors M.A. thesis „Der Diskurs über Juden in China" [The discourse on Jews in China] written under the supervision of Mechthild Leutner and Bettina Gransow at the Institute of East Asian Studies, Free University Berlin, 2005, forthcoming. This paper concentrates on the developments taken place within or initiated by the Chinese academic community. The outline of the developments outside of China is provided briefly where required.

[1] Regarding the academic community after 1949 I use "China" and "People's Republic of China" interchangeably. Taiwanese academic discourse on Jews in China is not included here.

[2] Several Jewish communities existed in traditional China, but only one of them, in Kaifeng, left signs of its existence. In modern China there were three different waves of Jewish migration: in the middle of 19th century Baghdadi Jews came to China, Jews from Russia settled mainly in Northeastern China in the first decades of the 20th century and Jewish refugees from Europe found refuge in Shanghai in the end of 1930s. Most of the Jews left China after 1949.

[3] See for example: Weir/Hutchings 2005, Hutchings 2005.

[4] I could only find a few studies on the internationalization of social studies and humanities in China: Spakowski 2001, Yang 2004 and special issue of Chinese education and society 2001.

[5] The lack of research on the internationalization of humanities and social sciences was even identified by Transatlantic Science and Humanities Advisory Board in the Alexander von Humboldt Foundation

It is generally assumed that the "soft" sciences like the social sciences and the humanities achieve a lower rate of international cooperation than the "hard" ones (Yang 2004: 1, Rampelmann 2005: 5). This situation is explained with the importance of national languages (ibid.), but also with the assumption that varied ideologies and domestic considerations "are given more weight in these fields" (Yang 2004: 1). Rui Yang's paper suggests that this assumption proved true for educational research in China (Yang 2004). Yet, Nicola Spakowski has shown a very high level of internationalization of China's women's studies due to actively promotion and financing (Spakowski 2001).

Building upon a large body of Chinese studies on Jews in China and analyzing the development of this research field as well as interactions between Chinese and Western scholars, I argue that Chinese research on Jews in China is undergoing a process of internationalization, while at the same time maintaining strong autonomy. Since this article concentrates on the internationalization of the Chinese discourse, Chinese publications will be studied in detail. My general impression of non-Chinese discourse is that specialists on Chinese studies try to integrate Chinese research into their works.[6] See for example Leslie's bibliography on Jews and Judaism in traditional China which also includes studies of Chinese scholars (Leslie 1998). However, most of the Western scholars dealing with Chinese Jews are not sinologists, they do not read Chinese and therefore cannot refer to the Chinese discourse in their studies.

After briefly reviewing the Chinese academic discourse on Jews in China before the 1980s to provide the background of more recent developments, this article will examine the academic, economical and political motives for internationalization of the discourse after 1980. Then, the agents of internationalization – institutions and persons – and different modes of internationalization such as international conferences, scholars' mobility etc. will be introduced. The next part will deal with signs of internationalization and its limits, which – if possible – will be explained through political, economical and social contexts.

The Internationalization Takes Root: Chinese Research on Jews in China Before the 1980s

"Jew" as a concept and as a research topic was brought to China by Westerners in the 19th century and was therefore – from the very beginning – a product of intercultural knowledge transfer.[7] The initial knowledge Chinese gained about Jews and Judaism in China and abroad came from protestant missionaries in the beginning of 19th century (Zhou Xun 2001: 12ff). The first Chinese to report on the Jews of Kaifeng were Chui Tiansheng and Jiang Rongji – two Chinese converts, who had been sent to explore the situation of the Jewish community of Kaifeng by the Protestant mission.[8] Since then the Jews of Kaifeng became a frequent topic in numerous magazines published in China by western missionaries. Consequently more and more Chinese readers got familiar with the Jewish presence in China (ibid. : 22).

In 1897 the Jews in China for the first time became a topic of Chinese academic research when the historian Hong Jun, who had lived abroad for a long time and had actually learned from Westerners about the existence of Jews in China (Shapiro 1984: 3, Pollak

---

as "an issue that needed special attention" (Rampelmann 2005: 5).

[6] See for example Leslie 2000, Betta 2000a.

[7] For Chinese perceptions of Jews and Judaism see Zhou 2001.

[8] Their report is published in White 1966 (White 1966: 184ff).

1988: 140f), dealt with possible names for Chinese Jews in his "Study on terms for various religions during the Yuan dynasty" (元史各教名考).

Until 1949 about 20 articles were published in China dealing with Jews in China. Most of the Chinese scholars publishing on this issue had contacts to Westerners – like Hong Jun – or close connections to Christian missionaries in China and were familiar with their publications. Zhang Xiangwen, the famous Chinese geographer, who was the first Chinese to mention the stone inscriptions in Kaifeng (Zhang 1910) for example, often visited the Christian mission, where he could read newspapers and read various books on geography published by the Jesuit mission press in Xujiahui (Hahn 2002). The Director of Xujiahui (Zikawei) Library in Shanghai, Chinese Jesuit Xu Zongze, also studied the Jews in Kaifeng (Xu 1936). Sometimes the interest of Chinese scholars was a reaction to actions of the Christian Mission: Shi Jingxun, for instance, was a Chinese official in Kaifeng, who tried to stop Bishop White of the Canadian Church of England from buying the synagogue site and the stone stele (Pollak 1993: 93), before publishing an article in 1913 (Shi 1913).

The most prominent and important study of this period was written by one of the most eminent Chinese historians of the 20th century, Chen Yuan, who was president of the catholic Furen-University (Shapiro 1984: 15) and co-editor of the journal "Monumenta Serica" (Yang 2000: 206). His series of articles "A Study of the Jewish Religion in Kaifeng" (开封一赐乐业教考) (Chen 1920) is still considered as "the point of departure for almost every Chinese scholar who subsequently researches the history of the Jews in China" (Shapiro 1984: XVII). Chen examined the stone inscriptions and made conclusions about various aspects of the history of Jews in Kaifeng.

In this period nothing was published on Jewish communities in modern China. Maybe because the Baghdadi Jewish merchants like Victor Sassoon as well as the Jewish refugees were not seen as Jews, but much rather as representatives of Shanghai's foreign population (Zhou 2001: 59, Kreissler 1991: 296f).

After the foundation of People's Republlic of China in 1949 the academic research on Jews in general and on Chinese Jews in particular became impossible. Various political movements like the "Anti-Rightist"-Campaign (1957) and the Cultural Revolution (1966-1976) had a negative impact on Chinese academic research (Xu 2000a: 5). The Jews of Kaifeng were not officially recognized as an "ethnic minority" and therefore could not be studied within the field of studies of ethnic minorities. Nevertheless there was one scholar, who dealt with Jews in China during this period: the well-known eugenics scholar Pan Guangdan, who like other Chinese scholars involved in studies on Chinese Jews, also studied abroad – in the USA (Pan 1991: 1467). His manuscript "Some historical questions on Jews in China" (中国境内犹太人的若干历史问) was written in 1953, but was not published till 1980 (Pan 1980). Pan used the Jews of Kaifeng as a perfect example for his theory of "ethnic harmony" (民族团结), which according to him was necessary in order to establish the "great superior Chinese race" (伟大优秀的中华民族) (Zhou 2001: 158). The publication of Pan's study in 1980 marked the new beginning of the Chinese academic discourse on Jews in China.

The Stimuli for Internationalization

Before analyzing the signs of internationalization of the Chinese research on Jews in China since 1980, it is essential to understand the three main categories of stimuli which motivated the Chinese scholars[9] to be engaged in this process: academic, economic and political.

Providing a solid basis for further research: At the beginning of the 1980s Chinese scholars of Jewish studies did not have much academic basis or indigenous scholarly tradition to rely on. A few historians and social scientists dealt with Jews during the Republican period, but nothing had been done in this field since the foundation of the People's Republic of China in 1949. There were no Chinese professors and very little Chinese publications to learn from, no universities or research institutes to study or work in. Knowledge on Jews and Judaism could at this stage only be provided through international knowledge transfer in its different modes: knowledge media (publications, films, letters etc.), physical mobility of scholars and joint research and teaching projects[10]. Later, the involvement of Chinese scholars in the international academic community allowed them and foreign scholars to benefit mutually from academic achievements all over the world.

Looking for funding and serving the national economy: There are two aspects of the economic side of the internationalization: the first concerns the economic situation of research institutions, the second refers to the profitability of the economy at national or provincial level.

The economic reforms directly affect universities and research institutions. Since the governmental support is decreasing, there is a growing need in other funding sources. Science becomes a commodity in the rapidly growing market economy (Leutner 2003: 109). Already in the 1980s Chinese scholars of Jewish studies started looking for foreign financial support and book donations. International associations initiated by Chinese or foreigners were established in China and abroad in order to provide necessary support, which is still very important for Chinese educational and research institutions working in the field of Jewish studies in general or studies on Jews in China in particular[11].

---

[9] Though this chapter focuses on the motives of Chinese scholars, some stimuli of their colleagues abroad should be mentioned here. Since the Reform and Open Door Policy was launched by Deng Xiaoping in 1979, foreign scholars became able to do their research in China, which made new approaches, such as fieldwork and oral history, possible and new sources available. Moreover, the communication between Western and Chinese scholars became possible. Although the political context played an important role in internationalizing Chinese studies, some developments within the Western academia were of enormous importance. There has been a long tradition of border-crossing academic communication in the West, which has been "viewed as almost identical with 'quality,' the most positive thing in academia" (Teichler 2004: 8), but it was usually applied only to the Western discourse. Influenced by Said's orientalism thesis as well as Foucault's power and knowledge concepts, the social studies and humanities experienced some major changes in the 1980s, which on the one hand involved the emergence of "cultural" and "post-colonial" studies (for the "paradigm shift" in Chinese studies see Mühlhahn 1997) and on the other hand brought a strong critics on Eurocentrism of the academia and an increased interest in academic works by non-western foreign scholars. Already in 1996 Gail Hershatter noted that "regular interchange with scholars in the PR has broadened the boundaries of 'the China field'" (Hershatter et al. 1996: 2).

[10] These modes of international knowledge transfer were formulated by Ulrich Teichler (Teichler 2004: 13).

[11] For more detailed account of the importance of international funding for Chinese institutions see Part 4 of this paper.

In addition to the responsibility for their own profitability Chinese academic institutions should serve the economy at national, provincial and city level. In the last twenty years ethnic groups became increasingly commercialized. This commercialization affects the academics: Local historians try to show, that their cities or provinces on the one hand hold an important place in Chinese culture, and on the other hand have some special characteristics, which distinguish them from others (Thøgersen 2001: 308). The Center for Jewish Studies of the Heilongjiang Academy of Social sciences (黑龙江省社会科学院犹太研究中心) officially states the expansion of tourism[12] and serving the economic development of the province as two of its main goals (Ha'erbin 2006). Furthermore, it is "a challenge for Chinese scholars" to attract Jewish investors (Xu Xin 1999:23). The Sino-Judaic research in China as well as the construction of tourist sites should attract the attention of the Jews from Western countries to China.

Serving (inter-)national political aims: Academic activities cannot be placed outside the national and international political context. By internationalizing the academic institutions Chinese scholars follow the general governmental educational and research policies and long-term principles put forward by the Ministry of Education of the People's Republic of China and the Chinese academy of social sciences, which according to Deng Xiaoping's demand, that Chinese education should "face the world" (Ouyang 2004: 144), encourage foreign academic exchanges, Chinese-foreign cooperation, international conferences and the exchange of education materials (CASS 2006, MOE 2006).

Chinese scholars often emphasize the special importance of studies on Chinese Jews in the international arena. In the words of Pan Guang:

"[...] this topic has important practical significance in opposing racism and fascism, furthering friendly relations and cultural harmony between all peoples, and preserving a peace in the world. [...] it also plays a unique role on furthering the continued opening-up of China and developing relations between China and nations like Israel and United States" (Pan 2006).

Studies of Chinese scholars can also help to improve the image of the Chinese state outside of China. In the last twenty years minority rights became an important part of international relations (Mackerras 2003: 174). A positive policy of the Chinese government towards the descendants of Chinese Jews in Kaifeng could be profitable as a gain of prestige in the international arena. In the same way, academic research, which concentrates on the assimilation of Jews, the tolerance of Chinese society and the traditional friendship between Chinese and Jews, contributes to the image of China as a state of peaceful coexistence of various ethnic groups, which the Chinese government would like to create outside and inside of China (Zhou 2001: 160).

In order to achieve the mentioned goals, Chinese scholars must actively take part at the international discourse on Jews in China.

---

12 Along with the emergence of the market economy the old perceptions of Jews as being rich and powerful came out as well (Zhou 2001: 159). Jewish tourists are often seen as an important source of capital, which should be wisely exploited.

Agents of Internationalization since the 1980s[13]

Since the beginning of the „open-door-policy" in 1979, which offered a relatively liberal environment for academic matters, the topic of Chinese Jews became a research interest for Chinese scholars again. China has today at least 10 known and relatively active research centres (Treiman 2003) for different aspects of Jewish Studies such as Jewish religion and culture, Judaism in the USA, Israel and other countries (Huang 2000: 663ff). Although only about 20 Chinese scholars devote themselves completely to Judaic studies, up to 200 scholars work in this field on a part-time basis (Wald 2004: 52). The research on Jews and Judaism in China is of particular importance, it has become a "hotspot" (热点) (Wang 2005: 110): more than 100 studies dealing specifically with this issue have been published in China since 1980. Chinese scholars themselves consider the number of publications as relative high in comparison to many other cultures[14] (Wald 2004: 53). Chinese research on Jews in general as well as on Jews in China has undergone a very rapid development since the 1980s. This development is inseparably connected to the internationalization of this research field, which makes knowledge transfer between Chinese and foreign scholars possible. The impact of internationalization processes on the Chinese discourse on Jews in China is discussed in the next chapter.

The beginnings: the impact of personal and political international interactions: The development of this research field in those years is closely connected to personal interests and life stories of a few scholars. Though very different, they have one important aspect in common: all of them were influenced by intercultural interactions. Sydney Shapiro – an American Jew, who has been living in China – claims to have played an important role for the renewal of Chinese academic interest in Chinese Jews. After being repeatedly asked by his Jewish friends abroad, if he knew something on Jews in China, he personally travelled across China in the beginning of the 1980s and convinced some of Chinese historians, archaeologists and sociologists of the importance of research on Chinese Jews (Shapiro 1984: XVf).

The most dominant agents of the Chinese discourse and of its internationalization – Xu Xin[15] and Pan Guang[16] – also started to develop academic interest in Jews through international contacts. Xu Xin – "China's homegrown Jewish studies dynamo" (Treiman 2003) – taught American literature and started to deal with Jews and Judaism from a scholarly point of view after he went to the US as an exchange scholar in the mid 1980s and got familiar with Jewish life in America through his friendship with Jewish literature scholar James Friend (ibid.). A Friendship with a child of German-Jewish Refugees during his childhood in Shanghai sparked Pan Guang's interest in Jewish communities in Shanghai, especially the exile-community (Friend 2004b).

---

[13] Here both Chinese and Western agents, who were directly involved in promoting the integration of Chinese scholars in the international academic community, will be introduced.

[14] Judaism is most often referred to in China as "Jewish culture" (*Youtai wenhua* 犹太文化), that's why Chinese scholars compare research on Judaism with research on other cultures.

[15] In recognition of his contribution to Jewish studies in China the Bar-Ilan University (Israel) bestowed on Xu Xin an Honorary Doctorate in May 2003 (Xu 2003).

[16] Most of the publications of Chinese scholars published in English or/and abroad come from those two scholars. Pan has even published in Hebrew (Pan 1994b).

Personal life stories may have played an important role in the development of Jewish Studies in China, but the growing interest of Chinese scholars in Jews and Judaism and their ability to devote themselves to these studies were particularly enhanced by the establishment of diplomatic relations between the People's Republic of China and Israel in 1992. There had already been a few Chinese associations of Jewish studies established between 1988 and 1992[17], but the studies were not yet sanctioned by the government, so that the scholars faced quite a number of problems: they could not get genuine information and had difficulties to get their studies published (Gluckman 1997). After 1992 the establishment of new research institutes provided a basis for a better and broader research.

The role of institutions in the process of internationalization: There are a few organizations in China and abroad which have played an important role in internationalizing the Chinese discourse on Jews in China[18]. The most influential are: the "Sino-Judaic Institute", the "Center of Jewish Studies Shanghai", the "China Judaic Studies Association", the "Research Institute for Judaic Studies at Nanjing University" and the "Center for Judaic and Inter-Religious Studies of Shandong University".

The "Sino-Judaic Institute": Founded in 1985 in California by an international group of scholars and laypersons, the "Sino-Judaic Institute" was the first international organization, which aim was "to serve as a vehicle for the study and preservation of Jewish history in China" (History 2006). Providing support to Chinese scholars of Jewish studies very soon became one of the major projects of the institute. It has been active in facilitating the establishment of institutions of Jewish studies in China and translations of subject related foreign language publications into Chinese[19], enabling Chinese scholars to carry out their research and to attend meetings abroad, as well as donating books to scholars and institutions in China (ibid.), thus promoting not only the establishment of the Chinese academic research on Jews in general and on Jews in China in particular, but also the integration of Chinese scholars in the international academic community.

Center of Jewish Studies Shanghai (CJSS) (上海犹太研究中心): Established in 1988, CJSS was the first Chinese research institution on Jewish and Israeli studies in China. Headed by Pan Guang, the Center, which is affiliated with the Shanghai Academy of Social Sciences is one of the most influential Chinese institutions in this research field: not only coordinates it the research activities in Shanghai and China, but it also has strong links to institutions and scholars from abroad (Center 2006a).

---

17 For example: "Shanghai Research Institute of Jewish Studies" (上海犹太研究会), "The Department for Jewish Studies at Research Institute for Society and Culture of Tongji-University" (同济大学社会与文化研究所犹太学研究室), "Israeli-Judaic Research Centre at the Institute for Peace and Development" (和平与发展研究所以色列·犹研究中心) (Zhu/Jin 1992: 311f, Yang 2000: 214). All of these institutions in Shanghai had later blended into the Center of Jewish Studies (Gluckman 1997).

18 Most of the research institutions work on Jews in general, but integrate the studies on Jews in China in their research. Only the Center of Jewish Studies in Shanghai concentrates on Jews in Shanghai as a main field of research.

19 For example the translation of Tokayer, Martin, and Swartz, Mary (1979) *The Fugu Plan: The Untold Story of the Japanese and the Jews During World War II*, New York and London: Paddington, into Chinese: Mawen Tuokaye and Mali Siwozi (1992) *Hetun jihua, erzhan qijian Ribenren he Youtairen zhijian yiduan bu wei ren suo he de gushi, Shanghai: Sanlian shudian.*

The online-presentation of the center provides an idea of how important international ties are for CJSS: First, the website of CJSS is bilingual, so that it can be understood by non-Chinese-speakers. Second, sponsoring and organizing international conferences[20], reunions of Shanghai Jews and publishing bilingual books[21] count as some of the major academic accomplishments of the center. Third, a special column is dedicated to „the distinguished guests from abroad who visited CJS […]": politicians such as Yitzhak Rabin, Gerhard Schröder and Hillary Clinton as well as known scholars of Jewish Studies such as Alfred Gottschalk and Zorach Warhaftig (ibid.). Furthermore, the "What's New" page consists completely of a list of visits of foreign scholars, politicians and diplomats. The most often topics discusses with foreign visitors are "cooperation concerning books and reference materials", „plan to cooperate on related subjects", "development of cooperation" and "discuss details of further cooperation" (Center 2006b). The exchange program with Hebrew University and Tel Aviv University in Israel, which allows annually one or two scholars to go to Israel (Kirshner 2006), is one of the cooperations CJSS benefits from. "Cooperation concerning books" seems also to prove successful: some of the books in CJSS' library of Judaica were donated by Americans and Canadians (ibid.).

China Judaic Studies Association and Research Institute for Judaic Studies at Nanjing University (南京大学犹太文化研究所): The "China Judaic Studies Association" (CJSA), founded in 1989 by Xu Xin, differs from CJSS in two aspects: the character of the organization and its target group. CJSA is not a research institution, but an international organization providing financial aid to projects affiliated with Jewish Studies in China: university courses, Judaic conferences, publications etc. (CJSA 2006). Although established by a Chinese scholar, it does not have an official Chinese name or a Chinese web site: the official page is in English[22] – a fact, which predefines foreigners as potential members and as a target group that should be introduced to the activities of the association. Considering the main aim of CJSA – to provide financial aid and some common perceptions of Jews portrayed in the chapter above, this one-sided orientation is not surprising.

The research institute benefiting the most from the activities of CJSA is the Research institute for Judaic Studies at Nanjing University (南京大学犹太文化研究所[23]), which has been set up in 1992 and is headed by the president of CJSA – Xu Xin[24]. The importance of international cooperation is explicitly emphasized by the institute: international collaboration, invitations of foreign scholars to give lectures in Nanjing, joint efforts to organize international workshops and conferences and the promotion of international exchange belong to its main aims and also to its main achievements: exhibitions and

---

[20] The role of international conferences in the internationalization process will be discussed later in this chapter.

[21] Pan Guang's *The Jews in China* was first published in 1995 as a Chinese-English edition (Pan 1995). Since then a German-Chinese and a French-Chinese version came out.

[22] Http://servercc.oakton.edu/~friend/chinajews.html, accessed 7 July 2006.

[23] The institute was founded under the name Nanjing daxue youtai wenhua yanjiu zhongxin (南京大学犹太文化研究中心) and was renamed into Nanjing daxue youtai wenhua yanjiusuo (南京大学犹太文化研究所) in 2001 (Nanjing daxue youtai wenhua yanjiusuo 2006).

[24] CJSA requests help specifically for the Research institute for Judaic Studies at Nanjing University such as book donations, providing scholarships as well as funding lectures and publications (Building an Academic Judaic Center in China 2006).

international conferences have been organized jointly by the institute and foreign organisations and relations has been established to numerous foreign academic institutions in the USA, Israel and England (Nanjing 2006). However, the institute does not have an English presence on the internet, there is only a short description of it at the websites of CJSA (Building 2006). Thus, CJSA can in some sense be seen as an international office of the Research institute for Judaic Studies at Nanjing University.

The Center for Judaic and Inter-Religious Studies of Shandong University (山东大学犹太教与宗教研究中心) The Center for Judaic and Inter-Religious Studies of Shandong University was developed in 2003 from the Judaic Culture Study Center of Shandong University which was founded by Fu Youde in 1994. This institution went farthest in internationalization. Apart from hosting international conferences and sending members of the center abroad to study and attend conferences, inviting foreign experts to give lectures and collecting books and other publications from abroad (Brief Introduction 2006), the Shandong university is the first and only university in China to offer a senior post and full professorship to a foreign scholar, Professor M. Avrum Ehrlich, for the teaching of Jewish religion and philosophy. Furthermore, the university has international programs for master and doctorate candidates (A New School 2006). The center also keeps the most detailed English presence on internet[25].

Developing international programs and exchanges including international Diploma, Masters and Ph.D. programs and attracting high ranking scholars to visit and lecture at Shandong University are the main focuses of the center for the next years (Brief Introduction 2006). The attractiveness of the center for foreign scholars could be explained by the better governmental funding, since it has been designated by the State Ministry of Education as one of 100 prestigious key research institutes. Still, the Center for Judaic and Inter-Religious Studies needs book donations from abroad and has initiated a book exchange of Chinese books for books on Jewish subjects (ibid.).

Modes of Internationalization since the 1980s

The discussed organizations played an important role in promoting studies on Jews in general and on Chinese Jews in particular through funding and organizing such modes of internationalization as: international exchange and cooperation in the form of international conferences and workshops, personal mobility of Chinese and foreign scholars, enabling them to do research or attend conferences abroad, and knowledge transfer in form of publications exchanges and translations.

Chinese scholars of Jewish studies had to "upgrade their studies to meet international standards" (Xu 1995). But the Sino-Judaic studies experienced a dramatic development during the last twenty-five years outside China as well. So international conferences have been very important for both Chinese and foreign scholars to keep up to date and to contribute their part to the promotion of further research. Since the mid 1980s Chinese scholars participated at international conferences concerning solely Jews in China or Asia in Harvard (1992), Salzburg (1995), Sankt-Augustin (1997) and Germersheim (2003) and organized several international conferences and workshops in China like the international seminar "Jews in Shanghai" in Shanghai (1994), an international symposium "History of

---

[25] Http://www.cjs.sdu.edu.cn/english/, accessed 7 July 2006.

Jewish Diaspora in China" in Nanjing (2002) and an international seminar at ICAS (International Convention of Asia Scholars) 4 in Shanghai (2005).

Particularly significant was the leading part Chinese scholars played in the broadening of the research on Jewish communities of North-Eastern China and its internationalization. In the mid 1990s there was already more Chinese research on this topic than abroad. At that time, Fang Jianchang complained about the relatively small interest on Jewish communities in North-Eastern China and the absence of research institutes dealing with this issue (Fang 1997b: 91, Fang and Li 1997: 81). The Center for Jewish Studies of the Heilongjiang Academy of Social Sciences (黑龙江省社会科学院犹太研究中心) was established only in 2000 (Heilongjiang 2006), but already in 2004 it organized the "International Seminar on the History and Culture of the Jews of Harbin" together with the "Israel-China Friendship Association," established by former members of Russian-Jewish community in China (Jutai 2004). It was the first international conference with a special focus on the Russian Jewish communities in North-Eastern China.

Attending conferences abroad requires personal mobility of scholars, but there are also other goals of personal mobility. Xu Xin's detailed reports on 8 of his journeys to America, Israel and Great Britain exemplify the different goals and the importance of scholars' mobility.[26] Analyzing those reports showed that except doing research and establishing numerous contacts, Chinese Sino-Judaic scholars' going abroad serves three specific goals: negotiating and creating exchange programs for students and scholars as well as discussing possible ways of cooperation, search for financial support, and obtaining more books, mainly through donations (Xu 2006).

There are obvious reasons for obtaining books and other published materials being important for scholars. Knowledge media provides a fundamental basis for knowledge transfer – not only for those scholars, who are able to travel abroad, but also for those, who do not have the opportunity to do so. Publications give them the possibility to be a part of international academic community.

The works of contemporary Chinese Sino-Judaic scholars were first presented to the English speaking academic community by Sydney Shapiro in 1984 (Shapiro 1984). Unfortunately no compilations of translations of Chinese publications have come out since then. Donald Leslie gives shorts accounts on some of them in his comprehensive bibliography on Jews in traditional China (Leslie 1998), but books and papers dealing with Jews in modern China are not included.

Since the beginning of the 1990s some Chinese scholars publish abroad or in Chinese English-language journals. Most of the publications come from Pan Guang (Pan 1992, 2000a, 2000b) and Xu Xin (Xu Xin 1999, 2000a, 2000b)[27], but there are also some papers of other scholars, such as Xu Buzeng (Xu Buzeng 1999), Huang Lingyu (Huang 2000), Wei Qianzhi (Wei 2000) and Yang Haijun (Yang 2000) that came out abroad. There are

---

[26] Of course, other Chinese scholars went abroad as well: Pan Guang, for example, visited and did research amongst others in the USA, Israel, France, Germany and Hungary (Friend, Beverly 2004) and Fu Youde and other members of The Center for Judaic and Inter-Religious Studies of Shandong University were sent to Britain, the USA, Hong Kong and Taiwan (Brief Introduction 2006). Xu Xin's journeys are proper for exemplifying such a trips, because of his detailed accounts published on the website of CAJS (http://servercc.oakton.edu/~friend/ xuxin_trips.html).

[27] It is only a selection of Pan Guang's and Xu Xin's works in English.

also some studies in Chinese that were included in an international conference volume printed in Germany (Zhang/Li 2000, Fang 2000).

Different organizations were very active funding translations of books of foreign scholars into Chinese. Naturally, most of them consider general Judaic subjects, like the Encyclopaedia Judaica. A few books dealing with Jews in China were translated into Chinese: David Kranzler's *Japanese, Nazis and Jews: The Jewish Refugee Community of Shanghai, 1938-1945* (Kranzler 1976) was translated in 1991 (Daiwei Kelansile 1991) and the already mentioned Martin Tokayer's Mary and Swartz's *The Fugu Plan: The Untold Story of the Japanese and the Jews During World War II*, translated in 1992[28]. Thus, only very few foreign works are available to Chinese scholars in Chinese, therefore their English language ability is essential for being a part of international academic community as well as the accessibility of studies published abroad. Since most of the Chinese research institutions still need book supplies from abroad and Chinese published books are not easy to find outside of China, the internet[29] can provide Chinese and foreign scholars at least with some of the publications. Many foreign internet based databases such as Academic Search Elite, Social Science, Business Science Source or Dissertation Abstract Online are nowadays available at Chinese research and educational institutions. It could to some extent compensate the lack of appropriate materials in Chinese Judaic libraries. Foreign scholars can access Chinese databases, such as "China Academic Journals fulltext database" (CAJ), which includes 15.1 million articles from 7200 Chinese journals in different disciplines: Science and Engineering, Medicine, Literature, History, Philosophy etc.

Scope and Limits of Internationalization

Although there is no clear definition of the internationalization of academics, it is often opposed to globalization, which is perceived as a world-wide unification of discourses, because on the one hand it emphasizes an increase of border-crossing activities, but on the other hand implies a persistence of national discourses and education systems.[30] Therefore discourses within research fields undergoing internationalization would include both signs of internationalization and those of autonomous development. Moreover, some developments can be seen as a part of the both processes at the same time.

Internationalization: a matter of methodology: The majority of Chinese scholars still follow the paradigms of long existing patterns of Chinese historiography based on text critics and comparison in their studies on Chinese Jews. Those are mostly narrative accounts on the history of Jewish communities in China.[31] But the international integration led to

---

[28] For books and articles published in China I had to rely on a bibliography compiled by CJSS, which ends in 2000 (http://www.china10k.com/simp/main/jews/yanjiuchengguo/chengguosoying.htm). In is possible that some translations into Chinese were published since then.

[29] Chinese scholars recognized very early the usefulness of the internet for making international contacts. Already in 1990 – 4 years before China was integrated in the international internet-community (Abels 2004: 845) – Pan Guang made use of international Newsletter for Judaic Studies to inform the scholars abroad about the establishing of the first Jewish history research center in China (Judaic Studies 1990). He asked for support in providing books and materials and expressed his hopes, to establish relations with other organizations or persons interested in research on the same subject (ibid.)

[30] See for example Kehm 2003: 7, Teichler 2004: 7, Yang 2004: 1.

[31] See for example Wang 1994, Fang /Li 1997, Fang 2000, Sun 2000, Zang 2000, Ning 2001, Mao 2002.

some changes in research methods. The number of academic works using methods of cultural and ethnic history is continuously growing.

This change of paradigms can be explained with the "Social history turn" within the Chinese history studies. The new Chinese social history, enrooted mostly in studies of Eric Hobsbawm, includes histories of social formations, interclass relationships, political system, ideology, socio-economic relationships und therefore covers both political and economic as well as cultural history and the social problems (Leutner 2003: 112f). New research topics in the Chinese academic discourse on Jews in China can be seen as an outcome of this turn, such as: rites (Liu 1994b), religious sites (Fang 1997c, Zang 2001, Zhang/Zhao 2002), women and marriage (Li 2000), descendants of Chinese Jews (Wang 1984, 1992a, 1992b), music (Tang 1999, Xu Buzeng 1999), literature (Wang 1995) and organisations (Pan 1993, 1994, Fang 1997b).

Except for this methodological aspect academic internationalization does not seem to have had other influences: neither in studies following the traditional methods nor in those using the "adapted" ones. The analysis of argumentation lines of the Chinese scholars and the comparison with those of Western scholars show that in spite of the interactions there is no common homogeneous academic discourse on Jews in China.

The limits of internationalization: the lines of arguments: Though dealing with the same subjects, relying on the same primary sources and even sometimes sharing the same methods, the argumentation lines of Chinese discourse(s) on Jews in China differ from those of their foreign counterparts. They seem to serve particular (inter-)national goals such as constructing China as a place of historical tolerance towards various ethnic groups. In the following part of my article I will exemplify those differences and explain them within the Chinese political and social context.

The assimilation of Chinese Jews is one of the main topics of the Chinese and foreign discourses on Jews in traditional China. But the focuses within the discourses are different. While non-Chinese scholars tend to re-evaluate the assimilation process and to emphasize its positive aspects for the long-term survival of a distinct Jewish identity,[32] their Chinese colleagues usually view it as an inevitable and completed absorption of the Jewish minority into the tolerant and open Han-Chinese majority, which kindly allowed the Jews to integrate themselves into society.[33] The positive image of traditional China is often stressed by creating a Western-Chinese dichotomy and comparing Chinese tolerant attitudes toward the Jews with the oppression of Jews and their social isolation in the West.[34]

Since the 1980s the integration of ethnic minorities has become a sensitive issue in China. Not only because of its importance in international relations as mentioned above, but also because of growing ethnic consciousness and significant increase of ethnic conflicts in China itself. As already in the 1950s the Jews of Kaifeng exemplify the perfect integration of an alien minority into the Han-Chinese majority: their descendents are so assimilated that they are not even recognized as an ethnic minority (少数民族)[35].

---

[32] See for example Ross 1982, Eber 1993, Leslie 2000. For positive impacts in particular aspects see Katz 1999, Shatzman Steinhardt 1999, Plaks 1999, Blady 2000.

[33] See for example Wu 1984, Xu 1992, Gong 1992, Wang 1994, Liu 1994a, Chen 1994, Zhang Youmei 1995, Zhang Qianhong 1995a, 1995b, Li 1999, Zang 2001, Ning 2001.

[34] See for example Wu 1984: 165, Wang 1994: 62, Chen 1994: 76f, Liu 1994a: 36, Zhang Yongmei 1995: 22.

[35] Gong Fangzhan is the only Chinese scholar asking directly, if Jews form an ethnic minority in

China's traditional goodwill and tolerance towards the Jews is the main line of arguments uniting Chinese discourses on different Jewish communities. Studies on Jewish exile in Shanghai emphasize the good relations between Chinese and the Jewish refugees. Shanghai is referred to as a "bridge of ongoing development of traditional friendship between Chinese and Jews" (Pan 1995: 63f). The term "traditional friendship" (传统友谊) is used by Pan very often (Pan 1992: 373, 1995: 2, 2000a: 446, 2000b: 82), yet he does not explain what he refers to as "tradition" in the relatively short time of relations between Chinese and Jews. Based on accounts of one Chinese and a few Jewish witnesses Pan states that Chinese in Hongkou overcame difficulties in order to make living space available for Jewish refugees, that Chinese and Jews helped each other during the difficult times in 1943-1945 and cooperated during the bombardment of Hongkou on June 17th 1945 (Pan 2000b: 79f). This portrayal of the Sino-Jewish relations in Shanghai contradicts the testimonies of witnesses cited in non-Chinese literature. Though the relations between the Chinese and the Jews in exile are seldom brought up in the discourse outside of China, the few scholars dealing with these relations see them as problematic and negative, because Jews were perceived by the majority of Chinese as Western imperialists (Kreissler 1988, 1991, Löber 1997, Ristaino 2001).

As well as in studies on Jews in traditional China, China's "goodness" is contrasted with the bad treatment of Jews and the indifference toward their destiny in the West. While the rest of the world closed their gates for the Jewish refugees, Shanghai provided them an asylum (Pan 1992: 356f, 1995: 22f, 2000a: 439, Sun 2000: 12, Mao 2002: 34). Shanghai is called an "ideal haven" (Pan 1992: 354), "Noah's ark" (诺亚方舟) (Mao 2002: 34), which opened its doors and "reached out a helpful hand" (伸出了温暖之手) (Sun 2000:12, Mao 2002:34). Chinese scholars also tend to state a higher number of Jewish Refugees in Shanghai than the foreign experts: most of them speak of about 25,000 (Pan 1992: 363, 1995: 22f, Sun 2000: 12, Fang 1997c: 82) and one even of about 30,000 (Mao 2002: 35), while some foreign scholars speak of about 16,000 to 18,000 refugees (Dicker 1962: 101, Kranzler 1976: 19) and others of about 18,000 to 20,000 (Mars 1969: 291, Kreissler 1991: 294f).

Chinese tolerance is not only opposed to Western treatment, but also to the Japanese policy toward the Russian Jews and the European Jewish refugees. Though studies of Chinese scholars deal either with the relations between Jews and Chinese or with Japanese policy, those argumentation lines gain relevance in relation to each other. Japanese are mentioned in connection with the establishment of the "designated area" (Pan 1995: 22f), with the Fugu-plan (河豚计划), which goal was to use the Jewish capital for Japanese interests. The instrumentalization of Jews is emphasized in two aspects: the international (Fang/Li 1997, Wang 1998, Fang 1999, 2000) – to attract Jewish investors from abroad – and the municipal (Fang 1997a) – to support Japanese candidates in elections. Their "pol-

---

contemporary China. According to him, there are no "genuine" (真正) Jews in China, because they have been assimilated for a long time, do not have any common language or any common cultural tradition (Gong 1992: 297ff). This academic reference might have been very important because of the establishment of diplomatic relations between China and Israel in 1992. If the descendants of Jews of Kaifeng would have been recognized as an ethnic minority, they could have made use of the Israeli Law of Return, which grants every person with Jewish ancestors the right to become an Israeli citizen. The recognition of descendants of Jews of Kaifeng as Jews by the State of Israel is avoided according to a bilateral agreement (Urbach 2003, Fricker/Kupfer 2003).

icy of terror" is seen as the main reason for Russian Jews to escape from North-Eastern China to Shanghai (Sun 2000: 12). The ambivalence of Japanese policy towards the Jews, which was on the one hand anti-Semitic, but on the other hand allowed Jewish immigration into Chinese territory under their control, which is an important topic in non-Chinese academic discourse,[36] is not brought up.

The evaluation of the activities of Jewish Baghdadi community in Chinese and foreign discourses are completely different. While the western discourse on the Bagdadi community is dominated by the revision of the (semi-)colonial past[37], the current Chinese discourse almost completely ignores the negative aspects of "imperialistic activities," which were stressed by Marxist historiography not too long ago. The imperialism paradigm is replaced by the modernisation paradigm, which became common since 1990s and stresses the positive modernising effects of foreign presence in China[38]. The accomplishments of the Jewish Baghdadi community in the emergence of a modern urban culture in Shanghai and the interactions between Jews and Chinese are emphasized – particularly in articles published abroad in English. The background of the target audience seems to play quite an important role in choosing the content of the publications: the involvement of the Baghdadi Jews in opium trade is not mentioned in papers published in English (Pan 1993, 1995). Whereas Pan Guang's essay on Zionism in China published in English only notes the support of Chinese intellectuals (Pan 1993: 179), his article in Chinese also brings up the negative feelings Chinese had about Baghdadi Jewish capitalists, who became associated with the British Empire, and earned their money with opium and arms trade (Pan 1994a: 79). Foreign research does not seem to affect the Chinese discourse visibly, but foreign readership seems to do.

The analysis of the main lines of arguments shows that Chinese and non-Chinese scholars tend to emphasize different topics and choose different explanatory models for the same phenomena. If knowledge-transfer is taking place, it could not be found within the argumentation. Therefore the question comes up, if the Chinese discourse in undergoing a totally autonomous development.

Except of analyzing argumentation lines there is another possibility to examine, if foreign discourses are taken into account by Chinese scholars in their research: analyzing their references.

Table 1: Quantitative findings of referencing in 32 Chinese articles on Jews in China published in China 1992-2002 [39] (only references to publications on Jews in China)

Topic	Number of publications	Total number of references	References in Chinese	References in English
Jews in traditional China	19	105	65 (61,9%)	40 (38,1%)
Jews in modern China	13	38	21 (55,2%)	17 (44,8%)

---

[36] See for example Shickman-Bowman 1999, Bresler 1999, Altman 2000, Bowman 2000.

[37] See for example Betta 1999, 2000b, Geldermann 2000, Meyer 1999, 2003, Roland 1999.

[38] See for example Leutner 1996, Dirlik 1996, Wang 1998; specifically on Chinese Sino-Judaic discourse: Betta 2000a.

[39] All papers accessible through "China Academic Journals full-text database" were analyzed. Of totally 45, 13 did not include any references. For exact list, please contact the author.

As we can see from Table 1 a quantitative analysis shows a pretty balanced picture of secondary sources referred to in publications of Chinese scholars: about 58,5% cited literature were originally in Chinese and 41,5% in English.[40]

Chinese bibliographies on Jews in China include both Chinese and foreign sources to a different extent. In 2001 Xu Xin stated that there was no Chinese systematic bibliography on Jews in Kaifeng: a circumstance that hinders Chinese scholars in their research (Xu 2001: 28). For that reason he published "An essential bibliography for the study of the history of the Kaifeng Jewish Community" (Xu 2001), which includes both Chinese and foreign studies. The newest English-language publications listed are two bibliographies on Jews in traditional China (Pollak 1992, Leslie 1999). (Xu 2001: 31f). Another paper which introduces the western sinological reseach on Jews in Kaifeng concentrates mostly on the history of the research. Although it mentions a growing number of publications since the 1970s, only three works published lately are named because of space limit (Geng 2000: 12f). A quite complete bibliography compiled by CJSS can be found in internet[41]. It includes both Chinese and foreign studies on Jews in traditional and modern China ending in 2000 for Chinese and in 1999 for foreign publications.

Internationalization?

There are elements of internationalization of the Chinese academic discourse on Jews in China, such as the existence of personal and institutional cooperation, the integration of Chinese scholars into international networks through their participation in international conferences abroad and organization of international conferences in China itself, publication of Chinese scholars' findings in non-Chinese volumes, translation of foreign works into Chinese as well as using new research approaches developed by foreign scholars. At the same time the contemporary foreign discourse does not affect the argumentation lines of Chinese scholars visibly and the Chinese discourse is almost not referred to in the works of foreign scholars. The main subjects of Chinese and Western discourses oppose each other in almost a dichotomous way, so that no common Chinese-Western discourse emerge, but parallel discourses, which have some common points, but take very autonomous paths.

Though dependent on funding and book donations from abroad, Chinese research on Jews in China keeps its autonomy, thus taking a different path than Chinese gender-studies, where the dominance of Western promotion and financing has marginalized indigenous approaches (Spakowski 2001: 97). The assumption that varied ideologies and domestic

---

[40] No sources in other foreign languages were cited. The most often cited works of non-Chinese scholars were published in 1942, 1972 and 1973 (White 1966, second edition, Leslie 1972, Rhee 1973). Not a single foreign source that was published in the last twenty years is referred to in Chinese studies on Jews in traditional China. The situation is slightly different within the discourse on Jews in modern China, where most of the articles base on primary sources. The most often cited source is the translation of Kranzler's *Japanese, Nazis and Jews* (1976) from 1991 and Dicker's *Wanderers and Settlers in the Far East* from 1962. The newer sources are either exhibition catalogues or non academic publications. Shickman-Bowman's article "The Construction of the Chinese Eastern Railway and the Origin of the Harbin Jewish Community, 1898-1931" (Shickman-Bowman 1999) is the only reference to recent non-Chinese publications.

[41] Http://www.china10k.com/simp/main/jews/yanjiuchengguo/chengguosoying.htm, accessed 21 February 2006.

considerations play a more important role in the development of national discourses in "soft" sciences seems to prove correct, as it already did for educational research in China (Yang 2004: passim), since the choice of topics, approaches or argumentations, can often be explained by international and national political, economical and social contexts of the academic community. The Chinese academic discourse on Jews in China portrays China as a tolerant state and nation by emphasizing the tolerance of Chinese toward the Jews in traditional and modern China, which is important in political, social and economic contexts in China and abroad. But unlike Chinese scholars doing educational research the integration level of Chinese Sino-Judaic scholars into the international academic community is nevertheless very high. Compared to the two research fields mentioned above, Chinese research on Chinese Jews appears to take the middle course of "limited" internationalization by benefiting from international contacts and maintaining indigenous characteristics.

References

"A New School for Judaica opens in China" (2006), in *Points East*, http://www.sino-judaic.org/pointseast/anewschool.html, accessed 23 May 2006.

Abels, Sigrun (2004) "China," in Hans-Bredow-Institut (ed.) *Internationales Handbuch Medien*, Baden-Baden: Nomos, pp. 820-858.

Altman, Avraham (2000) "Controlling the Jews, Manchukuo Style," in Malek 2000, pp. 279-317.

Armbrüster, Georg, Michael Kohlstruck and Sonja Mühlberger (eds) (2000) *Exil Shanghai 1938-1947. Jüdisches Leben in der Emigration*, Teetz: Hentrich & Hentrich.

Betta, Chiara (1999) "Silas Aaron Hardoon and Cross-Cultural Adaptation in Shanghai," in Goldstein 1999, pp. 216-229.

Betta, Chiara (2000a) "Myth and Memory. Chinese Portrayal of Silas Aaron Hardoon, Luo Jialing and the Aili Garden Between 1924 and 1995", in Malek 2000, pp. 377-400.

Betta, Chiara (2000b) "Marginal Westerners in Shanghai: the Baghdadi Jewish Community", in Robert Bickers and Christian Henriot (eds) *New Frontiers. Imperialism's New Communities in East Asia, 1842-1953,* Manchester and New York: Manchester UP, pp. 38-54.

Blady, Ken (2000) "The 'Blue-Turbaned Muslims'," in Ken Blady, *Jewish Communities in Exotic Places*, Northvale, New Jersey, Jerusalem: Jason Aronson, pp. 253-284.

Bowman, Zvia (2000) "Unwilling Collaborators: The Jewish Community of Harbin under the Japanese Occupation 1931-1945," in Malek 2000, pp. 319-329.

Bresler, Boris (1999) "Harbin's Jewish Community, 1898-1958: Politics, Prosperity, and Adversity," in Goldstein 1999, pp. 200-215.

Brief Introduction to the Centre for Judaic and Inter-Religious Studies at Shandong University (2006), http://www.cjs.sdu.cn/english/jianjie.htm, accessed 21 February 2006.

"Building an Academic Judaic Center in China" (2006), http://servercc.oakton.edu/~friend/center.html, accessed 25 May 2006.

Center of Jewish Studies Shanghai (2006a), http://www.cjss.org.cn, accessed 05 May 2006.

Center of Jewish Studies Shanghai (2006b) *What's new*, http://www.cjss.org.cn/new_page_9.htm, accessed 05 May 2006.

Chen Yiyi 陈贻泽 (1994) "Zhongguo gudai Kaifeng youtairen bei tonghua xianxiang chutan" 中国古代开封犹太人被同化现象初探 [Interim analysis of the assimilation of Kaifeng Jews in old China], in *Shijie zongjiao yanjiu* 1 (1994), pp. 73-80.

Chen Yuan 陈垣 (1920) "Kaifeng Yicileyejiao kao" 开封一赐乐业教考 [A Study of Jewish Religion in Kaifeng]," in *Dongfang Zazhi* 17/5 (1920), pp. 117-122, 17/6 (1920), pp. 119-126, 17/7 (1920), pp. 103-107.

Chinese Academy of Social Sciences (CASS) (2006), http://bic.cass.cn/english/ InfoShow/Arcitle_Show_Cass.asp?BigClassID=1&Title=CASS, accessed 13 June 2006.

Chinese education and society. Special issue (2001) "Sociology of Education (I) Inter-nationalization or Inndigenization?" *Chinese education and society* 34/6 (2001).

Daiwei Kelansile 戴维·克兰兹勒 [David Kranzler] (1991) *Shanghai Youtai nanmin shetuan 1938-1945* 上海犹太难民社团 1938-1945 [The community of Jewish refu-gees in Shanghai 1938-1945], Shanghai: Sanlian shudian.

Dicker, Herman (1962) *Wanderers and Settlers in the Far East: A Century of Jewish Life in China and Japan*, New York: Twayne.

Dirlik, Arif (1996) "Reversals, Ironies, Hegemonies. Notes on the Contemporary Histo-riography of Modern China," in *Modern China* 22/3 (1996), pp. 243-284

Eber, Irene (1993) "K'aifeng Jews Revisited: Sinification as Affirmation of Identity," in *Monumenta Serica* 41 (1993), pp. 231-247.

Fang Jianchang 房建昌 (1997a) "Taipingyang zhanzheng baofa qianxi riben dui lai hu deguo youtairen nanmin de liyong" 太平洋战争爆发前夕日本对来沪德国犹太难民的利用 [The exploitation of German Jewish refugees through the Japanese in Shang-hai shortly before the outbreak of Pacific War], in *Deguo yanjiu* 12/4 (1997), pp. 49-53.

Fang Jianchang 房建昌 (1997b) "Shanghai he Haerbin youtai shengyishe shulüe" 上海和哈尔滨犹太圣裔社述略 [A short account on Jewish B'nai B'rith in Shanghai und Harbin], in *Shilin* 2 (1997), pp. 101-106.

Fang Jianchang 房建昌 (1997c) "Jindai Zhongguo youtaijiao huitang ji qidaosuo kao" 近代中国犹太教会堂及祈祷所考 [An analysis of synogogues and Jewish halls in mod-ern China], in *Shijie zongjiao yanjiu* 1 (1997), pp. 81-90.

Fang Jianchang 房建昌 (1999) "Xingya yuanhuazhong lianluo bu: Shanghai Youtairen mimi diaocha baogao" 兴亚院华中联络部 上海犹太人秘密调查报告 [A report of the contact office central China of Great-Asia house Zentrales China des Großasien-Hauses about a secret investigation of Jews in Shanghai], in *Archives and History* 3 (1999), pp. 7-9.

Fang Jianchang 房建昌 (2000) "Nei Menggu, Liaoning, Beijing, Tianjin ji Qingdao Youtairen shi (1911-1949 nian)" 内蒙古、辽宁、北京、天津、及青岛犹太人史 (1911-1949 年) [History of Jews in Inner Mongolia, Liaoning, Beijing, Tianjin, and Qingdao (1911-1949)], in Malek 2000, pp. 229-275.

Fang Jianchang 房建昌 and Li Wei 李微 (1997) "Jindai Liaoning youtairen shulun" 近代辽宁犹太人述论 [Discussion on Jews of Loiaoning in modern times], in *Liaoning shifan daxue xuebao* 4, pp. 81-88.

Fricker, Silvia and Peter Kupfer (2003) *Bericht vom internationalen Symposium mit Ausstellung: Youtai – Presence and Perception of Jews and Judaism in China*, http://www.judentum.net/geschichte/youtai.htm, accessed 18 August 2004.

Friend, Beverly (2004) *Interview with Pan Guang*, http://www.oakton.edu/ user/~friend/pan1b.htm, accessed 11 November 2004.

Geldermann, Barbara (2000) "Shanghai – a city of Immigrants: Shanghai und die Gründer der ersten jüdischen Gemeinde, die bagdadischen Juden," in Armbrüster/Kohlstruck/Mühlberger 2000, pp. 46-57.

Geng Sheng 耿昇 (2000) "Xifang hanxuejie dui Kaifeng Youtairen diaocha yanjiu de lishi yu xianzhuang" 西方汉学界对开封犹太人调查研究的历史与现状 [The history and the contemporary situation of the research of Western sinology on Jews in Kaifeng], in *Xibei dier minzu xueyuan yuebao (zhexueban)* 47/4 (2000), pp. 3-13.

Gluckman, Ron (1997) *The Ghosts of Shanghai*, http://www.asiaweek.com/asiaweek/97/0606/is1.html, accessed 21 February 2006.

Goldstein, Jonathan (ed.) (1999) *The Jews of China. Vol. I: Historical and Comparative Perspectives*, Armonk, New York, London: M.E. Sharpe.

Goldstein, Jonathan (ed.) (2000) *The Jews of China. Vol. II: A Sourcebook and Research Guide*, Armonk, New York, London: M.E. Sharpe.

Gong Fangzhen 龚方震 (1992) "Guanyu dui Zhongguo gudai Youtairen yanjiu de shuping" 关于对中国古代犹太人研究的述评 [About the research on Jews in old China], in Zhu/Jin 1992, pp. 290-303.

Ha'erbin Youtairen lishi wenhua yanjiu zhongxin 哈尔滨犹太人历史文化研究中心 [Research center for history und culture of Harbin Jews] (2006), http://www.hlass.com/jgsz3-3.htm, accessed 07 July 06.

Hahn, Thomas H. (2002) *Zhang Xiangwen – Biography and Important Dates*, http://wason.library.cornell.edu/zhang/bio.html, accessed 12 December 05.

Heberer, Thomas (2000) *Some Considerations on China's Minorities in the 21st Century: Conflict or Conciliation?* Duisburg: Institut für Ostasienwissenschaften (Duisburger Arbeitspapiere Ostasienwissenschaften, Nr.31).

Hershatter, Gail, Honig, Emily and Stross, Randall (1996) "Introduction," in Gail Hershatter, Emily Honig, Jonathan N. Lipman and Randall Stross (eds) *Remapping China. Fissures in Historical Terrain*, Stanford: Stanford UP, pp. 1-9.

History of the Sino-Judaic Institute (2006), http://www.sino-judaic.org/aboutus.html, accessed 26 February 2006.

Huang Lingyu (2000) "Research on Judaism in China", in: Malek 2000, pp. 654-669.

Hutchings, Kate (2005) "Examining the Impacts of Institutional Change on Knowledge Sharing and Management Learning in the People's Republic of China," in *Thunderbird International Business Review* 47/4 (2005), pp. 447-468.

Interview with Pan Guang (2006), http://servercc.oakton.edu/~friend/art_pan1b.html, accessed 21 February 06.

"Judaic Studies In China" (1990) in *Judaic Studies* 43 (1990), http://www.h-net.msu.edu/~judaic/heasif/HEASIF43.txt, accessed 05 May 06.

Jutaj Sin-I (2004) "Konferencija v Harbine, posvjaščennaja istorii evreev jetogo goroda" [The conference in Harbin dedicated to the history of Jews in the city], in *Bjulleten' Igud Iocej Sin* 51/382 (2004), pp. 12-14.

Katz, Nathan (1999) "The Judaisms of Kaifeng and Cochin: Parallels and Divergences," in Goldstein 1999, pp. 120-138.

Kehm, Barbara M. (2003) "Vom Regionalen zum Globalen. Auswirkungen auf Institutionen, System und Politik," in *Die Hochschule. Journal für Wissenschaft und Bildung* 1 (2003), pp. 6-18.

Kirshner, Sheldon (2006) "Jewish studies in China are growing," in *The Canadian Jewish News*, 18 May 2006, http://cjnews.com/viewarticle.asp?id=2215, accessed 23 May 2006.

Kranzler, David (1976) *Japanese, Nazis and Jews: The Jewish Refugee Community of Shanghai, 1938-1945*, New York: Yeshiva UP.

Kreissler, Françoise (1988) "Die Emigration nach Shanghai: ein Ghettoisierungs-Prozess?" in Stadler, Friedrich (ed.) *Vertriebene Vernunft II: Emigration und Exil Österreichischer Wissenschaft, 1930-1940*, Wien: Jugend und Volk, pp. 1028-1044.

Kreissler, Françoise (1991) "Exil in Shanghai: Problematik und Schwerpunktthemen," in: Kuo Heng-yü und Leutner, Mechthild (eds) *Deutsch-chinesische Beziehungen vom 19. Jahrhundert bis zur Gegenwart*, München: Minerva, pp. 293-314.

Leslie, Donald D. (1972) *The Survival of Chinese Jews: The Jewish Community of Kaifeng*, Leiden: Brill.

Leslie, Donald D. (1998) *Jews and Judaism in Traditional China. A Comprehensive Bibliography*, Sankt Augustin: Monumenta Serica Institute.

Leslie, Donald D. (2000) "Integration, Assimilation, and Survival of Minorities in China: The Case of the Kaifeng Jews," in Malek 2000, pp. 45-76.

Leutner, Mechthild (1996) "Sozialgeschichte in der VR China: Modernisierungsparadigma statt Marxismus?" in: *Berliner China-Hefte* 11 (1996), pp. 47-63.

Leutner, Mechthild (2003) "Die 'sozialgeschichtliche Wende' in China seit den 1980ern. Chinesische und westliche/deutsche Historiographie: ein Dialog?" in *Zeitschrift für Weltgeschichte. Interdisziplinäre Perspektiven* 4/2 (2003), pp. 103-119.

Li Linfeng 李林风 (1999) "Kaifeng youtairen bei tonghua de yuanyin zhi wo jian" 开封犹太人被同化的原因之我见 [My opinion about the assimilation of Kaifeng Jews], in *Gansu shehui kexue* 1 (1999), pp. 26-28.

Li Wei 李微 (2000) "Lühua youtai funü ji youtairen jiehun zhuangkuang yanjiu" 旅华犹太妇女及犹太人结婚状况研究 [An analysis of the situation of Jewish women and marriages of Jews in China], in *Liaoning shifan daxue xuebao* 23/6 (2000), pp. 106-109.

Liu Wushu 刘五书 (1994a) "Kaifeng youtairen shenghuo xisu kao" 开封犹太人生活习俗考 [About the life customs of Kaifeng Jews], in *Henan daxue xuebao* 34/1 (1994), pp. 33-39.

Liu Wushu 刘五书 (1994b) "Cong youtaibei kan Kaifeng youtairen de ruhua guocheng" 从犹太碑看开封犹太人的儒化过程 [The confucianisation process of Kaifeng Jews as seen from Kaifeng Stelae Inscriptions], in *Zhongyuan wenwu* 2 (1994), pp. 111-115.

Löber, Petra (1997) "Leben im Wartesaal. Exil in Shanghai. 1938-1947," in Barzel, Amnon (ed.) *Leben im Wartesaal: Exil in Shanghai, 1938-1947,* Berlin: Jüdisches Museum, pp. 10-41.

Mackerras, Colin (2003) *China's Ethnic Minorities and Globalization*, London, New York: Routledge Curzon.

Malek, Roman (ed.) (2000) *From Kaifeng ... to Shanghai: Jews in China*, Nettetal: Steyler.

Mao Qin 茂钦 (2002) "Shanghai – youtai nanmin de 'Nuoya fangzhou'" 上海–犹太难民的"诺亚方舟" [Shanghai – Noah's ark of Jewish refugees], in *Wenshi jinghua* 10/149 (2002), pp. 34-39.

Mars, Alvin (1969) "A Note on the Jewish Refugees in Shanghai," in *Jewish Social Studies* 31/4 (1969), pp. 286-291.

Meyer, Maisie (1999) "Baghdadi Jewish Merchants in Shanghai and the Opium Trade," in *Jewish Culture and History* 2/1 (1999), pp. 58-71.

Meyer, Maisie (2003) *From the Rivers of Babylon to the Wangpoo: A Century of Sephardi Jewish Life in Shanghai*, Lanham: University Press of America.

Ministry of Education of the People's Republic of China (MOE): The Department of International Cooperation and Exchanges, http://www.moe.edu.cn/english/ international_1.htm, accessed 29 May 2006.

Mühlhahn, Klaus (1997) "Nation und Moderne: Paradigmen der chinabezogenen Geschichtswissenschaft," in *Asien Afrika Lateinamerika* 25 (1997), pp. 629-250.

Nanjing daxue Youtai wenhua yanjiusuo [Research institute for Judaic Studies at Nanjing University] (2006) http://philo.nju.edu.cn/institute_demo1.asp?id=17&name=%C4%CF%BE%A9%B4%F3%D1%A7%D3%CC%CC%AB%CE%C4%BB%AF%D1%D0%BE%BF%CB%F9, accessed 07 July 2006.

Ning Ping 宁平 (2001) "Lishi shang de Kaifeng youtairen" 历史上的开封犹太人 [The Jews of Kaifeng in history], in *Laoning shiwei daxue xuebao (Shehui kexue bao)* 4/5 (2001), pp. 102-104.

Ouyang Kang (2004) "Higher Education Reform in China Today," in *Policy Futures in Education* 2/1 (2004), pp. 141-149.

Pan Guang (1992) "A New Quest for Jewish Refugees in Shanghai during World War II," in *SASS Papers* 4 (1992), pp. 354-374.

Pan Guang (1993) "Zionism in Shanghai, 1903-1949," in *Studies in Zionism* 14/2 (1993), pp. 169-181.

Pan Guang 潘光 (1994a) "Youtai fuguozhuyi zai Shanghai de xingshuai ji qi huodong tedian" 犹太复国主义在上海的兴衰及其活动特点 [Rise and decline of zionism in Shanghai and its characteristics], in *Historic review* 2 (1994), pp. 54-60.

Pan Guang (1994b) "Haaintishemiut ve-hatsionut be-einaim siniot" [The anti-Semitism and the Zionism in Chinese Eyes], in *Kivunim* 43 (1994), pp. 111-115.

Pan Guang 潘光 (ed.) (1995), *Youtairen zai Shanghai* 犹太人在上海 [The Jews in Shanghai], Shanghai: Shanghai huabao.

Pan Guang (2000a) "Uniqueness and Generality: the Case of Shanghai in the Annals of Jewish Diaspora," in Malek 2000, pp. 437-445.

Pan Guang (2000b) "The Relationship between Jewish Refugees and Chinese in Shanghai during Wartime," in Armbrüster/Kohlstruck/Mühlberger 2000, pp. 77-83.

Pan Guang (2006) *Jews in China: Legends, History and New Perspectives*, http://www.cjss.org.cn/newa1.htm, accessed 20 February 06.

Pan Guangdan 潘光旦 (1980) "Guanyu Zhongguo jing nei Youtairen de ruogan lishi wenti" 关于中国境内犹太人的若干问题 [About some historical questions on Jews in China], in *Zhongguo Shehui Kexue* 3, pp. 171-186.

"Pan Guangdan" 潘光旦 (1991), in Xu Youchun 徐友春 (ed.), *Minguo renwu da cidian* 民国人物大词典 (Republican biographical dictionary), Shijiazhuang: Hebei renmin chubanshe, p. 1467.

Plaks, Andrew (1999) "The Confucianization of the Chinese Jews: Interpretations of the Kaifeng Stelae Inscriptions," in Goldstein 1999, pp. 36-49.

Pollak, Michael (ed.) (1988) *The Sino-Judaic Bibliographies of Rudolf Loewenthal*, Cincinnati, Ohio: Hebrew Union College Press.

Pollak, Michael (1993) *The Jews of Dynastic China: A Critical Bibliography*, Cincinnati, Ohio: Hebrew Union College Press.

Rampelmann, Katja (2005) "Introduction," in Alexander-von-Humboldt-Stiftung (ed.) *What Factors impact the Internationalization of Scholarship in the Humanities and Social Sciences. Arbeits- und Diskussionspapier 3/2005*, Bonn: Alexander-von-Humboldt-Stiftung.

Rhee, Song Nai (1973) "Jewish Assimilation: The Case of Chinese Jews," in *Comparative Studies in Society and History* 15/1 (1973), pp. 115-126.

Ristaino, Marcia R. (2001) *Port of Last Resort: Diaspora Communities in Shanghai*, Stanford: Stanford UP.

Roland, Joan G. (1999) "Baghdadi Jews in India and China in the Nineteenth Century: A Comparison of Economic Roles," in Goldstein 1999, pp. 141-156.

Ross, Dan (1982) *Acts of Faith: A Journey to the Fringes of Jewish Identity*, New York: St. Martin's Press.

Shapiro, Sidney (ed.) (1984) *Jews in Old China: Studies by Chinese Scholars*, New York: Hippocrene Books.

Shatzman Steinhardt, Nancy (1999) "The Synagogue at Kaifeng: Sino-Judaic Architecture of the Diaspora," in Goldstein 1999, pp. 3-21.

Shi Jingxun 时经训 (1913) "Henan Tiaojinjiao yuanliu kao" 河南挑筋教源流考 [A Study of Origin and Development of The Sect which Plucks out the Sinews in Henan], in *Henan jiaoyu zazhi*.

Shickman-Bowman, Zvia (1999) "The Construction of the Chinese Eastern Railway and the Origin of the Harbin Jewish Community, 1898-1931," in Goldstein 1999, pp. 187-199.

Spakowski, Nicola (2001) "The Internationalization of China's Women Studies," in *Berliner China-Hefte* 20 (2001), pp.79-100.

Sun Shihong 孙世红 (2000) "Shanghai – youtai yimincheng" 上海–犹太移民城 [Shanghai – the city of Jewish emigrants], in *At Home & Overseas* 7 (2000), pp. 11-13.

Tang Yating 汤亚汀 (1999) "1943-1944 nian Shanghai Hongkou gedou de yinyue shenghuo" 1943~1944 年上海虹口隔都的音乐生活 [The musical life in Hongkou-Ghetto between 1943 and 1944 in Shanghai], in *Yinyue yishu* 3 (1999), pp. 21-26.

Teichler, Ulrich (2004) "The changing debate on internationalization of higher education," in *Higher Education* 48 (2004), pp. 5-26.

Treiman, Daniel (2003) "Far East of Eden, a Scholar's Fascination With the Jews, in *Forward*, 28 February 2003, http://www.forward.com/issues/2003/03.02.28/ faces.html, accessed 30 October 2004.

Urbach, Noam (2003) "What's holding back the Reconstruction of the Kaifeng Synagogue? Between Revival and Obliteration of Kaifeng Jewry," paper presented at international Symposium „*Youtai – Presence and Perception of Jews and Judaism in China*" in Germersheim, September 19-23, 2003 (not published, personal notes of the author).

Wald, Salomon Shalom (2004) *China and the Jewish People. Old Civilizations in a New Era. Strategy Paper*, Jerusalem: The Jewish People Policy Planning Institute.

Wang Hui (1998) "Contemporary Chinese Thought and the Question of Modernity" (transl. by Rebecca E. Karl), in *Social Text 55* 16/2 (1998), pp. 9-44.

Wang Jian 王健 (1998) "Haerbin youtai shequ xintan" 哈尔滨犹太社区新探 [New analysis of Jewish community in Harbin], in *Shilin* 2 (1998), pp. 98-105.

Wang Shenhong 王申红 (2005) "Jin wu nian lai Zhongguo dalu Youtai yanjiu zongshu" 近五年来中国大陆犹太教研究综述 [The research outline of Judaism from 2000 to 2004], in *Fuyang shifan xueyuan xuebao (shehui kexue ban)* 104/2 (2005), pp. 110-113.

Wang Yisha (1984) "The Descendents of the Kaifeng Jews," in Sidney Shapiro (ed.), *Jews in Old China: Studies by Chinese Scholars*, New York: Hippocrene Books , pp. 167-186.

Wang Yisha 王一沙 (1992a) "Zhongguo gudai Youtairen ji qihouyi de qianxi he fenbu" 中国古代犹太人及其后裔的迁徙和分布 [Migration and distribution of Jews in ancient China and their descendants], in Zhu/Jin 1992, pp. 286-289.

Wang Yisha 王一沙 (1992b) *Zhongguo Youtai chunqiu* 中国犹太春秋 [Annals of Chinese Jews], Beijing: Haiyang.

Wang Yisha 王一沙 (1995) "Zhongguo gudai youtairen de wenxue zuopin" 中国古代犹太人的文化与作品 [The literary works of Jews in old China], in *Tongji daxue xuebao* 6/1 (1995), pp. 39-42.

Wang Zili 王自力 (1994) "Zhongguo Kaifeng youtairen de ruogan wenti" 中国开封犹太人的若干问题 [Some questions on Chinese Jews in Kaifeng], in *Beijing lianhe daxue xuebao* 8/18 (1994), pp. 61-66.

Wei Qianzhi (2000) "An Invistigation of the Date of Jewish Settlement in Kaifeng," in Goldstein 2000, pp. 14-25.

Weir, David and Hutchings, Kate (2005) "Cultural Embeddedness and Contextual Constraints: Knowledge Sharing in Chinese and Arab Culture," in *Knowledge and Process Management* 12/2 (2005), pp. 89-98.

White, William (1966) (ed.) *Chinese Jews: A Compilation of Matters Relating to the Jews of K'ai-feng Fu*, New York: Paragon Book (second edition).

Wu Zelin (1984) "An Ethnic Historian Looks at China's Jews," in Shapiro 1984, pp. 160-166.

Xu Boyong 徐伯勇 (1992) "Kaifeng Youtairen de ji ge wenti" 开封犹太人的几个问题 [Some questions concerning Jews in Kaifeng], in Zhu/Jin 1992, pp. 270-285.

Xu Buzeng (1999) "Jews and the Musical Life of Shanghai," in Goldstein 1999, pp. 230-238.

Xu Xin (1995) *Xu Xin's Trip Report: 1995: Reaction to Year in the U.S.*, http://servercc.oakton.edu/~friend/xuxin1995.html, accessed 21 February 2006.

Xu Xin (1999) "Chinese Research on Jews in China," in Aharon Oppenheimer (ed.) *Sino-Judaica: Jews and Chinese in Historical Dialogue. An international colloquium, Nanjing, 11-19 October, 1996*, Tel Aviv: Tel Aviv University, pp. 15-26.

Xu Xin (2000a) "Chinese Research on Jewish Diasporas in China," in Goldstein 2000, pp. 3-12.

Xu Xin (2000b) "Some Thoughts on Our Policy Toward the Jewish Religion – Including a Discussion of Our Policy Toward the Kaifeng Jews," in Malek 2000, pp. 671-682.

Xu Xin 徐新 (2001) "Kaifeng Youtai shetuan shi yanjiu wexian juyao" 开封犹太人社团史研究文献举要 [An Essential Bibliography for the Study of the History of the Kaifeng Jewish Community], in *Henan daxue xuebao (Shehui kexue ban)* 41/1 (2001), pp. 28-32.

Xu Xin (2003) *Xu Xin's Trip Report. 2003 Trip to Israel: a Renewed Beginning*, http;//servercc.aokton.edu/~friend/xuxin2003.html, accessed 21 February 2006.

Xu Xin (2006) U.S. *Trip Number 10 in the Winter 2006: Highly Productive!*, http://servercc.oakton.edu/~friend/chinajews.html, accessed 25 May 06.

Xu Zongze 徐宗泽 (1936), "Kaifeng youtaijiao gailun" 开封犹太人概论 [A survey of Jewish Religion in Kaifeng], in *Shengjiao zazhi* 25/4 (1936), pp. 194-202.

Yang Haijun (2000) "Die Erforschung der Juden in China," in Malek 2000, pp. 205-226.

Yang, Rui (2004) "Internationalisation, indigenisation and educational research in China," paper presented to the Australian Association for Research in Education International Educational Research, 28th Nov-2nd Dec, 2004, Melbourne, http://www.aare.edu.au/04pap/yan04597.pdf, accessed 17 December 2006.

Zang Piwen 臧丕文 (2000) "Xishuo youtairen dingju Kaifeng" 析说犹太人定居开封 [An analysis of Jewish settlement in Kaifeng], in *Kaifeng jiaoye xueyuan xuebao* 4 (2000), pp. 11-13.

Zang Piwen 臧丕文 (2001) "Ming Qing shiqi Kaifeng de youtai qingzhensi" 明清时期开封的犹太清真寺 [The Kaifeng Synagogue during Ming and Qing dynasties], in *Kaifeng jiaoye xueyuan xuebao* 21/2 (2001), pp. 17-19.

Zhang Qianhong 张倩红 (1995a) "Guanyu Kaifeng youtairen bei tonghua yuanyin de jidian kanfa" 关于开封犹太人被同化原因的几点看法 [Some views about the causes for assimilation of Kaifeng Jews], in *Henan daxue xuebao* 35/4 (1995), pp. 56-60.

Zhang Qianhong 张倩红 (1995b) "Lun lishi shang Kaifeng Youtairen bei tonghua de yuanyin" 论历史上开封犹太人被同化的原因 [About the causes for assimilation of Kaifeng Jews in history], in *Minzu yanjiu* 3 (1995), pp. 79-87.

Zhang Qianhong 张倩红 and Li Jingwen 李景文 (2000) "Guanyu Kaifeng Youtairen houyi de ji ge wenti" 关于开封犹太人后裔的几个问题 [Some observations on the descendants of the Jews in Kaifeng], in Malek 2000, pp. 153-170.

Zhang Tiejiang 张铁江 and Zhao Liantai 赵连泰 (2002) "Haerbin youtairen mudi kacha yanjiu" 哈尔滨犹太人墓地考察研究 [An analysis of the Jewish cemetery in Harbin], in *Heilongjiang shehui kexue* 1 (2002), pp. 54-57.

Zhang Xiangwen 张相文 (1910) "Daliang fang bei ji" 大梁访碑记 [The Analysis of stone inscriptions in Daliang (Kaifeng)], in *Dongfang zazhi* 3 (1910).

Zhang Yongmei 张咏梅 (1995) "Tan Kaifeng youtairen de tonghua" 谈开封犹太人的同化 [About the assimilation of Kaifeng Jews], in *Lishi Wenhua* 3 (1995), pp. 22-23.

Zhou Xun (2001) *Chinese Perceptions of the 'Jews' and Judaism. A History of the Youtai*, Richmond, Surrey: Curzon.

Zhu Weilie 朱威烈 and Jin Yingzhong 金应忠 (eds) (1992) *'90 Zhongguo youtaixue yanjiu zonghui* '90 中国犹太学研究总汇 [Compendium of Chinese Research on Jewish Studies in the 1990s], Shanghai: Shanghai guoji guanxi xuehui.

Conference Reports

5. Internationale Tagung zur Geschichte der Republik China, Xikou, Zhejiang, 28. Juli bis 1. August 2006

Das Forschungszentrum zur Geschichte der Republik China der Nanjing Universität unter Leitung von Zhang Xianwen veranstaltete die fünfte Internationale Tagung zur Geschichte der Republik China nicht nur an einem Ort von großer symbolischer Bedeutung, dem Geburtsort Chiang Kai-sheks; auch von den nahezu achtzig Vorträgen, teils im Plenum, teils in kleinen Arbeitsgruppen, waren zahlreiche Themen dem Wirken und der Persönlichkeit Chiang Kai-sheks gewidmet. Die Jiang-Familie selbst war vertreten durch *Jiang Fang Zhiyi*, die Schwiegertochter Jiang Jingguos; auch *Shirley Soong*, die derzeit an der Hoover Institution der Stanford Universität forscht, wo die Tagebücher Chiang Kai-sheks inzwischen für wissenschaftliche Forschungen eingesehen werden können, repräsentierte ihre Familie, die Nachkommen T.V. Soongs. *Qiu Jinyi*, ein Guomindang-Berater, plädierte auf der Schlusssitzung erneut für die Überführung der sterblichen Überreste der Jiang-Familie in ihre alte Heimat. Dass diese Tagung auch große Anziehungskraft für die chinesischen Medien besaß und vielfach darüber berichtet wurde, konnte angesichts dieses politischen Aufgebots nicht ausbleiben.

Die große politische Bedeutung der Tagung war hingegen nur ein Aspekt: Der wichtigste Aspekt war die Sichtbarmachung des Forschungsstandes und rege Diskussion neuester Forschungsergebnisse zur Geschichte der Republik China, die in den letzten 15 Jahren einen immensen Aufschwung innerhalb und außerhalb Chinas erfahren hat. So konnten die Veranstalter selbst ihre gerade erst erschienene vierbändige Geschichte der Republik China präsentieren. Sie behandelt über die politischen Entwicklungen hinaus auch die Grundzüge der wirtschaftlichen, sozialen und kulturellen Entwicklung.

Die Zugänglichmachung neuer Quellenbestände; die Entwicklung der einstmals wesentlich als Geschichte der politischen Entwicklungen, als Revolutionsgeschichte oder als Geschichte der großen Männer verstandenen Republikgeschichte hin zu einer auch die Ökonomie, Gesellschaft und Kultur umfassenden Gesamtgeschichte; die Verbreiterung und Pluralisierung der wissenschaftlichen Ansätze und Standpunkte; der wachsende wissenschaftliche Austausch, insbesondere auch mit den Kollegen aus Taiwan: das waren die einmütig genannten positiven Punkte des derzeitigen Forschungsstandes, die sich auch in den Beiträgen der Tagung widerspiegelten. Am Forschungsstand anknüpfend gab es Plädoyers für die Verstärkung sozialhistorischer Forschungen (*Zhu Hanguo*, Beijing Shifandaxue), für die Nutzung von *oral history*, für die Einbeziehung der chinesischen Geschichte in die „Weltgeschichte" – bisher behandelt das Fach „Weltgeschichte" die Geschichte außerhalb Chinas (*Hu Dekun*, Wuhan-Universität) – und für die Öffnung weiterer Archive, insbesondere des Archivs der KPCh, sowie für eine tiefgehendere ideologische Öffnung.

Mehr als 20 Beiträge befassten sich mit der politischen Entwicklung, 17 mit politischen Persönlichkeiten, weitere 16 waren außenpolitischen Beziehungen gewidmet. Da nach wie vor die Geschichte der KPCh selbst nicht als integraler Bestandteil der Republikgeschichte behandelt wird, thematisierte die Mehrzahl dieser Beiträge die Revolution von 1911, die Politik der Guomindang und deren innerparteiliche Konflikte, Person und historische Rolle Sun Yat-sens, Chiang Kai-sheks, aber auch Hu Shis und Chen Duxius sowie nicht zuletzt die Aggression Japans. Zahlreiche Beiträge suchten neue Thesen aufzustellen. So wurde die Republikzeit insgesamt als eine notwendige Phase des Übergangs von einem traditionellen zu einem modernen Nationalstaat definiert, welche die erste von drei Etappen dargestellt habe, die notwendigerweise militärisch dominiert gewesen sei (*Tian Xu*, Militärakademie Chinas). *Yang Tianshi* (Chinesische Akademie für Sozialwissenschaften, Institut für Neuere Geschichte, Peking) zeigte in seinem Beitrag auf, dass Chiang Kai-shek den Ratschlägen Kong Xiangxis, mit Japan einen Verhandlungsfrieden herbeizuführen, nicht folgte. Andere Referenten stellten die Beziehungen Chiang Kai-sheks nach dem Zweiten Weltkrieg zu Korea vor (*Hu Chunhui*, Zhuhai Akademie, Hong Kong) oder suchten dessen Beeinflussung durch buddhistische Ideen zu proklamieren (*Qiu Guosong*, Fenghua, Xikou-Museum), was allerdings in der Diskussion entschieden zurückgewiesen wurde. Auch die Bedeutung des historischen Ortes Xikou wurde von *Zhou Jinkang* (Fenghua, Xikou-Museum) vorgestellt.

Einen Vergleich der nationalsozialistischen Verbrechen, begangen durch die Wehrmacht, mit den Massakern der japanischen Truppen in China unternahm *Ma Zhendu* (Zweites Historisches Archiv, Nanjing), während *Zhang Sheng* (Nanjing-Universität) auf die internationale Wirkung des Nanjing-Massakers verwies, *Zhang Lianhong* (Nanjing Shifandaxue) die Auswirkungen des Massakers auf die Einwohnerzahl und die soziale Zusammensetzung der Bevölkerung Nanjings aufzeigte und *Jiang Liangqin* und *Wu Runkai* (Nanjing-Universität) Materialien zu Art und Anzahl der Getöteten vorstellten. Daten und Zahlen zur japanischen Politik der systematischen „Vergiftung" des chinesischen Volkes, insbesondere der Beamten der Marionettenregierung, durch Opium präsentierte *Cao Dachen* (Nanjing-Universität): 30% der Bevölkerung in der Mandschurei waren opiumsüchtig. Neben Japan wurden die Beziehungen der unterschiedlichen innenpolitischen Kräfte zu den USA und zu Großbritannien um das Jahr 1930 herum thematisiert (*Shen Xiaoyun*, Nanjing-Universität); die Bemühungen Großbritanniens und Indiens, ihren Einfluss in Tibet auszuweiten, waren ebenso ein Thema (*Chen Qianping*, Nanjing-Universität) wie die Beschlüsse der Guomindang 1946 hinsichtlich der Haltung zur Sowjetunion und zur Mandschureifrage (*Wang Chaoguang*, Chinesische Akademie für Sozialwissenschaften, Institut für Neuere Geschichte, Peking) oder die Frage der Ryukyu-Inseln (*Shi Yuanhua*, Fudan-Universität, Shanghai).

13 Themen befassten sich mit Problemen der wirtschaftlichen Entwicklung: u.a. der Finanzpolitik der Guomindang, der Bedeutung der chinesischen Wirtschaftswissenschaften, den Wirtschaftsgesetzen der Guomindang-Regierung, der Wirtschaftspolitik Japans in Qingdao oder Einzelthemen wie den Ningbo'er Kaufleuten in Shanghai. *Tim Wright* (Sheffield-Universität) zeigte überzeugend den engen Zusammenhang von wirtschaftlicher Entwicklung und Naturkatastrophen in Nordost-China auf und verwies insbesondere auf den Anteil gesellschaftlich bedingter Faktoren an diesen Katastrophen.

Die Themen der Kategorie „Gesellschaft und soziale Schichten" behandelten einmal Fragen des Charakters der Gesellschaft – z.B. wie und in welchem Maße kann wo und wann in China von Agrargesellschaft gesprochen werden (*Zhu Hanguo*) – und der Entwicklung von Märkten und dörflichen Geheimgesellschaften in Hubei (*Yin Enzi*, Nanjing-Universität). Zum anderen wurden spannende Mikrostudien präsentiert: zu lokalen Wohlfahrtsinstitutionen (*Sun Shang'en*, Ningbo-Universität) und Wohltätern wie Zhu Baosan (*Ying Fangdan*, Tianyige-Museum, Ningbo), zum Waisenhaus in Fenghua (*Yang Conglin*, Ningbo-Universität), zur „hygienischen Modernisierung" in Beibei (*Zhang Jin*, Medizinische Universität Chongqing), zum Wahlsystem der Handelskammer in Tianjin zu Beginn der Republikzeit (*Zhu Ying*, Huadongshifandaxue, Wuhan) und zu den unterschiedlichen politischen Fraktionen der Intelligenz 1949 (*Chen Sanjing*, Academia Sinica, Institut für Neuere Geschichte, Taipeh).

In der Sektion für Geistesgeschichte waren sechs Themen zusammengefasst, u.a. zur Professionalisierung der Wissenschaften im Zuge der Etablierung der Academia Sinica (*Chen Shiwei*, Forest Hill University, USA), zu den Differenzen zwischen den Konstitutionalisten und den Revolutionären um 1911 (*Wang Ruicheng*, Ningbo-Universität) und zum Quellenwert einiger früher Tageszeitungen und deren Beilagen. Auch die Sektion „Quellen und Forschungssituation" mit neun Beiträgen präsentierte Materialien zu neuen Forschungsbereichen: U.a. gab *Huang Jianli* (Singapur-Universität) einen ausgezeichneten Überblick über die Historiographie zur Rolle der Überseechinesen in der Revolution von 1911 und stellte bisher dominante „chinazentrierte" Forschungsansätze in Frage.

Diese Tagung zeichnete sich über ihre politische und wissenschaftspolitische Bedeutung hinaus neben den neuen Akzenten der Einschätzung von Persönlichkeiten und Hauptströmungen vor allem durch quellenbasierte empirische Studien aus, die insbesondere im sozialhistorischen Bereich wichtige Aspekte der Republikzeit erstmals beleuchtete. Nach wie vor ist allerdings bei zahlreichen Historikern das Bemühen stark, bestimmte Hauptlinien und Bewertungen der historischen Entwicklung als „positiv" oder „negativ" zu bewerten und die historische Rolle einzelner Persönlichkeiten „korrekt" einzuschätzen: So wurde u.a. von einem Historiker aus Taiwan vorgeschlagen, für die Geschichte Chinas im 20. Jahrhundert vier große Persönlichkeiten als entscheidend anzuerkennen: Sun Yat-sen, Chiang Kai-shek, Mao Zedong und Deng Xiaoping. Insgesamt stand die Tagung für einen breiten, auch kontroversen akademischen Diskurs, der im Unterschied zu anderen wissenschaftlichen Disziplinen in China sich seine Eigenständigkeit und Autonomie gegenüber westlichen Diskursen und akademischen Trends erhalten hat.

(Mechthild Leutner)

„The Internationalization of China. International Symposium in Honor of Dr. Dr. h.c. William C. Kirby", Berlin, 22. Juni 2006

Die Zusammenarbeit zwischen der Fachrichtung Sinologie der FU Berlin und der Harvard University, Fairbank Center for East Asian Research, im Bereich "Internationalisierung Chinas" hat inzwischen gewissermaßen Tradition: Organisiert u.a. von *Mechthild Leutner* (FU Berlin) und *William C. Kirby* (Harvard University) fand im August 2000 der erste einer Reihe von Workshops zu diesem Thema an der Harvard University, Cambridge, statt. Im Dezember 2001 folgte ein Workshop an der FU Berlin und im Jahre 2004 an der Peking Universität. Anlässlich der Verleihung der Ehrendoktorwürde an William C. Kirby durch den Fachbereich Geschichts- und Kulturwissenschaften der Freien Universität Berlin wurde nun am 22. Juni 2006 ein Symposium in dieser Thematik durchgeführt. Die Zusammensetzung der Referenten und Teilnehmer aus Geschichtswissenschaft, Sinologie, Politikwissenschaft und den Sozialwissenschaften ermöglichten einen intensiven Austausch.

William C. Kirby fasste in seinem Vortrag am Abend der Verleihung zusammen, welches Erkenntnisinteresse heute im Bereich Internationalisierung Chinas leitend sei: Zunächst sei es die Erforschung dessen, was man als Internationalisierung der internationalen kulturellen Gepflogenheiten in China – im politischen Handeln, in Geschäftspraktiken, im Rechts- und Gefängnissystem u.ä. - bezeichnen könne, wobei den chinesischen Akteuren genauso viel Bedeutung zukäme wie internationalen Einflüssen. Eine zweite umfassende Aufgabe, die zum Teil noch bevorstünde, sei die Erforschung von Chinas Rolle *in* der Welt unter Berücksichtigung derjenigen Bereiche, in denen Chinas internationale Präsenz globale Gemeinschaften und Praktiken neu definiert habe (z.B. Kommunistische Internationale, Internationales Rotes Kreuz, Vereinte Nationen). Das Verständnis solch prägender Faktoren sei bedeutsam auch im Hinblick auf die künftige internationale Zusammenarbeit mit China.

In ihren einführenden Bemerkungen zum Symposium betonte *Mechthild Leutner* (Berlin) zunächst die Bedeutung des Perspektivwechsels in der Internationalisierungsforschung hin zur Akteursebene. So sensibilisiert offenbare sich zum einen die Vielheit von Akteuren (Staaten, Institutionen, Individuen, kollektive Akteure) von Internationalisierung in der historischen Rückschau. Zum anderen werde die Rolle von Wissenschaftlern als Akteure und Träger von Internationalisierung, als Mittler und als Übersetzer offenkundig.

In seinem Beitrag „Rethinking China in a Global World" verortete *Klaus Mühlhahn* (Turku) die Entstehung des Forschungsgebietes Internationalisierung in China zeitlich in den späten 1980er Jahren: Es sei in Reaktion auf Globalisierungsprozesse, -diskurse und die daraus resultierende Infragestellung gängiger Forschungskategorien, wie z.B. Nationalstaat, kulturelle Identität als Entitäten sowie den Dichothomien Tradition-Moderne und China-Westen entstanden. In China selbst handle es sich um einen dialektischen Prozess von Internationalisierung und Wiederaneignung der Geschichtsschreibung, letzteres durch die Wiederbelebung nationalistischer Narrative und die Etablierung des „Nationalen Lernens" (国学) als wissenschaftliche Disziplin. Im Rahmen eines solchen wechselseitigen Prozesses haben sich nationale Geschichten zu verwobenen Geschichten (*entangled history, histoire croisée*) entwickelt; die chinesische Geschichte werde „neu geschrieben". Mühlhahn benannte drei Themengebiete, die unter dem Internationalisierungsaspekt neu zu erforschen und bewerten wären: Hybridität, Verhandlungskultur zwischen China und den Westmächten sowie die Definition chinesischer Kultur.

Marianne Bastid-Bruguière (Paris) sprach über „China's Internationalization and Foreign Language Learning".[1] Sie stellte überzeugend dar, dass im Grunde erst mit der Einführung des HSK-Tests für Ausländer zu Anfang der 1990er Jahre, die sie als „linguistic turn in Chinese policy" bezeichnete, eine nationale Politik der Internationalisierung von Chinesisch als Fremdsprache (ChaF) verfolgt worden sei. Kein chinesischer Herrscher habe im Altertum gezielt für Kommunikationsmöglichkeiten mit Ausländern gesorgt; der Umgang mit diesen sei vielmehr ethnischen Minderheiten überlassen gewesen. Die weltweite Gründung von Konfuzius-Instituten zur Verbreitung der chinesischen Sprache markiere einen erneuten „turn". Die chinesische Regierung sei allerdings nicht Initiator, sondern habe lediglich auf bestehende Trends der Internationalisierung von ChaF reagiert. Tatsächlich entglitten chinesische Sprach- und Kulturoffensiven immer mehr staatlichen Händen und würden auf die Ebene der nicht-staatlichen Beziehungen (民间关系) verlagert. Am Beispiel der Konfuzius-Institute sei auch ein Richtungswechsel der Internationalisierung zu verzeichnen, nämlich von China nach außen.

Eine vergleichbare Tendenz beobachtet *Susanne Weigelin-Schwiedrzik* (Wien) in der Internationalisierung chinesischer Außenpolitik. In ihrem Beitrag „Methodological Prob-

---

[1] Siehe Artikel in diesem Heft, S. 97-105.

lems in the Analysis of Chinese Foreign Policy" charakterisierte sie zunächst den außenpolitischen Paradigmenwechsel vom Realismus zum Sozialkonstruktivismus. Für einige außenpolitische Schritte der VR China (Beteiligung an Kriegshandlungen, UN-Bei-
tritt) habe jedoch keines dieser Modelle Erklärungskraft gehabt. Aktuell dominiere das
Perzeptionsparadigma: Die chinesische Wahrnehmung Europas sei bestimmend für die
europäisch-chinesischen Beziehungen. China betrachte Europa als Entität, vernachlässige
dabei Einzelinteressen der EU-Mitgliedsländer und setze zudem eigenständig neue Themen auf die Agenda, wie z.B. die Forderung nach einer Internationalisierung der Taiwan-
frage. Um die Erklärungskraft politikwissenschaftlicher Ansätze auf diesem Gebiet zu
erhöhen, sei daher die Entwicklung neuer Instrumente über die Analyse gegenseitiger
Perzeptionen hinaus und vor allem die Fähigkeit zur Einnahme der chinesischen Perspektive auf internationale Beziehungen ein dringendes Desiderat.

Abschließend sprach *Nicola Spakowski* (Bremen) über „The Internationalization of the
Humanities and Social Sciences in China – Transfers and Interactions". Ihrer Beobach-
tung nach ist in den chinesischen Geistes- und Sozialwissenschaften weniger eine
Internationalisierung als deren Gegenbewegung (regionalistische Tendenzen) zu
verzeichnen. Sie prognostizierte, dass sich der akademische Markt in China möglicher-
weise auch in Zukunft sehr stark selbst genügen könne. Im Westen anerkannte Theorean-
sätze über die Internationalisierung von Wissen (Universalismus, Partikularismus,
Hybridität) und ihre entsprechenden Implikationen (Dichothomien Staat-Gesellschaft,
Ost-West; Einebnung von Machtgefällen) würden in der Übertragung auf die
wissenschaftliche Gemeinde in China hinfällig. Maßgeblich sei vielmehr die Vielzahl und
Unterschiedlichkeit von Akteuren, Interessen und Loyalitäten in den diversen Disziplinen. Als weitere Beispiele für regionalistische Aneignungsprozesse nannte sie den
chinesischen Diskurs über Zivilgesellschaft und die Institutionalisierung von Sinologie-in
China.

Insgesamt wurden in den Beiträgen folgende, auch gegenläufige Tendenzen chinesischer
Internationalisierungsprozesse sichtbar: (1) Staatliche Initiativen werden zunehmend von
transnationalen überlagert. (2) Internationalisierung Chinas bedeutet auch, historisch und
aktuell immer stärker, Externalisierung chinesischer Konzepte. (3) Auch gegenläufige
Tendenzen wie Nationalismus, Regionalismus und „Nationales Lernen" (国学) müssen
als Ausdruck von Internationalisierung gewertet werden. (4) Internationalisierungsfor-
scher sind zugleich Träger und Analysten von Internationalisierung. (5)
Internationalisierungsforschung dient auch der Revision der Geschichts*schreibung*.
Insbesondere die letzten beiden Punkte verdeutlichen einmal mehr die Verantwortung des
Wissenschaftlers als Mittler. (Nathalie van Looy)

**"China's Internet and Chinese Cultures": The Fourth Annual Chinese Internet
Research Conference 2006, Singapore, 21-22 July 2006**
The conference was hosted by the Singapore Internet Research Centre and the School of
Communication and Information at Nanyang Technological University; cosponsors were
the China Internet Project of UC Berkeley Graduate School of Journalism, the Intellectual
Property & Communications Law Program at the Michigan State University College of
Law, the School of Journalism and Communication at Chinese University of Hong Kong
and the School of Journalism and Communication at Peking University. The welcome address was given by *Ang Peng Hwa* (Singapore), the Dean of the School of Communica-

tion at NTU, who stressed the importance of the Internet for political and societal developments in general and for China, in particular, as one of the fastest growing Internet regions in the world today, with more than 120 million users.

The first panel dealt with "Internet Use and Social Transformation" and was presided over by *Eddie Kuo* (Singapore), Interim Executive Director of the Singapore Internet Research Center (SIRC). *Guo Liang* (Beijing) then presented a comprehensive picture of the most recent information and developments regarding the Internet in China in: "Internet Use in China: Trends and Projections," which focused on the changes in the gender gap – the gap is closing – and the still existing digital divide between the urban centers, where the use of the Internet is almost as ubiquitous as in Europe or North-America, and the rural areas, where only a small percentage of the people are considered to be Internet users. In "Comparing Popular Online Activities in the US and China," *Deb Fallows* (Washington, DC), from the Pew Internet and American Life Project, offered a comparison of Internet developments in China and the US. According to the results of her research, there are three main differences: first of all, developments in China are much more dominated by entertainment, including probably infotainment, than they are in the US. Secondly, men and women use the Internet differently to each other in the US, but in very similar ways in China, where no significant differences could be traced. Thirdly, the use of email, still dominant in the USA, is comparatively low in China, but gaming and other entertainment activities are increasing world-wide. *Bu Wei* (Beijing) talked about "Digital Divide Issues in China – Neglected and Excluded Aspects," presenting research from places such as Hohhot and Xining, where most users use Internet Cafés to go online. She called for more research on minority groups, ranging from ethnic minorities and migrants workers to gays and lesbians. She also mentioned the very interesting information that migrant workers, particularly when working in the service sector such as hotels, regularly employ the Internet to stay in contact with friends and family. The panel, "Uses and Perspectives in and outside China" presented three studies on very specific uses of the Internet; *Pamela Koch, Wei Chen* und *Brad Koch* (all Singapore) in "Beauty is in the Eye of the QQ" presented their research on the use of QQ (the specific Chinese form of Instant Messenger), and also sought to explain how the partly negative view of QQ found in the public discourse in China has come into being. *Lim Sun Sun* (Singapore), who had carried out a more ethnographic study of Internet use, asked in "A Study of Urban China's Media-Rich Households", how ICT has become a signifier for consumerism and status within contemporary Chinese society: for the new urban middle class, ICT products such as computers, mobile phones and digital cameras have replaced the former "four important things" (四大件) (watch, bicycle, sewing machine, radio) and the former "six important things" (六大件) (TV, fridge, recorder, washing machine, fan and camera). She concluded that when China is compared with other Asian countries, such as Korea and Singapore, the one child policy in China plays an enormous role in how the relationship between parents and their child is combined with the role of ICTs. In general, a very positive view of ICTs prevails and children are expected to know much more than parents. *Li Ziwei* (Beijing) talked on "Personal Ads on a 'Dating' BBS" and the influence of the new communication technologies on marriage and relationships. The lunchtime symposium brought the keynote speech by Isaac Mao, one of the best known bloggers and the co-founder of CNBlog.org, and his insights into how blogs have changed China's intellectual and journalistic scene. "Blogging in China: Social and Political Implications" then continued to discuss that topic: *Roland Soong* (Hong Kong) talked about the importance of blogging for spreading news all over the world and was convinced that blogging in China, where the press is still severely restricted by censorship laws, plays a very important role. He mentioned, as one example, the case of *Bingdian* 冰點, that is, the closing down of the famous supplement of the *Qingnianbao* 青年報. *Ashey Esarey* (Middlebury) and *Xiao Qiang* (Berkeley), "Zhenghua Fanshuo by Chinese Bloggers," dealt with the use of satire (正話反說) by bloggers and how the Internet has created a sphere for the free use of words. The panel "Digital Gaming in China" offered a comparative approach on gaming in the Chinese-speaking world, including Taiwan. "Driving Factors and their Interactions in China's Online Game Business" was the title of the paper by *Hu Zhengrong* and *Gao Di* (Beijing), who offered more of an inside view of gaming in China, while *Michael Fu* (Taipei), who has been involved in creating games for the Chinese market for years, described the Chinese market from a business perspective in "The Paradigm Shift of Taiwan's PC Game Market." The following discussion dwelt on two topics: firstly, on the question of how cultural differences influence the design of games, that is to say, why do Asians prefer Manga-like games, while in the West, games have to be designed in a "realistic" environment. Secondly, it was asked how Asian governments (China, Singapore, Taiwan) are dealing with the obviously conflicting demands confronting them as a result of their attempts to implement strict controls on games in order to protect young people, while at the same time promoting the development of these same games which are regarded as an important part of the new economy. In "Hibiscus Bloomed on the Internet – For a Short Time: A Case of Interaction Between Online Discourse and Celebrity Culture," *Chen Yanru* (Xiamen) described how "Sister Hibiscus," a 28-year-old female college graduate shot to fame almost overnight on the Internet after posting sexually assertive but not revealing personal photos on the BBS of one of the most prestigious universities. The following panel, one of the most interesting, dealt with the use of the Internet in underdeveloped regions: "ICT for Development in China: The Internet in Rural Areas." The first paper, "Network Technology and Social Impacts: Investigation of Farmers' Internet Application and Social Transformations in Northwest Rural Areas" by *Wang Xiling* (Beijing) described theoretically qualitative methodologies for measuring the success of the Internet in empowering undeveloped regions. "Chinese Rural Residents' Adoption of and Attitude Toward the Internet: An Exploratory Research," by *Zhang Mingxin* (Wuhan), presented field studies and the opinions of China's rural population on the Internet: the persons interviewed saw the Internet, to some extent, as an opportunity and as bringing change to China's rural economy, but the dominant view was that ICT is a "toy for the middle class" – whether in bigger towns or in rural areas. "Farmers' Internet Access and Usage in Western China: A Case Study" by *Chao Naipeng* (Nanjing) came to the conclusion that e-commerce has a certain influence on rural society, but that this influence is neither very solid nor large-scale. It may, however, lead to the diffusion of innovation if the "right persons" are involved. "The Internet Adoption and Usage: A Case Study of Rural Users in China's Shandong Province" by *Zhao Jinqiu*, *Hao Xiaoming*, and *Indrajit Banerjee* (Singapore) also concluded that the influence of the Internet is overestimated and mentioned, in addition to occasional success stories about some farmers or rural production units in the marketing of their products, the high cost of computers and the lack of infrastructure

The second day began with a panel on the "Internet and the Transformation of Chinese Communities." *Peter Marolt* (Berkeley) talked about "Identity Formation in a Chinese Online Community", and the close resemblance between off-line and online identities. In "New Media and Changes in Social Structure in Urban China: A Network Approach," *Yang Boxu*, *Li Li*, and *Bo Gai* (Beijing) dealt with other ICTs: mobile phones and their influences. Their empirical research concluded that mobile communication is used by lovers, hobby-oriented networks, and – surprisingly – for lower income groups to connect with friends. The panel "The Internet-based Distribution of R&D and the Chance for China's Scientific Community" was opened with a paper entitled "Distributed R&D" by *Zhao Chen* from the State Intellectual Property Office of the PRC, who showed proof of China's increasing embeddedness in international structures. In "Internet, Can You Sustain Media Hegemony? The War between "Mantou" and "Wuji," *Wang Wei* (Beijing) dealt with the law suit of Chen Kaige, the famous filmmaker, against Hu Ge's video, Mantou, which has been spread over the Internet. "Digital Media in Asia: Legal, Economic, and Social Implications" by *Susie Lindsay* and "The Future of Music and Film Piracy in China" by *Eric Priest* (both Cambridge, Mass.) dealt with the problem of "piracy": Eric Priest declared that China had made significant progress towards introducing formal legislation to deal with this problem, but underground channels still exist and he saw a solution only in a compulsory licensing system, which was rejected by a large majority of the other participants as this would increase the role of state and government and hinder "grey channels" of publication. The lunch symposium by *Rebecca McKinnon* (Cambridge, MA) on "Corporate Responsibility and the Internet in China" warned against any unilateral action being taken by the US or the West as this could counteract the desired aims of making China's Internet freer. McKinnon opted for more openness when "censorship" is carried out for various reasons (traditional, religious, and political): the user should at least be aware of any ongoing control – she quoted, as good examples, Singapore with its anti-racist laws or Germany with its anti-Nazi laws. The panel, "National Identity and Political Action," began with "China's e-Government Portal: a Discourse on National Identity"; *Raymond Fei Loi Lai* (Macau) compared Chinese and English language versions of China's official websites. *Jens Damm* (Berlin) in "China's Internet and the Creation of Public Spaces: Examples from BLOGS; BBSs and Interviews" showed the limitations of Western discourses on China's Internet and how Western interference could even lead to the fraternization of Chinese critical intellectuals with their government. "Urban Conservation Online: Chinese Civic Action Groups and the Internet" by *Nicolai Volland* (Taipei) showed how the Internet helped to form a community out of people from varied backgrounds and very different geographical locations, drawing them together in their efforts to save some of Beijing's old architecture. The conference ended with two papers on the panel, "Internet Governance and Regulation," "Chinese Network Ethics: Native Resources and Global Consensus on Morality," by *Lü Yao-huai* (Central South University) and "Promises and Problems of Civil Society in Internet Governance: Lessons from China" by *Ang Peng Hwa* and *Wang Guozhen* (Singapore).

To summarize, the conference brought to light new topics on China's Internet; the focus was shifted away from the questions of censorship and control towards the societal and economic use of the Internet, and the influence of new ICTs on society in general. These topics, including a focus on methodology, will be subjected to further analysis in the following conferences in Texas, Beijing and Hong Kong. (Jens Damm)

16. Akademische Konferenz „China, die chinesische Zivilisation und die Welt: Vergangenheit, Gegenwart und Zukunft", Moskau 27.-28. Oktober 2006
Die Konferenz wurde vom Institut für den Fernen Osten der Russischen Akademie der Wissenschaften im Zusammenhang mit dessen 50-jährigen Gründungsjubiläum durchgeführt. Es gab zwei Plenartagungen und vier Arbeitsgruppen. Diese befassten sich mit den Themen: die wirtschaftlichen Aspekte der russisch-chinesischen Zusammenarbeit, die gegenseitige Rezeption im Kontext von internationalen Beziehungen und Globalisierung, geschichtliche und aktuelle Aspekte der Interaktion sowie der Fragen des kulturellen und Zivilisationsdialoges zwischen Russland und China als Weg zum gegenseitigen Verständnis.
Außer den russischen und chinesischen Teilnehmern waren Gäste aus Japan, Südkorea und Indien gekommen. Von der Freien Universität nahmen die beiden Mitglieder des russisch-deutschen Redaktionskollegiums der Dokumentenpublikation „KPdSU(B), Komintern und China 1921-1943" teil. Der fünfte Band dieser Publikation wird im Frühjahr 2007 in Russisch erscheinen.
Das Institut hatte zwei Broschüren (424 Seiten) vorbereitet, die Thesen der Beiträge von über 70 Mitarbeitern, 35 Autoren anderer russischer Forschungseinrichtungen und Diplomaten sowie sieben chinesischen Gästen enthielten. Diese konnten natürlich nicht alle zu Wort kommen. Die Beiträge bezogen sich überwiegend auf aktuelle Fragen der russisch-chinesischen Beziehungen. Außerdem hat das Institut anlässlich seines Jubiläums zwei Sammelbände herausgegeben. Der eine („Menschen und Ideen") würdigt die drei bisherigen Direktoren und weitere profilierte Angehörige des Instituts. Darüber hinaus behandelt er die Hauptrichtungen der Forschung sowie Überlegungen zu Forschungsschwerpunkten und Entwicklungsproblemen. Der andere („Das Institut für den Fernen Osten – Jahre, Menschen, Arbeiten") stellt die heutige Einrichtung in ihrer Struktur vor. Den Hauptteil bildet eine Bibliographie der Mitarbeiter über die Jahre 1996 bis 2006 (eine Bibliographie 1966 bis 1996 erschien im Jahre 1996).
In seinen grundlegenden Ausführungen zur komplexen Erforschung des modernen China verwies Institutsdirektor *M.L. Titarenko* insbesondere auf einen politisch bedeutsamen Aspekt: Die öffentliche Wahrnehmung in Russland bleibe weit hinter dem Stand der intensiven und vielseitigen russisch-chinesischen Beziehungen zurück. Das daraus resultierende Defizit in der geistig-kulturellen Atmosphäre müsse unbedingt überwunden werden, wozu nicht zuletzt Anstrengungen der Wissenschaftler gefragt seien.
Auffallend waren die vielen Beiträge zur regionalen und grenznahen Zusammenarbeit, die hohe Veranschlagung der Shanghaier Organisation in ihrer Bedeutung für das Kräfteverhältnis in Mittelasien und die Zurückweisung des USA-Einflusses aber auch die Betonung einer strategischen Partnerschaft zwischen beiden Staaten.
In den Beiträgen spiegelten sich die Bemühungen um eine Förderung der intensiven russisch-chinesischen Zusammenarbeit. Da Chinawissenschaftler aus den USA und Westeuropa an der Konferenz kaum vertreten waren, wurde die Tagung nahezu zu einer russisch-chinesischen Veranstaltung zu den Beziehungen zwischen beiden Ländern, und zwar von führenden Repräsentanten maßgeblicher wissenschaftlicher Einrichtungen beider Länder. Von chinesischer Seite waren u.a. vertreten: das ZK der KPCh, die Akademie für Gesell-

schaftswissenschaften in Peking, die Peking-Universität, das Pekinger Institut für internationale Beziehungen und das Pekinger Verwaltungsinstitut sowie wissenschaftliche Einrichtungen aus Heilongjiang, Xinjiang, Yunnan und Shandong.

Die 16. Konferenz des Instituts für den Fernen Osten war ein kennzeichnender Bestandteil der gegenwärtigen Anstrengungen der russischen Sinologie zur Intensivierung des Verständnisses im beiderseitigen Interesse Russlands und Chinas. Eine Leistungsschau des Moskauer Instituts und seiner Kompetenz war sie allemal.

(Joachim Krüger)

Research Center for Yi Culture and the Arts Founded in Xichang, 16. September 2006

With support from the Committee for Minority Affairs of Sichuan Province, the Committee for Minority Affairs of Liangshan Yi Autonomous District, as well as local government departments and Yi culture researchers, the Liangshan Research Center for Yi Culture and the Arts (hereafter called LRCYCA) was founded in Xichang, district capital of Liangshan Autonomous Yi District on September 16, 2006. Directly responsible for the center's activities is the Liangshan Yi Language Middle School, which also acts as a host unit and provides the center with office space and staff. The center is also subject to the management and directives of departments at district government level. The center's board consists of 92 local (partially international renowned) Yi and Han scholars and political personnel as well as one international researcher (German). The LRCYCA currently has a staff of 14 people, mainly teachers and specialists on Yi language and culture, who are part of the Liangshan Yi Language Middle School's original staff. The center's research focus will mainly be concerned with the collection, development and publication/data production of Yi cultural heritage. More information of what this research focus entails can be found on the LRCYCA's website, which features regularly updated information on different aspects of Da Liangshan Yi intangible (as well as tangible) cultural heritage, such as religion (Bimo culture), Yi songs and literature, etc. and which is meant to serve as platform for the proliferation of Yi culture to the wider, Chinese-speaking public. The website can be visited at www.sclswhysw.home.sunbo.net. There are also plans for the LRCYCA to publish its own annual research journal.

The LRCYCA was initiated by the current principal of the Liangshan Yi Language Middle School, *Yang Chaoqing*, members of the school's staff (now also research staff), and a German researcher. Its constituting targets include specifically the research, development, performance and proliferation of Yi culture and the arts. Apart from focusing on the description and protection/development of the Liangshan Yi ethnic minority's intangible cultural heritage the center also aims at cooperating with scholars and institutions in China and abroad to jointly develop new methodologies for culture and language policies, and to make aspects of its work usable for an increased representation and expansion of the local cultural sector and the local government's cultural promotion activities.

China has been witnessing a revival in cultural awareness recently, specifically in the awareness for the "protection" and "development" of China's intangible cultural heritage. In line with a row of new policies now being implemented to realize this new and in itself often ideologically intangible policy, exhibitions, directives, meetings and institutions have been launched. The founding of the LRCYCA must also be seen in light of China's new cultural drive. With around 2,1 million Yi inhabitants, Da Liangshan Autonomous Yi

District is the largest and densest settlement area of China's Yi ethnic minority, which is spread out over the provinces of Sichuan, Yunnan, Guizhou and Guangxi. As a result of its long geographic, social and cultural seclusion the area has been one of the last to be opened for Chinese (and international) tourism. Consequently, the Da Liangshan Yi community can be culturally regarded to be the most well-preserved of all other provinces' Yi communities. Both local and central governments as well as Yi researchers, intellectuals and individuals from the arts and media circles have been paying an increasing amount of attention to the process of this opening up, its marketing and its future as an ethnically distinct cultural entity.

The founding of the research center can be seen to bear larger implications for ethnic minority studies in a Chinese context. Firstly, the founding of this type of center is in itself witness to the fact that a certain re-orientation has taken place within minority cultural policies on a central and a local level. This change in policy is not to be underestimated as it means a big step forward from only a year ago, where any project that was applied for along the lines of cultural preservation as an interdisciplinary approach between politics and academia was put on indeterminate hold. It remains to be seen however what the center can realistically accomplish, both in terms of research as well as politically, as it is part of (and influenced by) the local party and government structure (albeit not deriving its funding from this structure). Moreover, local politics and especially social relations in Liangshan tend to be extremely complicated. Especially the latter sport a long history and go back to the times before the area's liberation in 1956, when there existed fierce power struggles and regular and bloody clashes between the ruling clans of the Liangshan Yi. Often enough, research institutions in Liangshan can be "split down the middle" due to such persisting clan relations. Moreover, the center's board of constituting members is quite large and reflects a corresponding diversity of viewpoints and interests. For now, though, the center is still in its beginning stages, acquiring support and funding from sources within and outside of China. For more information on the center's activities and future projects and development the author can be contacted at olivia.kraef@gmx.de.

(Olivia Kraef)

"The Party-State System and the Cross Strait Social Economy during the Early Cold War," 12-13 October 2006, Taipei.

The Institute of Modern History at Academia Sinica has begun the new century with a new initiative to study the cross-Strait Cold War. It has held three international conferences since. In December 2001, a newly formed research group held its first conference, titled "Historical Developments of the 1950s across the Straits." This was the first academic conference ever to breach the formerly insurmountable barrier of 1949 to host scholars in Taiwan from Japan, the PRC, the United States, England and Israel. The active discussions shattered many myths including the so-called harmony within the eastern and western camps. Some papers explored the domestic employment of propaganda by the Chinese Communist Party. Others discussed the impact of ideology on economic development. Some papers were published in the *Bulletin of the Institute of Modern History Academia Sinica, Special Issue: The Two Sides of the Taiwan Straits during the 1950s* (volume 40, June 2003). The second conference, titled "Political and Economic Development across the Straits in Early Period of the Cold War," was held in November 2004. Most of the conference papers after review and revision were published in the book, *Parting Ways: Politics and Economics across the Taiwan Straits since 1949* (Taipei: Institute of Modern History, Academia Sinica, 2006) with an introduction by Chen Yung-fa. These papers focused on the similar challenges faced by the GMD and the CCP in the 1950s concerning regime consolidation, the cultivation of popular acquiescence, the control of intellectuals, resource mobilization, post-war reconstruction, and the selection of foreign models for economic development and state building. The book offers some answers to these challenges.

In October 2006, the research group hosted its third conference, titled "The Party-State System, the Economy and Society across the Taiwan Straits in the Early Cold War Period." Nineteen papers were presented. *Julia Strauss'* (London) paper, "Feeding the People, Establishing the State: Rice Supply in Jiangnan and Taiwan in the early 1950s," is the only one dealing with both sides of the Straits. Other papers focus either on China or Taiwan to show that both the GMD and the CCP used state power to guide the economy but chose very different strategies to do so. *Chen Siyu* focused on the transformation of central planning, *Chen Ciyu* (Taipei) on the Taiwanese aluminium industry, and *Liu Sufen* (Taipei) examined the China Development Corporation in Taiwan. *Zhang Xule* (Shanghai) discussed private banks in Shanghai, *Wu Jingping* (Shanghai) wrote on the Shanghai Clearing House, and *Lin Meili* analyzed industrial and commercial taxation in Shanghai.

These papers show that whereas the GMD and the CCP both emphasized economic development, the CCP focused more on political and ideological outcomes instead. The CCP tried to use "reform" to attain the desirable outcomes. *Zheng Chenglin* (Wuhan) explained how the CCP reformed the union of industrial and commercial organizations, *Lian Lingling* (Taipei) how the CCP took over the decision-making of the department stores of Shanghai, *Feng Xiaocai* (Shanghai) how the CCP asserted control over Shanghai businessmen, and *Xie Guoxing* (Taipei) how the CCP fixed interest rates. In order to raise productivity, the CCP used model workers to reform others. Papers by *Xing Long* and *Yu Miinling* (Taipei) deal with the Chinese agricultural and industrial Stakhanovites. The panelists agreed that the reforms initiated by the CCP in the 1950s could never able be complete. Whenever the party had political needs, it began a new reform campaign. It was impossible to reach the ideal state through reforms. From today's hindsight, they all failed. Also, studies of land reform on Taiwan by *Xu Shirong* (Taipei) and in Jiangsu by *Cao Shuji* (Shanghai) demonstrate that the pre-reform social stratification was not as serious as either the GMD and the CCP had claimed.

These exciting new findings have been made possible in part by the rich archival sources available on Taiwan and the PRC. The Institute of Modern History holds all the archives from the Ministry of Economy of the GMD government while Academia Historica has the archives from other government ministries. The library of the Institute of Modern History has a rich collection of local gazetteers of the PRC as well as many other general materials. In a word, the Institute of Modern History is one of the best places to study Taiwan or to do preliminary research before going to the PRC in search of primary sources on the CCP.

As to the background of the research initiative, the research group consists of eight institute research fellows and one professor from National Taiwan University under the leadership of a distinguished scholar of the People's Republic of China and director of the Institute of Modern History, Chen Yung-fa. The research group will study not only the international dimension of the Cold War, but also its economic, social, and cultural dimensions. Although the group will bound its research emphasis chronologically with the Communist victory in the Chinese Civil War in 1949 and the collapse of the Soviet Union in 1991, it will focus not on the global Cold War but on the Cold War between the rival governments of Taiwan and the People's Republic of China.

Until very recently political issues and limited archival access impeded the study of cross-Strait relations. Social scientists, not historians, generally examined the topic. In Taiwan, research on the People's Republic of China was called "bandit studies" and on Taiwan only emphasized the "White Terror" of Chiang Kai-shek. With achievement of full democracy in Taiwan in 2000, when for the first time in Chinese history an opposition came to power peacefully through elections, it is time to examine the Cold War period in detail. The rapidly expanding archival access in Taiwan and relative openness in the PRC make this research particularly exciting. The endurance of the Cold War to the present day and the continuing political rivalry with the increasing economic and cultural interactions, sometimes cooperation, make the examination of this topic of global significance.

The Cross-strait Cold War study initiative will examine many issues comparatively because in 1949 both Taiwan and the PRC faced the same problem of state building and economic development. There have been many historical parallels: For instance, both the Guomindang (GMD) and the Chinese Communist Party (CCP) relied on authoritarian leaders with significant political and military experience. Initially both established political and military institutions based on the Soviet one-party model. After 1949 they were engaged in land reform, aimed rectification campaigns at intellectuals, relied on state-sponsored economic development, received aid from great powers that later fell apart, mobilized the population through cultural issues, and promoted the national integration of minority peoples. Often they did these things differently. China mobilized its population by rejecting traditional culture while Taiwan embraced it. China focused on the development of heavy over light industry, while Taiwan did the reverse. The research group also encourages study on one side of the Straits, but hope to keep the comparative aspect or the international context of the cold war in mind.

The activities of the research group include lectures, seminars, workshops, and conferences. Since 2004 there have been graduate workshops to encourage young scholars actively to participate in the field. So far there have been three very well-attended workshops with participants not only from Taiwanese universities but also from Japan. Because of the growing graduate-student interest in the field, from 2006 forward there will be a graduate-student workshop every spring.

The Institute of Modern History will hold a conference on culture in 2008. All the past and upcoming events can be found on the website:
http://www.sinica.edu.tw/~bsts50/news.html.

(Yu Miinling)

Georg Lehner und Monika Lehner, *Österreich-Ungarn und der „Boxeraufstand" in China* (Mitteilungen des Österreichischen Staatsarchivs, Sonderband 6), Innsbruck: Studien-Verlag 2002, 738 S. (ISBN 3-7065-1713-2)

Georg Baur, *China um 1900. Aufzeichnungen eines Krupp-Direktors*, herausgegeben und kommentiert von **Elisabeth Kaske**, Köln, Weimar, Wien: Böhlau 2005, 782 S. (ISBN 3-412-19305-4)

Georg und Monika Lehner haben einen umfangreichen Band österreichischen Archivmaterials zusammengestellt und ausgewertet, um zu zeigen, wie der „Umgang mit den ‚Wirren' in China" sich gestaltete. „Umgang" bezieht sich auf die „politisch-diplomatischen Abläufe als auch die maritim-militärischen Operationen"; „Wirren" bezieht sich auf den so genannten Boxeraufstand in China, zu deren Niederschlagung eben die untersuchte so genannte Ostasienexpedition alliierter Mächte im Jahre 1900, unter ihnen Österreich-Ungarn, dienen sollte. Ausdrücklich wollen die Autoren dabei keine „Beurteilung der europäischen Intervention insgesamt vornehmen".

Diese Selbstbeschränkung der Autoren hat denn auch Konsequenzen: Die Präsentation der historischen Ereignisse aus der Brille der österreichischen Beteiligten bzw. Österreichs macht die Akteure der chinesischen Seite auch auf der Textebene zu Objekten: Deren Interessen, Positionen und Aktionen scheinen lediglich am Rande der ausführlichen Berichterstattung auf. Interaktionen finden vor allem innerhalb der alliierten Truppen bzw. der Ausländer insgesamt statt. Es ist eine europäische Welt, deren Dynamiken und Querelen, Interessen und Argumentationen hier entfaltet werden, und über die eine Fülle von Informationen vermittelt werden: Die Interessengegensätze in nahezu allen Detail-Fragen zwischen den ausländischen Vertretern werden ausführlich geschildert und dokumentiert – hier hat der Band denn auch einen hohen Erkenntniswert. Das betrifft auch die Friedensverhandlungen, das Geschacher um die hohen Entschädigungssummen und die genaue Auflistung der österreichischen Schäden. Letztlich erhält Österreich allein eine weitaus höhere Summe zugesprochen als es überhaupt an Kosten für entstandene Schäden, die Entsendung der Expedition oder den Neuaufbau der Gesandtschaft aufzulisten imstande war: 10 Mill. Kronen wurden (großzügig) geschätzt, 14 Mill. hatte die chinesische Seite in den nachfolgenden Jahrzehnten allein an Österreich zu zahlen.

Der Krieg wird als „Anteil der k. u. k. Detachments an den Operationen der kooperierenden Truppen" (bis Juni 1900) oder „maritim-militärische Präsenz in China" (bis Januar 1901) bezeichnet. Entsprechend wird von den verschiedenen Expeditionen berichtet – vielfach auf der Suche nach Boxern; lediglich „eine" Strafexpedition habe es im Unterschied zu den immerhin 35 der Deutschen gegeben. Das Requirieren von Unterkünften, Lebensmitteln etc. und die Gefangennahme und Erschießung von „Boxern" (aus den Quellen wird nicht deutlich, wie diese identifiziert wurden; auch die Autoren werfen diese Frage nicht auf) nimmt in den Schilderungen der Expeditionen einen selbstverständlichen und von Georg und Monika Lehner nicht hinterfragten Platz ein. So gerät, wie viele unmittelbar nach der Expedition veröffentlichte Darstellungen, auch diese noch, 100 Jahre nach den Geschehnissen, mit ihrer unkritischen Präsentation des Materials zu einer Geschichte von österreichischem Heldentum in fernen Landen.

Die Zeit der Boxerbewegung um 1900 wird – der Titel ist hier irreführend – gerade nicht in den Aufzeichnungen Baurs behandelt bzw. die Aufzeichnungen aus dieser Zeit sind nicht in die Publikation aufgenommen worden. Der vorliegende Band enthält

Aufzeichnungen Baurs aus drei Perioden: Tagebücher aus den Jahren 1890 bis 1893, als Baur Lehrer für Eisenbahnbau in Tianjin war, ein Reisetagebuch vom November 1911 bis April 1912 und Tagebücher und Briefe aus Baurs kurzer Zeit als Berater des Präsidenten der neuen Republik, die vom Februar bis Juli 1913 datieren. Es sind insgesamt, leider häufig gekürzte, aussagekräftige Dokumente über die frühen deutsch-chinesischen Handels- und Wirtschaftsbeziehungen, aber auch über viele Aspekte chinesischen Lebens. Nicht zuletzt sind diese Selbstzeugnisse ein wunderbares Dokument zum Selbstbild von Europäern im China dieser Jahre. Denn auch hier ist es die europäische bzw. die deutsche Perspektive, das ökonomische Interesse Baurs und der Firmen, die er vertritt, welche die chinesische Welt konstruierten. Und aus dieser Perspektive argumentiert auch die Herausgeberin in ihrer ansonsten kundigen Einführung zur Geschichte Krupps in China und zur Biographie Baurs. Elisabeth Kaske hat die Aufzeichnungen Baurs zudem mit nützlichen Anmerkungen versehen und äußerst hilfreiche Personen-, Orts- und Institutionenverzeichnisse angefertigt, die eine künftige Auswertung dieser Dokumente erleichtern werden.

(Mechthild Leutner)

Mechthild Leutner (Hrsg.), Andreas Steen (Verf.), *Deutsch-chinesische Beziehungen 1911-1927. Vom Kolonialismus zur „Gleichberechtigung". Eine Quellensammlung*, Akademie Verlag, Berlin 2006, 603 S. (ISBN-13: 978-3-05-004243-5, ISBN-10: 3-05-004243-5)

Die deutsch-chinesischen Beziehungen vom Kaiserreich zur Weimarer Republik, von der chinesischen Revolution bis zum Beginn der Nanjing-Periode sind von Umbrüchen gekennzeichnet. Nach Deutschlands Ausscheiden aus dem Reigen der Vertragsmächte durch die Niederlage im Ersten Weltkrieg wurden das Verhältnis auf eine völlig neue Grundlage gestellt, die gleichzeitig von der verworrenen innenpolitischen Situation der chinesischen Republik gekennzeichnet war. Fragen nach Unterschieden und Brüchen, wie auch nach Anknüpfungspunkten und Kontinuitäten bieten viel versprechende Ansätze für eine Analyse der bilateralen Beziehungen, wie auch der Bedeutung des deutsch-chinesischen Verhältnisses in dieser Zeit.

Der Titel des vorliegenden Bandes steckt das Feld mit den Begriffen „Kolonialismus" und „Gleichberechtigung" präzise ab. Die Periodisierung richtet sich nach Zäsuren der chinesischen Geschichte und leitet ihre Logik auch aus der Einordnung dieser Quellenedition in die Reihe der „Quellen zur Geschichte der deutsch-chinesischen Beziehungen 1897-1995" ab. Das Werk zeichnet den Gang der deutsch-chinesischen Beziehungen nach und vertritt dabei den Anspruch, über die Ebenen von Politik und Wirtschaft auch die Rolle des Kulturaustauschs, der gegenseitigen Wahrnehmung und die Rolle von Individuen und Netzwerken aufzuzeigen. Die Bezeichnung „Quellensammlung" ist dabei eher tief gestapelt, denn diese Edition bietet deutlich mehr als die Zusammenstellung einiger Quellen. Sie leistet einen Überblick über verschiedene Aspekte der deutsch-chinesischen Beziehungen, der jeder Anforderung an eine Quellenedition gerecht wird.

Der Aufbau des Werks folgt den gleichen Prinzipien wie die vorausgehenden Bände der Reihe. Nach den üblichen editorischen Vorbemerkungen vermittelt ein Verzeichnis der Dokumente einen guten Überblick über das aufgenommene Material. Darauf folgt eine ausführliche Einleitung in das Thema. Der Band ist in Abschnitte unterteilt, die chronologisch und thematisch die Entwicklung umreißen. Vorangestellt sind jeweils einleitende

Bemerkungen, denen dann die Quellen folgen. Die Gesamteinleitung wie die den einzelnen Abschnitten vorangestellten Abschnitte geben neben einer inhaltlichen Einführung auch den jeweiligen Forschungsstand wieder und korrespondieren gut mit dem folgenden Quellenmaterial.

Die ersten drei Kapitel widmen sich chronologisch den deutsch-chinesischen Beziehungen zwischen 1911 und 1927. Im Kapitel 1 wird die Situation von der Xinhai-Revolution bis zur Anerkennung der Republik China durch das Deutsche Reich behandelt. Dabei spielen neben der deutschen Stellung zur Revolution und der Regierung Yuan Shikais auch die Debatte um eine Rückgabe des Pachtgebietes Kiautschou und die Debatte und der Abschluss der so genannten Reorganisationsanleihe eine Rolle. Das zweite Kapitel befasst sich mit den deutsch-chinesischen Beziehungen vom Ausbruch des Ersten Weltkriegs bis zu den Pariser Vorortverträgen 1919. Hier ist besonders das Material der chinesischen Diskussion und der deutschen diplomatischen Bemühungen bis zur chinesischen Kriegserklärung hervorzuheben; Aufmerksamkeit verdienen aber genauso die Quellen zu den Folgen des chinesischen Kriegseintritts und der Niederlage für die Deutschen in China. Der Neubeginn der Beziehungen ist dann Objekt des dritten Kapitels, das sich vor allem an den verschiedenen Abkommen und der deutsch-chinesischen Kooperation im Völkerbund orientiert.

Den chronologischen Kapiteln folgen vier thematische Abschnitte. Sie überschneiden sich notwendigerweise teilweise mit den ersten drei Kapiteln, aber der Versuch, das komplexe Beziehungsgeflecht zwischen Deutschland und China so von verschiedenen Seiten anzugehen, darf insgesamt als gelungen betrachtet werden. Kapitel 4 trägt der zersplitterten inneren Lage Chinas Rechnung und behandelt Deutschlands Verhältnis zur nationalrevolutionären Bewegung unter Sun Yat-sen bis zur Errichtung der Nanjing-Regierung. Die folgenden Kapitel behandeln die Wirtschaftsbeziehungen, die Kultur- und Wissenschaftsbeziehungen sowie schließlich die gegenseitige Wahrnehmung.

Im Zentrum einer Quellenedition steht das publizierte Material. Der Band fasst den Begriff der Quelle weit und berücksichtigt neben Archivmaterial auch veröffentlichte Quellen wie die Reichstagsprotokolle, die zeitgenössische Presse und Auszüge aus Publikationen. Der Löwenanteil des archivalischen Materials stammt aus den Beständen des Bundesarchivs Berlin-Lichterfelde (vor allem Deutsche Botschaft China) und dem Politischen Archiv des Auswärtigen Amts. Zusätzlich wurden ausgewählte Bestände weiterer Archive hinzugezogen, darunter neben staatlichen Archiven wie dem Geheimen Staatsarchiv Preußischer Kulturbesitz auch die für wirtschaftliche Belange materialreichen Archive von Schering und Siemens. Hervorzuheben ist die Verwendung von Material aus dem Zweiten Historischen Archiv in Nanjing. Obwohl die Einbeziehung chinesischer Quellen in die Geschichte der Beziehungen zwischen China und dem Westen inzwischen als internationaler Standard zu sehen ist, bestehen in dieser Hinsicht von deutscher Seite oft noch Defizite – die Reihe der Quelleneditionen zu den deutsch-chinesischen Beziehungen hat hier neue Maßstäbe gesetzt, die hoffentlich auch als Impuls begriffen werden.

Insgesamt ist der Band und die Fülle der darin behandelten Themen zu komplex, um in einer Rezension gebührend gewürdigt zu werden. Die Quellen zeichnen ein oftmals farbigeres Bild, als mitunter zu erwarten wäre. So beispielsweise die Erinnerungen Zhu Des, des späteren Mitbegründers der Roten Armee, an seine Studienzeit in Deutschland. Bemerkenswert ist die Wissbegierde, mit der sich Zhu in das Berliner Leben stürzte und von der Kirche bis zum Konzert versuchte, etwas über Deutschland zu lernen. Dies zeigt die andere Seite des späteren Marschalls, von dessen Aufenthalt sonst vor allem seine Verhaftung nach der illegalen Teilnahme an einer Kundgebung im Berliner Sportpalast erwähnt wird. Wie es in einer guten Quellenedition der Fall sein sollte, illustrieren die Quellen nicht nur die Darstellung, sondern gehen darüber hinaus und bieten Ansätze für weitere Fragestellungen.

Mit dem besprochenen Band hat die Reihe der „Quellen zur Geschichte der deutsch-chinesischen Beziehungen" ihren Abschluss gefunden. Damit liegt jetzt ein sechsbändiges Standardwerk vor, das eine Fülle von Material bietet, das nicht nur darstellt, sondern auf seine Verwendung für die Forschung wartet. Dem Rezensenten bleibt nur zu bedauern, dass die jeweils anderen Bände in den einzelnen Publikationen nicht verzeichnet sind, was den Überblick nicht vereinfacht. Aber vielleicht ist dies auch ein Verweis, dass jeder Einzelband auch die Handschrift seiner Bearbeiter trägt und damit für sich stehen kann.

(Cord Eberspächer)

Xu Guoqi, *China and the Great War: China's Pursuit of a New National Identity and Internationalization*, Cambridge, New York u.a.: Cambridge University Press 2005, 316 S. (ISBN: 13 978-0-521-84212-9)

In einigen Publikationen zum Ersten Weltkrieg bleibt China unerwähnt; in der Regel gilt das Interesse der japanischen Besetzung der deutschen Kolonie Qingdao, der daraus resultierenden „Shandong question" sowie den Friedensverhandlungen in Versailles und ihren Folgen. Weniger Aufmerksamkeit erfuhr der Umstand, dass chinesische Arbeiter von England und Frankreich angeworben wurden. Xu Guoqi berücksichtigt beides wie auch die innenpolitischen Konflikte des Kriegsbeitritts und bietet durch eine ebenso einfache wie folgenreiche These eine neue Perspektive auf die Bedeutung des Krieges für China: Er argumentiert und belegt, dass China sich ab 1914 aus wohlüberlegten Gründen aktiv um eine Kriegsteilnahme bemühte und nicht erst 1917 der Überredung durch die Alliierten bedurfte.

Xu untersucht das Thema auf der Grundlage theoretischer Überlegungen zur internationalen Geschichte bzw. zur Internationalisierung Chinas. Allerdings konzentriert er sich nicht auf das Kriegsgeschehen selbst, sondern sieht den Krieg als ein Vehikel für Chinas Regeneration, Erneuerung und Transformation. Der europäische Krieg, so Xu, „was considered an excellent opportunity for joining the emerging world order" (S. 10). Ausgehend von dieser Prämisse werden die Handlungen chinesischer Akteure als Strategien zur Erlangung der nationalen Souveränität interpretiert. Auch der Umstand, dass China auf Seiten Japans – seines ärgsten Feindes – in den Krieg eintrat, diente dem höheren Ziel, womit die Beziehungen zu Deutschland „geopfert" wurden: „Germany became a victim – or vehicle – in China's big-picture strategy. Germany was in fact a friend in disguise since it helped China springboard into the world arena" (S. 12). Nur durch das aktive Vorgehen Chinas sollte es gelingen, sich der Boxer-Rückzahlungen an Deutschland und Österreich zu entledigen, 1919 an den Verhandlungstisch in Versailles geladen zu werden und mit seinem Kriegsgegner Deutschland 1921 den ersten „gleichberechtigten Vertrag" in seiner Geschichte zu schließen. All dies wäre ohne den Kriegsbeitritt unvorstellbar gewesen, so dass Xu Chinas Kriegspolitik insgesamt als „a brilliant diplomatic move" bezeichnet (S. 14).

Die Arbeit gliedert sich in drei Hauptkapitel, welche gleichermaßen die Stadien der Anstrengungen zur angestrebten Internationalisierung Chinas in Anlehnung an den

Kriegsverlauf aus chinesischer Perspektive reflektieren. In „The stage is set" erfolgt zunächst der Rückblick auf die gesellschaftspolitische Entwicklung Chinas nach der Niederlage im Krieg gegen Japan (1895) bis 1914. Hier rekurriert Xu auf die Herausbildung einer neuen Öffentlichkeit (Zeitungen, Presse), die Aktivitäten von u.a. Kang Youwei, Liang Qichao und Sun Zhongshan, und die Ausprägung einer nationalen Identität. Mit der Revolution und dem Sturz des Kaiserhauses begann eine neue Phase, in welcher Presse und Zeitungswesen wesentlich zur Definition eines Nationalbewusstseins und modernen Nationalismus' beitrugen (S. 53). Im Zuge umfangreich geführter Diskussionen um Chinas Rolle in der Welt entwickelte sich eine „foreign policy public", die in der Öffentlichkeit durch drei unterschiedliche Stimmen, „the government, the press, and citizens' groups (elite and non-elite)", getragen wurde (S. 71). Die dort noch als statisch wahrgenommene internationale Ordnung, definiert durch das Gleichgewicht zwischen Europa und Asien, erfuhr ab 1914 einen Wandel, nicht zuletzt weil die USA, Japan und auch China ihre Stunde gekommen sahen (S. 77).

Das zweite Kapitel, „China attempts to join the war", behandelt Chinas Bemühungen um die Kriegsteilnahme. Hier gelingt es Xu aufzuzeigen, dass nicht nur Liang Qichao, sondern auch Intellektuelle wie Chen Duxiu, Li Dazhao und Teile der Öffentlichkeit die Kriegsereignisse in Europa als eine Chance für China begriffen, international Stellung zu beziehen. Präsident Yuan Shikai erklärte zwar Chinas Neutralität, war zur Rückgewinnung Qingdaos aber durchaus zum Kriegseintritt bereit. England lehnte ab, Japan besetzte Shandong und Qingdao und offenbarte im Januar 1915 mit den „21 Forderungen" an China seine weiteren Pläne. Stärker als zuvor strebte China nun nach einem Sitz auf der Friedenskonferenz, scheiterte 1915 aber am Widerspruch Japans. Im selben Jahr entwickelte China die Strategie des „laborers in the place of soldiers" (一工代兵) – die ersten Arbeiter erreichten Frankreich im August 1916. Xu unterstreicht Chinas Bemühen um den Arbeitertransfer, gewährt Einblicke in die konkrete Organisation und die in Europa geführten Debatten. Als die USA zu Beginn des uneingeschränkten U-Boot-Krieges im Februar 1917 dazu aufforderten, die diplomatischen Beziehungen zu Deutschland abzubrechen, ergriff China schnell die Gelegenheit, im August folgte die Kriegserklärung. Bereits Ende 1917 standen 40.000 chinesische Soldaten zum Abmarsch nach Europa bereit. Aus finanziellen Gründen kamen sie nie dort an. Indessen stellten die Alliierten hohe Forderungen, insbesondere was den Umgang mit dem Kriegsgegner betraf, und versprachen Vieles, was sie nicht hielten. Angesichts des Ausgangs der Versailler Friedensverhandlungen kommt Xu zu dem Schluss: „China's involvement in the First World War is thus a story of frustrations." (S. 198)

Das dritten Kapitel, „The war within", richtet den Fokus auf die innenpolitischen Konflikte Chinas. Zentral sind die Ereignisse des Jahres 1917. Xu analysiert die Standpunkte der Kriegsbefürworter und -gegner und gewährt u.a. neue Einblicke in die Entscheidungsprozesse Duan Qiruis und seine Beziehung zu Liang Qichao. An der Kriegserklärung zerbrach Chinas ohnehin instabile innenpolitische Lage, das Land zerfiel endgültig in die Machtbereiche diverser Militärherren, auf deren Interessen wiederum die ausländischen Mächte Einfluss zu nehmen versuchten, am effektivsten Japan. Die Verhandlungen und Enttäuschungen der „Paris Peace Conference" bilden den Schluss des Kapitels, wobei Xu – jenseits der „Shandong question" – auf Chinas weit reichende Ziele hinweist: „its internationalization and joining the world community, as well as the recovery of overall national sovereignity." (S. 272). In dieser Hinsicht sei China durchaus erfolgreich gewesen, kurzum: die Bedeutung des Krieges für Chinas moderne Geschichte wird erst jenseits der Kriegsereignisse und des Desasters der Friedenskonferenz erfahrbar. Am Ende heißt es: „In a sense, this book is about China's unacknowledged successes und its shared experience with the wider world during the First World War" (S. 280).

Schon aufgrund des verwendeten Quellenmaterials und der neuen Perspektive, welche die inneren und äußeren Faktoren des Kriegsverlaufs in China sorgfältig herausarbeitet, darf diese Arbeit als Standardwerk zum Thema gelten. Gleichwohl ist hervorzuheben, dass es sich um eine Studie handelt, die ausschließlich auf die angloamerikanische Sekundärliteratur Bezug nimmt und dadurch gewissen Verzerrungen nicht entgeht. Hierzu gehört z.B. der Umstand, dass es für viele Chinesen eben nicht einsichtig war, weshalb man einen Krieg gegen das in China relativ schwache Deutschland führen sollte, wo doch die eigentlichen Feinde – England und Japan – vor der Tür standen. Des Weiteren irritieren die Verallgemeinerungen, die Chinas gesamtes Streben einschließlich der „foreign policy public" dem Postulat der Internationalisierung unterordnen. In der Rückschau mag dies so erscheinen, sollte aber nicht an einer letztlich übersichtlichen Zahl chinesischer Akteure und Kontrahenten festgemacht werden. Selbstverständlich trat auch China nach dem Krieg in eine international neue Epoche ein, hatte somit Anteil an einer kollektiven Welterfahrung. Es ist jedoch eine zu verkürzte Sicht, dieses *der* chinesischen Kriegspolitik zuzuschreiben, die es so nicht gab. China war „pseudo-neutral", befand sich in einer Art Warteschleife und machte Angebote, die je nach Nation, Strategie und Kriegssituation abgelehnt oder befürwortet wurden. Eine Kriegspolitik wurde erst ab Ende 1917 „einheitlich" getragen, jedoch geographisch und zeitlich unterschiedlich umgesetzt und durch diverse innenpolitische Machtstrategien gelenkt. Dass dieses Vorgehen letztlich seine „Belohnung" in der Aufnahme in den Völkerbund, der Teilnahme an der Washingtoner-Konferenz und der Klärung der „Shandong-Frage" sah, ist alles andere als erfolgreich. Auch wenn dieses ohne die Kriegsbeteiligung kaum möglich gewesen wäre und der Krieg eine deutliche Wende in der modernen Geschichte Chinas darstellt, bleibt überdies die Tatsache bestehen, dass die Ergebnisse aus Washington später umfangreich kritisiert wurden, die ungleichen Verträge weiterhin ihre Gültigkeit behielten und China noch lange Jahre ein Spielball des informellen Imperialismus der Mächte blieb.

(Andreas Steen)

Marchetti, Gina, *From Tian'anmen to Times Square. Transnational China and the Chinese Diaspora on Global Screens, 1989-1997*, Philadelphia: Temple University Press 2006, 322 S. (ISBN 1-59213-278-2)

In ihrem Buch untersucht Gina Marchetti das „Bild" (*image*) Chinas und der Chinesen im Film einer von zwei Ereignissen überschatteten Periode. Sie beginnt mit der Niederschlagung der Demokratiebewegung auf dem Tian'anmen-Platz in Beijing 1989, deren Folgen lange Jahre spürbar bleiben und „den Platz" zu einem globalen Medienevent werden ließen. Sie endet mit der Rückgabe Hongkongs an die VR China am 1. Juli 1997, die bereits vorher vielfältige Diskussion und Ängste schürte. Beide Ereignisse, eines unerwartet, das andere lange bekannt, prägten auch das chinesische Filmschaffen. Parallel hierzu resultierte der gesellschaftliche Wandel Chinas dieser Dekade, national wie auch international, politisch, wirtschaftlich und kulturell, in eine postmoderne Situation, so dass „time and space warp, and Tian'anmen and Times Square move closer together connected by an instantaneous stream of motion pictures" (S. xi). So seltsam dieser Vergleich (historisch) im ersten Augenblick anmuten mag, gelingt der Autorin in ihrer Studie eine überzeugende Verbindung.

Die Autorin stellt die Frage, in welcher Weise das globale Filmschaffen dieses Zeitraums unterschiedliche Konzeptionen von China geprägt und mit gestaltet hat. In ihrer Untersuchung verbindet sie drei Ebenen: Erstens, die Bedingungen und kreativen Ansprüche der chinesischen Filmschaffenden unterschiedlicher Regionen: VR China, Taiwan, Hongkong, Singapur und den USA. Zweitens, die generelle Lebenssituation, d.h. die mit diesen Ereignissen erhöhte chinesische Emigration in die USA und nach England wie auch die Lebensumstände der chinesischen Diaspora in erweiterten transnationalen Zusammenhängen. Drittens, die Bedeutung bzw. der Einfluss, den diese Ereignisse auf das chinesische Filmschaffen hatten (und haben), ihre künstlerische Ver- und Bearbeitung wie auch die Frage, inwieweit diese filmischen Repräsentationen die Transformation der chinesischen Gesellschaft reflektieren.

Gegenstand des Buches ist letztlich eine konkrete Generation Chinas, die ihr Leben inmitten einer bis dato ungekannten Mobilität und Unsicherheit, politischen Freiheit und globalen Konsumkultur zu organisieren sucht. Gemeint ist die sog. „GenerAsian X", d.h. Personen, die zwischen 1989 und 1997 in ihren späten zehner oder frühen dreißiger Jahren waren, deren Leben und Weltsicht entschieden durch die rasanten Veränderungen dieses Zeitraums geprägt wurden. Den neuen ökonomischen Möglichkeiten der Globalisierung gegenüber stehen vielerlei Unsicherheiten, der Identität sowie der sozialen und kulturellen Beziehungen, die teilweise durch die Erwartungen eines transnationalen Konsumverhaltens geschürt werden. In diesem Zusammenhang, so Marchetti, „youth culture ... ekes out a transnational space for critique and the negotiation of competing demands" (S. 23). Das Medium Film nimmt hier eine wichtige Rolle ein. Die Autorin konzentriert sich aber nicht nur auf die bekannten Namen des chinesischen Mainstream-Kinos, sondern richtet den Blick auch auf die technologisch neuen Möglichkeiten und gegenwärtige Tendenzen des experimentellen Films, dem sie eine generelle Kapitalismuskritik unterstellt (S. 24). Zur Bearbeitung dieses komplexen Gegenstands greift die Autorin überzeugend auf wissenschaftliche Ansätze der Soziologie und Anthropologie, der gender studies, Filmwissenschaften und postmodernen sowie postkolonialen Studien zurück.

Das Buch besteht aus zwei großen Kapiteln, die sich in jeweils vier Unterkapitel gliedern, an deren Ende das Interview mit jeweils einem Filmregisseur steht. Das erste Kapitel, „Global Economies, Commodities, and Labor", nimmt konkrete Auswirkungen der Globalisierung ins Visier und behandelt ausgewählte „charakteristische" Filme aus bzw. über die genannten Regionen. Zunächst wird anhand des Films *Chunking Express* dem Einfluss der US-amerikanischen Konsumkultur in Hongkong nachgespürt. Ein anderes Bild vermittelt die VR-Produktion *The Opium War*, die 1997 in die Kinos kam. *Almost a Love Story* (1996) thematisiert die Emigration, von der VR nach Hongkong, sowie von Hongkong in die USA. Der folgende Abschnitt untersucht drei Filme, die den Wandel und die Migration arbeitender Frauen in der Volksrepublik China zum Inhalt haben. Die Perspektive auf Taiwan konzentriert sich auf den Aspekt "Gangland Taiwan in the Transnational Imagination". Im Vordergrund stehen kriminelle und internationale Subkulturen und Geheimgesellschaften, eingebettet in den gesellschaftlichen Hintergrund der Kolonialgeschichte, eine unsichere politische Zukunft und deshalb nicht leichte Beziehung zur globalen Modernisierung. Im Gegensatz hierzu ist die „Postmodern Condition in Singapore" durch eine nach Außen moderne, konfuzianisch moralische, kapitalistische und geordnete Welt gekennzeichnet, deren Widersprüche der Regisseur Eric Khoo in seinen Filmen zwischen amerikanischer Pop-Unterhaltung, Sex- und Brauthandel (*sex traffic*) und traditionellem Aberglauben aufdeckt.

Das zweite Kapitel trägt die Überschrift „Identities in Question: The Chinese Diaspora" und beginnt mit einem Beitrag zum transnationalen Kino und hybriden Identitäten. Was Marchetti hiermit meint, verdeutlichen die folgenden Zeilen zur Biographie des Regisseurs Evans Chan: „Born in Mainland China, bred in Macao, educated in Hong Kong and the United States, Evans Chan, currently based in New York City, makes independent narrative films primarily for a Hong Kong, overseas Chinese, „Greater China" audience" (S. 157). Es sind diese Biographien – zwischen Tian'anmen und Times Square – die nicht nur die Regisseure, sondern eine ganzen Generation betreffen, die sich in den Filmen spiegeln, die Fragen der Identität, des Sinns der Emigration sowie der globalen bzw. lokalen Verortung aufwerfen, denn: „the diasporic intellectual works from the perspective of exile and/or immigration, from the pain as well as the freedom of displacement" (S. 167). Der folgende Abschnitt wendet sich den Filmen der Regisseurin Clara Law zu und bietet – endlich – eine tiefer gehende Definition der „GenerAsian X", u.a. heißt es: „On the move around the world, this is a polyglott generation in which English as a second language dominates much of the popular imagination. It is a generation marked by its class and class aspirations, defined by consumption and its ability to consume, forging an identity out of commodities" (S. 190). Die hieraus resultierenden Widersprüche und Konflikte zeigen sich in den Filmen, z.B. in Fragen zur Gleichberechtigung der Frau und zur Ehe, zu Rassismus und Hass („I hate being Chinese.") und den konfuzianischen Werten. In gewisser Weise leiten diese Fragen über zum nächsten Kapitel, welches die Legende Bruce Lee und dessen Sohn Brandon behandelt. Es war – zur Erinnerung – Bruce Lee, der gegen böse Elemente in der chinesischen Diaspora und Rassismus kämpfte. Brandon (halbasiatisch, halbweiß) scheint zur Versöhnung ausersehen, um diesen Konflikt in einer Hollywood-Produktion beizulegen: „Hollywood, through Brandon, reconstructs a Bruce Lee that never existed and allows Brandon to attempt to transcend him" (S. 218). Das Schlusskapitel gilt im weitesten Sinne dem Dokumentarfilm *The Gate of Heavenly Peace* (1995) von Carma Hinton und Richard Gordon. Im engeren Sinne geht es um die Interpretation und mediale Verarbeitung der Ereignisse des „4. Juni", um ihre transnationale Verbreitung und Bedeutung, um den Wandel eben dieses Platzes, der durch die Errichtung einer filmbegleitenden Internetadresse zur „cyber entity" wurde (S. 220). Wenn Tian'anmen im Internet eine Plattform für den politischen Diskurs bietet, der Platz in Beijing aber eine Touristenattraktion ist, die parallel auch Chinas Eintritt in die globale Marktwirtschaft zelebriert, dann, so die Autorin, darf auch dem Times Square eine wachsende politische Identität innerhalb eines transnationalen China zugesprochen werden – zumal 1993 bereits eine Shopping-Meile unter diesem Namen in Hongkong eingerichtet wurde.

From Tian'anmen to Times Square sprudelt von Namen und Filmtiteln und demonstriert, inwieweit „Tian'anmen" und „die Rückgabe" auf das Leben einer ganzen Generation wirkten, in der Realität ebenso wie im Film. Darüber hinaus verdeutlicht Marchetti zweierlei: Erstens, dass die Regisseure der chinesischen Diaspora zunehmend erfolgreich Einfluss auf die Konstruktion eines transnationalen China nehmen, und zweitens, dass

Hollywood und Beijing diesen Diskurs aktiv zu manipulieren versuchen: James Bond, der gemeinsam mit der VR-Agentin Wai Lin gegen das Böse kämpft (1997), konkurriert mit „The Opium War" (1997), dem Hinweis auf das Ende kolonialer Vormundschaft und Unterdrückung. Das Medium Film ist somit ein Kampfplatz unterschiedlicher Ideologien, auf dem, bedingt durch die gestiegene Mobilität von Kapital, Regisseuren und Schauspielern, neue Akteure, Lebensentwürfe und Problemlösungen konkurrieren und vormalige Grenzen überschreiten. Allerdings muss man den Filminterpretationen Marchettis nicht immer zustimmen, auch bleibt zu hinterfragen, ob das „kritische Potential" der Filme wirklich so kritisch angelegt ist. Schließlich geht es – wie die Autorin deutlich hervorhebt – trotz allem um Konsum und Erfolg, d.h. um die Erfüllung bestehender Erwartungen und vermutlich auch Klischees.

Das Buch ist in mehrfacher Hinsicht empfehlenswert. Zum einen stellt es Regisseure und Filmtitel vor, die nicht unbedingt außerhalb Asiens bekannt sind, zum anderen analysiert es die Filminhalte vor dem Hintergrund der gesellschaftlichen Umbrüche in „Greater China". Dabei ist es gerade die Vernetzung dieser Ebenen, die ein neues Licht auf die Aktivitäten der chinesischen Diaspora wirft und unsere Perspektive erweitert.

(Andreas Steen)

Sepp Linhart, „*Niedliche Japaner*" oder *Gelbe Gefahr? Westliche Kriegspostkarten 1900-1945.* „*Dainty Japanese! Or Yellow Peril? Western War Postcards 1900-1945*, LIT Verlag Wien. Münster 2005, 164 S. (ISBN 3-8258-8655-7)

Ende des 19. Jahrhunderts kam die Ansichtskarte als neues, modernes Massenmedium auf. Es spielte dann über mehrere Jahrzehnte die Rolle eines die öffentliche Meinung erheblich prägenden Instruments und ist so zugleich ein historisches Zeugnis dieser Zeit. Ansichtskarten dienten der Information über Land und Leute der Nähe und der Ferne. Sie blieben für das einfache Volk lange Zeit die einzige Informationsquelle über die Welt, die es selbst nicht erleben konnte. Postkarten wurden auch zur Werbung, zu Glückwünschen an Feiertagen und zur Propaganda verwendet. In die historische Forschung sind sie bisher eher sporadisch und wenig intensiv einbezogen worden. Und so ist es höchste Zeit, dass ihnen die gebührende Aufmerksamkeit zuteil wird.

In den ersten vier Jahrzehnten des 20. Jahrhunderts hat Japan mit allen westlichen Großmächten Krieg geführt. Das Bild im Westen von diesem Land änderte sich grundlegend. Einen anfangs niedlichen, lächelnden und zu belächelnden Staat gab es nicht mehr. Da war ein ernst zu nehmender Rivale herangewachsen. Alle Aspekte zur Mobilisierung der eigenen Völker gegen diese reale Gefahr mit den spezifischen Möglichkeiten der Propaganda fanden auf den Propagandapostkarten ihren Ausdruck.

Der Japanologieprofessor Sepp Linhart von der Wiener Universität hat aus seiner Sammlung 191 Postkarten aus 12 Ländern, die entweder interessierte Beobachter, Verbündete, zumeist jedoch Kriegsgegner Japans waren, ausgewählt. Die Karten widerspiegeln insgesamt eine Entwicklung vom „Amüsement zum blanken Hass" (S. 13). In den unbeteiligten Ländern blieben die Japaner niedlich und lächerlich, die verbündeten Länder betonten deren Heroismus, in den Feindstaaten aber waren sie die grausamen, hinterlistigen „Gelben".

Linhart hat seine Auswahl chronologisch aufgebaut. Die Karten sind der Inbesitznahme Jiaozhous und dem „Boxeraufstand", dem russisch-japanischen Krieg, dem Kampf um

Reviews

Qingdao, den japanisch-sowjetischen Konflikten 1938/39 sowie dem Pazifischen Krieg 1941-1945 zugeordnet.

Einem knappen kommentierenden Teil folgt der umfangreiche Bildteil. 20 Karten zeigen deutschen Triumph (Nr. 1), westliche Rivalität bei der Aufteilung Chinas (Nr. 20) und eine diffuse „gelbe Gefahr", die fratzenhaft daherkommt (Nr. 12). Um 1900 waren die japanischen Attribute im europäischen Verständnis so dominierend, dass zwischen Japanerinnen und Chinesinnen noch nicht unterschieden wurde (Nr. 2-10).

85 Karten sind mit Karikaturen auf den japanisch-russischen Krieg versehen. Erstmals erlitt eine europäische Macht eine militärische Niederlage. Mit wenigen Ausnahmen (Nr. 50, 51) werden die Japaner noch nicht entstellt oder fratzenhaft dargestellt.

31 Karten beziehen sich auf Japans Angriff gegen Qingdao. Auf den deutschen werden der Japaner oder Japan nun vorherrschend als listig, verschlagen und hässlich gezeichnet (Nr. 112, 113). Ganz anders das Bild auf den Karten der Alliierten: Der Verbündete ist der Heroe (Nr. 125), ein niedliches Küken (Nr. 27), der sympathische Waffenbruder (Nr. 128).

Sieben Karten lassen schon die sowjetische Kriegspropaganda ab 1941 erkennen. Drei geben Aussprüche von Vorošilov, Molotov und Kaganovič auf dem XVIII. Parteitag der KPdSU 1939 wieder und illustrieren sie (Nr. 140-142). Klein und fratzenhaft verzerrt wird der Japaner dargestellt. Zugleich fällt eine Besonderheit auf, die schon die russischen Karten vom Beginn des Jahrhunderts kennzeichnet: Sie tragen zwei- und vierzeilige Reime, die an die russische častučka erinnern – ein lustiges Spottlied, dem bayerischen Schnaderhüpfel ähnlich (Nr. 37). Karte Nr. 138 zeigt allerdings keinen Sowjetsoldaten, sondern einen Chinesen. Hier handelt es sich um eine Solidaritätskarte für das China auf dem Weg der Befreiung vom Imperialismus.

48 Postkarten, davon fünf der Achsenmächte beziehen sich auf den Pazifischen Krieg. Nun ist der Japaner wieder der Affe (Nr. 153), das Stinktier (Nr. 158) oder die Schlange (Nr. 167). Er ist durchgängig der hässliche Gelbe.

Dieses Buch ist die überzeugende Eröffnung einer neuen Reihe des Verlages: „Visuell: Bilder und Weltbilder". Der erklärende Textteil zu den Karten ist in Deutsch und Englisch abgefasst. In ausreichender Größe und farbig genügt die Ausführung der Abbildungen allen Ansprüchen. Es sind also die Voraussetzungen für eine weite Verbreitung dieses interessanten und vergnüglichen Buches gegeben. Historiker wie Postkartensammler werden das gewiss bestätigen.   (Joachim Krüger)

Zvi Ben-Dor Benite, *The Dao of Muhammad. A Cultural History of Muslims in Late Imperial China.* **Cambridge: Harvard University Asia Center (Harvard East Asian Monographs 248), 2005, 400 S. (ISBN: 0-674-01774-9)**

Wenn die Rede ist von der historischen muslimischen Präsenz in China, denken wir in der Regel an die Moslems auf dem Territorium des heutigen Nordwestchina. Eine Serie von Rebellionen nach 1780 beeinflusste die einschlägige Historiographie dahingehend, dass diese Moslems in Abgrenzung und als Gegenpol zum monolithisch-konfuzianischen imperialen China projektiert wurden. Dieses Buch zeigt uns ein ganz anderes Gesicht der Geschichte von Moslems in China. Es lenkt unsere Aufmerksamkeit auf ein muslimisches Bildungs- und Gelehrtennetzwerk, welches sich zwischen der Mitte des 17. Jahrhunderts und dem späten 18. Jahrhundert von der Jiangnan-Region über Henan bis nach Shandong erstreckte und das so genannte *Han Kitab* hervorbrachte, ein Gesamtwerk von über 100 chinesischsprachigen wissenschaftlichen Texten mit Bezug zum Islam.

Die Eckpfeiler von Ben-Dor Benites Studie sind zunächst ein einführendes Plädoyer für eine nuanciertere Historiographie der Qing-Ära durch die Integration von Han-chinesischer Geschichte und der Geschichte von Minderheiten, anschließend die ausführliche Rekonstruktion des oben genannten Gelehrtennetzwerkes, und schließlich und hauptsächlich, die Konstruktion einer muslimisch-konfuzianischen Literati-Identität. Die bisherige Ignoranz der Existenz eines chinesisch-muslimischen Bildungsnetzwerkes zu jener Zeit ist, dem Autor zufolge, zurückzuführen auf eine Historiographie, welche leichtgläubig dem Anspruch der Han-chinesischen Gesellschaft auf das Bildungsmonopol verfällt (S.25). Ben-Dor Benite beweist, dass parallel zum imperialen Prüfungssystem ein muslimisches Ausbildungssystem existierte. Dieses Netzwerk von Schulen brachte wiederum ein Netzwerk von Gelehrten hervor, dessen kulturelles Milieu der Nährboden für die Produktion des *Han Kitab* war.

Auf der Basis einer bisher nicht studierten, umfangreichen muslimischen Gelehrtengenealogie, die in den 1670er Jahren in Kaifeng (Henan) entstand und 1987 in einer Moschee in Peking entdeckt wurde, rekonstruiert der Autor zunächst ein Netzwerk von Schulen, Lehrern und Schülern sowie wissenschaftlicher Textproduktion. Darüber hinaus werden die begünstigenden Bedingungen für die Entstehung eines solchen Netzwerkes und seiner überaus aktiven literarischen Produktion umrissen. Ein begünstigender Faktor war beispielsweise die große Anzahl von gut ausgebildeten, aus urbanem Großbürgermilieu (*gentry*) stammenden Muslimen in Ostchina, welche die natürliche Zielgruppe einer muslimischen Bildungsinitiative waren (68f.).

Das folgende Kapitel ist der Selbstwahrnehmung und Identität gewidmet. Hier geht es um das chinesisch-islamische Wertesystem. Auf der Grundlage der in der oben genannten Genealogie enthaltenen Texte werden Lernen und literarische Produktion, Bescheidenheit, Pädagogik und Gemeinschaftssinn als höchste Werte herausgearbeitet (89). „For Chinese Muslim scholars, Islam – what they called "the Dao of Muhammad" – was learning itself." (74). Die häufige Verwendung des Terminus *shi* 士 (literatus) weist dabei darauf hin, dass sich die muslimischen Gelehrten als Gelehrte im konfuzianischen Sinne verstanden. Dieses Verständnis findet einen Höhepunkt in einer Anekdote aus der Genealogie: "The ethics of our teaching and those of the Confucian teachings are the same. Whoever follows our precepts and laws takes loyalty to rulers and obedience to parents as a duty. How can this be compared with fatherless and rulerless ill-behaved Buddhists and Daoists?" (101). Ergänzend hierzu zieht Ben-Dor Benite eine interessante Parallele zwischen konfuzianischem und muslimischem Lernen im Hinblick auf die identitätsstiftende Methode des Auswendiglernens von Texten. Ähnlich wie im offiziellen kaiserlichen Bildungssystem war auch im muslimischen Bildungssystem die Beherrschung von Texten ein Ausdruck größter Gelehrtheit (92f.).

Das dritte Kapitel widmet sich ausführlich den einzelnen *Han Kitab*-Autoren und deren Werken, um zu demonstrieren, dass dieses Gesamtwerk der chinesisch-islamischen Schule der externe Ausdruck einer spezifischen chinesisch-islamischen Literati-Identität ist. Ben-Dor Benite betont, dass es sich bei dieser literarischen Produktion um ein Gemeinschaftswerk handelt, dass die Lehrer, Schüler, Übersetzer, Herausgeber und Sponsoren alle Teil und Produkt des bereits ausführlich rekonstruierten Bildungsnetzwerkes sind (160f.). Auf diese Weise erschafft der Autor die Gemeinschaft sowie deren kulturelle Identität und Geistesgeschichte.

Im vierten Kapitel skizziert der Autor, auf welche Weise es den muslimischen Gelehrten gelang, zwei Identitäten zu synchronisieren. Einerseits mussten sie sich ihrer Gesellschaft als Gelehrte präsentieren, und zwar in genau dem Sinne, wie diese soziale Kategorie von der konfuzianischen Elite konstruiert und verstanden wurde. Andererseits versuchten sie, ihre islamische Tradition vor dem Hintergrund der dominanten chinesischen kulturellen Paradigmen zu interpretieren (163). Ihre Integration in diese Paradigmen erreichen die muslimischen Gelehrten durch die Porträtierung Muhammads als „alten Weisen" (*sage*) und als „gerechten Herrscher" (*righteous ruler*), das heißt in Kategorien, die zentral und anerkannt sind, und in Harmonie mit dem konfuzianischen Gelehrtensein stehen (168). Damit wird Muhammad, zumindest für die *Han Kitab*-Autoren, nicht nur ein Teil der chinesischen Tradition, sondern auch ein notwendiges Studienobjekt, und damit zum Bestandteil des intellektuellen Diskurses der späten Kaiserzeit (181). Die Zentralität von Muhammad im chinesisch-muslimischen Denken bleibt bestehen, doch Muhammad im chinesischen Kontext ist kein Prophet im religiösen Sinne, sondern ein „alter Weiser", in der Tradition von Yao, Shun, dem Herzog von Zhou und Konfuzius selbst (184). Durch diese *de facto* „Säkularisierung" wird die Konstruktion einer muslimischen Gelehrtenidentität in Harmonie mit dem konfuzianischen Literati-Status ermöglicht.

Im abschließenden Kapitel werden die verschiedenen Komponenten der chinesisch-muslimischen Gemeinschaft (Bildungsnetzwerk, literarisches Gesamtwerk, Identität und Integration von islamischen Literati) wieder zusammengeführt. Der Autor fasst noch einmal zusammen, wie vor allem das Studium und die Verbreitung von Genealogien zur Entwicklung und Propagierung eines chinesisch-muslimischen Gründungsmythos beitragen. Das Netzwerk von islamischen Schulen wiederum perpetuiert diesen Mythos und kreiert die spezifisch islamisch-konfuzianische Identität:

This simultaneity of identity rested on myths that explained Chinese Muslim origins in such a way as to validate both Chinese Muslims' centrality to Chinese tradition and their direct descent from the closest companions of the Prophet. It was an identity that was lived, preserved, and developed through scholarship (S. 232).

Die Porträtierung von Muhammad als Gelehrten im konfuzianischen Sinne und damit die Auslegung von Islam in vorrangig wissenschaftlichen anstatt religiösen Dimensionen, ermöglichte den Protagonisten eine logische Positionierung innerhalb beider Systeme, Islam und Konfuzianismus. Einige der *Han Kitab*-Autoren hatten erfolgreich an den kaiserlichen Prüfungen teilgenommen und trugen offizielle Titel (S. 63), waren also auch formal integrierte Protagonisten beider Systeme.

Eine der Schlussfolgerungen des Buches ist diejenige, dass sich, durch die zu eben jener Zeit stattfindenden militärischen, politischen und kulturellen Kampagnen der Manchu und den Versuch der Konstruktion einer Manchu-Identität, viele kulturelle Kategorien verschoben und neu verhandelt wurden. Ein unbeabsichtigtes und indirektes Resultat der frühen Qing-Politik war die Entstehung einer spezifischen kulturellen, und nicht ethnischen, Identität (S. 233). Der muslimisch-konfuzianische Literatus ist Personifikation einer solchen.

Das Buch ist unterhaltsam, gut lesbar und überaus interessant für Kulturhistoriker der späten Kaiserzeit und Interessierte an der Geschichte des Islam in China. Vielfältige Referenzen zu anderen „fremden" Religionen in China, z.B. zum Christentum, und zu

anderen Minderheiten, vor allem den Manchus, zeichnen ein lebhaftes Bild vom
Wechselspiel und der Verhandlung von Identität und Integration im kulturellen Diskurs
der Qing-Ära.

(Karin-Irene Eiermann)

Timothy Brook: *Collaboration: Japanese Agents and Local Elites in Wartime China.*
Cambridge: Harvard University Press 2005, 302 S. (ISBN 0674015630)

Timothy Brook's latest book is published at a crucial moment: sixty years after World
War II, tensions between Japan and China accrue again to an anxious degree, and history
in both countries is being simplified as well as exploited for political reasons. With
Collaboration: Japanese Agents and Local Elites in Wartime China the author provides
access into the problematical but overdue discussion about this largely unacknowledged
topic in modern Chinese historiography. Brook reconstructs the collaboration between
Chinese elites and Japanese occupiers on the local level, namely in the Yangtze-delta,
during the immediate aftermath of the invasion (1937-1938). He argues that "the story of
China under Japanese occupation, hitherto told as a tale of resistance," (S. 240) was as
well a story of collaboration: some people resisted, others remained inertly, and again
others supported the invaders actively or passively. Although there was a significant number of Chinese elites willing to cooperate with the Japanese conquerors, their liaison remained often tense, finds the author. Brook is very ambitious as he vigorously claims history to be more complex than often narrated: He aims to suspend judgments, which have
kept collaboration from becoming a major topic in Chinese history, namely the nationalis-
tic, political, humanitarian and – most important – the moral ones. He furthermore
complicates the conventional picture of collaboration itself, as he contradicts the simple
moral judgment of this frowning alliance and shifts the fault lines in the moral landscape
of occupation from a small group of top-level collaborators to a broader "more intricate
pattern of interaction and accommodation" (S. 13).

Framed by the two first chapters, which accurately describe the conceptual approach as
well as the theoretical preparatory work of the Japanese occupiers, and the last, retrospec-
tive and assembling chapter, the author's modus operandi is a selection of five different
places in above named region, discussing five different themes: Firstly, he investigates in
Jiading the transformation process of the occupier's aggression into the appearance of
normalcy. The occupation resulted often solely in a "camera pacification" with eye-catch-
ing policies – "appearances might be the most a pacification agent could hope for" (S.
69). Secondly, Brook examines the occupation-costs considering as an example the
county of Zhejiang, followed, thirdly, by Nanjing and a survey of the complexity of
complicities. Fourthly, exemplifying Shanghai, he depicts the rivalries, thus the question
how politics actually get played out. Latterly, on the basis of the island county Chong-
ming, the author investigates the Chinese resistance movement, asking what impact had
ongoing resistance on the work of collaboration. Brook draws in the end the conclusion
that "collaboration proved to be politically unstable and morally awkward for both sides
of the relationship" (S: 248). Hence, the Japanese failed to create a competing legitimate
state with viable collaboration structures, undermining a long-term perspective of the
imperatorial authority.

The timeline and places of this thoughtful study, albeit provoking some minor handicaps,
seem carefully chosen by the author. Analyzing mainly the initial phase of occupation allows, on the one hand, an examination of collaboration among local elites at the country

level, which lost much ground after the inauguration of the national government in 1939. In doing so, Brook successfully depicts the personal relationships between Chinese local elites and Japanese supervisors in their ordinary life. But on the other hand, such a short-term analysis must widely ignore long-term effects of occupation. Doubtlessly, immediately after the invasion organizational structures are messy. But what happened later? Did the too sparsely spread Japanese pacification teams (*senbu han*) (often composed of young, euphoric men), the collaborating self-government committees (a rather marginal, equivocal elite among the Chinese), and other institutions of the occupation regime later become more effective? How successful was the further development of resistance and propaganda against the occupying force? Furthermore, in this study by virtue of historiographical considerations – emphasizing the collaboration – the author seems to downplay the resistance movement.

The occupation of Manchuria, a hybrid between the pure colony of Taiwan and the occupied areas after 1937, proved to be a comparatively easier case for the Japanese conquerors, since Japan, due to the acquiring of the South Manchurian Railway in 1906, developed already tight economical ties with that region, and the natural resources became indispensable for the country's imperial ambitions. Brook's investigated area, along the lower Yangtze, omits this and other often more violent northern and northeastern puppet states, but it focuses at the same time on the Chinese allegory of Japanese evil: Nanjing, where occupation felt hardest. Regrettably, due to this narrow focus the reader will also miss some other aspects, e.g. areas under Communist control.

At times Brook has taken up the topic too carefully, so that his decisiveness in supporting and emphasizing his thesis is afflicted. The reader will find many descriptive passages but insufficient interpretation. Brilliant in contrast is the choice of characters, such as the candid Guo Zhicheng or the more humanly behaving Jimmy Wang, vitalizing the different paths of collaboration. Furthermore, the extensive amount of primary sources and the transparent way in which they are presented are impressive. Brook thoroughly utilizes Japanese official records and personal testimonies as well as interviews of both conflict sides, which unearth significant new facts. It is not overstated to sum up that with this collection of case studies, Brook has opened scholarly research in this still sensitive field of Chinese collaboration. (Sören Urbansky)

Joanna McMillan, *Sex, Science and Morality in China*. London and New York: Routledge 2006, pp. 187, (ISBN 0-415-37632-7)

Joanna McMillan's work provides a comprehensive overview of the mainstream discourse on sex in the People's Republic of China during the last decade. Using a Foucauldian approach, she analyzes the discourse as produced by China's best-known sex experts and the media. She argues convincingly that this discourse sets out "natural ways of being a man or woman." In her analysis, this discourse reveals an image of monogamous heterosexual marriage as the most advanced form of social bond, based not on morality but on today's "scientific knowledge of sex."

Chapter I, "The sexed body and naturalized gender differences", gives an illustrative description of how gender differences are seen as being natural: firstly, McMillan describes the rather pragmatic approach of surgeons in China who deal with intersexuality and transsexuality. In contrast to the West, where at least in the Anglo-Saxon countries, powerful Christian groups oppose any surgery for transsexuals, a very much more pragmatic approach can be observed: they do not "argue over gender theory and causal distinctions, psychiatric disorder or lifestyle choice, they agree on one thing: she wants an operation, and he carries them out!" (p. 13). The aim is that the "patients" conform "completely" with gender roles. The second part of this chapter deals with the dominant perception of the naturalized differences between men and women ("tertiary sex characteristics", 第三性征) (p. 15); interestingly enough, the new market economy is described as a task for the "real man", while the former socialist system with its state-run enterprises is seen as a task for *taijian* (eunuchs) (16). Women, however, are expected to fulfill role expectations by being "passive and receptive" (17) and a completely new sector of cosmetic industry and surgeons has specialized in providing adaptations to the new "norms for female beauty" (18).

Chapter 2, "The sexual body and its normal function", deals with the linguistic interchangeability of the terms, "sex organs" (性器官) and "reproductive organs" (生殖器官), which lead to the strong linking of sex with reproduction (p. 24). McMillan points out that the subject of masturbation is also treated with some caution: it is sometimes still linked with physical weaknesses, such as tinnitus, dizziness, impaired memory, etc, and also sometimes treated more as a "yardstick of self-control" (35). The "Chinese discourse", according to McMillan, "demonstrates, if anything, distaste for the body. It sanitizes it with numbers and norms, writing out individuals, and therefore individual differences" (p. 39).

Chapter 3, "Sexual dysfunction and treatments in sex shops and sex clinics", describes the specific feature of China's sex shops where "Chinese sex aids appeal to nature, medicine, biomechanics and biochemistry in their attempts to repair the failed sexual function" (p. 41). McMillan also dwells, at length, on the arrival of Viagra and related drugs on the Chinese market, but also mentions briefly the more critical voices of such outstanding scholars as Li Yinhe at the Academy of Social Sciences, who regards these drugs as a tool for reinforcing gender roles. In the mainstream discourse, however, specific care is taken to relate the new drugs to the only legitimate relationships where they may be used: heterosexual, monogamous relationships (p. 55).

Chapter 4, "controlling sex outside marriage, eugenics, and quality children", is one of the most fascinating chapters. Eugenics and the production of healthy children (or one healthy child to be more precise) play an essential role in the discourse of sexuality, and here, Chinese morality is contrasted with "negative Western sexual culture", the latter being related to pornography prostitution, sexually transmitted diseases, AIDS, gambling and drugs", which is described as a threat to China. Regarding Safer Sex and the propagation of condoms, China has slowly shifted her position and, in China, the struggle between the International Education Foundation (國際教育基金會), influenced by American evangelists, and UNAIDS more and more frequently results in victory for the latter (pp. 60-62). Regarding eugenics, McMillan describes the long tradition of scientific discourses from the Republican period to the present day, which has been strengthened by the introduction of the one-child-policy.

Chapter 5, "Marriage manuals and instructions for harmonious sex", presents the common view that many Chinese couples are considered to be lacking in the scientific knowledge required for harmonious sex (p. 78), which has led to the publication of many handbooks and manuals. A newer trend is the establishment of successful advisory hotlines. One feature common to all these manuals and hotlines is that they all focus on heterosexual sex within marriage, "Sexual abnormality" – the title of Chapter 6 – such as "homosexuality, pornography and fetishism" is not encouraged. Nevertheless, "homosexuality has become a non-pathological abnormality – and for some academics, the stuff of newly legitimate and cutting-edge research" (p. 93). Although a "cure" is seldom offered, families are provided with regular advice on what action to take to prevent their children becoming homosexual (p. 95). One of the greatest problems for gays and lesbians in China remains the pressure to marry; only in a very few middle class circles in urban China, has this pressure somewhat diminished as a result of greater tolerance towards academic, medical and legal circles (p. 97). Fetishism and pornography, however, are regarded as alien and have been heavily attacked in various campaigns.

Chapter 7, "The sale and purchase of sex", describes, first of all, the historical developments since the 1950s when prostitution was said to have been eradicated after Liberation, pointing out that it has now become widespread everywhere in China. The legal position is simple: prostitution is considered to be illegal and offenders are sent to re-education centers or labor camps; hotels, which offer the services of prostitutes, can face stiff penalties. In reality, however, there are millions of prostitutes and many segmented markets have arisen. The Public Security Bureau and the People's Liberation Army also operate tourism and leisure venues where prostitution occurs. McMillan concludes that the discourse on sex remains a "positivist tradition, where science is presented as neutral and reified as modernity and progress."

To summarize, McMillan offers a rather gloomy and dark picture of the Chinese scientific and academic discourse on sex: she does not accept the idea that greater openness has resulted from the marketing of sex, from advertising, or, that with some exceptions, such as in the case of homosexuality, a mixture of marketization, the influence of global Christian groups, conservative and traditional values together with a positivist scientific approach regulate sex as the norm for monogamous, heterosexual relations in the public discourse. She cites a vast number of sources, and refers to interviews with various experts in the field, but fails to search for counter-discourses, which she only mentions briefly in a few instances, for example, regarding gay and lesbian venues. Instead of showing how more recent developments, such as marketization, have led to the re-emergence of prostitution and the stereotyped presentation of "the male" and "the female", postmodern approaches could be employed to show how consumerism and the presentations of sex and gender in the public sphere can lead to changes in attitude in the long-term, how sexual minority groups use the newly established private and semi-private field of the Internet with its forums and blogs, and the role which could be played by the new openness in literature. In my opinion, McMillan has focused too heavily on the positivist and conservative approach found in the mainstream media and supported by mainstream experts; the interesting developments in China today, however, are the counter-discourses which are not only to be found in the established media and academic world, but in various parts of the public sphere.

(Jens Damm)

Pun Ngai, *Made in China: Women Factory Workers in a Global Workplace*, Durham: Duke University Press 2005, xi + 225 S. (ISBN 1-932643-00-1)
Seit Mitte der 1990er Jahre hat es in der wissenschaftlichen Beschäftigung mit industriellen Beziehungen in der Volksrepublik China eine kontinuierliche Verlagerung der Aufmerksamkeit „von oben nach unten" einerseits, sowie eine konsequente Diversifizierung der beobachteten Teilgruppen der chinesischen Arbeiterschaft andererseits gegeben. *Made in China*, eine überarbeitete Version der Doktorarbeit von Pun Ngai, Assistant

Professor der Sozialwissenschaften an der Hongkong University of Science and Technology, ist nun das jüngste Beispiel für diese Mikro-Perspektive. Eine besondere Leistung
der Monographie ist, dass sie Forschungen über industrielle Beziehungen und
Geschlechterbeziehungen unter dem Einfluss der Globalisierung miteinander verbindet,
indem sie nicht allgemeine, sondern geschlechtsspezifische Erfahrungen von Ausbeutung
und Entfremdung beschreibt.

Pun Ngai hat acht Monate lang (11/1995-6/1996) mit den *dagongmei* 打工妹 (Arbeits-
mädchen) einer Hongkonger Elektronikfabrik in Shenzhen gelebt und gearbeitet. Ihre daraus entstandene, theoretisch anspruchsvoll eingebettete Forschungsarbeit gliedert sich in
sieben Kapitel, angefangen mit „State Meets Capital: The Making and Unmaking of a
New Chinese Working Class", der Schilderung der politischen und ideologischen
Voraussetzungen für die Herausbildung einer klassenbewussten Arbeiterschaft unter Mao
und heute, im Zeitalter der Reformen. Pun geht davon aus, dass Mao Zedongs
Klassenanalyse aufgrund ihres hegemonistischen Charakters, des Ziels einer Proletarisie-
rung von oben, gescheitert sei (S. 12f.). Im Umkehrschluss daraus stellt sie ihr eigenes, in
dem vorliegenden Band verfolgtes Forschungsvorhaben vor: ein Studium gegenwärtiger
Klassenerfahrungen von unten.

Im zweiten Kapitel mit dem Titel „Marching from the Village: Women's Struggle between Work and Family" benennt die Autorin Push- und Pullfaktoren, die Frauen dazu
bewegen, das Land zu verlassen und vorübergehende Beschäftigungen in den Städten
anzunehmen. Die Frauen träfen ihre Entscheidung in voller Kenntnis der sie erwartenden
Arbeitsbedingungen. Häufig flüchteten sie vor den patriarchalischen Strukturen auf dem
Land; gleichzeitig aber wüssten sie gerade ihre verwandtschaftlichen und *tong* 同 -
Beziehungen (basierend auf gemeinsamer Herkunft, schulischer Laufbahn, Erfahrungen,
Bekanntschaften u.ä.) beim Zuzug in die Städte und als Sicherheitsnetze in der fremden
Umgebung zu nutzen und flexibel anzupassen.

Kapitel 3, „The Social Body, the Art of Discipline and Resistance", beinhaltet eine genaue Dokumentation der Techniken der Disziplinierung, der "microphyics of power"
(Foucault) in der Werkhalle: vorgeschriebene Arbeitsabläufe, Maschinentempo, räumli-
che Gestaltung der Arbeits- und Wohnbereiche, Hausordnung und Verhaltensregeln,
physische Anforderungen der Fließbandarbeit, Kontrollmechanismen und disziplinarische
Maßnahmen. Sie geben Aufschluss über Entfremdungs- und Kommodifikationsprozesse,
die Kontrolle und Instrumentalisierung des Körpers, insgesamt eine Kultur der
Entpersonalisierung und Entwertung des Individuums, vor allem aber des weiblichen
Körpers ländlicher Herkunft. Gleichzeitig vertritt Pun ein Konzept der „tactical bodies"
(S. 78), welche nie vollständig gefügig seien: Sie beschreibt subtile Strategien des Wider-
stands, z.B. durch kollektive Verlangsamung des Arbeitstempos, durch kollektive
Krankmeldungen, in einem Fall sogar kollektive Arbeitsverweigerung, welche
innerbetriebliche Herrschaftsstrukturen, wenigstens für Momente, in Frage stellen.

Die Kapitel 4 („Becoming Dagongmei") und 5 („Imagining Sex and Gender in the
Workplace") widmen sich den Identifikationsprozessen der jungen Frauen als *dagongmei*.
Pun vertritt hier die These, dass erst die willentliche Konstruktion von Selbst- und
Fremdbildern innerhalb der Arbeiterschaft, entlang der Trennlinien „Status", „Klasse"
und „Geschlecht", die Legitimation für kapitalistische Arbeitsbedingungen und
Hierarchisierungen im Arbeitssystem schaffe (S. 110). Diese „politics of difference"
(ebd.) würden sowohl von Staat und Kapital als auch von den Betroffenen selbst betrie-

ben. Ein Beispiel sind gezielte verbale und tätliche Diskriminierungshandlungen gegen Landfrauen durch Staat und Kapital, aber auch durch die örtliche Bevölkerung, sowie diskriminierende Entlohnungs- und Bonuspraktiken, welche Unterschiede festschrieben. Zudem erinnerten Vorgesetzte in dem gewählten Fallbeispiel die Frauen ständig an Rollenerwartungen, ermahnten sie zu „weiblichem", das heißt gefügigem, und nicht ländlich-verrohtem Verhalten. Staatliche Medien wiederum beteiligten sich durch Negativdarstellungen über Wanderarbeiter wie auch über eine Generation einst als geschlechtsneutral konzipierter und heute als faul und parasitär stigmatisierter *gongren* (Arbeiter) unter Mao (S. 159). Diese Darstellungen machen eine Emanzipation aus dem Stigma und die Identität als „moderne" Lohnarbeiterinnen und Konsumentinnen attraktiv. Des weiteren schildert Pun identitätsstiftende Abgrenzungsstrategien von kantonesischen Arbeiterinnen untereinander, in diesem Fall von kantonesischen Arbeiterinnen gegenüber solchen aus nördlicheren Provinzen (北妹), welche sich in Shenzhen häufig prostituierten (S. 141), sowie auch gegenüber dem Management und der Stadtbevölkerung, welche negativ erlebt würden. Aufgrund all dessen werde eine als modern, urban und weiblich empfundene Identität als *dagongmei* schließlich als erstrebenswert erachtet.

Die letzten beiden Kapitel („Scream, Dream, and Transgression in the Workplace" und „Approaching Minor Genre of Resistance") widmen sich den Auswirkungen der Arbeitsverhältnisse auf Physis und Psyche der Arbeiterinnen: Schmerzen, Menstruationsbeschwerden, Albträume. Hier kommt Pun auf ihre Ausgangsthese geschlechtsspezifischen Entfremdungserlebens zurück: Die körperliche Verfassung und das zyklische Zeitempfinden von Frauen erschwerten ihre Eingliederung in die kapitalistische Produktionsweise. Sei die Eingliederung jedoch erfolgt, so erlebten sie eine doppelte Entfremdung: als Arbeiterin wie als Frau (S. 177). Pun interpretiert die Leiden der Frauen als Abbild ihrer inneren Zerrissenheit und des dreifachen Drucks durch staatlichen Sozialismus, globalen Kapitalismus und patriarchalische Strukturen, dem sie ausgesetzt sind (S. 186).

Insbesondere aus diesen letzten Kapiteln sprechen die Sympathie der Autorin für die *dagongmei* und ihr impliziter Aufruf zu handeln, welche wohl auch maßgeblich dazu beigetragen haben, das Werk im August 2006 mit dem kanadischen C. Wright Mills Award auszuzeichnen.

Die Bewertung von Krankheit und vereinzelter und spontaner kollektiver Leistungsverweigerung als *Strategien* der Durchbrechung und des Widerstands scheint alles in allem etwas wohlwollend. Hier wäre eine detailliertere und strukturiertere Beschreibung der Infragestellung bestehender Arbeitshierarchien und Geschlechterordnungen überzeugender gewesen. Auch die Traumdeutung im letzten Kapitel ist letztlich nicht belegbar. Allerdings sollte der Band nicht in Erwartung politischen Bewusstseins und organisierten Widerstands auf Werkhallenebene gelesen werden, sondern vielmehr als Zeugnis einer „silent…social revolution" (S. 55, 190) mit den *dagongmei* als *ein* Träger, in der bisher gültige soziale Gefüge aufgebrochen werden und neue Identitäten entstehen. Als solches ist es lehrreich und eindrücklich für all jene, die sich für ethnographische Ansätze in den Bereichen industrielle Beziehungen, Geschlechterforschung, Globalisierung und Glokalisierung, auch unabhängig von China, interessieren. Durch seine Anschaulichkeit wird es Studierenden zudem leicht zugänglich sein. (Nathalie van Looy)

Notes on Contributors

Marianne Bastid-Bruguière is a Research Professor at the Centre Nationale des Recherches Scientifiques (CNRS), Paris, affiliated with the Center for Studies of Modern and Contemporary China. Her research areas include: history of modern China and history of education.

Jens Damm is a Research Associate at the Institute of East Asian Studies, Free University Berlin. His research interests include the Chinese diaspora in Southeast Asia, gender studies, and new media.

Cord Eberspächer is a Research Fellow at the Secret Prussian State Archive in Berlin. He is currently working about the Prusso-German-Chinese relations 1842-1911. His research interests further include military history, history of shipping, Germany in the 19th and early 20th century and Qing history.

Karin-Irene Eiermann is a PhD student in Chinese Studies at Free University Berlin. Her PhD project is on Chinese communists in Moscow during the 1920s and 1930s. Currently, she is carrying out research at the Party and Comintern Archives in Moscow.

Izabella Goikhman is a Research Associate and PhD candidate at the Institute for East Asian Studies, Free University Berlin. Her main research interests are: Jews in China, history of science, cross-cultural science- and knowledge-transfer and gender studies.

Olivia Kraef is a PhD candidate at the Institute for East Asian Studies, Free University Berlin. Her main areas of research include identity issues, specifically Chinese ethnic identity and culture, majority-minority relations as well as questions of gender and education in the PRC.

Joachim Krüger (Dr. rer. pol.) was a Professor at the Institute for International Relations at Potsdam-Babelsberg; he is currently involved as a co-editor in the research project "The Comintern and China" at Free University Berlin. Other research interests include the history of GDR-China relations.

Mechthild Leutner is a Professor and currently holding the chair of Chinese Studies at the Institute for East Asian Studies, Free University Berlin. Her main research interests are on Chinese social and political history, German-Chinese relations, and Chinese women's history.

Luvsanvandan Manlajav is Head of the Foreign Language Department, School of Social Sciences, University of the Humanities in Ulaanbaatar, Mongolia. Her main research interests are: Mongolian and Chinese philology, linguistics and foreign language teaching methodology.

Klaus Mühlhahn is a Professor of Contemporary Chinese History and Director of the Centre for East Asian Studies, University of Turku, Finland. His research interests include legal history, human rights, Sino-Western interactions, modern Chinese social and cultural history.

Song Shaopeng is an Associate Professor in the Chinese Communist Party History Department, Renmin University of China. Her main area of research is the History of Contemporary China, including gender and politics in contemporary China, feminist political theory and cultural history in the PRC (main focus: the 1980s).

Andreas Steen is a Research Associate at the Institute of East Asian Studies, Free University Berlin. His research focuses on modern Chinese history and culture (popular music, film, cultural industry), and on the Sino-German relations. He is currently working in a project on the Prussian-German Relation (1842-1911).

Julia Strauss is the Editor of The China Quarterly and a Senior Lecturer in Chinese Politics at the School of Oriental and African Studies (SOAS). Her main areas of research include state building and institution building and governance in China and Taiwan, and she is currently working on a monograph that compares regime consolidation on the two sides of the Taiwan Straits in the 1950s.

Sören Urbansky is a Visiting Scholar at the History Department of University of California at Berkeley, USA. His current research interests include urbanisation processes and social interactions along the Chinese-Russian border during 20th century.

Nathalie van Looy is a Research Associate and PhD candidate at the Institute for East Asian Studies, Free University Berlin. Her main research interests are: labor relations and conflict, transformation processes, and development policies in the People's Republic of China, as well as the history of Chinese education.

Susanne Weigelin-Schwiedrzik is full professor of Sinology at the University of Vienna. Her research interest is focused on 20th century Chinese history and historiography, Chinese politics and global history.

Yu Miinling is an Associate Research Fellow at the Institute of Modern History, Academia Sinica (Taipei). Her academic interests are Sino-Soviet cultural relations, Soviet history, and history of modern China.

China
aktuell

Journal of Current Chinese Affairs

bietet systematisch und kontinuierlich
- Information und Analysen
- zu Hintergründen und Perspektiven

in Form von
- verlässlicher, konziser Dokumentation
- fundierten Analysen und wissenschaftlichen Studien

zu den Bereichen
- Wirtschaft, Politik und Gesellschaft
- in der VR China, in Hongkong, Macau und Taiwan

Themen
- Die Rolle ausländischer Unternehmen im Innovationssystem Shanghais
- Die Wirtschaftsbeziehungen zwischen China und Lateinamerika: Mehr als große Hoffnungen?
- Der deutsch-chinesische Rechtsstaatsdialog auf dem Prüfstand
- Der IKT-Sektor in China und Indien. Sektorüberblick und Hintergrundanalyse
- Chinas neues Arbeitsvertragsgesetz
- Probleme sozialer Gerechtigkeit in der VR China
- Die Regierung als Vorreiter ins Informationszeitalter: Eine Analyse des Hongkonger E-Government
- Perspektiven der chinesisch-taiwanesischen Beziehungen

Abonnement:	6 Hefte pro Jahr für € 82.00 (Studierende € 40.00) zuzüglich Versandkostenanteil
Online-Ausgabe:	Gebühren pro Download

Institut für Asienkunde
GIGA German Institute of Global and Area Studies
Leibniz-Institut für Globale und Regionale Studien
Rothenbaumchaussee 32 ▪ 20148 Hamburg
Tel.: +49 40 4288740 ▪ Fax: +49 40 4107945
E-Mail: ifa@giga-hamburg.de
Internet: www.giga-hamburg.de/ifa

Wir senden Ihnen gern ein Probeheft

GIGA
German ▪ Institute of Global and Area Studies
Institut für Asien-Studien

Berliner China-Hefte
Chinese History and Society
Edited by Mechthild Leutner (FU Berlin)

Zehn Jahre Berliner China-Hefte
Mechthil Leutner, Nicola Spakowski: *Zehn Jahre Berliner China-Hefte – aktuell, interdisziplinär, innovativ, kritisch, kontrovers;* Mechthild Leutner: *Politik und Wissenschaft: Die Marginalisierung nicht-philologischer Ansätze und die Konstruktion der Sinologie als Philologie;* Klaus Mühlhahn: *"Komparatistik des Wesentlichen" – Zur Relevanz der Sozialanthropologie Pierre Bourdieus für die Chinawissenschaften;* Doris Fischer: *Chinas "Großer Sprung" in die Globalisierung: Der WTO-Beitritt und seine Auswirkungen auf die chinesische Wirtschaftspolitik;* Jens Damm: *The WorldWideWeb in China and Taiwan. The Effects of Heterogenization and Homogenization in a Global Discourse;* Nicola Spakowski: *The Internationalization of China's Women's Studies;* Ole Döring: *Globalisierung durch Biotechnologie: Soziale und kulturelle Aspekte am Beispiel Humangenetik und China.*
Bd. 20, 2001, 144 S., Jahresabonnement (2 Hefte) 25,00€ plus Versandkosten, Einzelheft 20,90€ plus Versandkosten, br.

Devlopment and Development Projects
Klaus Birk: *Poverty Alleviation in Rural China: A Preliminary Assessment;* Arthur N. Holcombe: *The Impacts of Economic Policies and Philanphry on Ethnic Minority Population Living Standards in China: The Case of Tibet;* Axel Dörken: *GTZ's Mission in China – Supporting Economic and Social Reforms and Environmental Protection;* Jane Sayers/Eva Sternfeld: *Environmental Education in China;* Johanna Pennarz: *Conversion to Organic Agriculture in Poverty Areas: Experiences from Yuexi, Anhui Province, PR China;* Karin Janz: *"Through You We Learned the Meaning of Democracy" – Participatory Approaches in Natural Resource Management in China;* Monika Gaenssbauer: *Women in the Protestant Church in China – An Attempt to Describe the Situation at the Beginning of the 21st Century;* Zhu Min: *"Lebend aus einem KZ zu entkommen, war wie ein Märchen." Erinnerungen an die Zwangsarbeit in einem nationalsozialistischen Konzentrationslager in Ostpreußen*
Bd. 21, 2002, 120 S., Jahresabonnement (2 Hefte) 25,00€ plus Versandkosten, Einzelheft 20,90€ plus Versandkosten, br.

Recht und Rechtsgeschichte Chinas
Bd. 22, 2002, 128 S., Jahresabonnement (2 Hefte) 25,00€ plus Versandkosten, Einzelheft 20,90€ plus Versandkosten, br.

Interkulturelle Begegnungen
Bd. 23, 2003, 128 S., Jahresabonnement (2 Hefte) 25,00€ plus Versandkosten, Einzelheft 20,90€ plus Versandkosten, br.

Sozialgeschichte Chinas
Hsiung Ping-chen: *A Secret Garden or a Paradise Lost? Dislodging Intimacy between Sons and Mothers in Ming-Ch'ing China;* Li Changli: *The Rise of Socio-Cultural History in China;* Maria Khayutina: *Welcoming Guests – Constructing Corporate Privacy?;* Mechthild Leutner: *The Concept of Family Economy and Marriage Practices in Rural China in the Late Nineteenth Century and Today;* Selina Ching Chan: *Questioning the Patriarchal Inheritance Model in Hong Kong: Daughters, Sons and the Colonial Government;* Rachel Fabritius: *Frauen im Shanghaier Exil (1933 – 45)*
Bd. 24, 2003, 128 S., Jahresabonnement (2 Hefte) 25,00€ plus Versandkosten, Einzelheft 20,90€ plus Versandkosten, br.

Soziale Probleme
Marianne Bastid-Bruguière: *The Ebbs and Flows of Illiteracy in Present Day China;* Nina Y. Borevskaya: *The PRC Educational Modernization Strategy: The Shift of a Paradigm?;* Bettina Gransow: *Social Assessment in China – Action Learning for the Risk Society?;* Heike Schmidbauer: *Living on the Fringes – Urban Experiences of Rural Migrant Women in Reform China;* Nathalie van Looy: *From Revolution to Institutionalisation? Labour Relations and Conflict in the People's Republic of China;* Xia Hongwei: *The Indirectness of Chineses Communication;* Mechthild Leutner: *Sinologen als kulturelle Mittler: Versuch einer Typologie „gebrochener Identitäten"*
Bd. 25, 2004, 120 S., Jahresabonnement (2 Hefte) 25,00€ plus Versandkosten, Einzelheft 20,90€ plus Versandkosten, br.

China and Modern Historiography
Q. E. Wang: *The German Nexus in the East Asian Project on Modern Historiography;* D. Leese: *German Sinologists and the Question of "Orientalism" at the Turn of the 20th Century;* H. Ping-chen: *World History Texts in Republican China and Post-War Taiwan;* K. Siu-tong: *Cultural Migration and Historiography in the Regions of China since the End of World War II;* M. Leutner: *Chinese Historiography and (West) German/Western Historiography;* L. Paltemaa: *Western Historiography on China and Criticism of Its Euro-Centricity*
Bd. 26, 2004, 112 S., Jahresabonnement (2 Hefte) 25,00€ plus Versandkosten, Einzelheft 20,90€ plus Versandkosten, br.

LIT Verlag Berlin – Hamburg – London – Münster – Wien – Zürich
Fresnostr. 2 48159 Münster
Tel.: 0251 – 62 032 22 – Fax: 0251 – 23 19 72
e-Mail: vertrieb@lit-verlag.de – http://www.lit-verlag.de

Chinesische Literatur
Zum siebzigsten Geburtstag von Eva Müller.
Herausgegeben von Mechthild Leutner und
Jens Damm
Irmtraud Fessen-Henjes: *Laudatio zum 70.Geburtstag von Eva Müller*; Lutz Bieg: *Schriftenverzeichnis Eva Müller*; Wolfgang Kubin: *Ding Lings Yan'aner Erzählung „Die Nacht" (1940)*; Hans Kühner: *Von der (Un)Produktivität des Ressentiments in der Literatur. Einige aktuelle chinesische Beispiele*; Raoul Findeisen: *„Cherchez la femme": Eine kritische Hommage an die Schriftstellerin Zhang Zhaohe (1910–2003), Nachlassverwalterin von Shen Congwen (1902–1988)*; Dorothee Dauber: *Blumen und Blüten als Spiegel der Frau in der klassischen chinesischen Lyrik*; Kathleen Wittek: *Chen Ran und Kafka – eine unilaterale freundschaftliche Beziehung*; Mechthild Leutner: *Richard Wilhelms chinesische Netzwerke: Von kolonialen Abhängigkeiten zur Gleichrangigkeit*; Andreas Steen: *„Im Frühjahr kehrt Lei Feng zurück!" – Zur gesellschaftlichen und politischen Relevanz eines „Mustersoldaten" in der Postmoderne*
Bd. 27, 2005, 144 S., Jahresabonnement (2 Hefte) 25,00€ plus Versandkosten, Einzelheft 20,90€ plus Versandkosten €, br., ISBN 3-8258-8434-1, ISSN 1860-2290

Bettina Gransow; Pál Nyíri;
Shiaw-Chian Fong (Eds.)
China
New Faces of Ethnography
Twenty years ago, foreign researchers were just (or to be more exact: again) beginning to venture into China for fieldwork. Today, „the field" itself has become mobile, ephemeral and virtual as more research focuses on human mobility and communication. This issue of the Berliner China-Hefte takes a look at some of the trends and problems of fieldwork in and about China today, touching on issues that range from Internet research to sexual harassment in the field, foreign investors in China and Chinese tourists abroad as research subjects, and the role of social and poverty assessment in development.
Bd. 28, 2005, 168 S., 20,90 €, br., ISBN 3-8258-8806-1

Nicola Spakowski; Cecilia Milwertz (Eds.)
Women and Gender in Chinese Studies
Women and gender studies increasingly contribute to a more differentiated knowledge of China. This issue presents research on a variety of topics related to women and gender in modern and contemporary China including the question of women's citizenship in the Republican period, health issues of women soldiers on the Long March, the problem of and activities against domestic violence and the revision of the marriage law. By exploring how gender interacts with other categories and how processes of modernization and transformation are gendered the articles shed new light on the structures of Chinese society.
Bd. 29, 2006, 168 S., 20,90 €, br., ISBN 3-8258-9304-9

William C. Kirby; Mechthild Leutner;
Klaus Mühlhahn (Eds.)
Global Conjectures:
China in Transnational Perspective
This issue deals with the integration of modern China into processes of global exchange and cross-border interaction. The articles explore the broader theme in different ways and in different subfields, ranging from the history of political ideas to the history of institutions, from global migration of people to the transmigration of academic discourses. Focusing on modern as well as contemporary periods, the studies demonstrate that China in the course of the twentieth century became an ever more important nodal point in a complex set of worldwide networks and engagements. The integration into global networks, together with the global consciousness that corresponded with it, made possible significant connections transcending national borders. The essays also show that the effects could be homogenizing (or globalizing), but at the same time the growing interactions also produced opposition and fragmentation.
Bd. 30, 2006, 168 S., 20,90 €, br., ISBN 3-8258-9481-9

Wissenschaftliche Paperbacks
Politikwissenschaft

Hartmut Elsenhans
Das Internationale System zwischen Zivilgesellschaft und Rente
Bd. 6, 2001, 140 S., 12,90 €, br., ISBN 3-8258-4837-x

Klaus Schubert
Innovation und Ordnung
In einer evolutionär voranschreitenden Welt sind statische Politikmodelle und -theorien problematisch. Deshalb lohnt es sich, die wichtigste Quelle für die Entstehung der policy-analysis, den Pragmatismus, als dynamische, demokratieendogene politisch-philosophische Strömung zu rekonstruieren. Dies geschieht im ersten Teil der Studie. Der zweite Teil trägt zum Verständnis des daraus folgenden politikwissenschaftlichen Ansatzes bei. Darüber hinaus wird durch eine konstruktiv-spekulative Argumentation versucht, die z. Z. wenig innovative Theorie- und Methodendiskussion in der Politikwissenschaft anzuregen.
Bd. 7, 2003, 224 S., 25,90 €, br., ISBN 3-8258-6091-4

LIT Verlag Berlin – Hamburg – London – Münster – Wien – Zürich
Fresnostr. 2 48159 Münster
Tel.: 0251 – 62 032 22 – Fax: 0251 – 23 19 72
e-Mail: vertrieb@lit-verlag.de – http://www.lit-verlag.de